SECOND CUSTOM EDITION FOR JROTC
A CHARACTER AND LEADERSHIP DEVELOPMENT PROGRAM

CITIZENSHIP IN ACTION AND LEADERSHIP THEORY AND APPLICATION

Short excerpts taken from:

Developing Leadership Abilities
by Arthur H. Bell, Ph.D. and Dayle M. Smith, Ph.D.

Managing Diversity: People Skills for a Multicultural Workplace, Third Edition
by Norma Carr-Ruffino

Keys to Preparing for College
by Carol Carter, Joyce Bishop, and Sarah Lyman Kravits, with Lesa Hadley

PEARSON
Custom Publishing

PEARSON
Prentice Hall

PEARSON CUSTOM PUBLISHING
75 Arlington Street, Suite 300, Boston, MA 02116
A Pearson Education Company

Brief Contents

Table of Contents

Unit 2   Leadership Theory and Application   194

Chapter 1   Being a Leader   195

Chapter 2   Leadership Skills   246

Chapter 3   Leadership Planning   283

Citizenship in Action

Unit 1

Chapter 1

Foundations of Army JROTC and Getting Involved

Army JROTC– The Making of a Better Citizen

Key Terms

cadet
challenges
JROTC
mission
motivate
opportunities
unique

What You Will Learn to Do

- Identify how Army JROTC can impact your future

Linked Core Abilities

- Take responsibility for your actions and choices

Skills and Knowledge You Will Gain Along the Way

- Explain the mission of Army JROTC
- Identify the challenges in the Army JROTC program
- Identify the opportunities of the Army JROTC program
- Define the key words contained in this lesson

Introduction

Key Note Terms

JROTC –a program that teaches high school students the values of good citizenship while giving them an introduction to the US Army

mission – a specific job given to a person or group of persons to accomplish

cadet – a high school student enrolled in the leadership and citizenship activities through JROTC

unique – being the only one of its kind

motivate – provide a need or a purpose that causes a person to want to do something

challenges – to arouse the interest of one's actions or efforts; to stimulate; the quality of requiring full use of one's abilities, energy, and resources; to demand identification from someone before they are allowed to enter or pass

opportunities – favorable or advantageous circumstances or a combination of circumstances

This lesson introduces you to the US Army Junior Reserve Officers' Training Corps (**JROTC**) Program, its **mission**, and the Leadership Education and Training (LET) curriculum for this first level of your instruction. Completing the material in this course requires discipline and hard work, but the reward is well worth your effort. Through Army JROTC, you are building a foundation that will last a lifetime.

If this is your first adventure into the Army JROTC Program—*welcome to the team!* You are among a special group of high school students headed for success.

Your participation as a student or **cadet** in this program shows your willingness to make the most of your high school education. Whatever your reason for taking this course, every member of Army JROTC is special and brings a different cultural dimension to the program. We are proud that you elected to be a part of a **unique** team—a team of winners!

Mission of Army JROTC

The mission of JROTC is "to **motivate** young people to be better citizens." *You* are the focus of Army JROTC's mission. In fact, you are the whole point of Army JROTC; it is devoted to your growth, both as a student and as a person. JROTC is designed to teach the value of citizenship, leadership, service to the community, personal responsibility, and a sense of accomplishment while instilling a sense of self-esteem, teamwork, and self-discipline. This course prepares you for responsible leadership roles while making you aware of your rights, responsibilities, and privileges as an American citizen. JROTC stimulates your career potential and provides you with rewarding opportunities as a student that will benefit you, your community, and the nation. This program is a cooperative effort on the part of the Army and the host institution to give you an opportunity for total development and improve yourself in many ways. JROTC teaches self-discipline, confidence, and pride in a job well done, and it offers you the following **challenges** and **opportunities**:

- **Sharpen your communication skills**
- **Promote and encourage citizenship through participation in community service projects**
- **Develop your leadership potential**
- **Strengthen your self-esteem**
- **Improve your physical fitness**
- **Provide incentives to live drug-free**
- **Promote your graduation from high school and develop a solid foundation for career development**

Some employers spend millions of dollars training their employees to excel in many of these same skills and attitudes. By taking the JROTC course, you have an advantage over thousands of other young people who are seeking their place in the world.

Course Descriptions

The JROTC course is divided into seven sections or units. Each unit offers you new opportunities, challenges, and different perspectives from which you can see yourself and the world around you. Unit 7 is the only optional unit in the JROTC course. Take a quick look at what courses JROTC has to offer.

Unit 1: Citizenship in Action

This unit engages students in the practice of basic citizenship customs and traditions and in the exploration of opportunities for national service. Students learn the purpose of Army JROTC and their roles as cadets. Unit 1 provides opportunities to become familiar with the Department of Defense by examining how all branches of the US armed forces work together to serve the nation by defending democracy and maintaining peace. It also provides opportunities to learn about other service organizations.

Unit 2: Leadership Theory and Application

Unit 2 helps you develop cadet leadership potential through the application of principles, values, and strategies. It prepares you to work effectively as a team member and leader and act as a mentor to other cadets. You are taught the roles of leaders in promoting equal opportunity, addressing prejudice, and preventing sexual harassment and assault. You also compare how those with varied leadership styles approach planning, decision making, problem solving, negotiation, and supervision. In Leadership Lab, you apply leadership skills to drill movements, techniques, and commands as you move from novice to expert.

Unit 3: Foundations for Success

Unit 3 builds essential skills needed to maximize learning potential and future success. This unit lays the groundwork for service learning. You learn to recognize the value of varied learning styles and multiple levels of intelligence. You apply different learning strategies to improve critical thinking, study habits, and communication skills. As you progress through the program, you acquire new learning strategies by taking on responsibilities for teaching younger cadets. You also develop and expand your abilities to resolve conflict and prevent violence. In addition, this unit helps you prepare for life after high school by focusing on career planning and engaging in personal financial planning.

Unit 4: Wellness, Fitness, and First Aid

Unit 4 provides information and tools you need to take responsibility for physical and mental wellness. As a cadet, you learn to assess your personal status and develop plans for improving nutrition and exercise habits and controlling stress. This unit also helps you make responsible choices about substance use and prevent abuse. In addition, you develop proficiency in basic first aid techniques.

Unit 5: Geography, Map Skills, and Environmental Awareness

This unit helps you build map reading and land navigation skills and apply them in learning the art of orienteering and air navigation. This unit develops global awareness as you compare physical, political, economic, and cultural elements of continents, regions, and countries. Finally, this unit examines the global nature of environmental issues.

Unit 6: Citizenship in History and Government

Unit 6 builds the basic skills and interest for participation in civic and political life. You actively engage in the *We the People* curriculum to explore the origins, structure, rights, and responsibilities accorded by the American constitutional form of government. This unit actively engages you in applying problem-solving strategies to current political and social issues.

Unit 7: Cadet Safety and Civilian Marksmanship Program

This final and optional unit teaches elements of air rifle safety and marksmanship. The focus is on history, safety, and operation of air rifles, including taking aim, firing techniques, positions, scoring, and firing for record.

Conclusion

Your success as a cadet is the main goal of all Army JROTC learning experiences. This course focuses on the development of better citizens by building skills in leadership, citizenship, life success, geography, and wellness in a structured interactive environment. The JROTC program is one of the Army's contributions to assisting America's youth to become better citizens. It can prepare you for life by providing a framework for the qualities (skills, knowledge, and positive attitudes) that will help you to succeed—qualities such as courage, candor, competence, commitment, confidence, and character. JROTC offers many opportunities for teamwork, advancement, and self-enrichment that are not available in other high school courses. The effort you put into mastering this program and developing your personal skills will help you become a successful student and productive adult. Several components of this course have been evaluated and identified for college credits after successful completion of the specified requirements.

By enrolling in Army JROTC and joining the ranks of millions of other cadets who know the meaning of success, you have taken the first step toward a promising future.

Lesson Review

1. What is the mission of Army JROTC?
2. What JROTC skills do you look forward to learning?
3. Give an overview of one unit in the JROTC course.
4. Define the term *cadet*.

Lesson 2

The Past and Purpose of Army JROTC

Key Terms

conflict resolution
culturally diverse
leadership
National Defense Act

What You Will Learn to Do

- Analyze the purpose of the Army JROTC program

Linked Core Abilities

- Apply Critical Thinking Techniques

Skills and Knowledge You Will Gain Along the Way

- Describe the US congressional act that created JROTC
- Identify the JROTC program outcomes
- Explain significant historical events that combined military training and education
- Evaluate how the organization supports the operation of the Army
- Define the key words contained in this lesson

Introduction

The JROTC program is designed to teach high school students the value of citizenship, leadership, service to the community, personal responsibility, and a sense of accomplishment, while instilling in them self-esteem, teamwork, and self-discipline. This lesson reviews the birth of the JROTC program as well as its purpose of enabling students to meet their goals for success.

Military and Education: Historical Connections

The tradition of combining formal education with military studies goes back as far as the ancient Greeks. Centuries before JROTC existed, the Greeks, Romans, feudal Europeans, and Japanese had their own versions. In the United States, JROTC had its beginnings in Norwich, Vermont.

In 1819, Captain Alden Partridge, a former superintendent of the US Military Academy at West Point, founded the American Literary, Scientific, and Military Academy in Norwich, Vermont. This academy is now known as Norwich University. Military studies were a major part of the academy's course work. Captain Partridge felt that if his cadets were not prepared to defend their country's rights, their education was incomplete.

In addition to extensive drill practice and physical training (including marches of up to 50 miles per day), the cadets studied Latin, Greek, Hebrew, French, English, 10 types of mathematics, five types of law, and military history dating back to biblical times.

Captain Partridge's academy was so successful that the idea of combining military studies with regular classes spread to other schools in the United States.

The US Army Junior Reserve Officers' Training Corps (JROTC) formally came into being with the passage of the **National Defense Act** of 1916. Under the provisions of the act, high schools were authorized the loan of federal military equipment and the assignment of active duty military personnel as instructors. There was a condition that the instructors follow a prescribed course of training and maintain a minimum enrollment of 100 students over the age of 14 years who were U.S. citizens. Figure 1.2.1 shows an ROTC class from 1919.

The mission of the JROTC program, "To motivate young people to be better citizens," has changed very little since its inception in 1916 (see Figure 1.2.2); however, the JROTC program has changed greatly. Once looked upon primarily as a source of enlisted recruits and officer candidates, it became a citizenship program devoted to the moral, physical and educational uplift of American youth. Although the program retained its military structure and the resultant ability to infuse in its student cadets a sense of discipline and order, it shed its early military content.

The study of ethics, citizenship, communications, leadership, life skills, and other subjects designed to prepare young men and woman to take their place in adult

Key Note Term

National Defense Act – enacted in 1916, this act officially created the Reserve Officers' Training Corps (ROTC) of which Junior ROTC is a part

Figure 1.2.1: An ROTC
drill team in 1919
Courtesy of the US Army.

society, evolved as the core of the program. More recently, an improved student-centered curriculum focusing on character building and civic responsibility is being presented in every JROTC classroom.

JROTC is a continuing success story. From a modest beginning of six units in 1916, JROTC has expanded to 1,645 schools in 2005 and to every state in the nation and American schools overseas in 2005. Cadet enrollment has grown to approximately 273,000 cadets with 3,900 professional instructors in the classrooms. Comprised solely of active duty Army retirees, the JROTC instructors serve as mentors developing the outstanding young citizens of our country.

*Figure 1.2.2: The original
JROTC mission statement*
Courtesy of the US Army.

Where you will find Army JROTC

As of the 2005/2006 school year, the Army JROTC program is active in 1,645 high schools worldwide: in all 50 states, the District of Columbia, Asia, Europe, the Caribbean, and other locations where the United States has an extended presence.

Purpose of JROTC

The US Army's Junior Reserve Officers' Training Corps is designed to teach high school students the value of citizenship, leadership, service to the community, personal responsibility, and a sense of accomplishment, while instilling in them self-esteem, teamwork, and self-discipline. Its focus is reflected in its mission statement: "To motivate young people to be better citizens." It prepares high school students for responsible leadership roles while making them aware of their rights, responsibilities, and privileges as American citizens. The program is a stimulus for promoting graduation from high school, and it provides instruction and rewarding opportunities that will benefit the student, community, and nation.

JROTC prepares high school students for responsible **leadership** roles while making them aware of the benefits of citizenship. Classroom and outside activities, including service learning projects, become opportunities to acquire the knowledge, discipline, and sense of responsibility that are necessary to take charge of one's future. The result is responsible cadets who are sure of themselves, can think on their own, and can express their ideas and opinions clearly and concisely.

Key Note Term

leadership – the ability to influence, lead, or guide others so as to accomplish a mission in the manner desired

The JROTC program teaches cadets to

- Appreciate the ethical values and principles that underlie good citizenship
- Develop leadership potential while living and working cooperatively with others
- Be able to think logically and to communicate effectively with others, both orally and in writing
- Appreciate the importance of physical fitness in maintaining good health
- Understand the importance of high school graduation for a successful future and learn about college and other advanced educations and employment opportunities.
- Develop mental management abilities
- Become familiar with military history as it relates to America's culture and understand the history, purpose, and structure of the military services
- Develop the skills necessary to work effectively as a member of a team

Desired Goals

The JROTC program is a cooperative effort on the part of the Army and the host institution to provide secondary school students with opportunities for total development. The flexibility of the program allows it to bear the scrutiny of professional educators and to meet the needs of the community. Satisfactory completion of the program can lead to advanced placement credit in the Senior ROTC program or advanced rank in the armed forces. Some of the course has been reviewed, and college credit is awarded to cadets after completion of the specified requirements.

The JROTC program is one of the Army's contributions to assisting America's youth to become better citizens. The program produces successful students and productive adults, while fostering in each school a more constructive and disciplined learning environment. This program makes substantial contributions to many communities and ultimately to the nation's future. It is the centerpiece of the Department of Defense's commitment to America's Promise for Youth through its emphasis on community service and teen antidrug efforts.

Leadership education and training goals for cadets are:

- **Graduate from high school**

- **Be good citizens by knowing and exercising the rights, responsibilities, privileges, and freedoms of good citizenship**

- **Gain leadership potential and the ability to live and work cooperatively with others; demonstrate leadership in situations involving conflict resolution**

- **Achieve positive self-esteem and winning behavioral concepts in a culturally diverse society**

- **Learn the ability to think logically and to communicate effectively, with emphasis on effective oral communication**

- **Learn the importance of diet and of physical fitness in maintaining good health and appearance**

- **Gain an understanding of the history, purpose, and structure of Army JROTC**

- **Acquire proficiency in basic military skills (such as drill and ceremonies, first aid, and map reading) that are necessary for working effectively as a member of a team**

- **Learn the importance of citizenship through American history as it relates to America's culture and future from the Revolutionary War period to the present**

- **Learn about the dangers of substance abuse and the importance of mental management, including goal setting and positive self-talk**

Key Note Terms

conflict resolution – the solutions utilized by a society to settle disputes in a cohesive manner

culturally diverse – the presence of multiple and different cultural groups and their behaviors within an organization or institution

Conclusion

JROTC cadets are part of a proud tradition. Similar to their predecessors at Captain Partridge's American Literary, Scientific, and Military Academy, today's cadets are learning to lead and to motivate others while preparing to take part in today's competitive world. The program is a stimulus for promoting graduation from high school, and it provides instruction and rewarding opportunities that will benefit the cadet, community, and ultimately the nation's future. The program produces successful students and productive adults while fostering in each school a more constructive and disciplined learning environment. It is the centerpiece of the Department of Defense's commitment to America's Promise for Youth through its emphasis on community service and teen antidrug efforts. The JROTC program is one of the Army's contributions to assisting America's youth to become better citizens.

In the next lesson will learn about the rank and structure of JROTC, and how you can move up and advance within the program. You will also learn about the benefits of advancing your rank and doing your best.

Lesson Review

1. Where is Army JROTC active?
2. What is the purpose of JROTC? Choose one purpose and discuss how it pertains to you.
3. Name two desired goals from leadership education and training.
4. Discuss the National Defense Act.

Lesson 3

Moving Up in Army JROTC (Rank and Structure)

Key Terms

battalion
company
enlisted
platoons
specialist
squad
subordinate
succession
team

What You Will Learn to Do

- Illustrate the rank and structure of Army JROTC

Linked Core Abilities

- Communicate using verbal, nonverbal, visual, and written techniques

Skills and Knowledge You Will Gain Along the Way

- Identify Army JROTC enlisted and officer insignia
- Correlate cadet ranks to positions on the JROTC cadet battalion organization diagram
- Correlate duties and responsibilities with positions in an Army JROTC cadet battalion
- Evaluate how the organization supports the operation of the Army
- Define the key words contained in this lesson

Introduction

Army JROTC has a well-defined structure of organization. Each person in the unit has an individual job that is part of a larger task, which is part of a much larger mission. This lesson introduces you to the major concepts of command within the military, it shows you the various US Army and Army JROTC **enlisted** and officer ranks, and it presents a typical organizational structure for a JROTC cadet **battalion**.

Pyramid of Authority

There is a pyramid of authority within most organizations. For JROTC and the military, this pyramid of authority, (see Figure 1.3.1), includes individual and group responsibility. In this lesson, you find out how this pyramid works and the ranks and structure of your cadet battalion.

From the top to the bottom of this pyramid is a chain of command. The chain of command is a **succession** of leaders through which authority and commands pass from the leader to **subordinate** and then down through the ranks.

Chain of Command

An effective chain of command can guarantee that all members are on the same **team**, working hard to accomplish their individual tasks and those of the unit. A chain of command depends on team members having various duties.

Span of Control

Span of control is the number of immediate subordinates, one commander or leader can effectively control, supervise, or direct. Maximum and minimum limits of control vary with the conditions under which the unit operates and the complexity of the functions performed.

Unity of Command

In every effective military unit, there must be only one commander who is responsible for all that the unit does or all that it fails to do. This commander must have the necessary authority to carry out the responsibilities of the unit.

Key Note Terms

enlisted – relating to or constituting the part of the military force below officers

battalion – a military unit made up of two or more companies or batteries and a headquarters that is commanded by a lieutenant colonel, is the smallest unit to have a staff, and is administratively self-sufficient

succession – the order of persons next in line for an office or rank that is held by another

subordinate – a person lower in rank or grade

team – a group of people approximating one-half of a squad and normally led by a junior noncommissioned officer

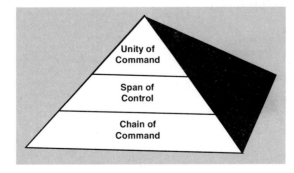

Figure 1.3.1: JROTC Pyramid of Authority
Courtesy the US Army.

Rank and Grade

Rank and *grade* are terms used by the military to classify soldiers. Rank is a title indicating a soldier's position and responsibility; grade is a letter/number combination denoting a soldier's pay rate. Soldiers are classified as either enlisted or officers. Figure 1.3.2 identifies the rank and grade for soldiers in the US Army.

Within the enlisted ranks are two divisions based on experience and skill. The first three enlisted positions are usually entry level.

Figure 1.3.2: Rank and grade for US Army soldiers
Courtesy of US Army JROTC.

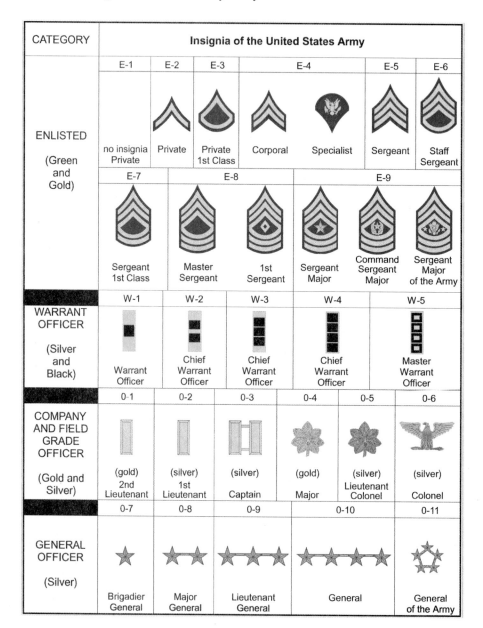

CATEGORY	Insignia of the United States Army						
	E-1	E-2	E-3	E-4		E-5	E-6
ENLISTED (Green and Gold)	no insignia Private	Private	Private 1st Class	Corporal	Specialist	Sergeant	Staff Sergeant
	E-7	E-8		E-9			
	Sergeant 1st Class	Master Sergeant	1st Sergeant	Sergeant Major	Command Sergeant Major	Sergeant Major of the Army	
	W-1	W-2	W-3	W-4	W-5		
WARRANT OFFICER (Silver and Black)	Warrant Officer	Chief Warrant Officer	Chief Warrant Officer	Chief Warrant Officer	Master Warrant Officer		
	0-1	0-2	0-3	0-4	0-5	0-6	
COMPANY AND FIELD GRADE OFFICER (Gold and Silver)	(gold) 2nd Lieutenant	(silver) 1st Lieutenant	(silver) Captain	(gold) Major	(silver) Lieutenant Colonel	(silver) Colonel	
	0-7	0-8	0-9	0-10		0-11	
GENERAL OFFICER (Silver)	Brigadier General	Major General	Lieutenant General	General		General of the Army	

Noncommissioned officers are those personnel who have advanced above the first three entry level positions and are in a supervisory position over personnel in lower grades.

Commissioned officers are appointed by the president and confirmed by the Senate. Commissioned officers have authority over lower ranking officers, warrant officers, and enlisted personnel. Warrant officers rank between an enlisted person and a second lieutenant and primarily hold positions as technicians or administrative supervisors.

Advancement to higher ranks and grades is based on ability, skill, experience, and potential.

A similar structure exists for cadet officers and noncommissioned officers in the Army JROTC program. The *insignia of grade for cadet officers and noncommissioned (enlisted) officers* is shown in Figure 1.3.3. The grade of warrant officer does not exist in Army JROTC. Figure 1.3.4 illustrates a model cadet battalion organizational structure that establishes a clearly defined chain of command and pyramid of authority—much the same as in the Army. A similar organization exists within your own cadet battalion.

The cadet battalion commander reports to the Army instructors and to the principal. All other officers and noncommissioned officers report to the cadet battalion commander through the chain of command.

Each **company** consists of a headquarters section and at least two **platoons**. The company headquarters contains the following key personnel:

- **Company commander**
- **Company executive officer**
- **Company first sergeant**
- **Guidon bearer**

Each platoon is composed of a headquarters section and at least two or three **squads**, with two teams per squad. The key platoon personnel are as follows:

- **Platoon leader**
- **Platoon sergeant**
- **Two or three squad leaders**
- **Two or three assistant squad leaders (if the number of enrolled cadets permits)**
- **Four to six team leaders**

INSIGNIA OF GRADE FOR CADET OFFICERS

| CADET COLONEL | CADET LIEUTENANT COLONEL | CADET MAJOR | CADET CAPTAIN | CADET FIRST LIEUTENANT | CADET SECOND LIEUTENANT |

INSIGNIA OF GRADE FOR CADET ENLISTED PERSONNEL

| CADET COMMAND SERGEANT MAJOR | CADET SERGEANT MAJOR | CADET FIRST SERGEANT | CADET MASTER SERGEANT | CADET SERGEANT FIRST CLASS |

| CADET STAFF SERGEANT | CADET SERGEANT | CADET CORPORAL | CADET PRIVATE FIRST CLASS | CADET PRIVATE |

Duties and Responsibilities

This section provides an outline of the duties and responsibilities for the personnel in a model cadet battalion organization. Your cadet battalion may contain additional positions or list duties and responsibilities different from these; however, the JROTC instructor staff will determine the exact positions and duties for your organization. Cadet leaders are expected to become familiar with their own duties and responsibilities as well as those of their superiors and subordinates.

Use the following duties and responsibilities as a guide only. As you can see in Figure 1.3.4, a model cadet battalion organization has a clearly defined chain of command.

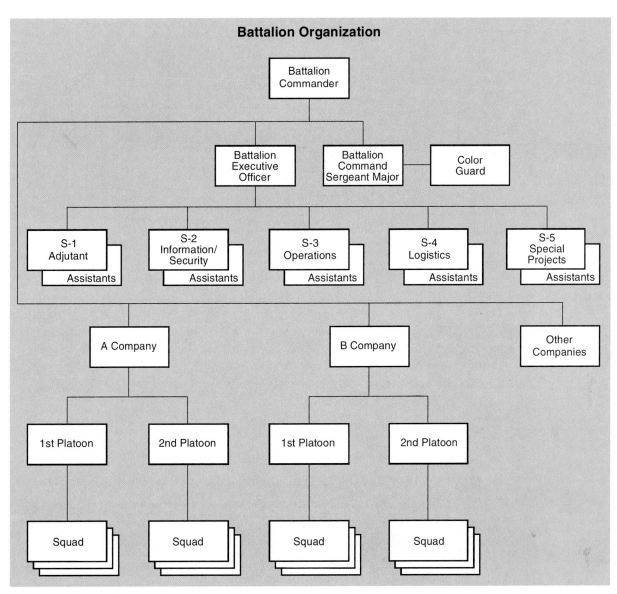

Battalion Organization

Figure 1.3.4: Battalion organization
Courtesy of US Army JROTC.

A. Command Positions

The Army command positions are battalion commander and company commander. These positions are covered in the following sections.

1. Battalion Commander (Cadet Lieutenant Colonel)

This position is the most demanding in a cadet battalion. The instructor staff selects the cadet for this position based on demonstrated leadership ability and academic standing. The appointed cadet must be able to apply common sense and judgment in the solving of problems that affect the entire cadet corps. Specific chain of command is shown in Figure 1.3.5.

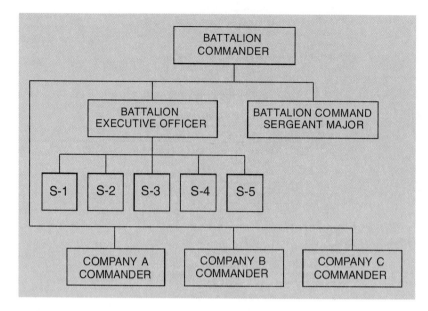

The battalion commander must be mature, willing to accept responsibility, and able to effectively delegate authority and supervise subordinates. The battalion commander controls the staff through the battalion executive officer and the companies through the company commanders while maintaining the final approval authority in the cadet chain of command.

The specific duties of the battalion commander are as follows:

(a) **Command the battalion at all formations.**

(b) **Prepare for and conduct the training of the battalion on drill days.**

(c) **Maintain a direct and personal relationship with the staff and the company commanders.**

(d) **Encourage the company commanders to communicate freely.**

(e) **Use the staff to assist in gathering information and preparing plans for conducting training and controlling the battalion.**

(f) **Designate staff officers to assist in the preparation, execution, and supervision of orders.**

(g) **Ensure that feelings of mutual respect and confidence exist between the staff and company commanders.**

(h) **Ensure that staff members are capable and that they understand their responsibilities to the battalion commander, battalion executive officer, and to the corps of cadets.**

(i) **Ensure orders and actions are in compliance with JROTC regulations, policies, and directives and with local school regulations and policies.**

(j) **Execute all responsibilities in the name of the senior Army instructor; seek advice and assistance from the instructor staff and carry out all of their directives quickly and completely.**

(k) **Arrange the required meetings and assemble the required command or staff personnel to determine any actions that may be necessary in fulfilling the obligations of the cadet battalion.**

(l) **Be prepared to evaluate any member of the battalion, specifically the battalion headquarters personnel and the company commanders.**

(m) Make operational decisions for the cadet battalion.

(n) Preside over officer calls.

(o) Work with school authorities in coordinating activities of the cadet battalion with the organizations of the school, ensuring that battalion activities are in accordance with school policy.

(p) In coordination with the senior Army instructor, assign missions to all extracurricular team captains (such as drill, rifle, and color guard).

(q) Be responsible for all the battalion does or fails to do.

2. Company Commanders (Cadet Captains)

A good company commander is an outstanding leader with lots of initiative. Company commanders get things done. Until orders reach a company commander, they are just plans, something that someone would like to have accomplished. Rather than waiting to be told what to do, company commanders think and plan ahead what seems best for the company. They use common sense action and try not to worry about making mistakes, knowing that the greatest mistake is to do nothing when action is required. Company commanders use all available help to accomplish company duties and to keep subordinates informed, at the same time ensuring that the goals of the mission remain in focus.

A company commander provides the why and how to accomplish the assigned mission. They must check and inspect to ensure that what needed to be done is being accomplished. They must be outstanding leaders with plenty of initiative. Company commanders do not wait for someone to tell them what to do; they think ahead and plan what is best for the company.

> **Note**
>
> In some organizations where actions go from the battalion staff to class leaders, the company commander has the duties of a special assignment officer.

The company commander

- **Is responsible for all the company does or fails to do**
- **Keeps the battalion commander apprised of the status of the company at all times**
- **Ensures the company is prepared to accomplish its assigned mission in a satisfactory manner**
- **Is an expert in drill**

The principal duties of the company commander are as follows:

(a) Command the company at all formations.

(b) Ensure that all members of the company know and use the chain of command.

(c) Consult the training schedule, study the drill references, and ensure that subordinates are prepared to instruct.

(d) Check with the instructor staff daily prior to formation to obtain any changes or other information they may want announced.

(e) Seek advice from the battalion commander or the instructor staff when encountering problems to which answers are not known.

(f)   Execute the orders of the battalion commander even though the company commander may personally disagree with them.

(g)   Conduct short inspections at every formation, making on-the-spot corrections as necessary; follow up to ensure that deficiencies from earlier inspections are corrected.

(h)   Make each cadet an effective member of the team; take an interest in the cadets and their problems; offer advice and help them to solve their problems.

(i)   Make on-the-spot corrections at any time to ensure that all members of the company understand and comply with cadet regulations.

(j)   Keep the company executive officer informed in case of absence.

B. Battalion Executive Officer (Cadet Major)

The cadet battalion executive officer (XO) supervises, directs, and coordinates the cadet battalion staff to prevent overlapping efforts and to ensure that the commander's desires are understood and achieved. The cadet battalion XO keeps the staff informed of the commander's policies and keeps the cadet battalion commander informed of the status of projects assigned to the staff. The cadet battalion XO assumes command of the cadet battalion in the absence of the cadet battalion commander.

The primary duties of the cadet battalion XO are as follows:

(a)   Organize the cadet battalion staff properly and ensure that it works as a team.

(b)   Inspect the work of the cadet battalion staff and make other inspections as directed by the cadet battalion commander.

(c)   Ensure that the battalion staff officers prepare and submit reports on time and that they are engaged in future planning.

(d)   Act as the commander of troops during ceremonies.

(e)   Ensure that instructions and orders issued to the cadet battalion are in accordance with the established policies of the cadet battalion commander and report all violations of orders to the cadet battalion commander.

(f)   Perform other duties as assigned by the cadet battalion commander or the instructor staff.

C. Battalion Coordinating Staff Officers (Usually Cadet Captains/Majors)

The battalion coordinating staff officers are divided into five different categories. The following sections detail these positions and their responsibilities.

1. Battalion Adjutant (S-1)

The battalion adjutant is the administrative assistant to the battalion commander. The adjutant is also responsible for performing other administrative duties as assigned by the battalion commander, the battalion executive officer, or the instructor staff. The specific duties of the battalion adjutant are as follows:

(a) Assist in aligning the battalion at all battalion formations.

(b) Receive the report at battalion formations from the company commanders and receive the names of absentees from the sergeant major.

(c) Plan for the conduct of special ceremonies in coordination with the operations and training officer.

(d) Prepare and publish any orders necessary for the operation of the cadet battalion.

(e) Maintain the qualification records and personal files on all cadets.

(f) Publish and execute the cadet battalion's recruiting plan.

(g) Collect, consolidate, post, and maintain all merit and demerit reports and records.

(h) Coordinate with the company commanders and the battalion staff on recommendations to the instructor staff on reassignments and organization; assign cadets to the various companies and maintain a record of those assignments.

(i) Prepare periodic strength reports under the supervision of the instructor staff and keep the manning board posted and up to date.

(j) Report incidents that are prejudicial to good order and discipline, and submit reports to the instructor staff, the cadet battalion commander, and the executive officer.

(k) In coordination with the S-2, make recommendations to improve morale and welfare of the cadet battalion.

(l) Perform other duties as assigned by the battalion commander, the battalion executive officer, or the instructor staff.

2. Battalion Intelligence or Security Officer (S-2)

The battalion S-2 assists the battalion commander and the instructor staff in matters pertaining to unit security and enforces the provisions of the security requirements for the battalion. The specific duties of the S-2 are as follows:

(a) Assist in making periodic inspections of the security of weapons (if available within the unit).

(b) Make periodic inspections of the security of the supply room and equipment storage areas.

(c) Make necessary on-the-spot corrections resulting from security inspections and keep the battalion commander and instructor staff informed.

(d) In coordination with the S-1, report incidents that are prejudicial to good order and discipline, and submit reports to the instructor staff, the cadet battalion commander, and the executive officer.

(e) Perform other duties as assigned by the battalion commander, battalion executive officer, or the instructor staff. For example, in some JROTC units, the S-2 may also be responsible for the information center and the duties of a public affairs officer if one is not assigned or for the duties of an ordnance officer if one is not assigned.

3. Battalion Operations and Training Officer (S-3)

The battalion S-3 assists the battalion commander in the preparation, conduct, and supervision of all training activities of the cadet battalion. Additionally, the S-3 keeps the commander advised on the progress of training within the battalion. Specifically, the principal duties of the S-3 are as follows:

(a) Prepare the weekly training schedules.

(b) Select and designate cadet instructors in coordination with the instructor staff; post the weekly training schedules not later than one week in advance of training on all bulletin boards.

(c) Assign areas for outdoor training and ensure classrooms are available and prepared for instruction.

(d) Inspect the drill field prior to use by the battalion and prepare it for ceremonies.

(e) Coordinate the training of the rifle team(s), drill team(s), color guard, and the honor guard; also coordinate training for guidon bearers and manual of the saber for cadet officers.

(f) Organize events such as reviews, parades, and extracurricular activities.

(g) Plan and supervise field events.

(h) Inspect cadet training for compliance.

(i) Maintain the unit reference library.

(j) Maintain the training portion of cadet records.

(k) Assume command of the battalion in the absence of both the battalion commander and XO.

(l) Supervise the activities of the battalion communications officer.

(m) Perform other duties as assigned by the battalion commander, the battalion executive officer, or the instructor staff.

4. Battalion Logistics or Supply Officer (S-4)

The battalion logistics or supply officer is responsible for the maintenance, security, record keeping, issue, and turn-in of all US government property (except ordnance). The S-4 coordinates the securing of property with the S-2. Some of the duties of the S-4 are as follows:

(a) Create a JROTC Clothing and Equipment Record for each cadet. Maintain all cadet supply records in proper order.

(b) Maintain accountability of all equipment and supplies used by the unit.

(c) Conduct periodic inventories of the on-hand supplies and equipment; submit weekly reports to the instructor staff on the availability of supplies and on the condition of equipment.

(d) Ensure that adequate cleaning materials are available for use during assigned maintenance activities.

(e) In coordination with the battalion sergeant major, make periodic inspections of the national, state, and organizational colors for serviceability.

(f) Maintain security of all items of clothing and equipment in the supply room and training aids storage area.

(g) Maintain the supply room in a neat and orderly fashion at all times.

(h) Maintain a running inventory of all supplies/property, determine supply requirements, and prepare requisitions for equipment and supplies required for the cadet battalion.

(i) Issue clothing, insignia, and other supply items as directed by the battalion commander, the battalion executive officer, or the instructor staff.

(j) Collect and dispose of excess salvage equipment and clothing.

(k) Supervise the activities of the battalion ordnance officer (if assigned).

(l) Perform other duties as assigned by the battalion commander, the battalion executive officer, or the instructor staff.

5. Special Projects Officer (S-5) (Optional)

The duties of the cadet battalion special projects officer, if assigned, are as follows:

(a) Plan and coordinate special projects as outlined by the cadet battalion commander, the cadet battalion XO, or the instructor staff.

(b) Maintain records on all activities and coordination as they pertain to each project.

(c) Keep the cadet battalion commander, the cadet battalion XO, and the instructor staff informed as to the progress of, or any problems encountered with, the projects.

D. Battalion Special Staff Officers

Battalion special staff officers are covered in the following sections.

1. Battalion Communications (Signal) Officer

The communications officer is responsible for setting up and maintaining all signal or public address/projection/sound equipment issued to the cadet battalion. Additionally, this officer ensures that all equipment is operational and that spare parts are on hand at all times.

2. Battalion Ordnance Officer

The ordnance officer advises the S-4, battalion commander, and instructor staff on the condition of all weapons. This officer supervises the issue, maintenance, and turn-in of all weapons; maintains the weapons roster; and prepares and issues weapons cards to cadets.

3. Battalion Public Affairs (Information) Officer

This officer acts as the contact between the corps of cadets and all news media and student publications. This officer publicizes as many of the activities of the Army JROTC program as possible to create an outstanding image of the cadet battalion and to reinforce the image of the school. Some of the specific duties of the public affairs/information officer are as follows:

(a) Maintain the cadet information board in the correct state showing news events of local, national, and international interest.

(b) Keep abreast of newsworthy events in the cadet battalion; prepare and distribute news releases, articles, or announcements on events of the JROTC program to appropriate news agencies. Submit all articles to the instructor staff for approval prior to their release.

(c) Act as the battalion's point of contact with the school newspaper and yearbook committees. Ensure at least one item of JROTC interest makes every publication of the school newspaper.

(d) Maintain the cadet battalion scrapbook.

(e) Make recommendations to improve morale and welfare of the cadet battalion.

E. Battalion Staff

The battalion staff works directly for the battalion commander.

Battalion Command Sergeant Major

The battalion command sergeant major is the principal cadet enlisted assistant to the battalion commander. As the senior enlisted member of the cadet corps, the command sergeant major supervises the other noncommissioned officers (NCOs) of the battalion and companies. Specific duties of the command sergeant major are as follows:

(a) Assist subordinate NCOs, the battalion XO, and the adjutant with administrative duties/details.

(b) Advise and assist the battalion commander in all matters pertaining to the enlisted members of the cadet battalion.

(c) Assist the adjutant in the formation and alignment of the battalion at all battalion formations.

(d) Receive lists of absentees from the companies and submit them to the adjutant.

(e) Supervise the color guard and all flag details. Ensure that company first sergeants submit their weekly flag details on time, post those rosters, and ensure that members selected for detail receive their notification slips prior to the assignment.

(f) Ensure the flag details are properly trained.

(g) Ensure that the battalion area, including the drill field, is maintained in a high state of neatness at all times and that JROTC offices and classrooms are kept neat and orderly.

(h) Preside over all noncommissioned officer promotion boards.

(i) Assume command of the battalion in the absence of all officers.

(j) Perform other duties as assigned by the battalion commander, the battalion executive officer, or the instructor staff.

F. Other Staff Assistants (Optional)

There are other staff assistants that need to be mentioned, and these positions are detailed in the following sections.

1. Rifle Team Captain

Primary duties are as follows:

(a) Organize the training schedule for the rifle marksmanship team.

(b) Schedule matches/competitions for the rifle marksmanship team; coordinate these activities with the S-3 and the cadet battalion training schedule.

(c) Supervise maintenance and care of the JROTC rifle range.

(d) Develop the rifle marksmanship program for the cadet battalion.

(e) Coordinate weapon requirements with the S-4.

2. Drill Team Captain

Primary duties are as follows:

(a) Recruit members and organize the cadet drill team.

(b) Schedule the drill team training program.

(c) Coordinate uniform and weapon requirements with the S-4.

(d) Schedule drill programs, parades, and competitions for the drill team; coordinate these activities with the S-3 and the cadet battalion training schedule.

3. Color Guard Commander

Primary duties are as follows:

(a) Train members of the color guard.

(b) Represent the cadet battalion at activities as directed by the cadet battalion commander, the cadet battalion XO, or the instructor staff.

(c) Coordinate uniform, flag, and weapon requirements with the S-4.

(d) Schedule competitions for the color guard; coordinate these activities with the S-3 and the cadet battalion training schedule.

(e) Inspect uniform and personal appearance of color guard members.

(f) Be thoroughly familiar with FM 22-5.

G. Other Company, Platoon, and Squad Personnel

Other company, platoon, and squad personnel are important, and those positions are covered in the following sections.

1. Company Executive Officer (Cadet 1st Lieutenant)

The company executive officer (XO) assists the company commander in the training of the company and performs such administrative duties as designated by the commander. The company XO should be well versed in all functions of the company and prepared to assume command of the company in the absence of the company commander.

2. Company First Sergeant

The company first sergeant is responsible to the company XO (if assigned) or to the company commander for administrative matters. The company first sergeant is responsible for company formations, submits absentee reports to the battalion sergeant major, checks all merits and demerits with the company commander before submitting them to the S-1, and keeps the company commander informed on all matters pertaining to health and welfare of the unit. The first sergeant assumes command of the company in the absence of all officers.

3. Platoon Leader (Cadet 2nd Lieutenant)

The platoon leader is a very desirable position. A platoon leader has a platoon of cadets for whom they are directly responsible. Primarily, the job is one of leadership, training, and discipline. Platoon leaders also have the opportunity and privilege to be a role model, coach, and counselor. The duties and responsibilities of a platoon leader are as follows:

(a) **Keep the company commander apprised of the status of the platoon at all times.**

(b) **Organize and maintain an effective chain of command. Learn the name of everyone in the platoon and use their names when addressing them.**

(c) **Conduct an inspection of the platoon at formations.**

(d) **Use the chain of command to accomplish tasks; work mainly with the platoon sergeant and the squad leaders.**

(e) **Know all cadet regulations and ensure that all members of the platoon also know and follow them.**

(f) **Enforce orders from superiors whether in agreement with them or not; however, if the platoon leader thinks an order is wrong, it should be discussed with the chain of command or the instructors, as necessary. Develop a spirit of teamwork so as to instill respect, obedience, and cooperation in the unit.**

(g) **Know all phases of drill; supervise and conduct platoon drills. If the platoon leader is the senior officer present in a formation, conduct company drills.**

(h) **Set high standards of personal appearance and conduct for yourself. The platoon leader sets the example for the platoon to follow.**

(i) **Make an effort to resolve all leadership, training, and disciplinary problems at this level; if a problem cannot be solved, seek the advice and assistance of the company commander, company XO, or first sergeant.**

(j) **Provide assistance/counseling to personnel in the platoon, especially when requested by a squad leader or the platoon sergeant, and/or when necessary for performance or disciplinary reasons.**

4. Platoon Sergeant (Cadet Staff Sergeant)

Platoon sergeants set the example at all times; assist in the supervision of the squad leaders; develop a spirit of teamwork in the platoon; submit absentee reports to the company first sergeant; assist the platoon leader in training the platoon; counsel personnel at a squad leader's request; and assume control of the platoon in the absence of the platoon leader.

5. Squad Leaders (Other Cadet NCOs)

Squad leaders are responsible to their platoon leader/sergeant for the appearance, conduct, training, and discipline of their squad. They ensure that each squad member learns and does what is expected and maintains high standards of behavior. Squad leaders must

(a) Set the example at all times.

(b) Know the number, names, and personal information on all assigned personnel.

(c) Counsel/assist squad members with JROTC matters or help them find solutions to other issues when possible; refer to the platoon sergeant/leader if unable to handle/resolve an issue.

(d) Form the squad correctly. Make an accurate report by name of those persons present and absent during common hour activities, company platoon formations, and other cadet battalion activities.

(e) Be thoroughly familiar with individual, squad, and platoon drill. When conducting drill, instruct/demonstrate the movement and allow time for individual performance; then supervise team leaders and squad members to ensure they perform properly. Conduct inspections to ensure personnel are prepared for training.

(f) Develop responsibility and leadership in team leaders and be the first person they turn to for assistance and advice.

6. Team Leaders (NCOs)

Team leaders are responsible for the formation, appearance, training, and discipline of their team members and must be ready to assume control of the squad in the absence of the squad leader. Team leaders assist their squad leaders as directed and must

(a) Set the example at all times.

(b) Know the number, names, and personal information on all assigned personnel.

(c) Assist team members with JROTC matters when possible; refer them to the squad leader for assistance if you are unable to handle/resolve an issue.

(d) Be thoroughly familiar with individual and squad drill; inspect team members during formations, ensuring they know what is required of them.

7. Team Members

The duties and responsibilities of a team member are as follows:

(a) Maintain and wear the entire uniform immaculately when prescribed.

(b) Properly safeguard and care for all equipment and materials for which you are responsible.

(c) Ensure you are on time for all official formations requiring your presence.

(d) Conduct yourself in a manner that brings credit to yourself, the cadet battalion, and your school.

Conclusion

The cadet battalion structure is set up to ensure a quick and clear flow of commands. Each individual cadet has a job to do, which is part of a squad task, that then proceeds up the chain of command until that individual task is a part of the battalion's overall mission.

How far you climb in rank is up to you. Each cadet battalion, depending on unit requirements, has opportunities for advancement. You will receive the necessary training and have the opportunity to demonstrate excellence in what skills and knowledge you have learned. Your actions and abilities ultimately will let your battalion leaders know if you are ready to move up.

Taking on added responsibility in a leadership position is part of what JROTC is all about. Moving up in JROTC takes three things: desire, time, and work. JROTC will give you the time, but you must have the desire and be willing to put in the work.

The following lesson deals with the different types of awards for which you can be eligible. You will learn about unit, individual, and institutional awards, and how they can benefit you in your career and educational goals.

Chapter 1

Lesson Review

1. Define the terms *rank* and *grade*.
2. List the five key platoon personnel positions.
3. What are the primary duties of the color guard commander?
4. Which position interests you the most? Why?

The Signs of Success

Key Terms

academic awards
athletic awards
commitment
decorations
individual awards
initiative
military awards
miscellaneous awards
motivation
responsibility
unit awards

What You Will Learn to Do

- Determine which signs of success you plan to accomplish within JROTC

Linked Core Abilities

- Build your capacity for life-long learning
- Take responsibility for your actions and choices

Skills and Knowledge You Will Gain Along the Way

- Compare the three types of unit decorations
- Identify the components of individual award categories
- Identify the four institutional award categories
- Define award criteria
- Define the key words contained in this lesson

Chapter 1

Introduction

This lesson covers the various types of award programs you can work toward while in JROTC. You learn about unit awards as well as individual awards, and you are also introduced to the four types of institutional awards. This lesson also examines the criteria you need to meet to be eligible for awards, and how these awards can further your educational and career opportunities.

JROTC Awards Program

Key Note Terms

unit awards – recognition given to a JROTC unit for being an honor unit or an honor unit with distinction

individual awards – recognition given to an individual for outstanding academic, athletic, or military achievement or for excellence in competition, contribution to unit goals, or outstanding service

The JROTC Awards Program is for *any* JROTC cadet who excels. It recognizes high levels of performance, excellence, and achievement. Because the JROTC program recognizes that not all cadets have the same abilities and skills, the Army designed its awards program to recognize as many personal traits as possible in cadets. There are two kinds of awards: **unit awards** that recognize unit excellence, and **individual awards** that recognize personal achievement. Both of these types of awards are covered in this lesson.

The Army rewards cadets for extracurricular activities, excellence in competition, contributions to unit goals, and outstanding service. Also, you may receive national recognition from patriotic and civic organizations for outstanding academic and military achievements. To achieve any of these awards, however, you must prepare yourself for success. You learn those preparation skills in this lesson.

Strive for Success

Success is a process in motion, not a fixed mark. A successful person is one who is consistently learning, growing, and working toward a goal. When people perceive success as an end point to a process instead of the process itself, they often wonder why they feel unsatisfied when they get there. If you don't continually grow and add new goals, you may feel dissatisfied, empty, aimless, or "stuck."

Striving for success takes effort. It requires motivation, commitment, initiative, responsibility, and a willingness to face your fears. In combination, these strategies will help you father and retain knowledge as well as create new knowledge.

Getting Motivated

Key Note Term

motivation – a force that moves a person to action; often inspired by an idea, fact, event, or goal

Motivation is the energy that fuels your drive to achieve, and a motivator is anything that moves you forward. There are at least as many motivators as there are people, and what motivates any given person can change from situation to situation. For example, some potential motivators for attending school could be learning a marketable skill, supporting a family, or improving yourself.

It's human to lose your motivation from time to time. For reasons ranging from a stressful life change to simply a period of low energy, sometimes you might not feel like accomplishing anything. The following can help you build or renew motivation.

- **Spend time reflecting on why your goal is meaningful to you**
- **Make a decision to take one step toward your goal, rather than feeling overwhelmed by the "big picture"**
- **Reward yourself for a job well done**
- **Examine and deal with obstacles**
- **Begin or begin again**

Making a Commitment

So, how do you focus the energy of motivation? Make a **commitment**. Commitment means that you do what you say you will do. When you honor a commitment, you prove to yourself and others that your intentions can be trusted.

Commitment requires that you focus your energy on something specific. A decision to change your life or make a million dollars might intimidate you into staying motionless on the couch. Instead, break any goal into manageable pieces, naming the steps you will use to achieve it.

To make and keep a commitment, consider the following:

- **State your commitment concretely**
- **Get started and note your progress**
- **Renew your commitment on a regular basis**
- **Keep track of each commitment**

Making and keeping commitments help you maintain a steady focus on your most important goals. You feel a sense of accomplishment as you experience gradual change.

Showing Initiative

When you show **initiative**, you push yourself to take the first difficult step toward achieving your goal. Initiative jump-starts your journey and helps to renew motivation.

Initiative requires you to keep on top of your goals and to listen to your instincts. You may discover that you want to do more than what is expected of you, which can be positive at school, in JROTC, and in the workplace.

Being Responsible

Being responsible is all about living up to your obligations, both those that are imposed on you as well as those that you impose on yourself. Through action, you prove that you are responsible. When something needs to be done, responsible people do the work as efficiently as possible and to the best of their ability.

Responsibility can take enormous effort. Throughout your life, you will have moments when you just don't want to respond. In those moments, you need to weigh the positive and negative effects and decide what to do. Being responsible has definite benefits, such as making a crucial impression on others and earning the trust and respect of your instructors, supervisors, relatives, friends, and family. When people trust you, they may give you increasing power and opportunities for growth because you have shown you are capable of making the best of both.

> **Key Note Term**
>
> **commitment** – a pledge or promise to do something; dedication to a long-term course of action

> **Key Note Term**
>
> **initiative** – the power to begin or follow through energetically with a plan or task; determination

> **Key Note Term**
>
> **responsibility** – the quality of being responsible, trustworthy, and accountable for your actions

Facing Your Fears

Everyone experiences fear at some point in their lives. New experiences are often frightening and exciting at the same time. The changes involved in pursuing an education can incite fear. You may wonder if you can handle the work, if you will get along with your instructors, of if you have chosen the right school or program. You may worry that family and friends expect too much or might stand in your way. You may also have fears about the future: Will your education prepare you to find a job that you like and that pays well?

Education presents challenges that demand a willingness to push your limits and face your fears. The following can help you face your fears with courage.

- **Acknowledge and examine your fears**
- **Develop a plan of attack to overcome your fears**
- **Move ahead with your plan**

As you work through your fears, talk about them with people you trust. Often, the ideas other people have about gaining control of fear can help you. When you acknowledge and evaluate your fears, it can provide valuable clues as to what blocks your success. Facing your fears and taking action promote healthy self-esteem.

Unit Awards

Key Note Term

decorations – an indication of honor, such as a badge, medal, or ribbon

JROTC enables you to succeed in a variety of ways. One way to show your success is to strive for unit awards. The JROTC Awards Program offers three types of unit **decorations**: Merit Unit, Honor Unit, and Honor Unit with Distinction. The Merit Unit, Honor Unit, and the Honor Unit with Distinction awards are chosen based on results of a formal inspection and on exceptionally high standards of training and discipline throughout the school year. All service academies reserve 20 appointments for honor graduates of schools that have been designated Honor Units with Distinction. These cadets may apply for appointment to one of these service academies.

The Department of the Army adopted the Merit Unit insignia for Army JROTC cadets in units designated as Merit Units. The Merit Unit insignia is a small white enamel five-pointed star. You wear this insignia above the right pocket of Class A or B uniforms.

The Honor Unit insignia for Army JROTC cadets in units designated as Honor Units. It is a small blue enamel five-pointed star. This insignia is worn in the same manner as the Merit Unit insignia.

The Honor Unit with Distinction insignia is similar to the Honor Unit insignia, except that it is yellow. The Department of the Army also adopted this device for all Army JROTC cadets in units designated as Honor Units with Distinction. This insignia is worn in the same manner as the Honor Unit insignia, which is above the right pocket of Class A or B uniforms..

Individual Awards

Each Army JROTC unit can award various types of individual awards to its cadets for recognition of excellence, outstanding achievement, or superior performance. There are two main categories of individual awards: institutional and national awards.

Institutional Awards

Superintendents, principals, and Army instructors can present institutional awards to individual JROTC cadets for reasons of academic excellence, military and athletic achievement or performance, participation in community parades, excelling in recruiting programs, and other reasons determined by instructors. Each cadet has an opportunity to earn these awards.

The following is the order of merit (or importance) for these awards along with the number of ribbons available for each type. Within each category, these awards (or ribbons) are worn in their numerical order.

1. **Academic Awards—10 ribbons**
2. **Military Awards—15 ribbons**
3. **Athletic Awards—5 ribbons**
4. **Miscellaneous Awards—5 ribbons**

National Awards

National awards recognize individual JROTC cadets for heroic, distinguished, meritorious, and other commendable acts and achievements.

Army JROTC Awards

JROTC offers numerous awards to those who are willing to go above and beyond the minimum effort asked of them. These categories include academic, military, athletic, and miscellaneous awards as well as national awards. The following sections offer you more detail on each award and what it takes to earn them.

Academic Awards

Table 1.4.1 shows the various types of **academic awards** that you can earn.

> **Key Note Term**
>
> **academic awards –** recognition given to individual cadets for scholastic achievement or excellence

Table 1.4.1: Academic Awards

Award	Awarded By	Criteria
Distinguished Cadet Award for Scholastic Excellence (N-1-1)	Superintendent	Awarded annually to one cadet who exhibits the highest degree of excellence in scholastics
Academic Excellence Award (N-1-2)	Principal	Awarded annually to one cadet in each LET level for maintaining highest school academic grades
Academic Achievement Ribbon (N-1-3)	DAI/SAI (awarded by the DAI, except for in single units; then awarded by the SAI)	Awarded annually to those cadets who maintain a grade of A in all academic subjects
Perfect Attendance Ribbon (N-1-4)	SAI	Awarded to cadets with no unexcused absences during each quarter/semester
Student Government Ribbon (N-1-5)	Principal	Awarded to cadets elected to student government offices
LET Service Ribbon (N-1-6)	SAI	Awarded to cadets successfully completing first quarter/semester of training of each LET year
N-1-7 through N-1-10	DAI/SAI	Awarded based on criteria developed locally and approved by region commanders

Military Awards

Table 1.4.2 lists the various types of **military awards** that are available to you through hard work and effort.

Key Note Term

military awards – recognition given to individuals for participating in JROTC-sponsored activities, or for leadership excellence

Table 1.4.2: Military Awards

Award	Awarded By	Criteria
DAI/SAI Leadership Ribbon (N-3-1)	SAI	Awarded annually to one cadet per LET level who displays the highest degree of leadership
Personal Appearance Ribbon (N-3-2)	SAI	Awarded annually to cadets who consistently present an outstanding appearance
Proficiency Ribbon (N-3-3)	DAI/SAI (awarded by the DAI, except for in single units where it is awarded by the SAI)	Awarded annually to those cadets who have demonstrated an exceptionally high degree of leadership, academic achievement, and performance of duty
Drill Team Ribbon (N-3-4)	SAI	Awarded annually to drill team members
Orienteering Ribbon (N-3-5)	SAI	Awarded annually to cadets who are members of orienteering teams
Color/Honor Guard Ribbon (N-3-6)	SAI	Awarded annually to members of the color/honor guards
Rifle Team Ribbon (N-3-7)	SAI	Awarded annually to members of the rifle team
Adventure Training Ribbon (N-3-8)	SAI	Awarded annually to cadets who are members of adventure training units
Commendation Ribbon (N-3-9)	SAI	Awarded to cadets whose performance of duty far exceeds that expected for grade and experience
Good Conduct Ribbon (N-3-10)	SAI	Awarded annually to the cadets who have demonstrated outstanding conduct and participation
Summer Camp Participation Ribbon (N-3-11)	SAI	Awarded to those cadets who participate in summer camp
N-3-12 through N-3-15	DAI/SAI	Awarded based on criteria developed locally and approved by region commanders

Athletic Awards

Athletic awards are achievable through JROTC. All you need is an attitude geared toward success.

Key Note Term

athletic awards – recognition given to individuals for athletic participation or excellence

Table 1.4.3: Athletic Awards

Award	Awarded By	Criteria
Varsity Athletic Ribbon (N-2-1)	Principal	Awarded annually to cadets who excel in varsity sports
Physical Fitness Award (N-2-2)	SAI	Awarded annually to cadets who maintain excellent physical fitness; male cadets must run one mile in 8:30 minutes or less and female cadets in 10:45 minutes or less
ROTC Athletic Ribbon (N-2-3)	SAI	Awarded annually to cadets who excel in ROTC athletics
N-2-4 through N-2-5	DAI/SAI (awarded by the DAI, except for in single units where it is awarded by the SAI)	Awarded based on criteria developed locally and approved by region commanders

Miscellaneous Awards

There are several **miscellaneous awards** that you can earn.

Key Note Term

miscellaneous awards – recognition given to individuals for participation in school or community service activities, or in activities that enhance the JROTC program

Table 1.4.3: Miscellaneous Awards

Award	Awarded By	Criteria
Parade Ribbon (N-4-1)	SAI	Awarded to cadets who have participated in local community parades (such as Veterans Day or Memorial Day parades)
Recruiting Ribbon (N-4-2)	SAI	Awarded to cadets who recruit students into the JROTC program.
N-4-3 through N-4-4	DAI/SAI (awarded by the DAI, except for in single units where it is awarded by the SAI)	Awarded based on criteria developed locally and approved by region commanders
Superior Cadet Award (N-4-5)	SAI	Awarded to cadet staff officers for outstanding performance
Service Learning Ribbon (N-4-6)	SAI	Awarded annually to cadets who participate in service learning projects

National Awards

With your eye on success, you can also earn national awards.

Table 1.4.5: National Awards

Award	Criteria
Medal for Heroism	Awarded to any JROTC/NDCC cadet who has been distinguished by an act of heroism
Superior Cadet Decoration	Awarded annually to the outstanding cadet of each LET level
Legion of Valor Bronze Cross for Achievement	Awarded annually to a LET 3 cadet for achievement of scholastic excellence in military and academic subjects and development of leadership
Sons of the American Revolution Award	Awarded to a cadet enrolled in ROTC for meritorious achievement
The Military Order of the World Wars Award	Awarded annually for overall improvement in military and scholastic studies
Daughters of the American Revolution Award	Awarded annually to a cadet at each institution for outstanding ability and achievement
Association of Military Colleges and Schools of the US Award	Awarded annually to a full-time cadet who has completed at least two full years of JROTC
American Legion and American Legion Auxiliary Awards	Awarded annually to outstanding cadets at each institution for general military excellence and scholastic achievement
The National Sojourners Award	Awarded annually to an outstanding cadet at each installation who contributed the most to encourage and demonstrate Americanism
US Army Recruiting Command Award for JROTC	Awarded annually to a cadet at each school in recognition of outstanding achievement and contributions to the JROTC program
Association of the US Army Award	Presented at the discretion of the DAI/SAI and the local AUSA chapter according to criteria that best suit the school's program

Conclusion

The JROTC Awards Program has much to offer. It can give you the chance to be recognized either individually or as a member of a unit for your accomplishments and excellence. To earn these awards, you must be as competitive as your abilities and skills will allow, perhaps putting forth extra effort to be competitive. The result, however, is self-satisfaction and sometimes public recognition for your accomplishments.

In Lesson 5 you will learn what it takes to maintain your personal appearance and your uniform. You will learn how to keep your uniform and shoes in top-notch shape, and how you can present yourself in the most professional and flattering light at all times.

Lesson Review

1. Compare and contrast unit awards and individual awards.

2. Which type of award interests you the most?

3. How do you wear the unit awards?

4. Define the term *decoration*.

Lesson 5

Your Personal Appearance and Uniform

Key Terms

align
Battle Dress Uniforms
bisecting
Class A and B uniforms
chevron
ferrule
fitted
formal inspections
garrison cap
gigline
hemmed
insignia
nap
nonsubdued
precedence
pre-inspection
shoulder marks
sized
tarnish

What You Will Learn to Do

- Demonstrate proper cadet appearance

Linked Core Abilities

- Take responsibility for your actions and choices

Skills and Knowledge You Will Gain Along the Way

- Describe the uniform-wearing guidelines
- Demonstrate placement of uniform awards, insignias, and decorations
- Conduct a uniform pre-inspection
- Prepare for uniform inspection
- Define the key words contained in this lesson

Introduction

People often form opinions of others based on their personal appearance. A good personal appearance complements the wearing of your uniform. A neatly pressed and clean uniform, with properly placed ribbons, awards, and insignia, demonstrates that JROTC cadets have pride in themselves as well as in their unit, and they use self-discipline to get things done. To assist you in this effort, this lesson covers the proper placement for the awards, decorations, and **insignia** you will be required to wear on your uniform. This lesson also presents four factors you can use to assess your personal appearance, reinforces the importance of a neat and clean appearance, and explains how those factors relate to your appearance in uniform.

Army JROTC Uniforms

The word *uniform* comes from two Latin words, *unus* and *forma*, that mean "one form." Your JROTC uniform sets you apart from others and tells who and what you are. Uniforms date back to ancient times; for example, certain Romans wore togas. Today, society has uniforms to identify jobs and groups. Policemen, firefighters, athletic teams, and school bands all have uniforms.

Wear the JROTC uniform with pride! Every part of the uniform has a place and a reason. Later in this lesson you learn how to place insignias, awards, rank, and decorations on your uniform. First, however, take a look at the different types of JROTC uniforms.

Class A, B, and Battle Dress Uniforms

Figure 1.5.1 shows **Class A uniforms** for men and women. You wear them during ceremonies, social functions, **formal inspections**, and as required by your instructor.

Figure 1.5.2 shows **Class B uniforms** for men and women. These uniforms are worn during all occasions except field training and formal social occasions. The Class B uniforms are also worn at other times as required by your instructors.

Figure 1.5.3 shows the **Battle Dress Uniforms** (BDUs) for men and women. They are worn at Junior Reserve Officer Training Course Cadet Leadership Course (JCLC) and for participation on special teams.

Key Note Terms

insignia – an emblem, badge, medal, or other distinguishing mark of office, honor, or position; denotes grade and branch; may also indicate capacity and duty assignment in the U.S. Army

Class A uniforms – service uniforms that consist of an Army green coat, trousers, or slacks; a long or short sleeve shirt; a black four-in-hand tie or black neck tab; and other authorized accessories

formal inspection – an official examination of JROTC units that takes place on a prescribed schedule

Class B uniforms – service uniforms that are the same as the Class A uniform except the service coat is not worn. The black tie and black neck tab are required when wearing the long sleeve shirt; both tie and tab are optional with the short sleeve shirt

Battle Dress Uniforms – a camouflage uniform worn by members of the U.S. Army, Army National Guard, Army Reserve, and Army ROTC

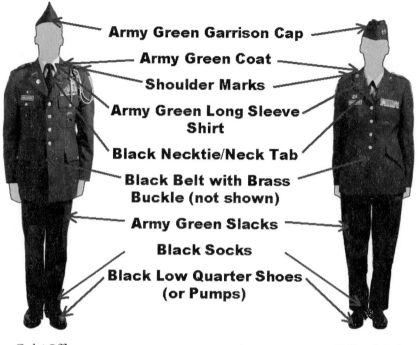

Figure 1.5.1: The Class A uniform
Courtesy of US Army JROTC.

Army Green Garrison Cap

Army Green Coat

Shoulder Marks

Army Green Long Sleeve Shirt

Black Necktie/Neck Tab

Black Belt with Brass Buckle (not shown)

Army Green Slacks

Black Socks

Black Low Quarter Shoes (or Pumps)

Cadet Officer   Enlisted Cadet

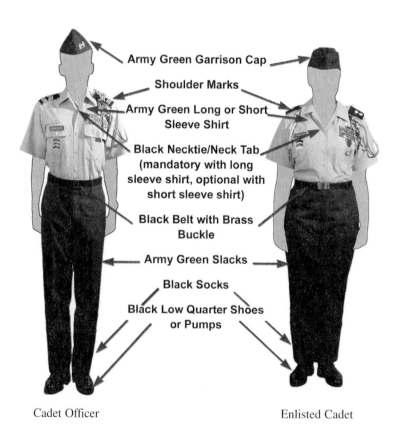

Figure 1.5.2: The Class B uniform
Courtesy of US Army JROTC.

Army Green Garrison Cap

Shoulder Marks

Army Green Long or Short Sleeve Shirt

Black Necktie/Neck Tab (mandatory with long sleeve shirt, optional with short sleeve shirt)

Black Belt with Brass Buckle

Army Green Slacks

Black Socks

Black Low Quarter Shoes or Pumps

Cadet Officer   Enlisted Cadet

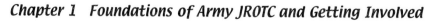

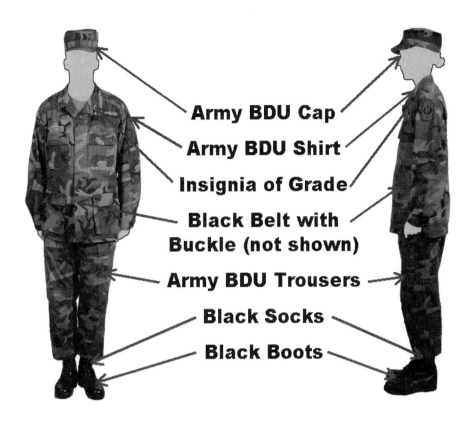

Army BDU Cap

Army BDU Shirt

Insignia of Grade

**Black Belt with
Buckle (not shown)**

Army BDU Trousers

Black Socks

Black Boots

Proper Placement of Insignia

Insignia are a way to show your advancement in JROTC. Insignia can include a
badge, medal, or other mark of honor or position. Insignia can also represent your
military branch and indicate a duty assignment. Depending on the type of insignia,
where it's placed on your uniform is important. This section covers many insignia
as well as the proper placement.

The Army Garrison Cap

Before positioning the appropriate cadet officer or enlisted cadet insignia on the
garrison cap, you should first know how to wear it. Place it on top of your head
with the front vertical crease of the cap centered on your forehead in a straight line
with your nose. Tilt the cap slightly to your right but do not let it touch or rest on
the top of your ear. Do not crush or shape the garrison cap to form peaks at the top
front or top rear of it.

> **Note**
>
> The term *garrison* refers to a military post or to station soldiers in a town or post.

In Figure 1.5.4 you can see that cadet officers wear grade insignia, or rank, on the
garrison cap while enlisted cadets wear the ROTC insignia. Position either insignia
on the left side of the cap one inch from the crease and centered vertically between
the top braid and the bottom of the cap.

Key Note Terms

garrison cap – head-
gear that may be worn
with the Class A or B
uniforms; for JROTC,
the braid (piping used
for identification pur-
poses) will have a cord
edge of the same mate-
rial as the cap (or Army
green shade 344)

Insignia of Grade

Key Note Terms

shoulder marks – a pair of broad pieces of stiffened cloth worn on the shoulders of the Class A or B uniforms to display the insignia of grade; blank shoulder marks do not display an insignia of grade so that pin-on insignia may be used instead

chevron – insignia consisting of stripes meeting at an angle to indicate (enlisted) grade or rank

nonsubdued – bright and shining, not dull or flat, such as polished brass pin-on insignia

bisecting – to cut or divide into two equal parts

align – to arrange in a line; alignment: the arrangement of several elements on the same line

To wear the grade insignia on long or short sleeve JROTC shirts, you normally wear **shoulder marks** (rank or shoulder boards). For cadet officers, place the narrow, pointed end toward the collar and the flat end toward the edge of the shoulder; for enlisted cadets, place the side with the pointed **chevron** (stripe) toward the collar, as shown in Figure 1.5.5.

The wearing of grade insignia for certain enlisted grades, such as cadet private and cadet private first class, may differ between schools. In some units, those cadets may wear **nonsubdued** pin-on grade insignia on both shirt collars or pinned to *blank* shoulder marks.

As seen in Figure 1.5.5, place these insignia centered on the collar, with the centerline of the insignia **bisecting** the point of each collar and one inch up from the edge of the collar point.

The area of both shirt pockets is where you place your nameplate, honor unit insignia, and personal awards. For female cadets, the pocket area (because those shirts do not have pockets) is where you also position these items. Imagine a horizontal line slightly above the top button on your shirt or one to two inches above the top button. This imaginary line allows you to properly **align** your awards, insignia, and nameplate in the same manner as male cadets do.

Nameplate

Center the nameplate on the right pocket between the top pocket seam and the top of the pocket buttonhole (see Figure 1.5.6). On the female uniform center the nameplate horizontally on the right side with the bottom of the nameplate on the imaginary line.

Honor Unit Insignia

Center the Honor Unit Star one-fourth of an inch above the top seam of the right pocket. On a female uniform, the Honor Unit star should be one-half inch above the nameplate and centered. You can wear the Honor Unit Star either by itself or joined with the Academic Achievement Wreath. In either case, center them as described.

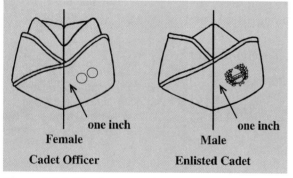

Figure 1.5.4: The Army garrison cap
Courtesy of US Army JROTC.

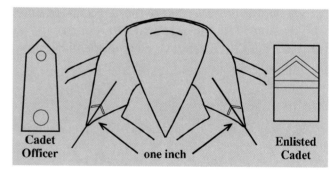

Figure 1.5.5: Placing the grade insignia
Courtesy of US Army JROTC.

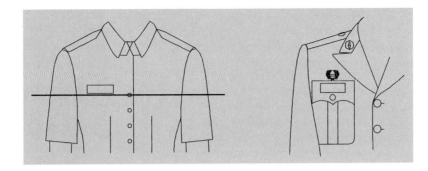

Figure 1.5.6: Placing the nameplate: female uniform (left) and male uniform (right)

Courtesy of US Army JROTC.

Awards and Decorations

Position individual awards for academic, athletic, and military excellence on the left pocket (or left pocket area); however, you cannot wear both the ribbon and the medal for the same award at the same time.

Center your ribbons on the pocket button one-eighth of an inch above the top seam of the left pocket (centered above the horizontal line for female cadets). Place awards of this type no more than three across. Do not start a second row until you have four or more ribbons; also, the first and second rows must have the same number before you can start a third row. Center the top row on the row beneath it. Wear your ribbons in order of **precedence** from top to bottom and from your right to left in one or more rows. This is shown in Figure 1.5.7.

Wear medals and place badges for excellence in marksmanship one-eighth of an inch below the top seam on the left pocket flap (or in a similar position for female uniforms), again in the order of precedence from your right to left.

When not wearing medals, center your badge or badges or space them equally from your left to right on your pocket flap. The upper portion of the badge or badges should be one-eighth of an inch below the top seam of the left pocket. If you only have one medal or badge, center it from left to right on your left pocket flap. Place the top of it one-eighth of an inch below the top seam of the pocket.

Key Note Term

precedence – the act or right of preceding or placing in order according to rank or importance; priority

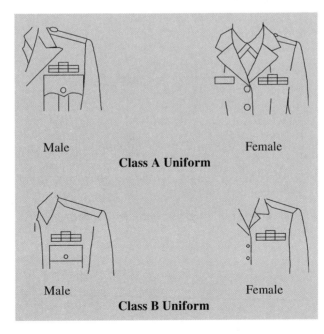

Male   Female
Class A Uniform

Male   Female
Class B Uniform

Figure 1.5.7: Award and decoration placement for Class A and Class B uniforms

Courtesy of US Army JROTC.

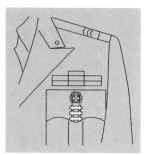

Figure 1.5.8: Wearing two badges or medals

Courtesy of US Army JROTC.

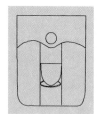

Figure 1.5.9: Wearing the unit crest on the pocket

Courtesy of US Army JROTC.

Wear two medals or badges equally spaced from left to right on the left pocket flap. Keep the top portion of them one-eighth of an inch below the seam, at least one inch between them, and special skill badges to the right. Figure 1.5.8 shows how to wear two medals or badges.

If you are wearing a special medal with one or more marksmanship badges, equally space all awards (but not more than three) from left to the right on the left pocket flap. Place the upper portion of the medals one-eighth of an inch below the top pocket seam. Wear the special medal to your right of any marksmanship badges.

These same rules apply for female cadets, except you wear your medals and/or marksmanship badges one-fourth of an inch below the bottom row of ribbons.

Miscellaneous Uniform Accessories

Certain units may authorize the wearing of approved unit crests. You can wear these crests in one of two places on the uniform.

The first option is on both shoulder marks, midway between the button and the insignia of grade; however, enlisted cadets who wear pin-on grade insignia on their collars should center these crests on blank shoulder marks.

The second option is to center the unit crest below the button on the right pocket, between the bottom of the pocket flap and the bottom seam of the pocket, as seen in Figure 1.5.9.

At the discretion of the senior Army instructor, you may wear scholar or service program insignia, such as national or local military honor societies, centered on the left pocket between the bottom of the pocket flap and the bottom pocket seam. The instructor staff may authorize you to wear shoulder cords for participation in certain JROTC activities, including the color/honor guard, drill team, and rifle team. Wear one cord by itself on the left shoulder, and any other cord on the right shoulder. When wearing cords with a **ferrule** (metal tip), keep the ferrule to the front; otherwise, wear these cords based on the procedures of your local unit.

Polishing Your Image

Neatness counts in JROTC. To achieve it, you must know the proper guidelines for wearing and cleaning your JROTC uniform.

Guidelines for Care and Cleaning of Your JROTC Uniform

The following are some basic guidelines for the care and cleaning of your uniform.

- **Place coats on hangers wide enough to keep the shoulders of the coat in shape. Do not use wire hangers.**
- **Keep shirts on hangers to prevent creasing.**
- **Clean and shine shoes and boots.**

- Keep trousers and slacks on hangers that allow them to hang at full length. Use a clothes brush with stiff bristles to loosen dust and dirt. This also helps freshen the **nap** and should be done each time the uniform is worn.

- Dry clean wool uniforms at a competent cleaner to take out stains or spots.

Guidelines for Personal Appearance in the JROTC Uniform

Keeping up your personal appearance will help you look great in your uniform. The following are guidelines for always looking your best.

- **Acceptable hairstyles for JROTC cadets do not include any extreme fads. The JROTC instructor staff will make all decisions on questionable hairstyles.**

- **Male cadets: Keep your hair neatly trimmed, with sideburns no lower than the bottom of the ear opening, and be clean shaven.**

- **Female cadets: Keep your hair styled so that it does not touch the top of the collar and so that the cap can be worn easily.**

- **Keep fingernails short and clean.**

- **A good personal appearance includes good grooming, which you can only achieve by cleaning your hair, teeth, and the rest of your body. It also includes maintenance (care) of your clothing—making sure that it is cleaned and pressed. In JROTC, you must maintain your uniform.**

Guidelines for Wearing Your JROTC Uniform

Now that you know how to care for your uniform and how to look your best, you need to know how to properly wear the uniform.

- **Wear a clean and neatly pressed uniform.**

- **Tuck shirt into trousers or skirt; keep its seam aligned with the seam of the zipper flap of the trousers and the edge of the belt buckle (gigline).**

- **Male cadets wear a T-shirt under the Class A and B uniforms. Male and female cadets wear a T-shirt under BDUs and as a physical training uniform. Wearing T-shirts prevents underarm perspiration from affecting your uniform.**

- **Button all buttons, with the exception of the top or collar button of the shirt.**

- **Clean, polish, and properly display all brass on the uniform.**

- **Push the belt through the left front loop of the trousers first and adjust to allow only the tip of the belt to protrude from the buckle.**

- **Wear only issued socks and shoes with the uniform.**

- **The wearing of a wrist watch, a wrist identification bracelet, and not more than two rings is authorized with Army uniforms (unless prohibited for safety or health reasons) as long as the style is conservative and in good taste.**

- **Female cadets may also wear small circular earrings (not to exceed one-quarter inch in diameter).**

- **Do not carry bulky objects in any pocket of the uniform.**

- **Wear the hat at all times when outdoors.**

Key Note Term

nap – a soft, fuzzy finish or cloth formed by short fibers raised on the surface

Key Note Term

gigline – line formed by the seam of the shirt aligned with the zipper flap and the edge of the belt buckle on certain JROTC uniforms

Guidelines for Taking Care of Brass Articles

Buttons, medals, and other articles made of brass need to be cleaned and shined on a regular basis. The following explains how to care for your brass items.

- **Brightly polish the lapel insignia, belt buckle, and cap insignia. The brass buttons are an exception. Do not use polish on the brass buttons; instead scrub them with ammonia and water.**

- **Perspiration tarnishes brass on contact, so be careful when putting the insignia back on the uniform and when handling the belt buckle. One helpful hint is to wipe any brass with cleaning fluid to remove the extra polish. This avoids dulling the shine that you worked hard to get and slows down any corrosion.**

Checking Your Look: The Pre-Inspection

Uniform inspection is an important part of JROTC. As a cadet, you should know how to care for your uniform and how to present yourself for inspection. Doing well on the inspection increases pride in yourself and in your accomplishments. Learning how to care for and maintain the JROTC uniform can also improve your self-discipline. When every cadet does well on the uniform inspection, it makes the unit look good and increases unit pride.

The **pre-inspection** is your chance to make sure that everything is in its proper place on your uniform and looks sharp. After learning how to wear your uniform and the placement of awards, it is now a matter of carefully checking your appearance. If your pre-inspection is done properly, there should be no surprises during the actual inspection.

Getting Ready

Inspect your uniform before you ask someone else to check it, so be sure that you have all the basics. The major parts of your uniform are identified in the uniform checklist.

UNIFORM CHECKLIST

_____	Garrison cap	_____	Placement of uniform accessories
_____	Coat	_____	Belt
_____	Shirt	_____	Shoes
_____	Neck tab/tie	_____	Socks
_____	Pants/slacks		

Placement

Follow the instructions you learned earlier in this lesson for the specific locations and proper placement of awards, insignia, and other uniform accessories.

A Preliminary Check

Table 1.5.1 lists you some of the items that the cadet staff and the instructors will look for during an inspection. You should use it only as a guide because your unit may have a different inspection form.

Table 1.5.1: Sample Inspection Criteria	
Headgear	Clean? Brass shined? Brass properly placed?
Hair	Properly styled/groomed? Off the ears/collar?
Shirt/Coat	Properly sized? Clean and pressed? Grade insignia placement? Nameplate placement? Honor Star placement? Ribbons/badges placement? Unit crest placement? Shoulder cord(s) placement? Pockets buttoned? Strings?
Trousers	Properly sized? Clean and pressed? Belt buckle shined? Gigline straight?
Shoes	Shined/dusted? Black socks?

For male cadets, the black belt with brass buckle is an important item. Line the tip of the belt (which will be either brass or black) with the end of the brass buckle so that none of the belt shows. This makes the belt buckle appear as one solid unit.

The most obvious sign of a correctly worn uniform is the formation of the gigline. Properly done, the edge of the shirt, belt buckle, and zipper flap should form an unbroken vertical line.

Head to Toe—The Inspection

Prior to the **formal inspection**, it is a good idea to ask a fellow cadet to look at your uniform and check it for anything that does not meet regulations. Make a final check yourself and then proudly present yourself for inspection. Always strive to be the cadet who scores the most points during each uniform inspection.

When to Wear the Uniform

You may wear the prescribed issued uniform in the United States and its possessions:

- **During military ceremonies; this shows that you are a proud part of the Army JROTC program**
- **When attending or participating in JROTC activities such as on the prescribed uniform day at school, during formal inspections, while instructing cadets in JROTC courses, and so on**
- **When traveling to and from school where you attend JROTC**
- **When visiting a military installation if you are taking part in drills, exercises, or JCLC**
- **When required by your instructors**

Your Personal Appearance

How do you look today? Do you have good posture? Do you have good grooming (personal hygiene) habits? In addition to these two areas, proper weight control and good muscle tone are all equally important factors in your personal appearance. In JROTC, being neat and clean is a way of life.

Good personal grooming is an important part of projecting a positive image. Your personal appearance can make all the difference in how you look in uniform. The following guidelines will give you that polished look.

- *Good posture* **involves more than just standing tall. It is sitting, walking, bending, and lifting properly. Poor posture can cause backaches, digestive trouble, and fatigue. You will become more relaxed and at the same time more energetic when you have good posture. It takes some practice to correct any bad habits, but in time the rewards are well worth the effort.**
- *Proper weight* **is a major health concern in our society. There is great pressure to be thin; however, being too thin (or overweight) can affect your self-image as well as your health. A balanced diet is the key to proper weight. Some people go to extremes by overeating or crash dieting; both are equally dangerous. See your family doctor for advice on weight reduction and dieting.**
- *Good muscle tone* **comes from a well-rounded exercise program. Swimming, bicycling, walking, and tennis are types of regular exercise that tone and build muscles. Exercise helps you feel good, both physically and mentally.**

- *Good grooming* means proper personal hygiene—taking care of your body. Daily showers or baths are vital, as is brushing your teeth. Proper amounts of sleep are also important to your mind and body.

Because many of your peers will now recognize you as an Army JROTC cadet, they will be watching you and your appearance more closely than before. Therefore, your appearance both in and out of uniform must be immaculate.

The importance of good grooming

Rick was applying for a new job. On the day of the interview, he woke up late and did not have time to take a shower or iron a shirt that he was wearing with his suit and tie. As Rick ran a brush through his hair, he told himself, "Confidence and credentials are what will get me this great job . . . and I have those."

When Rick arrived at the office, he told the secretary, "I have an appointment with Mr. Bender at one o'clock." As Rick was leaving the receptionist's area for the interview, dirt fell from one of his shoes. He meant to clean and polish them before the interview, but he did not have time. He apologized and told the secretary that he would clean up the dirt after the interview. She told him not to worry about it.

During the interview, Mr. Bender asked Rick several tough questions, which Rick felt he answered very well. Then, at the close of the interview, Rick expected to be offered the job. Instead, Mr. Bender thanked him for coming and told him that he would be in touch.

After a few days, Rick received a letter from Mr. Bender. It stated in part, "I appreciated your enthusiasm, and your qualifications were excellent, but the company has hired someone else for the position."

Did Rick present himself to Mr. Bender in the best possible way? Even though Rick thought that he was mentally alert, confident, and ready for the interview, was he really prepared for it? Although Rick thought that his qualifications would get him the job, should he have taken more time and care with his personal appearance?

A Properly Fitting JROTC Uniform

According to Army regulations on the wearing and appearance of uniforms, "all personnel will maintain a high standard of dress and appearance." This regulation means that your personal appearance in uniform should project the image to others that you are a part of one of the finest groups in the world.

Learning how to look your best in uniform takes time and effort. Your uniform must be **sized** and **fitted** to give you comfort and a good appearance. Pants, shirts, or coats that do not fit will make you look less than what you truly are. Your pants should be **hemmed** to the required length, and your shirt and coat, issued by size, should also fit well.

Key Note Terms

sized – the physical dimensions, proportions, magnitude, or extent of an object; any of a series of graduated categories of dimension whereby manufactured articles, such as shoes and clothing, are classified

fitted – to adapt to the proper size or shape

hemmed – to fold back and stitch down the edge of a garment

Factors That Affect Appearance

After you have a perfect fitting uniform, there are still other guidelines to follow for maintaining an outstanding appearance:

- **Have good personal grooming habits, such as caring for your hair and fingernails**
- **Know how to wear the uniform properly**
- **Know how to care and clean the uniform; a proper appearance requires a pressed and cleaned uniform**

These factors, as well as the guidelines given earlier in this lesson, are the basic keys to a good overall appearance in your JROTC uniform. By following these guidelines, you can ensure that your uniform and your personal appearance are in accordance with regulations.

Conclusion

Your personal appearance affects what others think about you. How you look can also influence your own self-confidence. Take some time to study yourself. Are you neat and presentable in and out of uniform? It is not hard to look your best. A clean uniform, good personal appearance (posture, weight, and muscle tone), and good grooming are keys to success.

In the next lesson, you will learn about the American flag. You will learn about its origins and the true meaning of the Stars and Stripes.

Lesson Review

1. What is the difference between a Class A and a Class B uniform?
2. What should you use to clean brass buttons?
3. When is the Battle Dress Uniform worn?
4. Define the word *ferrule*.

The Stars and Stripes

Key Terms

colors
ensign
garrison flag
half-staff
halyard
pennant
post flag
staff
standard
storm flag
union

What You Will Learn to Do

- Demonstrate protocol to show respect for and handle the U.S. flag

Linked Core Abilities

- Take responsibility for your actions and choices
- Do your share as a good citizen in your school, community, country, and the world

Skills and Knowledge You Will Gain Along the Way

- Explain the history of the U.S. flag
- Explain the symbolism of the various parts and colors on the flag
- Classify the size and use of each basic type of U.S. flag
- Describe how to show respect for the U.S. flag
- Compare the rules for displaying the flag in different situations
- Describe the correct way to fold the U.S. flag
- Define the key words contained in this lesson

Chapter 1

Introduction

The U.S. flag is the most notable of symbols for our nation. It is important that you know the respect the U.S. flag deserves. This lesson explores the history of the U.S. flag, rules for displaying and folding the flag, and paying respect to it in and out of uniform.

The United States Flag

Before the United States became a nation, the various colonies, represented by many countries, had their own flags. For example, the Norsemen explored our coastal waters sailing under the banner of a black raven. Columbus carried the Spanish flag across the seas, the Pilgrims carried the flag of Great Britain, and the Dutch colonists brought their flag to New Amsterdam. Additionally, each Native American Indian tribe had its own totem and insignia. The immigrants of many races and nationalities brought their symbols of loyalty to the shores of this country.

The first flags adopted by our colonial forefathers were symbolic of their struggles with the wilderness of a new land. Beavers, pine trees, rattlesnakes, anchors, and various mottoes such as "Hope," "Liberty," "Appeal to Heaven," or "Don't Tread on Me" adorned those early banners.

In 1776, when George Washington took command of the Continental Army at Cambridge, Massachusetts, he stood under the Grand Union flag (see Figure 1.6.1), which continued to show respect for Great Britain. To establish our independence and unity, however, the Continental Congress in Philadelphia created the first Stars and Stripes flag on June 14, 1777.

The flag of the United States in 1777 had 13 alternating red and white stripes and a **union**, an emblem standing for unity. The union was a blue rectangle with white stars, representing a constellation. Some historians give Betsy Ross credit for sewing the first flag, but there is no evidence that she designed it. Her fame is traced to a story told by her grandson. Also, there were problems with the design because there were no directions as to how the stars should look. Some had five

Key Note Term

Union – the emblem on a flag symbolizing unity, such as the blue rectangle and stars on the U.S. flag

Figure 1.6.1: The Grand Union flag

Courtesy of US Army JROTC.

THE GRAND UNION FLAG

THE FIRST STARS AND STRIPES

points, others had six or eight points; some had the stars in a circle, some had them in rows, and others scattered the stars without any apparent design. The Betsy Ross flag, shown in Figure 1.6.2, had the stars in a circle.

As the United States admitted new states to the union, the nation changed the flag to include them in its design. The first change took place in 1794 when Congress added two stars and two stripes for Vermont and Kentucky.

Fearing that too many stripes would spoil the true design of the flag, Congress passed legislation in 1818 returning the flag to its original design of 13 stripes and 20 white stars in a blue union. The stripes would represent the first 13 colonies, and the nation would continue to add a star for each state that joined the United States.

The arrangement of the stars varied until 1912 when President William Howard Taft issued an executive order to place the stars in six rows of eight stars each—acknowledging the admission of New Mexico and Arizona as the 47th and 48th states. President Dwight David Eisenhower ordered the last two changes to the flag in 1959 adding Alaska and Hawaii as the 49th and 50th states.

There is no fixed order for numbering the stars on the flag, and stars are not assigned to particular states. The stars represent the states collectively, not individually. The colors used in the flag are white for hope, purity, and innocence; red for hardiness and valor; and blue (the color of heaven) for reverence to God, loyalty, vigilance, perseverance, and justice.

> **Note**
>
> On June 14, 1889, George Balch, a kindergarten teacher in New York City, planned appropriate ceremonies for the children of his school, and his idea of observing Flag Day was later adopted by the State Board of Education of New York. On June 14, 1891, the Betsy Ross House in Philadelphia held a Flag Day celebration, and on June 14 of the following year, the New York Society of the Sons of the Revolution celebrated Flag Day. On August 3, 1949, President Truman signed an Act of Congress designating June 14th of each year as National Flag Day.

Types of Flags

Key Note Terms

Colors – the U.S. national flag

standard – a term now interchangeable with "the Colors," although formerly it was used for flags of mounted, motorized, and mechanized organizations

ensign – a flag that is displayed or flown from an aircraft, ship, or boat as the symbol of nationality

garrison flag – type of flag, flown on holidays and important occasions; 20 feet x 38 feet

post flag – type of flag used for everyday occasions; 10 feet by 19 feet

storm flag – type of flag flown in bad weather; 5 feet by 9½ feet

The branches of the military service use different names for the flag. These names include **Colors**, **standard**, or **ensign**; however, the term *flag* is correct regardless of size or use.

The three most commonly displayed flags at state and federal government buildings and on military installations are the garrison, post, and storm flags.

- **The garrison flag is 20 feet by 38 feet. Government buildings and military installations fly this flag on all national holidays and for special occasions, such as for special days or events proclaimed by the president.**
- **The post flag is 10 feet by 19 feet; it is for general display on days when it is not appropriate for the garrison flag.**
- **The storm flag is 5 feet by 9½ feet. State and federal governments fly this flag only during stormy or windy weather.**

Respect for the U.S. Flag

Because the flag symbolizes justice, unity, and pride in the United States, you should honor it with respect and dignity. Even after the flag becomes old and worn, you should not use it for banners or in any disrespectful way. If you do not preserve it, you should destroy it as a whole, privately, respectfully, and traditionally, by burning. Always show the flag the utmost respect, whether you are in uniform or in civilian attire.

In Uniform

When you are in your uniform, it is very important that you show respect for the flag. Because you wear the Army JROTC uniform, others look to you to be a leader and they will, in turn, follow your lead.

When you are in formation and the Colors are about to pass you, the commander calls the formation to *attention* and *present, arms* when the Colors come to within six steps of the unit. Everyone holds the salute until the Colors are six steps past the unit; then the commander calls *order, arms*, allowing you to drop your salute. If your formation is passing the Colors, six steps prior to reaching them the commander will call *present, arms*; then six steps past them, the commander will call *order, arms*.

When you are outdoors but not in formation, you should turn your head toward the flag and render the hand salute when you pass within six steps of the flag. If the flag passes you, stand at attention, render the hand salute, and hold it until the flag is six steps past you. When indoors, you should stand at attention until the flag is six steps past you.

In Civilian Clothes

When you are in civilian clothes, you must still take appropriate actions to honor the flag.

- **When you are outdoors and the Colors pass you, stand at attention with your right hand over your heart until the Colors are six steps beyond you. If you are wearing a hat, remove and hold it over your left breast with your right hand, ensuring that your hand is still over your heart. If you are outdoors and passing the Colors, remove your hat (if you have one on) and place your right hand over your heart about six steps before reaching the Colors; remove your hand when you are six steps past the Colors.**

- **When indoors and the Colors pass you, stand at attention until the Colors are six steps past you.**

Rules for Displaying the U.S. Flag

When displaying the flag, you should always raise it briskly and lower it ceremoniously.

It is customary to display the flag from sunrise to sunset, but you can display all-weather flags at all times if properly lit at night. The use of the flag at night, as well as during the day, should follow rules of custom.

Presidential proclamations contain the rules for displaying the flag at **half-staff**. For example, on Memorial Day, we display the flag at half-staff until noon, then raise it to the top of the **staff**. State and federal governments also fly the flag at half-staff when there is death of a president, former president, principal official, or foreign dignitary.

When flying the flag at half-staff, raise it to its peak and then lower it to the half-staff position. When lowering the flag for the day after it has been flown at half-staff, raise it to its peak and then lower it ceremoniously.

Key Note Terms

half-staff – the position of the flag about halfway down from the top of the pole or staff, used to honor and pay respect to military and nationally important deceased persons.

staff – another word for flagpole used to carry unit guidons or colors

Figure 1.6.3: The flag at full- and half-staff

Courtesy of US Army JROTC.

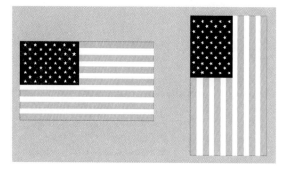

Display of the U.S. Flag Alone

When displaying the national flag from a staff projecting from a windowsill, balcony, or front of a building, the union of the flag should be at the staff's peak (unless displaying the flag at half-staff).

When displaying the flag flat against a wall, either horizontally or vertically, the union should be uppermost and to the flag's own right, or the observer's left, as shown in Figure 1.6.4.

When displaying the flag in a window, place it with the union to the left of the observer in the street.

When displayed suspended across a street, the flag should be vertical, with the union to the north on an east-west street, or to the east on a north-south street (Figure 1.6.5).

When suspending the flag at the edge of a sidewalk on the side of a building, raise the flag out from the building toward the pole, union first.

When using the flag over a casket, place it so the union is at the head and over the left shoulder, as seen as in Figure 1.6.6.

Note

Never lower the flag into the grave nor allow it to touch the ground.

Figure 1.6.5: Displaying a flag
across a street

Courtesy of US Army JROTC.

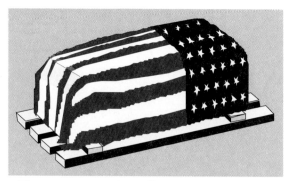

Figure 1.6.6: Draping a flag over a casket

Courtesy of US Army JROTC.

Group Display

When displaying the flags of two or more nations or states, fly them from separate flag staffs (or flagpoles) of the same height. The flags should be of similar size.

When grouping a number of flags and displaying them from staffs radiating from a central point, center the national flag or place it at the highest point of the group.

When carried in a procession with other flags, carry the national flag either on the far right of the row of marching persons or, if in a line of flags, carry it in the front and center position of that line.

When flying a **pennant** or another flag on the same **halyard** with the national flag, always fly the national flag at the peak of the staff. The only exceptions to this rule are displaying the United Nations flag at the United Nations Headquarters or a church pennant during services at sea.

When displaying the national flag with another flag from a crossed staff, place the national flag on its right with its staff in front of the staff of the other flag.

When displaying the U.S. flag from a staff in an auditorium, meeting hall, or chapel, whether on the same floor level or on a platform, it should be in the position of honor at the speaker's or chaplain's right facing the audience or congregation. Place other flags on the left of the speaker or chaplain; that is, to the right of the audience.

Folding the Flag Correctly

It is important that the flag be folded in the correct manner. The following is the correct procedure for folding the U.S. flag.

1. **Bring the lower striped section of the flag up over the blue field (Figure 1.6.8).**
2. **Fold the folded edge over to meet the open edge (Figure 1.6.9).**
3. **Start a triangular fold by bringing the lower striped corner to the open edge (Figure 1.6.10).**
4. **Fold the outer point inward and parallel with the open edge to form a second triangle (Figure 1.6.11).**
5. **Continue to fold the flag in triangles until the entire length of the flag is folded with only the blue field and the margin showing (Figure 1.6.12).**
6. **Tuck the margin into the pocket formed by the folds at the blue field edge of the flag (Figure 1.6.13).**

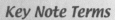

Key Note Terms

pennant – a long, narrow flag tapering to a point or a swallowtail at the end

halyard – a rope or tackle used for hoisting or lowering

Figure 1.6.7: Displaying a flag with a pennant on the same halyard

Courtesy of US Army JROTC.

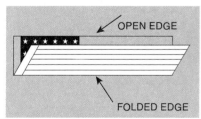

Figure 1.6.8: The first step to correctly fold a flag

Courtesy of US Army JROTC.

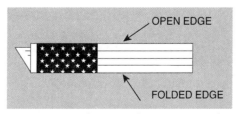

Figure 1.6.9: The second step to correctly fold a flag

Courtesy of US Army JROTC.

Figure 1.6.10: Start a triangle fold

Courtesy of US Army JROTC.

Figure 1.6.11: The next triangle fold
Courtesy of US Army JROTC.

Figure 1.6.12: Continue the triangular fold
Courtesy of US Army JROTC.

Figure 1.6.13: Tucking the margin into the pocket completes the folded flag
Courtesy of US Army JROTC.

When you have completely folded the flag, only the blue field should be visible, and it should have the triangular shape of a cocked hat.

Pledge of Allegiance

I pledge allegiance to the flag of the United States of America and to the Republic for which it stands, one Nation under God, indivisible, with liberty and justice for all.

This wording varies slightly from the original, which *The Youth's Companion* magazine in Boston drew up in 1892. Schools first used it in that same year to celebrate Columbus Day. Almost 50 years later, the Pledge of Allegiance received official recognition by Congress on June 22, 1942, and they added the phrase, "under God" on June 14, 1954. President Eisenhower said, "We are reaffirming the transcendence of religious faith in America's heritage and future; in this way we shall constantly strengthen those spiritual weapons which forever will be our country's most powerful resource in peace and war."

Conclusion

The flag of the United States has a rich heritage and interesting history, from the original Stars and Stripes to the present day 50-star version. It represents an independent nation in its own right. The traditions that it symbolizes will continue to exist as long as citizens treat the national flag with the respect it deserves. Always show respect, and remember; different people respect the flag for different reasons.

Lesson 7 covers the national anthem. You will learn when the anthem was written, by whom, and why. You will also learn the correct way to stand when the national anthem is sung.

Lesson Review

1. **Which flag did George Washington and the Continental Army use?**
2. **When was the Stars and Stripes flag created?**
3. **When is Flag Day?**
4. **When in civilian dress, what should you do when a flag passes in front of you?**

Proudly We Sing:
The National Anthem

Key Terms

anthems
bombardment
national march
symbol
"The Star-Spangled Banner"
under arms

What You Will Learn to Do

- Demonstrate courtesies during the playing of the National Anthem

Linked Core Abilities

- Take responsibility for your actions and choices
- Do your share as a good citizen in your school, community, country, and the world

Skills and Knowledge You Will Gain Along the Way

- Explain the history of the national anthem
- Describe cadet courtesies when the national anthem is played
- Explain the history of the official national march
- Define the key words contained in this lesson

Chapter 1

Introduction

When you hear the national anthem, do you know what to do? National **anthems** are usually songs already in a culture that become so popular that the people claim them as a **symbol** for themselves and their nation. The United States adopted "The Star-Spangled Banner" this way. In fact, it took Congress 117 years to ratify what the American people had decided in 1814. In addition to presenting the history of "**The Star-Spangled Banner**," this lesson explains how you should pay your respect to it, indoors or outdoors.

National anthems

National anthems are hymns or songs expressing patriotic sentiment and either governmentally authorized as an official national hymn or holding that position in popular feeling. During the 19th and early 20th centuries, most European countries followed Britain's example. Some national anthems were written especially for the purpose; others were adapted from existing tunes. The sentiments of national anthems vary, from prayers for the monarch to allusions to nationally important battles or uprisings.

History of Our National Anthem

Francis Scott Key wrote "The Star-Spangled Banner" as a result of a mission he was on during the War of 1812. Key was one of two people chosen to deliver official release papers for an American prisoner of war being held on a British ship in the harbor of Baltimore, Maryland.

The British agreed to release their prisoner only if the Americans did not immediately return to shore. The British were preparing to attack Fort McHenry, and they did not want Key and his companions to warn the American troops. The two Americans complied and returned to their boat to wait. At dusk, when the **bombardment** began, the British told the waiting Americans to take one last look at their flag because by morning it would be gone.

The bombardment continued throughout the night. At dawn, fog onshore hid Fort McHenry from view. Finally, the fog cleared, and the American flag could be seen. Inspired by the sight of his country's flag standing in defiance to the enemy, Francis Scott Key wrote the words to "The Star-Spangled Banner."

The next day, the commander of Fort McHenry printed and distributed the poem Key had written throughout Baltimore. That night, an actor sang the poem to the tune of a British drinking song. A few days later, the Baltimore newspaper printed the poem with directions that it be sung. In less than one week "The Star-Spangled Banner" had spread as far as New Orleans. Soon the whole country had taken it to heart; however, it was not until 117 years later, in 1931, that Congress passed an act making "The Star-Spangled Banner" the national anthem of the United States (36 USC 10, Sec. 170).

"The Star-Spangled Banner"

O say, can you see, by the dawn's early light,

What so proudly we hailed at the twilight's last gleaming,

Whose broad stripes and bright stars, through the perilous fight,

O'er the ramparts we watched were so gallantly streaming?

And the rockets' red glare, the bomb bursting in air

Gave proof through the night that our flag was still there,

O say, does that Star-Spangled Banner yet wave

O'er the land of the free and the home of the brave?

On the shore dimly seen through the mist of the deep,

Where the foe's haughty host in dread silence reposes,

What is that which the breeze, o'er the towering steep

As it fitfully blows, half conceals, half discloses?

Now it catches the gleam of the morning's first beam,

In full glory reflected now shines on the stream;

'Til the Star-Spangled Banner—O long may it wave

O'er the land of the free and the home of the brave.

O thus be it ever when free men shall stand

Between their loved homes and the war's desolation;

Blest with victory and peace, may the heaven rescued land

Praise the Power that has made and preserved us a nation.

Then conquer we must, when our cause it is just,

And this be our motto, "In God is our trust;"

And the Star-Spangled Banner in triumph shall wave

O'er the land of the free and the home of the brave.

When we sing the national anthem

The national anthem is performed and sung at a variety of events. Aside from official government functions, our national anthem is usually sung at the start of sporting events, sometimes at church events, and at funerals for government workers. In the aftermath of the 9/11 tragedies, the singing New York policeman Daniel Rodriguez captured America's hearts and spirits with his rendition of the national anthem. He sang this not only at official government functions but also many times on television and at nongovernmental events.

Courtesies to the National Anthem

A national anthem is a symbol of the people, their land, and their institutions. When we salute during the playing of "The Star-Spangled Banner," we are saluting the nation. Servicemen and women follow specific procedures in showing their respect to the U.S. anthem and to the anthems of friendly foreign nations.

Additionally, the armed forces give this same respect to the bugle call "To the Colors." The military uses "To the Colors" when a band is not available or during bad weather.

When Outdoors in Uniform

When you are outdoors in uniform and you hear the national anthem or "To the Colors," face the flag (if the flag is not visible, face the source of the music), stand at attention, and render the hand salute. Begin your salute on the first note of the music and hold the salute until the last note.

When Outdoors in Civilian Clothes

When you are outdoors in civilian clothes and you hear the national anthem or "To the Colors," face the flag (if the flag is not visible, again face the source of the music), stand at attention, and place your right hand over your heart. A male must remove his hat and hold it in his right hand over his heart. A woman does not remove her hat, but she must place her right hand over her heart.

During Indoor Ceremonies

If you are attending an indoor ceremony and you hear the national anthem or "To the Colors," stand, face the flag, and assume the position of attention. If the flag is not visible, face the source of the music or to the front and assume the position of attention. Do not salute unless you are **under arms**.

When in a Private Vehicle

On a military base, at the first note of the national anthem, all vehicles must come to a complete stop. If the driver is in uniform, that person must step out of the

vehicle and take the appropriate actions for being outdoors and in uniform. If the driver is a civilian or is a service member who is not in uniform, that person must step out of the vehicle and take the appropriate actions for being outdoors and in civilian clothes. All other occupants sit quietly inside the vehicle until the last note of music is played.

The Olympic anthem

Not only do countries adopt national anthems. The Greek poem "Ancient Eternal and Immortal Spirit," with music by Spyros Samaras, was performed for the first time at the first modern Olympic Games in Athens in 1896. Thereafter, a variety of musical offerings provided the backgrounds to the opening ceremonies until 1960. At the 55th session of the International Olympic Committee in Tokyo, the committee decided unanimously to adopt "Ancient Eternal and Immortal Spirit" as the official Olympic Games anthem.

The National March: "The Stars and Stripes Forever"

The composition by John Philip Sousa entitled "The Stars and Stripes Forever" is the **National March**.

In late 1896, Sousa and his wife took a much-deserved vacation to Europe. While there, Sousa received word that the manager of the Sousa Band, David Blakely, had died suddenly. The band was scheduled to begin another cross-country tour soon, and Sousa knew he must return to America at once to take over the band's business affairs. Sousa tells the rest of the story in his autobiography *Marching Along: Recollections of Men, Women and Music* (Westerville, Ohio: Integrity Press, 1994): "Here came one of the most vivid incidents of my career. As the vessel (the *Teutonic*) steamed out of the harbor, I was pacing on the deck, absorbed in thoughts of my manager's death and the many duties and decisions which awaited me in New York. Suddenly, I began to sense a rhythmic beat of a band playing within my brain. Throughout the whole tense voyage, that imaginary band continued to unfold the same themes, echoing and re-echoing the most distinct melody. I did not transfer a note of that music to paper while I was on the steamer, but when we reached shore,

Key Note Term

national march – "The Stars and Stripes Forever" as recognized in the U.S. Code of Federal Regulations

I set down the measures that my brain-band had been playing for me, and not a note of it has ever changed." The march was an immediate success, and Sousa's Band played it at almost every concert until his death over 25 years later. (http://www.dws.org/sousa/starsstripes.htm)

"The composition by John Philip Sousa entitled 'The Stars and Stripes Forever' is hereby designated as the national march of the United States of America." (36 USC 10, Sec. 188)

Conclusion

"The Star-Spangled Banner," the national anthem of the United States, is symbolic of the struggles and successes of this country. It is still as inspirational today as when it first swept throughout the country in 1814. Either as a JROTC cadet in uniform or as a private citizen out of uniform, render "The Star-Spangled Banner" the courtesies and respect it deserves. Remember, "To the Colors" receives the same respect as the national anthem. "The Stars and Stripes Forever" demonstrates the strength and the power of patriotic music in the development of a national spirit.

In Lesson 8, you will learn about American military traditions, customs, and courtesies. Through these actions, you develop pride in the military service and establish strong bonds of professional and personal friendships—patterns of behavior that enhance the military way of life.

Lesson Review

1. Who wrote "The Star-Spangled Banner" and why was it written?

2. When in a private vehicle on a military base, what should you do when you hear "The Star-Spangled Banner"?

3. What famous person wrote "The Stars and Stripes Forever"?

4. Define the term *under arms*.

Lesson 8

American Military Traditions, Customs, and Courtesies

Key Terms

courtesies
customs
dress
espirit de corps
mess
position of honor
reporting
ruffles and flourishes
salutes
self-propelled
traditions
uncasing
uncovered

What You Will Learn to Do

- Explore the purpose of military traditions, customs, and courtesies

Linked Core Abilities

- Treat self and others with respect

Skills and Knowledge You Will Gain Along the Way

- Distinguish among the types of personal salutes
- Relate Army ranks to their proper titles
- Determine situations requiring a salute
- Identify forms of respect to senior officers
- Define the key words contained in this lesson

Introduction

The purpose of military traditions, customs, and courtesies is to develop pride in the military service and to establish strong bonds of professional and personal friendships—patterns of behavior that enhance the military way of life. This lesson familiarizes you with these traditions, customs, and courtesies.

Traditions and Customs

Two of the more common military **traditions** and **customs** are dress and ceremonies. **Dress** sets the branches of the armed forces (the Army, Air Force, Navy, Marines, and Coast Guard) apart. Each branch has formal, semiformal, black tie, white tie, informal, and casual dress codes appropriate for various occasions and settings. All branches have a standard of dress that they require their members to follow.

Throughout history, military ceremonies represent the pride, discipline, and teamwork of the armed forces. Some of the more common ceremonies include parades, reviews, inspections, occasions that honor and recognize individuals with awards for outstanding service, and formal dining. Ceremonies help preserve tradition and to build **esprit de corps**.

Personal Salutes

Personal **salutes** are honors given to dignitaries, civil officials, and military officials. They include cannon salutes, **ruffles and flourishes**, and a march or anthem, depending on the official.

Cannon Salutes

A cannon salute honors civil or military officials from the United States or foreign countries. A commissioned officer directs the firing of the cannons, whether they are towed, **self-propelled**, or tank mounted. The time interval between rounds is three seconds. Usually, the U.S. armed forces does not fire a cannon salute on Sunday, between retreat and reveille, or on national holidays. Independence Day and Memorial Day are exceptions to this rule and have special cannon salutes.

The number of guns fired depends on the position of the official. For example, the military fires a 21-gun salute for the President, members of a reigning royal family, and the chiefs of state of foreign countries. The Vice President receives a 19-gun salute, as do ambassadors and the Speaker of the House of Representatives. Secretaries of the Army, Navy, and Air Force, and Generals of the Army and Air Force also receive a 19-gun salute.

What is the origin of the 21-gun salute?

The use of gun salutes for military occasions is traced to early warriors who demonstrated their peaceful intentions by placing their weapons in a position that rendered them ineffective. Apparently this custom was universal, with the specific act varying with time and place, depending on the weapons being used. A North African tribe, for example, trailed the points of their spears on the ground to indicate that they did not mean to be hostile.

The tradition of rendering a salute by cannon originated in the 14th century as firearms and cannons came into use. Because these early devices contained only one projectile, discharging them once rendered them ineffective. Originally warships fired seven-gun salutes, the number seven probably selected because of its astrological and biblical significance. Seven planets had been identified and the phases of the moon changed every seven days. The Bible states that God rested on the seventh day after Creation, that every seventh year was a sabbatical, and that the seven times seventh year ushered in the jubilee year.

Land batteries, having a greater supply of gunpowder, were able to fire three guns for every shot fired afloat; hence the salute by shore batteries was 21 guns. The multiple of three probably was chosen because of the mystical significance of the number three in many ancient civilizations. Early gunpowder, composed mainly of sodium nitrate, spoiled easily at sea, but it could be kept cooler and drier in land magazines. When potassium nitrate improved the quality of gunpowder, ships at sea adopted the salute of 21 guns.

The 21-gun salute became the highest honor a nation rendered. Varying customs among the maritime powers led to confusion in saluting and return of salutes. Great Britain, the world's preeminent seapower in the 18th and 19th centuries, compelled weaker nations to salute first, and for a time monarchies received more guns than did republics. Eventually, by agreement, the international salute was established at 21 guns, although the United States did not agree on this procedure until August 1875.

The gun salute system of the United States has changed considerably over the years. In 1810, the national salute was defined by the War Department as equal to the number of states in the Union—at that time 17. This salute was fired by all U.S. military installations at 1:00 p.m. (later at noon) on Independence Day. The president also received a salute equal to the number of states whenever he visited a military installation.

In 1842, the presidential salute was formally established at 21 guns. In 1890, regulations designated the national salute as 21 guns and redesignated the traditional Independence Day salute, the "Salute to the Union," equal to the number of states. Fifty guns are also fired on all military installations equipped to do so at the close of the day of the funeral of a president, ex-president, or president-elect.

Today the national salute of 21 guns is fired in honor of a national flag, the sovereign or chief of state of a foreign nation; a member of a reigning royal family; and the president, ex-president, and president-elect of the United States. It is also fired at noon on the day of the funeral of a president, ex-president, or president-elect.

Gun salutes are also rendered to other military and civilian leaders of this and other nations. The number of guns is based on their protocol rank. These salutes are always in odd numbers.

Source: Headquarters, Military District of Washington, *Fact Sheet: Gun Salutes*, May 1969.

When you are in the audience on such an occasion and in uniform, you should render the hand salute as the official party does. When in civilian clothing, you should remove any head covering to salute.

Ruffles and Flourishes

The armed forces plays ruffles and flourishes together—ruffles on drums and flourishes on bugles. The number of ruffles and flourishes also depends on the position of the official. The President; Vice President; the secretaries and assistant secretaries of the Army, Navy, and Air Force; cabinet members; and ambassadors all receive four ruffles and flourishes.

Additionally, a military band may play a march or anthem following the ruffles and flourishes as an honor to special officials. For example, the band may play the national anthem or "Hail to the Chief" for the President, ex-presidents, or president-elect; a march for the Vice President; the National Anthem of the United States or the anthem of another country for ambassadors; and a march for generals, admirals, and most other armed services officials.

Courtesies

Key Note Term

courtesies – acts of politeness or gracious manners; the use of polite gestures or remarks

Courtesies honor people with actions or words to show respect, authority, and achievement. The use of titles and salutes are two courtesies that honor members of the military.

Titles

One military courtesy is the use of titles to show respect for superiors. When you are talking to someone in the military, address that person by his or her rank. This form of a courtesy is a standard greeting in the military and shows respect for the responsibility that person has earned. Table 1.8.1 shows the correct titles by which you should address most individuals in the U.S. Army.

If you do not know the person's name, you may address privates as "Soldier," all medical officers by their rank, male officers as "Sir," and female officers as "Ma'am."

Conversation with others in the military should be formal and correct. Use proper titles to show respect and indicate rank. Senior JROTC cadets may address junior JROTC cadets by their first name, but not the other way around.

Saluting

In addition to honoring those senior in rank with a title, the military requires a hand salute in many cases. By properly executing the hand salute, you show respect for those in positions of authority. A sloppy or poorly given salute can mean a number of different problems, including the following:

- **An inappropriate attitude or possible disrespect for a person who deserves the honor**
- **A lack of understanding on how to execute the salute**

Table 1.8.1: Proper Titles

Title	How to Address
All Generals	"General"
Colonels and Lieutenant Colonels	"Colonel"
Majors	"Major"
Captains	"Captain"
Lieutenants	"Lieutenant"
Chaplains	"Chaplain"
Cadets	"Mister," "Miss," or "Cadet"
Officer Candidates	"Candidate"
Warrant Officers	"Mister" or "Miss"
Sergeant Majors	"Sergeant Major"
First Sergeants	"First Sergeant"
All other Sergeants	"Sergeant"
Corporals	"Corporal"
All Specialists	"Specialist"
Privates and Privates First Class	"Private"

Hand Salute

The hand salute is one of the most recognizable courtesies of the military way of life. Centuries ago, the salute was a greeting that indicated you were not holding a weapon in your hand. Today, it is a way to show respect.

Whom to Salute

You must render the salute to all commissioned and warrant officers. Generally, you do not salute noncommissioned officers or petty officers; however, there are exceptions. For example, when you act as a squad leader, salute your platoon sergeant when making reports.

How to Salute

When a leader who is in charge of a formation commands "*present, arms,*" you should execute a salute. If you are not carrying a rifle, you can give the hand salute in three different ways depending on whether you are wearing headgear, glasses, or both.

- **When wearing headgear with a visor (with or without glasses), raise your right hand sharply, fingers and thumb extended and joined, palm facing down. Place the tip of your right forefinger on the rim of the visor slightly to the right of your right eye. Barely turn the outer edge of your hand downward so neither the back of your hand nor the palm is clearly visible from the front. Keep your hand and wrist straight, your elbow inclined slightly forward, and the upper arm horizontal.**

- **When wearing headgear without a visor, or you are uncovered, and without glasses, execute the hand salute in the same manner as previously described except touch the tip of your right forefinger to the forehead near and slightly to the right of your right eyebrow.**

- **When wearing headgear without a visor, or you are uncovered, and with glasses, execute the hand salute in the same manner as above except touch the tip of your right forefinger to that point on the glasses where the temple piece of the frame meets the right edge of your right brow.**

When **reporting** or rendering a courtesy to an individual, turn your head and eyes toward the person and simultaneously salute. In this situation, execute the actions without command. The subordinate initiates the salute at the appropriate time and terminates it upon acknowledgment.

When to Salute

Military regulations on conduct require you to salute, even when carrying a rifle, when you meet and recognize a person entitled to the honor, except under the following conditions:

- **When on public transportation, including buses and trains**
- **When in public places such as stores and theaters**

> ### Key Note Terms
>
> **uncovered** – to remove a hat or other headgear; to be bareheaded or without a cover
>
> **reporting** – presenting oneself to a senior

Figure 1.8.1: Hand salute wearing headgear with a visor
Courtesy of US Army JROTC.

Figure 1.8.2: Hand salute without a visor or glasses
Courtesy of US Army JROTC.

Figure 1.8.3: Hand salute with glasses (without a visor)
Courtesy of US Army JROTC.

- When giving the salute would be inappropriate or physically impractical (such as when officers are acting as drivers or passengers of civilian vehicles or when both hands are occupied carrying articles)
- While indoors except when reporting to an officer or when on duty as a guard
- When one or both parties are in civilian clothes

Conditions under which you must salute are as follows:

- When you hear the national anthem, "To the Colors," or "Hail to the Chief" (if you are in uniform)
- When the Colors pass you
- During all official greetings
- During reveille and retreat, when within sight of the flag or the sound of the music and in uniform
- During the rendering/sounding of honors
- When first **uncasing** the Colors or later when casing them
- When pledging allegiance to the flag while outdoors and in uniform. Indoors in uniform requires that you stand at attention and face the flag, but you do not salute. Indoors in civilian clothing requires that you stand at attention, face the flag, and place your right hand over your heart.
- When reporting

Reporting

Reporting is requesting and obtaining permission to speak to a senior officer or being notified that a senior officer wants to speak with you. How you report to that officer may change according to local policy and to the location (in an office or outdoors), situation (under arms), or reason for reporting.

Showing Respect to Senior Officers

When an officer enters an office for the first time each day, the first person to see the officer calls the room to attention. If at any time, another, higher ranking officer enters the office, the first person to see that officer again calls the room to attention. This same practice holds true if an officer enters a barracks; that is, the first person to see the officer calls the room to attention. Everyone rises to attention except those personnel who are on work details; however, they must rise if the officer stops and addresses them directly.

When an officer enters the dining area, the first person to see the officer calls the **mess** to "at ease." You may remain seated and continue eating unless directed otherwise by the officer. If you are seated at a chair and the officer addresses you directly, rise to attention and respond. If you are seated on a bench, stop eating and sit at attention until the officer has ended the conversation.

Position of Honor

The **position of honor** dictates that those of lower rank walk, sit, or ride to the left of those with senior rank. When entering a vehicle (car or small boat), you should enter first, staying to the left of the officer. When you arrive at your destination and leave the vehicle, the senior officer should exit first.

Key Note Term

uncasing – removing the case from the Colors that are attached to a staff

Key Note Terms

mess – a group of persons, usually in the military, who regularly eat meals together; the place where such meals are served

position of honor – a military courtesy of usually keeping senior officers to your right while walking or sitting

Note

The position of honor originated during medieval times when knights fought primarily with their sword in their right hand. Because their left arm held a shield for defense, their right side—the fighting side—was their position of honor.

Conclusion

The pride and respect that come from traditions, customs, and courtesies make for a strong, well-run organization. Taking part in these traditions, customs, and courtesies builds esprit de corps and respect in your organization—indications of what success is all about.

Personal courtesies and good manners are a basic part of military courtesy. By showing proper respect, you gain respect from others and a sense of pride within yourself. Using the proper salutes and actions shows that you are proud of yourself, your unit, and Army JROTC.

Lesson Review

1. Give examples of three common ceremonies.
2. What is the proper form of address to all officers?
3. What is the purpose of the salute?
4. What do you do when a senior officer enters the room?

Basic Command and Staff Principles

Key Terms

coordinating staff
course of action
echelon
personal staff
special staff

What You Will Learn to Do

- Demonstrate command and staff principles while performing the duties of an earned leadership position within your cadet battalion

Linked Core Abilities

- Communicate using verbal, nonverbal, visual, and written techniques
- Apply critical thinking techniques

Skills and Knowledge You Will Gain Along the Way

- Describe staff responsibilities and three common procedures used to coordinate staff actions
- Compare the three types of staffs and their relationship to the commander
- List the nine-step sequence of command and staff actions in the correct order
- Clarify the scope and purpose of the commander's estimate
- Define the key words contained in this lesson

Introduction

As commanders or staff officers in your cadet battalion, being prepared to meet the challenges of your position is a major responsibility. Your success or failure may not depend only on your abilities as a leader but also on how well you execute command and staff actions and can work with the subordinate commanders and staff officers of the battalion.

After completing this lesson, you will have a better understanding of command and staff procedures and how they relate to your duties in your cadet battalion. This lesson explains command and staff authority and responsibilities, and the principles underlying delegation of authority, command and staff actions, staff organization and operations, and the sequence of actions in making and executing decisions.

Model Cadet Battalion Organization

Now that you are in a principal leadership position in your cadet battalion, your job may require you to coordinate activities or work in conjunction with the personnel assigned to those positions. To be an effective leader, therefore, you should know all of these positions and their related duties. Studying them will also reinforce your knowledge of the chain of command. These positions are shown in Figure 1.9.1.

Your cadet battalion may contain additional positions or list different duties for them; however, the information provided outlines a model cadet battalion organizational structure and its associated chain of command.

Command Authority and Responsibilities

Command is the authority that a commander lawfully exercises over subordinates by virtue of rank or assignment. With authority comes responsibility.

Figure 1.9.1: Battalion organization

Courtesy of US Army JROTC.

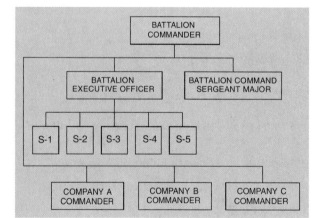

Command Responsibility

Command responsibility is a moral and legal obligation. Commanders alone are responsible for all that their unit does or fails to do. Through a chain of command, commanders hold each subordinate commander and staff officer responsible for all that their unit or section does or fails to do. If it becomes necessary to bypass the normal chain of command, both the commander issuing and the one receiving the order must notify any intermediate supervisors of the situation as soon as possible.

> **Note**
>
> Battalions are the lowest level at which the U.S. Army authorizes a staff.

Importance of a Staff

Commanders must effectively use available resources for planning, organizing, directing, coordinating, and controlling people and units to accomplish their missions. No one individual can personally direct, coordinate, and supervise the operation of a battalion-size unit or larger. Regardless of how capable, educated, experienced, or energetic commanders may be, they must have assistance. A group of officers and senior noncommissioned officers provide this assistance. They reduce their commander's burden by assuming responsibility for and accomplishing as many of the routine matters of command as possible. This leaves commanders to serve in leadership roles as intended.

Delegation of Authority

To be totally effective, commanders and their staffs must work as a cohesive team. Staffs achieve this by having a thorough understanding of the policies of their commander. Staff authority varies with the degree of authority delegated to it by the commander. Commanders can delegate as much authority to subordinates as considered necessary, but under no circumstances can they delegate any part of their responsibility. Additionally, the following command functions should remain with commanders.

- **Developing concepts for estimates and plans**
- **Processing and disseminating their guidance and concepts**
- **Ensuring coordination of the effort of the command**
- **Supervising the execution of decisions**

The normal delegation is for staffs to take final action on matters of command policy within their section's jurisdiction. This frees commanders to focus their attention on the essential aspects of command. Authority delegated to staff officers varies with the mission of the unit, the immediacy of the task, and the relationship of the staff section's area of interest to the unit's primary mission.

Command and Staff Actions

Command and staff actions must be accurate and timely. That is, the staff must identify promptly and define accurately the decisive elements of each problem. To this end, commanders organize their staffs to

- **Be immediately responsive to the needs of the command**
- **Remain abreast of the situation and to ensure that they consider all pertinent factors**
- **Reduce the time needed for control, integration, and coordination of tasks**
- **Minimize the possibilities of error**
- **Minimize their requirements for detailed supervision of routine matters**

Staff Authority and Responsibilities

Staffs do not have command authority and are not in the chain of command. The only authority they exercise is over the members of their own section and what their commander delegates to them.

Commanders assign staff officers certain specific functional areas of responsibility. To carry out these command responsibilities effectively, commanders then give each staff section specific duties. When commanders have chosen a **course of action**, it is the duty of the staffs to prepare and issue the necessary orders and to supervise their execution. Staff officers should always issue orders for, or in the name of, their commander; however, responsibility for those orders still remains with the commander. Other staff responsibilities include the following:

- **Securing information and furnishing advice as the commander may require. Staff officers also provide information to other staffs and to other agencies and units.**
- **Analyzing information as a basis for making recommendations to the commander and other agencies.**
- **Preparing the details of the commander's plans and orders. Each staff section prepares its appropriate part of the plan or order.**
- **Translating decisions and plans into orders and transmitting the orders to each command element.**
- **Supervising (to the extent authorized by the commander) the execution of the plans and/or orders. Staff officers accomplish supervision by way of conducting visits or inspections and preparing reports.**
- **Taking other actions as necessary to carry out the commander's intentions.**

The effectiveness of a staff depends on the professional qualifications of its members. Staff officers must possess the qualities of leadership and the ability to apply them in a staff role. They must have a thorough understanding of the organization, capabilities, limitations, and operating techniques of the command. As a rule, experience in a position that is of equal or lesser responsibility to the current or proposed staff position is a prerequisite to the assignment of a staff officer.

Key Note Term

course of action – a decision on how to proceed; a plan

Staff Organization

Good staff organization assists a commander by decreasing the number of routine items requiring decision. Through effective staff procedures, staffs can speed up the processing of information into material useful to the commander and can improve the quality of the product that they develop. Efficient staff techniques minimize possible delays in preparing and transmitting plans and instructions to subordinates.

> **Note**
>
> The U.S. Army General Staff established in 1903 forms the basis for the Army's present staff system.

Regardless of its organization, a staff must apply the principles of unity of command and direction, span of control, delegation of authority, and the grouping of compatible and related activities. Consequently, staff organization depends on the following factors:

- **The unit's mission.** This is the primary consideration for everything that the commander does and for the operation of the unit.

- **Activities conducted by the unit.** The unit's mission and its activities go hand-in-hand. For example, all of the duties and responsibilities that make up the unit's activities—especially those required to accomplish the unit's mission—are fundamental to the organization and functioning of a staff.

- **Emphasis on broad fields of interest.** Regardless of the mission, command interests can be divided into five broad fields: personnel (S-1), intelligence (S-2), operations and training (S-3), logistics (S-4), and civil-military operations (S-5). The emphasis placed on each of these broad fields of interest, and the specialized activities required for each, vary according to the mission and the activities required to accomplish the mission. For example, within your JROTC battalion, the S-2 may also handle public affairs matters, while the S-5 could be assigned as the special project's officer. Although military staffs may vary in organization and specific titles of its staff members, they do possess certain common characteristics. Functional responsibilities are the basis for military staff organization.

- **Laws and regulations.** Army regulations, the Uniform Code of Military Justice, and other directives require special relationships between certain staff officers and the commander.

To be successful, the staff must work together. No staff officer can work alone and expect to get the job done. Each staff officer must actively pursue every scrap of information that will help the commander operate. Staff officers continually exchange information with staff officers from higher headquarters, subordinate unit leaders, and among themselves.

Types of Staffs

Each type of staff consists of three groups of staff officers plus liaison officers. These three groups are the **coordinating staff** officers, **special staff** officers, and the commander's **personal staff** officers.

Key Note Terms

coordinating staff – principal staff assistants to the commander

special staff – assists the commander in professional, technical, and other areas of interest in the command

personal staff – officers who work under the immediate control of the commander

Coordinating staff officers are the principal staff assistants to the commander. Each staff officer specializes in one (or a combination) of the broad fields of interest mentioned for S-1 through S-5.

Special staff officers assist the commander in professional, technical, and other functional areas of interest in the command. The specific number and duties of special staff officers vary at each level of command, and they may also be unit commanders. Special staffs may include the following personnel:

- **Signal officer**
- **Maintenance officer**
- **Logistics readiness officer**
- **Aviation officer**
- **Chemical officer**
- **Provost marshal**
- **Public affairs officer**
- **Chaplain (see Figure 1.9.2)**
- **Surgeon**

Personal staff officers work under the immediate control of the commander. Typical personal staff members include the command sergeant major and, at higher levels, the inspector general and staff judge advocate.

Executive Officer

An executive officer (XO) directs, coordinates, and supervises the efforts of the coordinating and special staffs. The XO's other duties are as follows:

- **Formulating, recommending, and announcing staff operating policies**
- **Keeping the commander informed**

Figure 1.9.2: Special staff members include chaplains
Courtesy of the US Army.

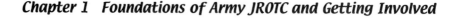

- **Assuming command in the absence of the commander**
- **Reviewing plans, orders, and staff actions**
- **Approving staff actions**
- **Supervising the execution of orders**

Common Staff Procedures

Staff officers use certain common procedures to coordinate staff action. In addition to staff coordination, these include visits and inspections, conferences, briefings, and reports.

Staff coordination is the process of making certain that all pieces of a staff action fit together. The responsible, or action, officer and all other interested staff officers examine and make adjustments to any subactions of the project. Staff officers then determine the proper action within their section's area of interest. Finally, the action officer has the added responsibility to complete the coordination with other commanders and staff sections, as appropriate.

Staff officers make staff visits to obtain information for the commander, observe the execution of orders, and assist subordinate unit commanders. Concerning the first two points, the information that staff officers obtain can indicate to their commander how effectively or efficiently subordinate units are executing command decisions. Concerning the last item, a vital part of the staff officer's job is to discover and help subordinate elements to resolve internal problems. On occasion, staffs may combine staff visits with command-directed inspections.

Commanders and/or staffs conduct inspections to ascertain the condition of the command. Using checklists prepared by the various staff sections, commanders and staffs conduct inspections to collect positive and negative information from which the commander can determine the readiness of the unit to accomplish its mission.

Commanders and staff officers frequently participate in conferences. Conferences often replace the need for staff visits and certain types of correspondence. Commanders and staffs call conferences to accomplish the following objectives.

- **Determine and evaluate facts by exchanging information and ideas**
- **Solve problems (particularly new ones)**
- **Coordinate actions, including arriving at the best possible decision or reaching agreement in a particular area**
- **Formulate policy**
- **Instruct, counsel, or advise**

Staff briefings ensure a coordinated or unified effort by the entire staff. The executive officer usually presides over these briefings. The XO calls on each staff section representative to exchange information or guidance, present matters of interest to the command, or present matters that require staff coordination and decision.

Command and staff channels are two of the channels through which orders, instructions, and information flow within a command.

Command channels transmit all orders and instructions to subordinate units. These channels are commander-to-commander, and all orders transmitted are in the name of the commander.

Staff channels coordinate and transmit information and operating instructions to comparable staff elements and to subordinate commanders. Both in planning and conducting operations, staff officers of a higher headquarters frequently need to contact comparable staff elements of subordinate headquarters. However, a staff officer of a higher headquarters has no authority over the staff of the subordinate headquarters.

Sequence of Command and Staff Actions

Commanders and their staffs often initiate planning an action before they receive a mission. After receipt of the mission, they continue to plan for contingencies that require a command decision. The tools used to assist commanders and staffs in making these decisions are the problem-solving/decision-making processes. Completing actions in a uniform sequence assures commanders that they are making decisions based on all available information and are using staff assistance to the maximum.

Additionally, a uniform sequence makes it possible for staff officers to anticipate the needs of each step. This results in faster and better prepared staff actions. Making and executing decisions involve a series of separate actions.

The following nine steps are those used by commanders and their staffs to arrive at decisions.

Step 1: Mission

Command and staff actions begin with the receipt of a mission from a higher headquarters and/or the development of a mission by the unit commander. The commander then analyzes the mission to identify the specific tasks the unit must accomplish.

Step 2: Information Available

The staff provides any available information to the commander, who also attempts to obtain additional information from the next higher commander as early as possible. After analyzing the mission and reviewing the available information, the commander issues the planning guidance (Step 3).

Step 3: Planning Guidance

The planning guidance is the commander's assistance to a staff in preparing or revising their estimates. This guidance spans more than one step. The amount of planning guidance varies with each mission, the volume and validity of the information available, the situation, and the experience of the commander and staff. The commander does not select a course of action at this time because doing so would prevent objective and unbiased staff estimates.

Step 4: Staff Estimates

Based on the mission and planning guidance, the coordinating staff sections prepare their staff estimates. The special staff, who may also prepare their own estimates, assists them. Coordinated staff estimates result in recommendations as to what specific actions the commander may take to accomplish the mission.

Step 5: Commander's Estimate and Decision

In this step, the commander considers the recommendations of the staff, completes his or her own estimate, and announces a decision. Following the decision (the last step of the estimate), the commander provides the staff with an overall concept of how the commander wants the operation conducted (known as the commander's concept, which is the basis for the preparation of orders).

Step 6: Preparation of Plans or Orders

After staff members completely understand the mission, they carefully analyze the decision and commander's concept to determine what actions the unit must take to conduct a successful operation. From this analysis comes the development of plans or orders.

Step 7: Approval

Staffs normally submit the plans or orders to the commander for approval before submitting them for publication; however, the staff may omit this step based on the urgency of the situation and/or if the commander previously delegated that authority.

Step 8: Publication of Plans or Orders

See Step 7.

Step 9: Command and Staff Supervision

Supervision of the orders must be continuous if the mission is to be successful. This could well be the most important step. Without proper supervision, the best plan may fail. Proper supervision also allows the commander and staff to be constantly abreast of the situation and able to make changes as necessary.

The Estimate of the Situation in the Sequence of Command and Staff Actions

The estimate of the situation is a vital part of the decision-making process. Estimates have been an integral part of military procedures ever since the first man fought his first war. The intellectual and perceptive reasoning that must go into the estimate form the basis for sound recommendations by staff officers and sound decisions by commanders. History tells us that great military leaders invariably adopted a logical sequence of thought in their planning processes, similar to those used in the modern estimate of the situation.

Commanders develop the ability to make sound decisions by habitually applying logic to each of the many problems that confront them during their careers. If this were not so, eventually commanders would become the victims of their own emotional decisions.

Purpose of the Estimate

The estimate of the situation is an analysis of all factors affecting accomplishment of the mission. It helps commanders to determine the most suitable course of action. Commanders and staffs need only to develop courses of action in sufficient detail to be readily distinguishable for analysis and comparison purposes with other courses of action.

Scope and Nature of the Estimate

The estimate of the situation is a logical and orderly examination of all factors affecting the accomplishment of the mission in order to reach a sound decision. The amount and nature of detail considered in the estimate varies with the level and type of command, the functions of the preparing agency, and other circumstances.

The basic approach used in the estimate of the situation is applicable to any situation, **echelon**, or type of command. Any individual may use it to arrive at a decision. Commanders use it to choose the course of action they want their command to follow. Staffs use it to determine the influence of factors within their particular field of interest on the courses of action under consideration. They also use it to arrive at recommendations for their commander.

The estimate of the situation is a continuing mental process. With each change in the situation, commanders and staffs must revise the estimate and modify the course of action as appropriate. The estimate is as thorough as time and circumstances will permit. It may vary from a short, almost instantaneous process when the requirement for a decision is urgent to a long, complex, and complete process requiring the effort of the entire staff.

Key Note Term

echelon – an arrangement of a body of troops in the form of steps; a section of a military group; an organizational level of importance

Conducting a Meeting

When members of an organization, such as the student government at your school, assemble to transact business, they are conducting a meeting. Within JROTC, your instructors or the chain of command may call on you to organize and conduct a meeting using the proper rules of order (see Figure 1.9.3).

The two types of meetings that you will conduct most often are the regular and special meetings. Hold regular meetings at set time intervals, such as weekly, monthly, or quarterly to discuss matters of routine business. You can convene a special meeting when important matters arise between the regular meetings that urgently require action before the next regular meeting.

The minimum essential officers for the conduct of business are a presiding officer (chairperson or president) and a secretary. The presiding officer conducts the meeting and sees that members observe the rules. The secretary makes a written record of the proceedings. These are called the *minutes*.

The Procedures of Order

When the time for the meeting arrives and sufficient members are present, the presiding officer opens it. An organization may adopt its own order of business (known as a *program* or *agenda*) or it may follow one addressed in its bylaws. Most organizations consider the following order as standard for their meetings:

- **Reading and approval of the minutes**
- **Reports of officers and special committees**
- **Unfinished business**
- **New business**

Figure 1.9.3: You might be called on to organize and lead a meeting
Courtesy of Corbis Images.

Normally, any member can introduce a legitimate issue at any time when there is no other business for consideration. Members do this through the use of motions. After a member makes a motion and another member seconds it, the presiding officer places it before the assembly for debate. Every member has the right to speak to every debatable motion before the membership votes on it. In most situations, the basic requirement for approval of an action is a majority vote. All members in good standing (not under a disciplinary suspension) have the right to vote. The regular methods of voting are by

- **Voice:** Normal method of voting on a motion
- **Rising:** Verifies a nonconclusive voice vote
- **Show of hands:** Alternative to the rising vote

An organization may use other methods of voting when prescribed by the bylaws. They are voting by ballot (used when there is a need for secrecy of each member's vote) and roll call vote (which has the opposite effect of a ballot vote because it places on record how each member votes).

To close a meeting, either a member can motion for adjournment, or under certain conditions, the presiding officer can declare the meeting adjourned.

Framework

Every organization should specify in its bylaws what officers it requires, how they will be elected or appointed, their terms of office, and any qualifications for holding those offices. The officers that most organizations require for a smooth running assembly are the presiding officer (chairperson or president), vice president, secretary, and treasurer. Other key, nonelected personnel are the sergeant-at-arms and the historian/librarian. Refer to the book *Robert's Rules of Order* for an explanation of the duties and responsibilities of these officers and for other key personnel not listed.

> **Note**
>
> To learn more about *Robert's Rules of Order*, go to http://www.robertsrules.com.

The basic reports essential for and during the conduct of a meeting are the minutes (or the report of the proceedings) and the reports by the various officers.

Conclusion

From past military history, the relationship between command and staff actions; staff organization, duties, and responsibilities; and the manner in which a unit successfully accomplishes its missions are very apparent. If you pursued this lesson with the intention of learning the "how" of command and staff procedures, you should have become better qualified to assume the top leadership positions in your cadet battalion.

This lesson ends Unit 1, "Citizenship in Action." The next unit, "Leadership Theory and Application," examines many aspects of leadership skill and principles. It also covers specific steps, marches, and squad drills as well as stationary movements.

Lesson Review

1. Why is it important to know how to work with subordinate commanders and staff officers?

2. What tasks might you delegate to subordinates?

3. Name the three groups of staff. Choose one and discuss it.

4. Define the term *echelon*. How does it relate to this lesson?

Chapter 2

Service to the Nation

Lesson 1

The Department of Defense

Key Terms

operational commands
specified
strategic
tactical
theater

What You Will Learn to Do

- Explore the purpose of the U.S. Department of Defense (DoD)

Linked Core Abilities

- Do your share as a good citizen in your school, community, country, and the world

Skills and Knowledge You Will Gain Along the Way

- Examine the mission of the Department of Defense
- Identify the four major responsibilities inherent to DoD's mission
- Explain civilian control over the military
- Show the relationship between the Joint Chiefs of Staff and the DoD
- Define the key words contained in this lesson

Chapter 2

Introduction

The executive department responsible for the nation's defense forces is the Department of Defense (DoD). It was created in 1947, when Congress combined the former Navy and War departments into a National Military Establishment, an executive department headed by a secretary of defense. This lesson offers you an in-depth look at the DoD, what it does, and who works for it.

The DoD's Roots

Nations have historically raised and maintained military forces to defend their borders, protect their citizens, and preserve their government. Military forces imbue a nation with military power, the ability to influence other nations based on the implied or explicit threat of military action. Military power is directly related to a nation's military strength, and the will of the nation's government to employ it. Military strength is predicated on the ability to meet and defeat any adversary on any battlefield, including air, land, and sea. Today, under the direction of the DoD, the United States enjoys the strongest, most respected military in the world.

In 1789, Congress created the Department of War to administer and conduct military affairs. Congress separated the naval forces from the land forces in 1798, creating the Department of the Navy. The Departments of War and Navy remained for almost 150 years as the only two military departments; however, the National Security Act of 1947 created the Department of the Air Force and replaced the Department of War with the Department of the Army. This act also created the National Military Establishment to oversee the three military departments (Army, Navy, and Air Force; the Marine Corps was included under the Navy). In 1949, Congress renamed the National Military Establishment the Department of Defense. The seal for the Department of Defense is shown in Figure 2.1.1.

Mission

The mission of the DoD is to "provide the military forces needed to deter war and protect the security of the United States." Inherent in this mission is the responsibility for planning military strategy, maintaining the armed forces, operating the military bases throughout the world, and defending the country from foreign threats. The DoD assigns these duties to the military departments.

Figure 2.1.1: The official seal of the Department of Defense.
Courtesy of US Army JROTC.

How the DoD Is Organized

The DoD is the organization through which the president exercises civilian control over the military. The major elements of DoD are covered in the following sections and are shown in Figure 2.1.2.

Secretary of Defense

The Secretary of Defense, a civilian appointed by the president but subject to Senate approval, is the principal defense policy adviser to the President. Although the president has final authority and responsibility on all defense matters, the Secretary of Defense is responsible for formulating general defense policy, executing approved policy, and exercising authority, direction, and control over the DoD. The annual report to the president and Congress is the premier document issued by the Secretary of Defense. In addition to fulfilling a statutory requirement, it serves as an important reference document for many people interested in national defense issues and programs.

> **Note**
>
> The Secretary of Defense is sixth in the order of presidential succession, following the vice president (VP), Speaker of the House, President Pro Tempore of the Senate (presiding officer of the Senate in the absence of the VP), Secretary of State, and Secretary of the Treasury. Beginning with the Secretary of State, succession is determined by the order in which the departments of the president's cabinet were created.

Deputy Secretary of Defense

The Deputy Secretary of Defense is delegated full authority to act for the Secretary of Defense and to exercise the powers of the Secretary on any and all matters for which the Secretary is authorized to act pursuant to law.

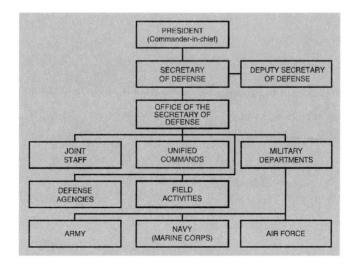

Figure 2.1.2: The elements of the Department of Defense.
Courtesy of US Army JROTC.

Office of the Secretary of Defense

This office is the principal staff element of the Secretary of Defense in the exercise of policy development, planning, resource management, fiscal, and program evaluation responsibilities. The office of the Secretary of Defense includes Under Secretaries for the following:

- **Acquisition and Technology.** Responsible for programs such as nuclear, chemical, and biological defense; acquisition reform; advanced technology; environmental security; logistics; space; and ballistic missile defense organization
- **Comptroller.** Responsible for programs in areas such as contract audit, program analysis and evaluation, and national performance review activities
- **Personnel and Readiness.** Responsible for programs such as force management, program integration, and health and reserve affairs
- **Policy.** Responsible for programs such as international security affairs, special operations and low-intensity conflict, and strategy and threat reduction

The office of the Secretary of Defense also includes Assistant Secretaries for the following:

- **Command, Control, Communications, and Intelligence**
- **Legislative and Public Affairs**

Other elements of the office are as follows:

- **General Counsel**
- **Inspector General**
- **Director of Operational Test and Evaluation**

The central headquarters for the DoD is at the world's largest office building, the Pentagon, located in Washington, D.C.

Joint Chiefs of Staff

The Joint Chiefs of Staff (JCS) constitute the immediate military staff of the Secretary of Defense and consist of the following general officers (four-star rank) from the U.S. Armed Forces:

- **Chairman (appointed by the president but subject to Senate approval)**
- **Vice chairman**
- **Chief of Staff of the Army**
- **Chief of Naval Operations**
- **Chief of Staff of the Air Force**
- **Commandant of the Marine Corps**

The collective body of the JCS is headed by the chairman, who sets the agenda and presides over JCS meetings. Additionally, the chairman is the principal adviser to the president, the Secretary of Defense, and the National Security Council.

All JCS members are, by law, military advisers, and they may respond to a request or voluntarily submit, through the chairman, advice or opinions to the president, the Secretary of Defense, or the National Security Council. Although responsibilities as members of the JCS take precedence over the duties as the Chiefs of the Military Services, these personnel are the senior military officers of their respective services. As such, they are also responsible for keeping the secretaries of the military departments fully informed on matters considered or acted upon by the JCS.

The main responsibilities of the Joint Chiefs of Staff, in conjunction with the military departments, are as follows:

- The **strategic** and **tactical** direction of the combatant forces
- The operation of the combatant forces under unified commands
- The integration of combatant forces into an efficient team of land, naval, and air forces
- Research and development

Executive Authority

During World War II, the Joint Chiefs of Staff acted as executive agents in dealing with **theater** and area commanders, but the original National Security Act of 1947 saw the Joint Chiefs as planners and advisers, not as commanders of combatant commands. In spite of this, the 1948 Key West Agreement allowed members of the Joint Chiefs to serve as executive agents for unified commands, a responsibility that allowed them to originate direct communication with the combatant command.

Congress abolished this authority in a 1953 amendment to the National Security Act. Today, the Joint Chiefs have no executive authority to command combatant forces. The issue of executive authority was clearly resolved by the Goldwater-Nichols DoD Reorganization Act of 1986: "The secretaries of the military departments shall assign all forces under their jurisdiction to unified and **specified** combatant commands to perform missions assigned to those commands . . . ;" the chain of command "runs from the president to the Secretary of Defense; and from the Secretary of Defense to the commander of the combatant command." The world is divided into nine geographical areas, each with a Commander-in-Chief (CINC) assigned. To facilitate mission accomplishment, these commanders have full **operational command** and control over all forces assigned to them.

Military Departments

The military departments of the Army, Navy, and Air Force are each headed by a secretary who does not have cabinet rank and is a civilian. These departments are responsible for maintaining the readiness of their assigned forces to ensure the security of the United States and to support the nation's policies and interests. The basic objectives of the military departments and the U.S. Armed Forces are as follows:

Key Note Terms

strategic – of or relating to the large-scale or global planning and conduct of military strategy, movements, and/or operations essential to the effective conduct of war

tactical – of or pertaining to tactics

theater – a large geographic area (including its land, sea, and air) in which active military operations are coordinated and conducted

specified – to state explicitly or in detail

operational command – commands performing the primary mission of the service as distinguished from support commands

- **Prevent military actions that threaten the safety of the United States or its allies**
- **Defend the United States' territories, waters, and airspace**
- **Engage in all necessary military operations and other assigned duties**
- **End hostilities on terms favorable to the United States**

> ### Note
> The Department of Defense maintains the academies for each of these departments. Can you name these academies?

The DoD is headed from the top by a unified leadership that exercises direction through three separate but mutually supportive chains of command:

- **The Operational Chain of Command**
- **The Advisory Chain of Command**
- **The Administrative Chain of Command**

The Operational Chain of Command

The Operational Chain of Command is the exclusive avenue for directing authority to employ force and move troops, otherwise known as combatant command authority (COCOM).

The Operational Chain of Command originates with the president of the United States and runs through the Secretary of Defense to the military generals in charge of the nine Unified Combatant Commands.

The U.S. Constitution invests the president as Commander-in-Chief with combatant command authority to employ force and move troops. The president's combatant command authority is tempered only by Congress' own constitutional authority to levy taxes and declare war.

Sending troops into harm's way is a profound responsibility that no president takes lightly. In addition to the life and death consequences and moral implications of the decision, presidents approach military intervention cautiously because they must answer to the electorate for their actions. Consequently, military action is typically the method of last resort only after all other nonlethal options have been exhausted. The different means available to the president to influence the actions and decisions of foreign governments are collectively known as the Instruments of National Power and include informational, diplomatic, economic, and military powers.

The president will employ all the Instruments of National Power to protect American national security interests. The Goldwater/Nichols Act of 1986 requires the president to present to Congress annually his plan for the national security of the United States. The published document is called the National Security Strategy.

The National Security Strategy identifies what is important to the American people as determined by their single common elected representative—the President. The National Security Strategy defines what are the national security interests of the United States and publicly declares the willingness of the President to take action when they are threatened. The National Security Strategy provides the framework for determining when the president will put American forces in harm's way and under what conditions he will invoke his constitutional authority to employ force and move troops.

When the President decides to invoke the military Instrument of National Power, he will plan and direct operations through the Secretary of Defense in charge of the nine Unified Combatant Commands.

Unity of Command has been a core principle of American military operations since the founding of our nation. General Washington directed both American and French naval and ground forces to corner General Cornwallis and decisively defeat the British at Yorktown in 1781. Unity of Command is the underlying principle supporting the concept behind today's Unified Combatant Commands.

Today's concept of a separate Unified Combatant Command to direct all military forces within a given region or performing the same function emerged directly from our experience in World War II. During World War II, General Marshall was the Chief of Staff of the Army, Admiral King was the Chief of Naval Operations, and General Arnold represented the Army Air Forces, yet each of these Service Chiefs turned over control of their forces to General Eisenhower who was appointed by President Roosevelt to command the war in Europe.

The National Security Act of 1947 formalized the ad hoc arrangement that won World War II and established the Unified Combatant Commands. The Goldwater/ Nichols Act of 1986 clarified lines of authority asserting that the Operational Chain of Command runs from the president, through the Secretary of Defense, to the commanders of the Unified Combatant Commands.

At present, there are nine Unified Combatant Commands. The scope of authority and responsibility assigned to each is determined by the Secretary of Defense in the Unified Command Plan:

- **U.S. Northern Command**
- **U.S. Southern Command**
- **U.S. Central Command**
- **U.S. Pacific Command**
- **U.S. European Command**
- **U.S. Joint Forces Command**
- **U.S. Strategic Command**
- **U.S. Transportation Command**
- **U.S. Special Operations Command**

Each Unified Combatant Command is distinguished by its area of resonsibility as either a geographic or functional command. A Geographic Command is responsible for a geographic region of the globe, for example, United States Pacific Command (USPACOM) is responsible for the region of the earth encompassing the entire Pacific Basin. A Funcational Command has functional responsibilities that span the entire globe, for example, United States Transportation Command (USTRANSCOM) is responsible for the shipment and movement of troops and supplies around the world by air, land, and sea.

Each Unified Combatant Command is headed by a four-star general designated the commander. The commander is appointed by the Secretary of Defense based on the recommendation of the chairman of the Joint Chiefs of Staff and approval by the president.

The commanders of the Unified Combatant Commands are distinguished as the warfighters. They bear total responsibility for conducting military operations within their assigned area of responsibility throughout peace, crisis, and war. The commanders have ambassadorial status and works with other nations to assure our allies, dissuade military competition, and deter potential adversaries. At the direction of the president of the United States, the commanders will use their assigned combatant command authority to employ force and move troops to decisively defeat all enemies across the spectrum of conflict.

The Advisory Chain of Command

The Advisory Chain of Command is designed to advise the President and help him make decisions in times of national crisis or emergency. The National Security Council is the primary forum for evaluating crisis and advising the President on all matters of national security. Established by the National Security Act of 1947, the National Security Council is composed of the following:

- **President**
- **Vice President**
- **Secretary of Defense**
- **Secretary of State**
- **Director of Central Intelligence**
- **Chairman of the Joint Chiefs of Staff**

The National Security Council convenes when necessary to evaluate threats or potential threats against the United States. The National Security Council considers using all Instruments of National Power when deciding how to respond to a threat. If the president wishes to consider a military option, he may call on the chairman of the Joint Chiefs of Staff to recommend a military course of action.

The chairman of the Joint Chiefs of Staff is the principal military adviser to the president of the United States. The chairman is nominated by the Secretary of Defense and serves at the appointment of the president for a period of two years. By virtue of his position, the chairman is the senior ranking officer in the military, and first among equals. To assist the chairman with providing sound military advice to the president, he is assisted by a vice chairman, Joint Staff, and the Joint Chiefs of Staff.

The Joint Chiefs of Staff is comprised of the Service Chiefs, the senior ranking officer from each of the four uniform services. The Joint Chiefs of Staff advise and consult the Chairman on the capabilities and readiness of their respective services. The complete membership of the Joint Chiefs of Staff is as follows:

- **Chairman**
- **Vice Chairman**
- **Chief of Staff of the Army**
- **Chief of Naval Operations**
- **Chief of Staff of the Air Force**
- **Commandant of the Marine Corps**

If the president decides to take military action, he will work with the Secretary of Defense and the commanders of the Unified Combatant Commands to plan and execute the recommended course of action.

The Administrative Chain of Command

The Administrative Chain of Command is charged with the responsibility of organizing, training, and equipping combat forces to provide to the Unified Combatant Commands. The Administrative Chain of Command begins with the president and extends through the Secretary of Defense to the three service departments:

- **Department of the Army**
- **Department of the Navy**
- **Department of the Air Force**

The U.S. Marine Corps is part of the Department of the Navy. There are only three Service Departments, but there are four Uniform Services:

- **Army**
- **Navy**
- **Air Force**
- **Marines**

> ### Note
>
> The Coast Guard is a uniform service assigned to the Department of Homeland Security. Similarly, personnel assigned to the Surgeon General's Office working for the Department of Public Health and the National Oceanic and Atmospheric Administration also wear uniforms and may report to the military when directed by the president.

Each service department is headed by a Civilian Service Secretary appointed by the president. The secretary positions are historic holdovers from when the Army and Navy were cabinet level positions and reported directly to the president. They were demoted when the services were consolidated under a single Secretary of Defense in 1947. The secretary positions remain to assert constitutional separation of powers and reinforce civilian control over the military. There are three Service Secretaries:

- **Secretary of the Army**
- **Secretary of the Navy**
- **Secretary of the Air Force**

The Service Chiefs advise and assist the Service Secretaries in organizing, training, and equipping their respective military services. The Service Chiefs represent the senior ranking officer from each of the four uniform services. There are four Service Chiefs:

- **Chief of Staff of the Army**
- **Chief of Naval Operations**
- **Chief of Staff of the Air Force**
- **Commandant of the Marine Corps**

The Service Chiefs have two jobs. They advise the chairman as members of the Joint Chiefs of Staff, and they organize, train, and equip their services as the senior military officers within their respective service departments. When they're not advising the chairman, the Service Chiefs exercise their authority to organize, train, and equip forces through direction of their individual service budgets. The primary responsibility of the Service Chiefs is to develop effective combat capability and ensure readiness for deployment by the commanders of the Unified Combatant Commands.

Conclusion

This lesson introduced you to the organization, background, and missions of the DoD. You saw a specific example of the constitutional requirement for civilian control of the military with the president, Secretary of Defense, and the secretaries of the military departments all being civilians. The highest military officers in the DoD are the Joint Chiefs of Staff. The missions and responsibilities of this department make it a vital part of the federal government and critical to the nation's defense.

In the following lesson, you will learn about the Active Army. You will learn about the origins of the U.S. Army, and why this is an Active Army.

Lesson Review

1. What is the mission of the DoD?
2. The Secretary of Defense is where in the line of presidential succession?
3. Identify one Under Secretary and the responsibilities for this position.
4. Define the term *theater*.

Lesson 2

The Active Army

Key Terms

counterintelligence
doctrine
nonaccession
unconventional

What You Will Learn to Do

- Relate the role of the Active Army to the U.S. Army

Linked Core Abilities

- Do your share as a good citizen in your school, community, country, and the world

Skills and Knowledge You Will Gain Along the Way

- Explain how the two Congressional acts impact the organizational structure of Armed Forces
- Identify the Congressional act that provides the basis for recent Army organization
- Distinguish between the fundamental roles of the Army and the Active Army
- Identify how the Active Army contributes to domestic affairs
- Correlate Army commands to the JROTC program
- Determine categories under which the Army classifies its branches
- Classify the basic/special branches of the Army
- Identify two nonaccession branches of the Army
- Define the key words contained in this lesson

Chapter 2

Introduction

The US Army dates back to June 1775. On June 14, 1775, the Continental Congress adopted the Continental Army when it appointed a committee to "draft the rules and regulations for the government of the Army." This authorization marks the birthday of the US Army, the oldest branch of the U.S. Armed Forces.

The Army is a major part of the U.S. Armed Forces, which collectively are responsible for defending American interests by:

- **Supporting and defending the Constitution of the United States against all enemies, foreign and domestic**
- **Ensuring, by timely and effective military action, the security of the United States, its possessions, and areas vital to its interests**
- **Upholding and advancing the national policies and interests of the United States**
- **Safeguarding the internal security of the United States**

Within that framework, the fundamental mission of the US Army is to deter war and to win in combat; however, there is much more to the Army than accomplishing that mission. In fact, the Army spends most of its time involved in peacetime activities. This lesson looks at the origins of the US Army, and why this is an Active Army.

Origins of the US Army

The legal basis for the establishment of the Army, as well as for the other branches of the armed forces, is set forth in the Constitution. The Constitution stipulates that the U.S. Armed Forces must answer to and be responsible for the needs and desires of the American people as expressed by their elected representatives. To achieve that, the Framers established the principle of civilian control over the military; that is, the president serves as Commander-in-Chief of the U.S. Armed Forces and Congress alone has the power to raise and support armies and to declare war.

Although the Constitution established the need for a system to "provide for the common defense," it did not define the organization of that system; therefore, in the course of our nation's history, the national defense structure has taken many forms. After the ratification of the *Constitution*, the newly formed Congress and President George Washington established the Department of War in 1789, as an executive department. The Secretary of War became its director and his powers were entrusted to him by the President.

Congress established our present military structure with the passage of two post-World War II legislations: the National Security Act of 1947 and its Amendments of 1949. The 1947 act

- Redesignated the Department of War as the Department of the Army, headed by the Secretary of the Army

- Created a separate Department of the Air Force and U.S. Air Force as a branch of the armed forces

- Loosely grouped the Departments of the Army, Navy, and Air Force under the title of the National Military Establishment

- Established the Joint Chiefs of Staff, composed of the military chiefs of the three services, as a council to advise the three department secretaries and the President on military matters

In 1949, Congress amended the National Security Act of 1947 by passing the National Security Act Amendments of 1949. These amendments:

- Established the Department of Defense (DoD) under the executive branch of the government and placed the Departments of the Army, Navy (including the Marine Corps), and Air Force subordinate to it.

- Established a Secretary of Defense to assist the President in providing direction, authority, and control of the three services. This secretary is appointed by the President and is a member of the President's cabinet.

- Stipulated that the president would appoint civilian secretaries to head of the Departments of the Army, Navy, and Air Force, and that those secretaries would come under the authority of the Secretary of Defense. These secretaries are responsible for and have the necessary authority to conduct, all the affairs of their departments.

- Established a chairman of the Joint Chiefs of Staff, also appointed by the President, who would have direct access to the Secretary of Defense.

Note

To learn more about the Department of Defense and the Secretary of Defense, review Chapter 2, Lesson 1.

Following the passage of the National Security Act and its Amendments, Congress passed the Army Organization Act of 1950. This act provides the legal basis for the present internal organization of the Army and the Department of the Army. It organizes the Army into a composite of commands, components, and branches all organized, trained, and equipped primarily for prompt and sustained combat operations on land. This act also

- Stipulated that the President would appoint civilian secretaries to head of the Departments of the Army, Navy, and Air Force, and that those secretaries would come under the authority of the Secretary of Defense. These secretaries are responsible for, and have the necessary authority to conduct, all the affairs of their departments.

- Established a chairman of the Joint Chiefs of Staff, also appointed by the President, who would have direct access to the Secretary of Defense.

The Army Concept

Under the Army concept, the US Army consists of the Active Army, the reserve components, and the Department of the Army civilian work force. The reserve components consist of the Army National Guard and the US Army Reserve. The purpose of these components is to provide trained units and qualified personnel to be available for active duty in time of war, national emergency, or at other times as dictated by national security requirements.

> **Note**
>
> The reserve components are detailed in the next lesson.

A bond of mutual agreement exists among the Active Army, the reserve components, and the Department of the Army civilian workforce to ensure the operational effectiveness of the total Army. This bond promotes

- **A balanced force structure**
- **Programs and projects designed to ensure modern equipment for both the active and reserve components**

There is cooperation and affiliation (teamwork) between active and reserve units, thus enhancing the mobilization potential of the reserve components and ensuring their timely availability to satisfy wartime reinforcement objectives.

Major Roles of the Total Army

In addition to its main mission—to deter war and to win in combat—the Army's major roles in executing U.S. military policies are as follows:

- **To maintain the ability to respond to any level of aggression**
- **To be well trained and equipped to prevent conflict**
- **To be employed at a level of strength necessary to ensure a swift and decisive end of the conflict if land forces are committed in combat**
- **To bring about an end to the conflict in terms favorable to the United States**
- **To fulfill a peacetime role by being able to contribute personnel and resources to domestic programs that support the general welfare of the people**

The Active Army

The Active (or Regular) Army is a component of the US Army maintained by the federal government in peace and in war. Congress authorizes its strength yearly under the provisions of Article 1 of the Constitution. At the same time, Congress appropriates money for its sustainment, modernization, and pay.

The Army must be able to respond to threats that occur anywhere in the world. In addition, the Army supports security assistance programs conducted by the

Departments of the State and Defense to friendly countries seeking economic and military assistance to maintain their stability and security. The Army makes an important contribution to those programs by providing military advisers, equipment, and other support. The results are positive because the Army's efforts are instrumental in implementing U.S. national security policies, and the Army shares in the benefits of mutual friendship, cooperation, and understanding, all of which serve the nation's interests.

Although maintaining national security is the determining factor in the need for an Army, the Active Army also contributes in peacetime to the nation's general welfare through domestic involvement. However, Congress limits this involvement by law, tradition, and the need for the Army to maintain a high level of readiness to fulfill its primary mission. Some of the ways the Army contributes to domestic affairs are as follows:

- **Providing assistance to communities during natural disasters (see Figure 2.2.1)**
- **Assisting civilian communities during civil disturbances by providing personnel and equipment in support of civilian police forces**
- **Assisting civilian communities with civic-action programs**
- **Improving flood control and navigation**
- **Adding to the nation's scientific and technological skills through extensive research and development programs**
- **Advising and assisting governmental agencies in fighting the war on drugs**

Organization

The Department of the Army is headed by the Secretary of the Army assisted by the Chief of Staff of the Army supported by the Army Staff. The Department of the Army directs a supporting establishment comprised of fourteen Major Commands that recruit, organize, train, equip, and support Army Operational Forces. Army Opera-

Figure 2.2.1: Members of the Army help communities when disaster strikes.
Courtesy of AP/Wide World Photos.

tional Forces are tactically organized into Corps, Divisions, Regiments, and Brigades. At the direction of the Secretary of Defense, the Chief of Staff of the Army will transfer operational control of tactical units to designated Unified Combatant Commands to conduct operations at the direction of the president of the United States.

A Corps is the Army's largest operational maneuver unit. A Division is the basic unit of maneuver at the tactical level; it is the largest Army fixed organization that trains and fights as a tactical team. There can be anywhere from two to five divisions assigned to a Corps. Divisions are tactically self-contained incorporating all elements of combat arms, combat support, and combat service support necessary to conduct prompt and sustained land combat operations. A Division is composed of three to five Brigades. Brigades are task organized to achieve Division objectives that may be part of a Corps operational plan. Brigades are not tactically self-contained but depend on Division and Corps support to conduct sustained combat operations. Regiments are Brigade-size cavalry units that are tactically self-contained to conduct independent reconnaissance and security operations supporting the Division scheme of maneuver.

Tactical Echelons

Missions are executed or carried out by different size elements or organizations within the Army. The Army task organizes to accomplish assigned missions. Task organizations are built from functionally oriented, standard size units.

> **Note**
>
> The basic building block of all Army organizations is the individual soldier.

Squad

The squad/section is the smallest element in the Army organizational structure. The leader is a noncommissioned officer (usually a Sergeant or a Staff Sergeant). The size is dependent on the function of the squad/section. The squad is the final step in completing the mission.

Platoon

A platoon consists of two to four squads/sections with a Lieutenant usually as the leader. A Staff Sergeant or Sergeant First Class is second in command. The platoon leader coordinates and tasks squads to accomplish assigned platoon objectives.

Company

Typically, three to five platoons form a company. A company is normally commanded by a Captain. A First Sergeant is the Company Commander's principal noncommissioned officer assistant. A troop is a company-size unit in a cavalry organization. A battery is a company-size unit in an artillery organization.

Battalion

A battalion is composed of four to six companies. A battalion is normally commanded by a Lieutenant Colonel. The Command Sergeant Major is the battalion commander's principal noncommissioned officer assistant. A squadron is the cavalry equivalent of a battalion. The commander has a staff typically overseeing the battalion's mission, training, administration, and logistics functions. A battalion is capable of independent operations of limited duration and scope.

Brigade

A brigade headquarters commands the tactical operations of two to five battalions. A brigade is normally commanded by a Colonel. The Command Sergeant Major is the senior, noncommissioned officer. Brigades may be employed on independent or semi-independent operations.

Organization of the Active Army

The Department of the Army organizes the Active Army in a number of ways. There are ten major commands in the Continental United States (CONUS) and four major commands located in Europe, Asia, and other regions of the world (OCONUS). The most well-known commands in CONUS are Forces Command (FORSCOM) at Fort McPherson, Georgia, and Training and Doctrine Command (TRADOC) at Fort Monroe, Virginia. Other CONUS commands include the following:

- **Army Material Command**
- **Military District of Washington**
- **Medical Command**
- **Army Intelligence and Security Command**
- **Criminal Investigation Command**
- **Corps of Engineers**
- **Surface Deployment and Distribution Command**
- **Army Special Operations Command**

OCONUS commands include US Army Europe, US Army Pacific, Eighth Army, and US Army South.

FORSCOM controls all the combat and support units at installations throughout the United States.

TRADOC is responsible for developing Army **doctrine** and training. TRADOC also exercises control over the training installations and schoolhouses throughout the United States. US Army ROTC Cadet Command, a major subordinate command of TRADOC, manages both the Senior and Junior ROTC programs.

Branches of the US Army

The Army classifies its units and personnel by branches. Branch names identify the types of units that personnel can select to enter (on enlistment) and the personnel who are trained in the primary functions of that branch. There are basic and special branches; the Army classifies the basic branches into the categories of Combat Arms, Combat Support, and Combat Service Support.

- **Combat Arms** are units and soldiers who close with and destroy enemy forces or provide firepower and destructive capabilities on the battlefield
- **Combat Support** encompasses critical combat functions necessary to secure victory
- **Combat Service Support** sustain Army forces and reconstitute tactical units

Table 2.2.1 shows the different branches.

Table 2.2.1: Branches of the United States Army			
Combat Arms		**Combat Service Support**	
Infantry	Aviation	Transportation	Surgeon
Artillery	Special Operations	Quartermaster	Dentist
Armor	Air Defense Artillery	Ordinance	Veterinarian
Combat Support		Finance	Medical Corps
Engineer	Intelligence	Legal	Chaplain
Chemical	Signal	Adjutant General	Rabbi
Military Police		Doctor	Muslim
		Nurse	Buddhist

The remaining two, Special Forces and Civil Affairs, are **nonaccession** branches.

Special Forces accomplish missions of **unconventional** warfare, foreign internal defense, direct action, strategic reconnaissance, and counterterrorism. Civil Affairs is only in the Army Reserve and it accomplishes missions of command, control, and coordination of civil-military operations.

Combat Arms

The Combat Arms branches are directly involved in the conduct of actual fighting. The Combat Arms branches are as follows:

- **Infantry.** Closes with the enemy by means of fire and maneuver, on foot or in armored vehicles, in order to destroy or capture the enemy or repel their assault by fire, close combat, or counterattack. Infantry is the nucleus around which the Army groups the other branches in combat operations.
- **Armor.** Conducts mobile land and cavalry warfare; the tank is the nucleus of its forces.
- **Field Artillery.** Provides indirect fire support for Infantry and Armor. Field Artillery uses cannons, missiles, and rockets and is capable of providing both nuclear and nonnuclear firepower.
- **Air Defense Artillery.** Provides air and missile defense on the battlefield by destroying enemy aircraft and missiles with automatic weapons or missiles.

Key Note Terms

nonaccession – the policy or practice of not accepting personnel directly from traditional officer or enlisted entrance sources

unconventional – not bound by or in accordance with international agreements dealing with a specific subject, such as the rules or laws of warfare; the use of nuclear, biological, or chemical weapons or energy

- **Aviation.** Provides prompt and sustained combat air operations. Aviation units participate in a variety of combat and support roles including attack, assault helicopter, aerial observation, transportation, lift, supply, and troop transport duties.
- **Corps of Engineers.** Combat Engineer units are part of the combined arms team in combat operations. Corps of Engineers units provide combat support including construction, demolition, amphibious operations, defensive barriers, camouflage/topographic activities, and minefield employment (see Figure 2.2.2).

> ### Note
>
> Depending on their mission, engineer units can be Combat Arms, Combat Support, or a Combat Service Support Branch.

Combat Support

The Combat Support branches provide operational assistance to the combat arms, and they participate in combat operations as part of the combined arms team. The combat support branches are as follows:

- **Corps of Engineers.** See description under combat arms.
- **Chemical Corps.** Provides the Army with highly trained people in nuclear, biological, and chemical (NBC) warfare defense programs. These programs include employment, logistical support, defensive procedures, equipment, training, scientific development, and management of NBC materials.

Figure 2.2.2: The Army Corps of Engineers contributes in part through construction.
Courtesy of Dean Conger/ Corbis Images.

- **Military Intelligence.** Plans, conducts, and supervises collection, analysis, production, and dissemination of intelligence, such as combat intelligence, and **counterintelligence** information pertaining to the enemy, weather, or terrain.

> **Note**
>
> The Signal Corps, Chemical Corps, and Military Police Corps can either be a combat support or a combat service support branch.

Key Note Term

counterintelligence – actions taken by intelligence personnel or units to prevent an enemy from gathering information about friendly forces, to deceive the enemy, to prevent sabotage, or to gather political and military information

Combat Service Support

The Combat Service Support branches perform combat service support activities or administrative functions for the Army. These branches may also provide specialized services to other departments of the federal government and to the people of the United States.

The Combat Service Support branches are as follows:

- **Adjutant General Corps.** Formulates policy and manages the Army's administrative and personnel systems.

- **Corps of Engineers.** See description under combat arms.

- **Finance Corps.** Responsible for the management of the Army's financial resources, which includes paying US Army personnel.

- **Quartermaster Corps.** Plans and directs the acquisition, receipt, storage, preservation, and issue of equipment, repair parts, fortification/construction material, subsistence, petroleum products, water, and other general supplies.

- **Signal Corps.** See description under combat support.

- **Chemical Corps.** See description under combat support.

- **Military Police Corps.** See description under combat support.

- **Ordnance Corps.** Responsible for the maintenance and management of armament, tracked, wheeled, and general purpose vehicles, conventional and special munitions, test equipment, management of air defense and land combat missile systems, and construction material.

- **Transportation Corps.** Responsible for the movement of personnel and equipment for the Army and for the Navy, Air Force, and government agencies as assigned.

- **Judge Advocate General's Corps.** Provides professional legal service and assistance in the fields of both military and civil law and supervises the Army's system of military justice.

- **Army Medical Department (includes Medical Corps, Dental Corps, Veterinary Corps, Army Nurse Corps, Army Medical Specialist Corps, and Medical Service Corps).** Provides medical, dental, and veterinary care. The chief functions of the Medical Department are care of the sick and wounded, physical examinations, prevention of disease, and the operation of hospitals and dispensaries.

- **Chaplains.** The duties of the Army chaplains are similar to those performed by their civilian counterparts. They are clergymen from recognized denominational groups who have volunteered to perform their ministry in the Army. The mission of the Chaplains branch is to promote religion and morality in the Army by providing religious services, education, and counseling.

> **Note**
>
> The eight special branches of the Army are all Combat Service support units: the Judge Advocate General's Corps, Medical Corps, Dental Corps, Veterinary Corps, Army Nurse Corps, Army Medical Specialist Corps, Medical Service Corps, and the Chaplains.

Conclusion

This lesson covered the inception of the modern US Army, from the adoption of the Continental Army in 1775 to the present. The concept of the US Army includes the Active Army, the reserve components, and the Department of the Army civilian work force, all of which work together to provide a balanced force structure as well as programs and projects designed to ensure modern equipment for both the active and reserve components. This lesson showed you the major roles of the total Army as well as the organization of the Active Army.

The following lesson takes a look at the US Army Reserve components. You will learn the difference between the Active Army and the Army Reserves.

Lesson Review

1. Which document sets forth the legal basis for the establishment of the Army?
2. List the three concepts of the US Army.
3. Choose one combat arms branch and explain it.
4. List three missions of the Active Army.

Lesson 3

The Army Reserve Components

Key Terms

citizen-soldiers
combatant
militia
mobilize
Reserve Corps

What You Will Learn to Do

- Distinguish among the reserve components of the US Army

Linked Core Abilities

- Do your share as a good citizen in your school, community, country, and the world

Skills and Knowledge You Will Gain Along the Way

- Identify the two Congressional acts that had an impact on the organization and structure of the Army reserve components
- Compare the missions of the Army National Guard and the Army Reserve
- Contrast the major types of units the Army National Guard and the Army Reserve contribute to the Army force
- Identify the three categories of the Army Reserve
- Define the key words contained in this lesson

Chapter 2

Introduction

The Army reserve component is an important part of the Total Force comprised of active duty forces, the National Guard, the Reserves, and Department of Defense (DoD) civilians. The Guard and Reserves are similar in that they are composed of citizen-soldiers who devote themselves only part-time to military duty. The Guard and Reserves differ in that the National Guard reports to the State Governor, while the Reserves are federal forces who report to the president. The great advantage of both the Guard and the Reserves is they represent significant military capability at relatively small cost; they pack a big bang for the buck. The Department of Defense can't do its job without civilian employees. DoD civilians are subject to deployment to combat zones. DoD civilians lend important capabilities and provide constitutional controls over the military.

This lesson examines each component of the US Army Reserve.

Total Force Policy

Prior to 1973, the Guard and Reserves were viewed as measures of last resort—America's last line of defense. In 1973, General Creighton Abrams penned the Total Force Policy, directing the complete integration of the Guard and Reserves into the federal military mission.

General Abrams' initial purpose was to ensure public support for future military actions, particularly in light of the failure in Vietnam. One of the reasons the United States lost the war in Vietnam was because the public lost faith in the military. What Abraham Lincoln said 140 years ago remains true today: "With public support anything is possible; without it nothing is possible." As citizen-soldiers, the Guard and the Reserves come from your city, town, neighborhood, and home. When they are called to duty, their absence is noticeable, and suddenly the crisis doesn't seem so distant, foreign, or remote. The community unites to wish them good luck and a safe, speedy return home.

An added benefit to General Abram's Total Force Policy is that the Guard and the Reserves provide highly cost effective military forces. Today, the Guard and the Reserves comprise 50 percent of the United States' military capability, yet they cost less than 10 percent of the military budget.

The Total Force is composed of the National Guard, the Reserves, and DoD civilians. Today, the Guard and the Reserves are indispensable to maintaining the defense of our nation as they stand on the frontlines alongside our Active Duty forces.

The Army National Guard

The Army National Guard (ARNG) is one component of the Army (which consists of the Active Army, the Army National Guard, and the Army Reserves.) The ARNG is composed primarily of traditional Guardsmen—civilians who serve their country, state, and community on a part-time basis (usually one weekend each month and two weeks during the summer). Each state, territory, and the District of Columbia have its own National Guard, as provided for by the Constitution of the United States.

The ARNG was founded on October 7, 1683, in the Massachusetts Bay Colony. The Massachusetts Bay Colony organized two units (one infantry regiment and one engineer battalion) as part of their local **militia**. These units also became part of the Continental Army during the Revolutionary War (1775–1783).

In August 1824, the New York State Militia was the first state to apply the label *National Guard*. New York took the title as a compliment to the famous French hero, Marquis de Lafayette, who had commanded the French National Guard in Paris in 1789 and who had made great contributions in America's war for independence. Gradually, other states adopted the popular term for their units, and by 1896, only three states retained the word *militia* in their official designation.

The National Defense Act of 1916 had a more profound impact on the Army National Guard than any other legislation of the past century. That act and its amendments

- **Officially designated state organized militias as the National Guard.**
- **Changed the organizational structure of the various National Guard units to conform to the structure of the Active Army.**
- **Provided increased assistance from the federal government to the National Guard. Although the National Guard would still be under the control of state authorities, this legislation meant that when Guard units reached established Army standards, they became eligible for federal support.**

Another law passed by Congress in 1933 organized all Guard units into the National Guard of the United States; therefore, Congress made it possible for the Commander-in-Chief to give the National Guard an Army mission (or order) without having to wait for state governors to call those forces to duty.

In the late 1940s, Department of the Army established the Air National Guard, which was first used in the Korean War (1951–1953).

Throughout our proud history, as the nation's oldest military organization, the Army National Guard has protected America—in war and peace—from all enemies, both foreign and domestic.

Contribution to the Army Force and Its Missions

The National Guard has a unique dual mission that consists of both federal and state roles. For state missions, the governor, through the state Adjutant General, commands Guard forces. The governor can call the National Guard into action during local or statewide emergencies, such as storms, fires, earthquakes, or civil disturbances.

In addition, the president of the United States can activate the National Guard for participation in federal missions. Examples of federal activations include Guard units deployed to Bosnia and Kosovo for stabilization operations and units deployed to the Middle East and other locations in the war on terrorism. When federalized, Guard units are commanded by the Combatant Commander of the theater in which they are operating.

Aiding America's Communities, Our State Mission

As previously mentioned, the Army National Guard exists in all 50 states, 3 territories, and the District of Columbia. The state, territory, or district leadership are the Commanders-in-Chief for each Guard. Their Adjutants General are answerable to them for the training and readiness of the units. At the state level, the governors reserve the ability, under the Constitution of the United States, to call up members of the National Guard in time of domestic emergencies or need.

The ARNG state mission is perhaps the most visible and well known. Nearly everyone has seen or heard of Guard units responding to battle fires or helping communities deal with floods, tornadoes, hurricanes, snowstorms, or other emergency situations. In times of civil unrest, the citizens of a state can rest assured that the Guard will be ready to respond, if needed. During 2001, 34,855 Guardsmen were called to duty in response to the needs of their community or state.

The ARNG is represented in more than 2,800 communities in 50 states, the District of Columbia, Guam, Puerto Rico, and the Virgin Islands.

Organization of the Army National Guard

As part of the Army, the ARNG has to comply with DoD and Department of the Army orders and regulations. Therefore, the Guard needs some way to gain access to the Secretary of the Army and the military chain of command (such as Army Chief of Staff). The organization that accomplishes this is the National Guard Bureau (NGB).

The NGB was formed to assist the states, territories, and District of Columbia in procuring funding for the Guard, administering policies, and acting as a liaison between the Departments of the Army and Air Force and the states.

The NGB is a joint bureau of the Departments of the Army and Air Force and functions in both a staff and an operating capacity for each component. The NGB performs the federal functions of the ARNG and the Air National Guard (ANG). The senior leader at NGB is the Chief, usually a Lieutenant General.

The ARNG and the ANG are each led by their own director. The two directors are selected by the Secretary of the Army (for the Director of the ARNG) and the Secretary of the Air Force (for the Director of the ANG). Both directors report to the Chief of the NGB. Full-time staffs support the Chief of the NGB and the directors of the ARNG and the ANG.

When ARNG units are not mobilized under federal control, they report to the Adjutant General of their state or territory, or in the case of the District of Columbia, the Commanding General. Each Adjutant General is responsible to the governor of his state (or in the case of the District of Columbia, the mayor).

Most members of the National Guard are part-time soldiers (referred to as **citizen-soldiers**). Typically, National Guard members are required to attend one drill weekend each month and one annual training period (usually two weeks in the summer) each year. Weekend drills usually consist of one Saturday and Sunday each month but occasionally include reporting for duty on Friday night. Initially, all nonprior service personnel are required to attend initial entry training (IET), also known as Basic Training. After Basic Training, soldiers go to their Advanced Individ-

Key Note Term

citizen-soldiers – members of the National Guard or Army Reserves

ual Training (AIT), which teaches them the special skills they will need for their job in the Guard.

Accomplishments of the Army National Guard

Since its founding in the 1600s, the National Guard has participated in every American conflict, including the current Iraqi War. In this century alone, ARNG units have fought and distinguished themselves in both World Wars, the Korean War, the Vietnam War, the Persian Gulf War, Afghanistan, and now Iraq. In fact, individual Guardsmen received 14 Medals of Honor during World War II.

The National Guard plays a vital role in the Army, it must be ready to **mobilize** and deploy on very short notice. The 9-11 terrorist attacks on the United States resulted in the activation of thousands of ARNG personnel. A total of 9,600 National Guard men and women were already on duty across the country September 14, 2001, when President George W. Bush approved an order to call up as many as 50,000 additional members of the National Guard and Reserves. Soon after the attacks, ARNG soldiers were ordered to the nation's airports to assist in security. The governors of many states also called on the Guard to protect critical facilities and infrastructure. The mission of homeland security for the Guard is not a new mission nor is it the only mission; it is only one of the many missions of the Guard.

President Bush's call for a temporary tour of active duty for up to 50,000 National Guard and Reserve troops in a military operation on American soil was the largest of its kind since 1916.

ARNG soldiers were an essential element in controlling wildfires throughout the western United States. Many of the Guard troops were called in August 2001 to assist civilian firefighters in Oregon, Nevada, Montana, California, South Dakota, Arizona, and Washington.

In 1996 and 1997, National Guard personnel deployed overseas to support **combatant** commands and U.N. peacekeeping forces and soldiers from 16 states and territories participated in a record 160 state emergency call-ups and local civil authority missions.

Today's National Guard is better trained and equipped to respond to any state or national emergency than at any time in its history. In peacetime, National Guard units train alongside active Army commands or units for which the Army has associated them through partnership agreements. In the event of mobilization, these Guard units would then deploy and serve with their Active Army units during wartime. The Army simply cannot enter into a major conventional war without the support of the ARNG.

The US Army Reserve (USAR)

Reserves are citizen-soldiers who augment the federal Active Duty military force. Every federal military service has a reserve component: Army Reserves, Navy Reserves, Air Force Reserves, Marine Corps Reserves, and Coast Guard Reserves.

Active Reserves are reservists who have been called to active duty or otherwise fill a small number of permanent positions.

> **Key Note Term**
>
> **mobilize** – to assemble, prepare, or put into operation (personnel, units, equipment, and so on) for war or a similar emergency

> **Key Note Term**
>
> **combatant** – engaged in combat

Ready Reserves are reservists who may be called to active duty to augment forces in times of war or national emergency. There are two categories of Ready Reserves:

- **Selected Reserves train regularly and are combat ready**
- **Individual Ready Reserves have a federal commitment and are subject to recall, but don't train regularly**

Standby Reserves are reservists who fulfill civilian jobs that are considered key to national defense, for example, port authority and doctors. Standby Reserves don't train and don't serve in units. Essentially they are federalized so they can't desert their jobs in times of war or national emergency.

Retired Reserves include anyone receiving or waiting to receive retirement pay.

Just like the Guard, the Reserves perform a vital role in service to the nation by supporting and fulfilling federal missions on a daily basis. Also like the Guard, the Reserves may be activated for federal duty by the president or Congress.

Public attitude and economics played an important role in the origins of the Army Reserves. In our country's early days, citizens were suspicious of a large Active Army, and they knew it would be difficult to financially support such a large standing army. Therefore, a reserve military structure became attractive because it provided a capability to mobilize military forces when the situation arose.

The USAR originated on April 23, 1908, the result of lessons learned from the Spanish-American War and the realization that the Regular Army could not provide enough medical personnel to take care of the needs of an expanded wartime force. Its beginnings were quite modest: commissions as first lieutenants were initially given to 160 Army contract physicians who became the first members of the Federal Reserve Corps. From that small beginning has grown the modern day Army Reserves of thousands of units and hundreds of thousands of well-trained men and women.

The National Defense Act of 1916 formally established the **Reserve Corps**. It also established the Junior Reserve Officers' Training Corps (JROTC), provided for an Officers' Reserve Corps through direct commissioning up to the grade of major, and formulated a Reserve Officers' Training Program at civilian colleges and universities.

The Reserve Forces Act of 1955 reorganized the Army Reserves. It was important legislation because although federal budget cuts forced the Active Army to cut its strength, that act increased the size of the Army Reserves (despite eliminating 15 Army Reserves divisions) and stipulated that Reserve units would receive more modern equipment over a 15-year period.

Contribution to the Total Army Force and its Missions

The Army Reserves proved itself during World War I, when over 160,000 officers and enlisted Reservists served their country. World War II saw over 200,000 Reserve officers and enlisted soldiers take part in the war. These Reservists, in the words of Army Chief of Staff General George C. Marshall, "constituted the principal available asset that we possessed at this time. Without their assistance, the program (expansion of the Army) could not have been carried out except in a superficial manner." The Korean War, and to a much lesser extent, the Vietnam War, also saw Army Reserves involvement.

The USAR really proved itself, though, during Operation Desert Shield/Desert Storm, when tens of thousands of Army Reservists and hundreds of units were called up and sent to the Persian Gulf region. It is fair to say that the victory in the Gulf could not have occurred without the contributions of the Army Reserves.

The Army Reserve has two major missions:

1. **To organize, train, equip, and provide units to help defend our nation with little or no advance notice in the event that Congress or the President mobilizes the armed forces.**

2. **To provide trained individual reinforcements, officer and enlisted, as prescribed by Department of the Army mobilization plans. These soldiers would replace initial battlefield casualties, reinforce active Army units, and provide reinforcement for reserve component units that are mobilized.**

Organization of the Army Reserve

Unlike the National Guard, the Army Reserves are under federal control during peacetime. As a part of the total Army, it fulfills the Army's need for units to meet its mission requirements in times of changing national priorities and limited resources. A recent Army Chief of Staff remarked that the Active Army could not be successfully committed to a major conflict in Europe without the Army Reserves.

The Chief of the Army Reserves is an adviser to the Army Chief of Staff on Army Reserve matters. Therefore, US Army Reserve Command (USARC) channels begin at the Department of the Army and flow through Forces Command (FORSCOM) to the 10 Regional Support Commands (RSCs), the 3 Regional Support Groups (RSGs), and to the 3 Army Reserve Commands (ARCOMs) located outside the continental United States.

The USAR is organized into three unique categories: Ready Reserves, Standby Reserves, and the Retired Reserves.

Ready Reserves

The Ready Reserves consists of the Selected Reserves and the Individual Ready Reserves (IRR).

The Selected Reserves consists of members assigned to Troop Program Units (TPU), Individual Mobilization Augmentation (IMA) Program positions, and the USAR portion of the Active Guard/Reserve (AGR) Program. The AGR Program offers Army Reserve soldiers an opportunity to serve in active duty positions supporting USAR programs. Here's how each works.

TPUs enjoy the adventure and camaraderie of soldiering while serving in a reserve status. TPUs are located throughout the United States and even overseas. Usually TPUs train just one weekend a month, plus two weeks of annual training. Normally, this comes out to only 38 days per year.

IMA affiliates with a particular Active Army unit, are assigned to a unit duty position, and wear the unit patch and insignia. They train with the unit at least two weeks during the year and are eligible for many USAR benefits, including the Montgomery GI Bill for the Selected Reserves.

The Ready Reserves include TPUs and the IRR that are liable for active duty as prescribed by law. The highest priority elements are the members of the TPUs who are in a paid drill status. More than 3,200 units of company or detachment size are located throughout the 50 states, Puerto Rico, Guam, and Europe. The IRR consists of members not assigned to a unit, but they can be mobilized by order of the President in response to a national emergency.

Each troop program unit is required to conduct 48 training assemblies (or drills) annually. For every 4-hour drill, the unit member receives one day's pay and one retirement point. Drills are usually conducted as four training assemblies one weekend per month at the unit's reserve center or at a training site. In addition, each unit performs at least 14 days of annual training.

The IRR is composed of trained individuals assigned to a central pool. These Reservists will augment and fill Active Army and Army Reserve units should there be a call for mobilization.

The IRR is made up of two groups. The first group is the USAR Control Group (Annual Training). The Annual Training Group consists of nonunit members (with less than three years of active duty) who have a military service/training obligation to complete.

The second group is the USAR Control Group (Reinforcement). The Reinforcement Group is comprised of nonunit members (over three years of active duty) with no training requirements.

Standby Reserves

The Standby Reserves are those units and members of the reserve components (other than those in the Ready Reserves or the Retired Reserves) who are liable for active duty only in time of declared war or national emergency. The Standby Reserves are composed of Reservists who have completed all Ready Reserve obligations but who have yet to complete their eight-year military service obligation. Members of the Standby Reserves can be in an active or an inactive status.

Active status refers to Reservists who are completing their statutory military service obligation were screened from the Ready Reserves as being key personnel or may be temporarily assigned to the Standby Reserves for hardship reasons.

Inactive status refers to individuals who are not required by law or regulation to remain members of an active status program but who desire to retain their Reserves affiliation in a nonparticipating status or have skills that may be of possible future use to the Army.

Retired Reserves

The Retired Reserves consist of individuals that completed a total of at least 20 years of creditable Federal Military Service in either the Active Army or one of the Reserve Components that the Army placed on a Reserve Retired list. In all cases, the last eight years must have been spent in a Reserve Component.

The Army may involuntarily order any of those people, if qualified, to active duty in time of declared war or national emergency when the Secretary of the Army determines that adequate numbers of qualified individuals are not available in the Ready or Standby Reserves.

Accomplishments of the Army Reserves

Since its establishment in 1916, reservists have served in both World Wars, the Korean War, the Berlin Crisis, the Vietnam War, the Persian Gulf War, and now in Iraq. In fact, of the personnel mobilized for the Korean War over one-half were Reservists. Additionally, during the U.S. Postal Service strike in 1970, the U.S. government called 8,000 Reservists to active duty to help deliver the mail. They are currently answering the call in Bosnia and other places around the globe, carrying the torch passed on by the citizen-soldiers 200 years before who left their homes, farms, and businesses to take up arms against tyranny.

Conclusion

From its formal beginning in 1908 until now, Army Reservists have played a vital role in our nation's defense. From the hedgerows of World War I to the desert sands of the Persian Gulf, when our country needed its citizen-soldiers, they were there.

A distinguishing feature of the USAR is the important contribution Reservists make in the cities, towns, and villages in which they live and work. Their excellent training and varied experience make them valuable members of their communities. Often, Reservists put in long hours at such diverse projects as running medical clinics and clearing land for playgrounds. They stand ready to help in times of crisis or national emergency. Their contributions of time, energy, and skill can make their towns a better place to live.

If you are considering a career in the Active Army or one of the Reserve Components of the US Army, you should now have a better understanding of their roles and structure. More important, you now should have an idea of the role that the Army plays in our American society.

In the next lesson, you learn about the U.S. Navy. You will learn about the different departments of the Navy and the opportunities available to you.

Lesson Review

1. What state was the first to apply the term *National Guard*?
2. Compare and contrast the National Guard and the Army Reserves.
3. What are the three major categories of the Army Reserves?
4. Define the term *citizen-soldiers*.

Chapter 2

Lesson Review

Lesson 4

The United States Navy

Key Terms

Battlespace
Command by Negation
Forward from the Sea
Numbered Fleets
Officer in Tactical Command
Operating Forces
Principle Warfare Commanders
Shore Establishment
task force
Underway Replenishment

What You Will Learn to Do

- Explore the organization and mission of the U.S. Navy

Linked Core Abilities

- Do your share as a good citizen in your school, community, country, and the world

Skills and Knowledge You Will Gain Along the Way

- Explain the mission of the U.S. Navy
- Describe the organization of the U.S. Navy
- Distinguish between the Shore Establishment and Operating Forces
- Explain how the U.S. Navy is able to maintain a global presence
- Identify the three standard force packages of the U.S. Navy
- Identify the Elements of Naval Power
- Describe the Navy's role in nuclear deterrence
- Explain the use of Composite Warfare and Command by Negation
- Define the key words contained in this lesson

Introduction

The U.S. Navy is the branch of the U.S. Armed Forces that maintains command of the seas. The Navy is able to seek out and destroy enemies on, under, or above the sea. If attacked, it can return the blow almost anywhere on earth from its warships. The Navy also serves as an instrument of international relations in times of peace. It is possible that the presence of naval vessels may be helpful in keeping a crisis from developing into war. Additionally, the Navy engages in actions such as carrying food and medical supplies to disaster areas and in assisting merchant and passenger ships in emergencies. In this lesson you explore the purpose and structure of the U.S. Navy.

The United States Navy

On October 13, 1775, the Continental Congress authorized the outfitting of a 10-gun warship marking the birth of the U.S. Navy.

The Department of the Navy organizes, trains, and equips forces for prompt and sustained combat incident to operations at sea. The official Navy seal is shown in Figure 2.4.1. Operational units are assigned to designated Unified Combatant Commands to maintain sea power, sea control, and nuclear deterrence at the direction of the president of the United States.

The mission of the U.S. Navy is to maintain, train, and equip combat-ready naval forces capable of winning wars, deterring aggression, and maintaining freedom of the seas.

Figure 2.4.1: The official seal of the U.S. Navy.
Courtesy of US Army JROTC.

Organization

The Department of the Navy is headed by the Secretary of the Navy assisted by the Chief of Naval Operations and Commandant of the Marine Corps supported by the Navy Staff. The Department of the Navy directs a **Shore Establishment** composed of 17 Naval Commands, Bureaus, Offices, and Centers that recruit, organize, train, equip, and support Navy **Operating Forces**. Navy Operating Forces are composed of the **Numbered Fleets**, the U.S. Marines, and in times of war, the U.S. Coast Guard. All Navy ships, submarines, and aircraft are permanently assigned to the Atlantic and Pacific Fleets. Navy Fleet Forces Command will temporarily assign ships, submarines, and aircraft as needed to the Numbered Fleets. The Numbered Fleets, as seen in Table 2.4.1, are forward deployed providing a U.S. naval presence around the world. The ships, submarines, and aircraft of the Numbered Fleet are tactically organized into Navy task forces. A **task force** is structured to perform a specific task or mission, such as amphibious assault, missile deterrence, submarine warfare, escort, patrol, battle, and so on. At the direction of the Secretary of Defense, the Chief of Naval Operations will transfer operational control of a task force to a designated Unified Combatant Command to conduct operations at the direction of the president of the United States.

Key Note Terms

Shore Establishment – organization that recruits, organizes, trains, equips, and supports Navy operating forces

Operating Forces – the combatant arm of the United States Navy

Numbered Fleets – forward deployed forces of the United States Navy

task force – structured force designed to perform a specific task or mission

Table 2.4.1: Navy Numbered Fleets

Fleet	Headquarters
2nd Fleet	Norfolk, Virginia
3rd Fleet	San Diego, California
5th Fleet	Bahrain
6th Fleet	Gaeta, Italy
7th Fleet	Yokosuka, Japan

Task Force Packages

A task force can be built from any naval component to perform any specified mission. There is no set requirement for a Navy task force; however, the Navy does maintain a standard set of task force packages including the Carrier Strike Group, Expeditionary Strike Group, and Surface Action Group.

A Carrier Strike Group (see Figure 2.4.2) is a task force built around the offensive power of an aircraft carrier. A Carrier Strike Group is the primary power projection force of the U.S. Navy. A Carrier Strike Group includes an aircraft carrier, two cruisers, two destroyers, two attack submarines, and a resupply ship. A Carrier Strike Group projects power far across the ocean and deep inland through the striking power of the Carrier Air Wing.

An Expeditionary Strike Group (see Figure 2.4.3) is a task force built around the offensive power of a Marine Amphibious Ready Group. An Expeditionary Strike Group is comprised of amphibious ships, cruisers, destroyers, and submarines. The Expeditionary Strike Group is designed to project Naval power deep inland by augmenting the striking power of an amphibious ready group with submarine launched cruise missiles and shipboard anti-air and antimissile capability.

Figure 2.4.2: Carrier Strike Group.
Courtesy of the US Department of Defense.

Figure 2.4.3: Expeditionary Strike Group.
Courtesy of AP/Wide World Photos.

A Surface Action Group (Figure 2.4.4) is a task force built around cruisers, destroyers, and frigates to conduct specified operations without the aide of an aircraft carrier or Marine amphibious-ready group.

Elements of Naval Combat Power

Elements of naval combat power include the Aircraft Carriers, Carrier Air Wing, Guided Missile Cruiser, Guided Missile Destroyer, Guided Missile Frigates, Nuclear Attack Submarines, Fleet Ballistic Missile Submarine, Sea Air Land Teams, and the U.S. Marines. The following sections tell you a little bit about each element.

Aircraft Carrier

The Aircraft Carrier, as shown in Figure 2.4.5, is a Navy strike warfare platform. The Aircraft Carrier carries a complement of 84 combat aircraft comprising the Carrier Air Wing.

Figure 2.4.4: Surface Action Group.
Courtesy of the US Department of Defense.

Figure 2.4.5: Aircraft Carrier.
Courtesy of the US Department of Defense.

The Aircraft Carrier surpassed the battleship as the capital ship of the U.S. Navy in World War II during the Battle of Midway when the American fleet crippled the Japanese through naval airpower without the two fleets ever coming within range of each other's naval gunfire. An Aircraft Carrier is a power projection platform. Operating from international waters, it provides 4½ acres of sovereign U.S. territory to stage carrier air operations without the need to request basing rights from foreign countries. Because it's forward deployed with the Numbered Fleets, as shown in Table 2.4.2, the Aircraft Carrier can respond quickly to crises anywhere around the world.

Carrier Air Wing

The Carrier Air Wing is composed of fighter and attack aircraft capable of engaging enemy aircraft, surface vessels, and land targets. The primary fighter jet is the F-18 Hornet, shown in Figure 2.4.6, capable of conducting air-to-air and air-to-surface

Figure 2.4.6: F-18 Hornet.
Courtesy of the US Department of Defense.

Table 2.4.2: Navy Aircraft Carriers

ID	Name	Fleet
CV 63	*Kitty Hawk*	Pacific
CVN 65	*Enterprise*	Atlantic
CV 67	*John F. Kennedy*	Atlantic
CVN 68	*Nimitz*	Pacific
CVN 69	*Dwight D. Eisenhower*	Atlantic
CVN 70	*Carl Vinson*	Pacific
CVN 71	*Theodore Roosevelt*	Atlantic
CVN 72	*Abraham Lincoln*	Pacific
CVN 73	*George Washington*	Atlantic
CVN 74	*John C. Stennis*	Pacific
CVN 75	*Harry S. Truman*	Atlantic
CVN 76	*Ronald Reagan*	Pacific
CVN 77	*George H. W. Bush*	TBD

missions. The Hornet is supplemented by the F-14 Tomcat. Initially designed as an air superiority fighter, the swing-wing design made the Tomcat a capable attack aircraft against enemy surface and land targets. The Tomcat is soon to be retired from naval operations, as is the S-3 Viking. Initially designed to hunt enemy submarines, the S-3 has proven capable as an in-flight refueling platform. Both the F-14 and S-3 will soon be supplanted by the F-18 and the new F-35 Joint Strike Fighter.

Guided Missile Cruiser

The Guided Missile Cruiser is an anti-air and antimissile warfare platform. Employing the Aegis weapon system, the Guided Missile Cruiser carries a complement of SM-2 missiles capable of engaging enemy aircraft and intermediate range missiles from a distance of 200 miles. The Aegis Cruiser is an important asset for defending the task force against enemy air and missile attack. The Aegis Cruiser can also be used to establish local air superiority within close proximity to shore. The Aegis Cruiser has a limited antisubmarine and antisurface capability.

Guided Missile Destroyer

The Guided Missile Destroyer is an antisubmarine warfare platform. Employing a sophisticated sonar system, the Guided Missile Destroyer carries a complement of ASROC rocket-launched MK-48 torpedoes that can fly out to a suspected target area, then drop in the water and initiate a self-seeking program to hone in and destroy an enemy submarine within 5 nautical miles. The Guided Missile Destroyer is an important asset for defending the task force against enemy submarine attack. The Guided Missile Destroyer has a limited strike, anti-air, and antisurface capability.

Guided Missile Frigates

The Guided Missile Frigate (see Figure 2.4.7) was designed as a cost-effective surface combatant. Guided Missile Frigates carry a mixed complement of SM-2, ASROC, and Harpoon missiles providing a wide ranging capability to conduct limited anti-air, antisubmarine, and antisurface operations. Because of its shallow draft, the Guided Missile Frigate is an important asset for operating close inland, in the littoral regions of the world.

Nuclear Attack Submarines

The Nuclear Attack Submarine (see Figure 2.4.8) is an antisubmarine, antisurface, and strike warfare platform. Operating deep in the ocean depths and employing a sophisticated sonar system, the Nuclear Attack Submarine is a stealth platform capable of locating enemy combatant vessels and closing in undetected. The Nuclear Attack Submarine carries a complement of MK-48 torpedoes to sink enemy submarines and surface combatants. The Nuclear Attack Submarine also carries a complement of Tomahawk Land Attack Cruise Missiles (TLAMs) capable of striking enemy targets deep inland.

Fleet Ballistic Missile Submarine

The Fleet Ballistic Missile Submarine is a nuclear deterrent vessel. The Ohio-class submarine carries 24 Trident D-II missiles, each capable of flying 4,000 nautical

Figure 2.4.7: Guided Missile Frigate.
Courtesy of the US Department of Defense.

Figure 2.4.8: Nuclear Attack Submarine.
Courtesy of the US Department of Defense.

miles and delivering 5 independently targetable nuclear warheads. The Fleet Ballistic Missile Submarine is an oceangoing stealth platform, very quiet and hard to find. It deters enemy nuclear attack with the threat of assured nuclear retaliation. One submarine carries 120 warheads. The Navy has 14 Fleet Ballistic Missile Submarines.

Sea Air Land Teams (SEALS)

Navy SEALS conduct special reconnaissance and other special operations as required. Navy Special Boat Units have high-speed, shallow-draft craft capable of operating close to shore and up-river estuaries to infiltrate and extract SEAL teams. SEALS can also operate Underwater Delivery Vehicles, miniature submarines that move in close to shore undetected.

United States Marines

The U.S. Marines provide another strike capability for the Navy. Operating as Fleet Marine Forces or part of an Expeditionary Strike Group, Marines provide the ability to strike enemy targets close inshore or far inland.

Naval Operations

The Unified Combatant Commands are given operational control of Navy forces to maintain sea power, sea control, and nuclear deterrence. Sea power asserts navigation rights, conducts ocean science, facilitates ocean industry, and promotes ocean commerce. Sea control is the capability to control airspace above the ocean surface, preserve sea lines of communication, and protect against undersea threats. Nuclear deterrence is provided by Fleet Ballistic Missile Submarines, which carry 40 percent of the nations' nuclear arsenal.

Under the direction of the president and Secretary of Defense, the Navy has four primary missions during times of war:

- **Seek out and destroy enemy forces at sea**
- **Destroy or reduce enemy sea commerce**
- **Maintain control of the seas**
- **Conduct land, sea, and air operations as needed to achieve these goals**

Naval Strategy

For most of the 20th century, the U.S. Navy focused on a Blue Water Strategy designed to fight a set battle at sea against a peer competitor to establish naval superiority and maintain vital seal lines of communication. The Blue Water Strategy rose to the challenge to defeat Japan in World War II and prepared to do the same against the Soviet Union during the Cold War. With the collapse of the Soviet Union in 1991, however, the U.S. Navy lost its one and only peer competitor, and the Blue Water Strategy became obsolete. The U.S. Navy consequently reformulated its strategy in the mid-1990s to meet the growing demand for a military presence around the world at the dawn of the 21st century.

With today's sea lines of communication more or less assured, the U.S. Navy has shifted focus to the littoral regions of the world and redirected its power inland in a strategy called **Forward from the Sea**. The unique capabilities of the Navy allow it to maintain a forward presence around the world and project power from 150 miles offshore to more than 100 miles inland where 75 percent of the world's population and 80 percent of nations' capitals reside.

Power Projection

The purpose of the U.S. Navy is to project U.S. military power to deter or defeat hostile threats. The U.S. Navy uniquely serves as a visible reminder of U.S. military power to potential adversaries by maintaining a forward presence around the globe. Forward presence also positions the U.S. Navy to respond quickly in crisis or conflict. The U.S. Navy routinely sails into harms way and is ready to leap into action at moment's notice.

A robust logistics chain underpins the U.S. Navy's capability to maintain a forward presence around the globe (see Figure 2.4.9). Although the capital ships of the Navy are nuclear powered and only need refueling every 30 years, consumable goods such as aviation fuel and food need to be replaced regularly. The U.S. Navy is uniquely capable of restocking its ships at sea using a technique called **Underway Replenishment** where a supply ship will pull up along side another vessel and transfer its cargo while matching the fleet's course and speed. The great advantage to Underway Replenishment is that the fleet need not halt or return to port to resupply and can sustain uninterrupted operations.

Composite Warfare

The Carrier Strike Group maintains an extensive range of weaponry capable of engaging threats on land, at sea, in the air, and below the surface. The maritime environment requires the U.S. Navy to be uniquely proficient in all warfare regimes and capable of projecting power within a sphere of influence termed the **battlespace**.

Key Note Term

Forward from the Sea – U.S. Naval strategy to project power in the littoral regions of the world

Key Note Term

Underway Replenishment – logistic supply method that allows ships to maintain forward Navy presence

Key Note Term

battlespace – the three-dimensional battle area above, upon, and below the surface of the ocean

Figure 2.4.9: The U.S. Navy maintains a presence the world around. Courtesy of the US Department of Defense.

Composite Warfare allows the Navy to achieve battlespace dominance by controlling the space above, on, and below the surface of the ocean. Composite Warfare was developed in the late 1970s in response to the rapid growth in potential air and surface threats facing U.S. naval forces during the Cold War. Composite Warfare delegates principle warfare functions to subordinate commanders under the overall direction of the **Officer in Tactical Command** (**OTC**). Composite Warfare's emphasis on decentralized authority facilitates quick response to threats, as well as efficient use of maritime resources supporting the Navy's primary mission of Power Projection.

The Officer in Tactical Command manages the battlespace through the efforts of assigned Principle Warfare Commanders. The **Principle Warfare Commanders** are given tactical control of task force assets to control different segments of the battlespace.

Air Defense Commander (ADC)

The Air Defense Commander directs defensive anti-air warfare operations to protect against enemy aircraft, cruise missiles, and theater ballistic missiles. The ADC may be given tactical control of cruisers and fighter aircraft to perform his mission.

Anti-Surface Warfare (ASuW)

The ASuW Commander directs offensive and defensive operations against enemy surface vessels. The ASuW Commander may be given tactical control of attack aircraft and frigates (firing the Harpoon missile) to engage enemy ships.

Anti-Submarine Warfare (ASW)

The ASW Commander directs offensive and defensive operations against enemy submarines. The ASW Commander may be given tactical control of attack submarines, destroyers, and helicopters to engage enemy submarines.

Strike Warfare

The Strike Warfare Commander directs offensive operations against enemy surface and land targets. The Strike Warfare Commander may be given tactical control of attack aircraft and attack submarines to perform his mission.

> **Key Note Terms**
>
> **Officer in Tactical Command** – commands warfare functions within the battlespace
>
> **Principle Warfare Commanders** – ADC, ASuW, ASW, and Strike Warfare Commanders

When sailing into hostile waters, time is of essence. To ensure prompt reaction to hostile threats, the Officer in Tactical Command will delegate warfare functions to the Principle Warfare Commanders. Once such functions are delegated, the Principle Warfare Commanders will take the required action without delay, always keeping the OTC informed of the situation. The Principle Warfare Commanders do not request permission to fire. The Principle Warfare Commanders continue to fire until told to stop by the OTC. This is called **Command by Negation**.

Conclusion

The Department of the Navy directs Shore Establishments to recruit, organize, train, equip, and support Operating Forces. The Operating Forces of the U.S. Navy are permanently assigned to the Atlantic and Pacific Fleets but are task assigned to the Numbered Fleets providing a forward deployed, permanent naval presence around the world. Navy assets are task organized for specific mission in Navy Task Forces. There are three standard Task Force Packages: Carrier Strike Group, Expeditionary Strike Group, and Surface Action Group. The Carrier Strike Group is comprised of an Aircraft Carrier, two Guided Missile Cruisers, two Guided Missile Destroyers, two Nuclear Attack Submarines, and a Replenishment Ship. The Carrier Strike Group is the Navy's primary Power Projection force. Current naval strategy provides for the Navy to operate in the littoral regions of the world projecting power from 150 miles offshore to 100 miles inland, where 75 percent of the world's population and 80 percent of nations' capitals reside. When the Carrier Strike Group enters hostile waters, the Officer in Tactical Command will direct the actions of Principle Warfare Commanders to maintain control within the three-dimensional battlespace. Because time is of essence, Officer in Tactical Command will use Command by Negation directing the Principle Warfare Commanders to continue actions until told to stop.

In the following lesson, you will be introduced to the U.S. Air Force, another branch of the U.S. military.

Key Note Term

Command by Negation – orders to continue operations until told to stop

Chapter 2

Lesson Review

1. What is the mission of the U. S. Navy?

2. What are the two major organizational components of the U. S. Navy?

3. What is the purpose of the Numbered Fleets?

4. How does the Navy organize its assets to conduct specific tasks and missions?

Lesson Review

Lesson 5

The United States Air Force

Key Terms

Air Expeditionary Force
Air Expeditionary Wing (AEW)
Air Superiority
Air Wing
Counterland
Countersea
Numbered Air Force
Strategic Attack
Strategic Triad

What You Will Learn to Do

- Explore the organization and mission of the U.S. Air Force

Linked Core Abilities

- Do your share as a good citizen in your school, community, country, and the world

Skills and Knowledge You Will Gain Along the Way

- Explain the mission of the U.S. Air Force.
- Distinguish between NAFs and AEFs.
- Explain the importance of Air Superiority.
- Describe the purpose of Strategic Attack.
- Distinguish between Counterland and Countersea missions.
- Identify U.S. Air Force space missions.
- Describe the Air Force's role in nuclear deterrence.
- Define the key words contained in this lesson.

Chapter 2

Introduction

The U.S. Air Force exemplifies the dominant role of air and space power in meeting this nation's security needs across the entire spectrum of peace and conflict, such as building U.S. influence globally through its presence and strengthening national capabilities to conduct decisive combat operations worldwide on short notice. In this lesson, you explore the role of the U.S. Air Force in the nation's defense forces.

The United States Air Force

The Department of the Air Forces organizes, trains, and equips forces for *prompt and sustained offensive and defensive air operations.* Operational units are assigned to designated Unified Combatant Commands to control and exploit the air and space environment at the direction of the president of the United States. The official seal of the U.S. Air Force is shown in Figure 2.5.1.

The U.S. Air Force originated as a separate branch within the United States Army but was granted independent service status by an act of Congress on September 18, 1947.

The mission of the U.S. Air Force is to defend the United States through control and exploitation of air and space.

Organization

The Department of the Air Force is headed by the Secretary of the Air Force assisted by the Chief of Staff of the Air Force and supported by the Air Staff. The Department of the Air Force directs a Supporting Establishment composed of nine Major Commands supplemented by five Direct Reporting Units and 33 Field Operating

Figure 2.5.1: U.S. Air Force Seal.
Courtesy of the US Department of Defense.

Agencies that recruit, organize, train, equip, and support Air Force Operational Forces. Air Force Operational Forces are tactically organized into Numbered Air Forces, **Air Expeditionary Forces**, and Wings. Upon the direction of the Secretary of Defense, the Chief of Staff of the Air Force will transfer operational control of tactical units to designated Unified Combatant Commands to conduct operations at the direction of the president of the United States.

Air Force MAJCOMs perform specific duties that are organized functionally within the United States and by geographical area overseas. Air Force major commands accomplish broad, overall missions. The Air Force has nine major commands, as shown in Table 2.5.1.

A **Numbered Air Force (NAF)** is the Air Force's largest operational unit. A Wing is the basic operational unit at the tactical level. It is the Air Force's largest fixed organization that trains and fights as a tactical team. Two or more wings may be assigned to a NAF.

NAFs were established in the European and Pacific theaters during World War II and became permanent fixtures to check Soviet aggression during the Cold War. NAFs are home based at locations in the United States, Europe, and Asia.

An **Air Wing** is a tactically self-contained combat unit. A Wing is composed of four Groups: Operations, Maintenance, Support, and Medical. The Operations Group is normally comprised of three air squadrons. Squadron size depends on the type of aircraft, but a fighter squadron may include anywhere from 18 to 24 aircraft. The Maintenance Group consists of the Aircraft Generation, Electronics Maintenance, Component Maintenance, squadrons necessary to sustain air combat operations. The Mission Support Group is composed of Security Forces, Communications, Civil Engineering, Contracting, Personnel, and Logistic Readiness squadrons. The Medical

Table 2.5.1: Major Air Force Commands

MAJCOM	Headquarters
Air Combat Command (ACC)	Langley AFB, Virginia
Air Education and Training Command (AETC)	Randolph AFB, Texas
Air Force Material Command (AFMC)	Wright-Patterson AFB, Ohio
Air Force Space Command (AFSPC)	Peterson AFB, Colorado
Air Force Special Operations Command (AFSOC)	Hurlburt Field, Florida
Air Mobility Command (AMC)	Scott AFB, Illinois
Air Force Reserve Command (AFRC)	Robins AFB, Georgia
Pacific Air Forces (PACAF)	Hickam AFB, Hawaii
United States Air Forces in Europe (USAFE)	Ramstein AB, Germany

Key Note Term

Air Expeditionary Wing – tactically self-contained, deployable wing-size unit

Group attends to the care and health of wing personnel. A Wing is typically comprised of a single type of aircraft. A Composite Wing is composed of different types of aircraft contributed by the NAFs to form a task organized, independently deployable **Air Expeditionary Wing** (AEW).

Air Force Operations

The purpose of the U.S. Air Force is to deter potential adversaries, and, if deterrence fails, decisively defeat them from the air. The U.S. Air Force retains a significant portion of the nation's nuclear arsenal to deter potential adversaries from employing weapons of mass destruction. The U.S. Air Force maintains a strong conventional capability to decisively defeat adversaries across the spectrum of conflict.

What distinguishes the U.S. Air Force from the other services is that it primarily seeks to destroy an enemy's ability to wage war. The U.S. Air Force specializes in Strategic Warfare by attacking an enemy's war production capacity to strangle his forces in the field. Precision Guided Munitions and Stealth Technology allow the U.S. Air Force to conduct surgical strikes and destroy high value targets deep inside enemy territory. Long-range bombers, as shown in Figure 2.5.2, allow the U.S. Air Force to strike anywhere at anytime.

The flexibility of airpower, however, also allows the U.S. Air Force to enhance the combat effectiveness of Army, Navy, and Marine operations. Air Mobility Command is the executive authority for providing Airlift to the military services. Airlift is essential to the rapid deployment of forces to combat theaters. Combat aircraft are capable of delivering ordinance anywhere on the battlefield, day or night, and provide Close Air Support to friendly forces in close proximity to the enemy or conduct Air Interdiction missions to reduce the flow of enemy troops and supplies to the front.

The main tenet of airpower is centralized control and decentralized execution. Centralized control is necessary to effectively mass air forces to attack priority targets.

Figure 2.5.2: Long-range bomber.
Courtesy of the US Department of Defense.

Centralized control is achieved today using an Air Tasking Order master attack plan. Air Superiority is the first objective in any campaign. **Air Superiority** affords freedom of action to friendly and allied forces while denying the same to the enemy.

Combat Air Forces

Fourteen Numbered Air Forces comprise the Combat Air Forces to the U.S. Air Force. The Combat Air Forces are composed of Fighter and Attack Aircraft, Long Range Bombers, and Intelligence, Surveillance, and Reconnaissance Aircraft.

Fighter and Attack Aircraft

Fighter and Attack Aircraft of the U.S. Air Force perform Counterair, Counterland, Countersea, and Strategic Attack missions. Counterair missions target enemy aircraft, airfields, and surface-to-air missiles to gain and maintain Air Superiority. Air Superiority entails freedom to conduct operations within enemy airspace. Since World War II, military commanders have understood the necessity of Air Superiority to conduct successful air, ground, and naval operations.

Fighter Aircraft of the U.S. Air Force help gain and maintain Air Superiority by engaging and defeating enemy fighter aircraft in air-to-air combat. All U.S. fighter aircraft are equipped with internal guns, but most modern engagements are fought with air-to-air missiles including the heat-seeking Sidewinder and the radar guided AMRAAM (Advanced Medium Range Air-to-Air Missile). The F-15C Eagle, shown in Figure 2.5.3, and F-16 Falcon are air superiority fighters capable of engaging the enemy in air-to-air combat. The F-15 and F-16 will eventually be replaced by the F/A-22 Raptor and F-35 Joint Strike Fighter. The new generation of air superiority fighters carry their missiles in internal weapons bays and incorporate stealth technology to be almost invisible on enemy radar.

Attack Aircraft drop bombs and fire missiles to destroy enemy ground targets. Attack Aircraft help gain and maintain Air Superiority by destroying enemy airfields and surface-to-air missiles. Attack Aircraft can also conduct Counterland and Countersea

Figure 2.5.3: F-15C Eagle. Courtesy of the US Department of Defense.

missions. **Counterland** missions interdict enemy supplies and reinforcements and provide close air support to Army forces engaged with enemy ground units. **Countersea** missions target enemy ships and submarines operating in proximity to land. The A-10 Thunderbolt, sometimes referred to as the "Warthog" (see Figure 2.5.4), F-15E Strike Eagle, and F-117 Nighthawk, are the primary Air Force Attack Aircraft. The A-10 was specially designed to provide close air support to the Army by flying low and slow over the battlefield, loitering long periods, and engaging enemy armor with a 30mm gatling gun that protrudes from the nose of the aircraft. The problem with flying low and slow is that the enemy can also acquire you as a target; consequently, the A-10 was designed to take heavy punishment. To the Air Force way of thinking, "speed is Life"; that's why the attack version of the F-15 flies high and fast over the battlefield, using a sophisticated navigation and targeting system to accurately strike enemy targets. The F-117 Nighthawk is a first-generation stealth platform specializing in precision strike. Carrying two precision guided bombs in its internal weapons bay, the F-117 flies at night, invisible to enemy radar to sneak in close and destroy heavily defended enemy targets. The next generation F/A-22 Raptor and F-35 Joint Strike Fighter are both multirole aircraft capable of flying both air-to-air and air-to-ground missions just by changing out the weapons load in the internal weapons bays.

Long-Range Bombers

Long-range bombers conduct Counterland, Countersea, and Strategic Attack missions. Air Force bombers carry bombs and missiles and attack surface and land targets the same as Attack Aircraft. Bombers are distinguished, however, by their greater range and larger payloads. Bombers specialize in **Strategic Attack**, striking the enemy's Centers of Gravity to destroy their will and ability to fight. From the airman's perspective, Strategic Attack is the quickest means to ending conflict. Strategic Attack proved its worth during World War II in bringing about the surrender of Japan. The Air Force bomber fleet is comprised of the B-52, B-1, and B-2 bombers. First introduced in 1953, the B-52 is the oldest aircraft in the active inventory. Initially designed as a high-altitude bomber, the B-52 was extensively modified during the Cold War to penetrate Soviet air defenses by flying close to the

Figure 2.5.4: The A-10 "Warthog."
Courtesy of the US Department of Defense.

ground, below radar coverage. The B-52 remains in the Air Force inventory because it can still carry a large payload over intercontinental distances. Carrying the latest in precision guided munitions, the B-52 no longer needs to overfly the target to strike it, and can avoid flying into hostile airspace. The B-1 operates much the same as the B-52, but it's newer, sleeker, and faster than the B-52. The B-1 also has a smaller profile and is harder to see on enemy radar. Because they're slower than fighter and attack aircraft, the B-52 and B-1 can operate in enemy airspace only after air superiority has been attained, or with fighter escorts. The B-2, however, is invisible to enemy radar and can conduct night attacks within hostile airspace without the need for fighter escort or air superiority. The payload and range advantages of the long-range bomber make it a force multiplier. Consider that during Operation Enduring Freedom the Navy, operating from aircraft carriers in the Arabian Gulf, flew 75 percent of the missions over Afghanistan, but the Air Force, operating from Diego Garcia in the Indian Ocean, dropped 75 percent of the bombs because they carried a much greater payload.

Precision is another force multiplier. Today's Air Force is much smaller than the Army Air Force that fought World War II because today's bombs are much more accurate. The B-17 with the Norden bombsight had an accuracy measured in Circular Error Probable (CEP) of a half-mile. This means half the bombs dropped from the B-17 fell within a half-mile of the intended target. In order to gain a statistical probability of actually hitting the target, the 8th Air Force massed large formations of bombers over the target. At the height of the bombing campaign in 1943, the 8th Air Force would launch as many as a thousand bombers against a single target. Before the advent of the P-51 escort fighter, the bombers sustained as high as 10 percent casualties. That's 1,000 aircraft, each bomber with a 10-man crew, meaning 1,000 airmen were lost in a single mission. Today's laser-guided and GPS-guided bombs provide a CEP of less than 6-feet. Today we don't need large bomber formations to hit the target. A one-man crew in an F-117 can destroy the intended target in a single mission. Instead of 1,000 bombers flying a single mission, today we have a single bomber flying multiple missions. Precision is a force multiplier.

Intelligence, Surveillance, and Reconnaissance Aircraft

Today, the Air Force is so good at hitting the target that the hardest task is finding the target. That's why the Air Force flies an array of Intelligence, Surveillance, and Reconnaissance (ISR) aircraft designed to pinpoint the enemy. The Air Force flies a set of airborne radar stations including the E-3 Airborne Warning and Control System (AWACS) and the E-8 Joint Surveillance, Targeting, and Radar System (JSTARS). AWACS establishes an air radar net to spot enemy aircraft closing in on friendly forces. Air controllers aboard the AWACS can then vector in friendly fighters to intercept. JSTARS has a synthetic aperture radar that's looking for targets on the ground. JSTARS can penetrate through clouds and darkness to locate enemy targets and then direct air and ground attack forces to engage them. The Air Force also employs the U-2 Dragon Lady photographic surveillance and RC-135 Rivet Joint electronic surveillance aircraft. With operations over Afghanistan and Iraq, the Air Force is now moving into the realm of Uninhabited Aerial Vehicles such as the RQ-1 Predator and RQ-4 Global Hawk that can spy the enemy without endangering the lives of any aircrew.

Mission and Support Forces

The U.S. Air Force provides most of the United States' Military Space capability, as well as the land-based segment of the nuclear deterrent force. The U.S. Air Force also provides Airlift and Refueling services, and conducts Special Operations.

Space and Missile

The U.S. Air Force provides 90 percent of the United States' Military Space capability. The U.S. Air Force provides Space Support, Space Control, and Force Enhancement to all the services.

Space Support launches payloads into space. Operating from its two launch sites at Patrick Air Force Base in Florida and Vandenberg Air Force Base in California, the U.S. Air Force can launch satellite payloads into equatorial and polar orbits.

The Air Force launches satellites that enhance the abilities of terrestrial forces by providing surveillance, warning, communications, and weather services. These services are collectively known as Force Enhancement.

Space Control manages and maintains satellites once they're on orbit. The Air Force Satellite Control Network operates satellites in orbit to control their attitude, manage their payloads, and monitor their functions to prolong systems in the harsh environment of space. Satellites are susceptible to the effects of the Van Allen radiation belts and solar discharges that can fry electrical components. Space Controllers can prolong the operation of a satellite by powering down systems, re-orienting it away from the sun, and activating backup systems to survive the effects of space weather.

The U.S. Air Force maintains the land-based segment of the **Strategic Triad** designed to deter nuclear missile attack against the United States. The Strategic Triad is comprised of land-based bombers and missiles, and fleet ballistic missile submarines. The Strategic Triad is designed such that at least one segment will survive a surprise enemy attack, and consequently deter attack through threat of retaliation. The Navy maintains the fleet ballistic missile submarines. The Air Force maintains the land-based bombers and missiles. All nuclear deterrent forces are under the control of U.S. Strategic Command.

Airlift and Refueling

The U.S. Air Force provides inter-theater and intra-theater airlift to military forces. Inter-theater airlift is accommodated with long-range heavy lifters such as the C-5 Galaxy and the C-17 Globemaster. Each is capable of carrying an Army M-1A2 Abrams tank. Equipment and forces can be rapidly moved in and about the theater with the C-130 Hercules, as seen in Figure 2.5.5. The C-130 can't carry a tank, but it can carry a Humvee and other equipment and troops to rapidly transport them anywhere within the theater of operations.

To give our aircraft range, the U.S. Air Force operates a fleet of tankers that can conduct in-flight refueling of all Air Force and most Navy aircraft. Both the KC-10 Extender and KC-135 Stratotanker can extend the range of aircraft giving the Air Force *global reach*.

Key Note Term

Strategic Triad – nuclear deterrent force of land-based bombers and missiles, and fleet ballistic missile submarines

Special Operations

The U.S. Air Force operates a variety of Special Operations aircraft designed to transport and support special operations forces. The MH-53J Pavelow helicopter refueled by the MC-130P Combat Shadow is long-range, day/night, all-weather capable for inserting and extracting special operations forces undetected deep inside enemy territory. The AC-130 Spectre gunship provides artillery fire support to ground forces engaged with the enemy. The AC-130 has a 105mm Howitzer mounted through its side fuselage connected to an electronic targeting system that's accurate to the first round. Because the AC-130 itself is such a big target, it can only operate in special circumstances or at night. The MC-130E Commando Solo (see Figure 2.5.6) is a flying radio and television station designed to override enemy signals to accommodate Psychological Operations (PSYOPS) against the enemy. Air Force Combat Control Teams work with other services to target the enemy with precision guided munitions. And Combat Weather teams are typically the first forces on the ground to establish the conditions for air support operations.

Conclusion

The Department of the Air Force directs Major Commands, Direct Reporting Units, and Field Operating Agencies to recruit, organize, train, equip, and support Operational Forces. The Numbered Air Force (NAF) and Air Expeditionary Force (AEF) are the Air Force's basic combat units. The NAF operates from permanent home bases in Asia, Europe, and the United States. The AEF is task organized using NAF assets to deploy and conduct operations where the United States doesn't have permanent basing rights. The purpose of the U.S. Air Force is to deter potential adversaries, and if deterrence fails, decisively defeat them from the air. The U.S. Air Force specializes in Strategic Warfare attacking an enemy's war production capacity to

Figure 2.5.5: C-130.
Courtesy of the US Department of Defense.

Figure 2.5.6: MC-130E Commando Solo.
Courtesy of the US Air Force.

strangle its forces in the field. Precision Guided Munitions and Stealth Technology allow the U.S. Air Force to conduct surgical strikes and destroy high value targets deep inside enemy territory. Long-range bombers allow the United States Air Force to strike anywhere at anytime. Airlift is essential to the rapid deployment of forces to combat theaters. With aerial refueling, combat aircraft are capable of delivering ordinance anywhere on the battlefield, day or night, and provide Close Air Support to friendly forces in close proximity to the enemy, or conduct Air Interdiction missions to reduce the flow of enemy troops and supplies to the front. Air Superiority is the first objective in any campaign. Air Superiority affords freedom of action to friendly and allied forces while denying the same to the enemy. The U.S. Air Force retains a significant portion of the nation's nuclear arsenal to deter potential adversaries from employing weapons of mass destruction. The U.S. Air Force maintains a strong conventional capability to decisively defeat adversaries across the spectrum of conflict.

Next, you will learn about the U.S. Marine Corps, its origin, and its place in the U.S. Military scheme.

Chapter 2

Lesson Review

Lesson Review

1. What is the mission of the U.S. Air Force?
2. What is the difference between a NAF and an AEF?
3. Why is Air Superiority important?
4. What is the purpose of Strategic Attack?

The United States Marine Corps

Key Terms

Marine Air Ground Task Force
Marine Expeditionary Unit
Marine Expeditionary Brigade
Marine Expeditionary Force
Maritime Prepositioned Squadron
Noncombatant Evacuation Operation
Vertical Envelopment
Operational Maneuver from the Sea

What You Will Learn to Do

- Explore the organization and mission of the U.S. Marine Corps

Linked Core Abilities

- Do your share as a good citizen in your school, community, country, and the world

Skills and Knowledge You Will Gain Along the Way

- Describe the organization of the U.S. Marine Corps
- Explain the mission of the U.S. Marine Corps
- Explain the combined arms organization of the U.S. Marine Corps and how it makes the Marines unique
- Identify the Marine Corps Elements of Combat Power
- Describe the two operational specialties of the U.S. Marines
- Define the key words contained in this lesson

Introduction

"First to Fight," the U.S. Marine Corps organizes, trains, and equips a force in readiness to respond in crisis and conduct prompt military action. Operational units are forward deployed and assigned to designated Unified Combatant Commands to conduct expeditionary and amphibious operations at the direction of the president of the United States. In this lesson, you learn about the U.S. Marine Corps–its origins, mission, and organization.

The United States Marine Corps

The U.S. Marine Corps (USMC) was founded on November 10, 1775, by an act of the Continental Congress authorizing two battalions of Marines to provide "soldiers of the sea." The USMC provides Fleet Marine Forces for service with the fleet in the seizure or defense of advanced naval bases and for the conduct of such land operations as may be essential to the prosecution of a naval campaign. The USMC also provides detachments and organizations for service on armed vessels of the Navy. The official seal of the U.S. Marine Corps is shown in Figure 2.6.1.

Organization

The U.S. Marine Corps is subordinate to the Department of the Navy. The Commandant of the Marine Corps is directly responsible to the Secretary of the Navy for the administration, discipline, organization, training, and readiness of the Marine Corps. The Commandant of the Marine Corps directs a Supporting Establishment composed of 15 major bases and stations in the United States and Japan that recruit, organize, train, equip, and support Marine Operating Forces. Marine Operating Forces include Marine Security Guards, Marine Corps Security Forces,

Figure 2.6.1: The official seal of the U.S. Marine Corps.
Courtesy of the US Department of Defense.

and Marine Forces. Marine Security Guards provide embassy security for 121 diplomatic posts in 115 countries. Marine Corps Security Forces protect naval installations. Marine Forces are assigned to Marine Forces Atlantic (MARFORLANT), Marine Forces Pacific (MAFORPAC), and Marine Forces Reserve (MAFORRES). The Marine Corps Reserve provides trained units and qualified individuals to be mobilized for active duty in times of war, national emergency, or contingency operations. Marine Forces Atlantic provides combat-ready Marine Forces to the U.S. Joint Forces Command. Marine Force Pacific provides combat-ready Marine Forces to the U.S. Pacific Command. Marine forces are apportioned to the remaining geographic commands for contingency planning and are provided when directed by the Secretary of Defense.

Marine Corps Philosophy

The U.S. Marine Corps is smallest among the four uniform services. Because it depends on the Department of the Navy for its budget, it is protected by law to ensure it maintains a force in readiness of at least corps strength. To maximize its operational capability, the Marine Corps operates on the principle "Every Marine a Rifleman." Every Marine attends the Marine Corps Basic School and qualifies as a marksman.

Task Organization

The U.S. Marine Corps is organized to make itself uniquely light and lethal. Every Marine unit is conceptually organized into a **Marine Air Ground Task Force** combining air and ground combat elements into a seamless operation. The MAGTF includes a Command Element (CE), Ground Combat Element (GCE), Air Combat Element (ACE), and Combat Service Support (CSS) element. The Air Combat Element provides mobility and firepower to the Ground Combat Element. Airlift elements rapidly deploy Marines into battle, maneuver them into a position of advantage, and redeploy them to exploit the enemy. Attack elements provide essential fire support, acting like flying artillery to eliminate the burden of carrying heavy weapons into battle. The MAGTF concept maximizes combined arms effectiveness and makes the U.S. Marine Corps light, lethal, and mobile on the battlefield.

> **Key Note Term**
>
> **Marine Air Ground Task Force** – organizational concept that makes the Marines uniquely light and lethal

Elements of Marine Combat Power

MARFORLANT and MARFORPAC are task organized into Marine Expeditionary Forces, Marine Expeditionary Brigades, and Marine Expeditionary Units.

Marine Expeditionary Unit (MEU)

The **Marine Expeditionary Unit** is the smallest combat unit composed of approximately 2,200 Marines. A MEU is a standard forward-deployed Marine expeditionary organization deployed as an Amphibious Ready Group (ARG). A MEU is a self-contained operating force capable of missions of limited scope and duration. The Air Combat Element is a squadron-size unit, and the Ground Combat Element is a battalion-size force. A MEU typically deploys with 15 days sustainment.

> **Key Note Term**
>
> **Marine Expeditionary Unit** – smallest combat organization, forward deployed with the amphibious ready group

Marine Expeditionary Brigade (MEB)

The **Marine Expeditionary Brigade** is an intermediate-size combat unit composed of approximately 16,500 Marines. A MEB is a crisis response force capable of forcible entry and enabling the introduction of follow-on forces. The MEB is not a standing organization but is rather embedded within the MEF. A MEB is capable of rapid deployment either by air, in combination with Maritime Prepositioned Squadrons (MPS), or by amphibious shipping. The Air Combat Element is a group-size unit, and the Ground Combat Element is a brigade-size force. A MEB is self-sustaining for 30 days.

Marine Expeditionary Force (MEF)

A **Marine Expeditionary Force** is the largest combat unit composed of approximately 42,000 Marines that can be quickly deployed in times of crisis. The Air Combat element is a Marine Air Wing, and the Ground Combat Element is a Marine Division. The MEF typically deploys with 60 days sustainment.

Marine Corps Operations

The U.S. Marine Corps provides a force in readiness prepared to respond at the direction of the President to crisis and contingencies around the world (see Figure 2.6.2). The unique capabilities that make the Marines "First to Fight" are that they're forward deployed, expeditionary by design, special operations capable, and amphibious specialists.

Forward Deployed

Marine Expeditionary Units are forward deployed near hot spots of the globe aboard Amphibious Ready Groups. The Amphibious Ready Group is a fleet of ships specially modified to carry Marine forces and support Marine amphibious opera-

Figure 2.6.2: The U.S. Marines are ready to respond at the direction of the President.
Courtesy of Jim McDonald/Corbis Images.

tions. The Amphibious Ready Group is commanded by a naval officer at sea but falls under Marine control once command is established ashore during amphibious operations. The Amphibious Ready Group puts Marines in the thick of action whenever crises flare around the world and makes the U.S. Marines Corps America's "911" reaction force, the first to respond to emergencies. The following sections describe the Amphibious Ready Group.

Amphibious Assault Ship

The Amphibious Assault Ship carries Marines, equipment, landing craft, and aircraft into battle. About the size of a World War II aircraft carrier, the Amphibious Assault Ship doesn't have a catapult system, so it can't launch fixed wing aircraft. Only vertical takeoff and landing aircraft can operate from its deck including helicopters, Harriers, and Ospreys. Depending on mission, the Amphibious Assault Ship can carry 2,000 Marines, 35 aircraft, and 7 landing craft. Marines board landing craft inside the relative safety of the Well Deck, which opens to the sea and allows water to come into the ship. All ships of the Amphibious Ready Group have a Well Deck.

Amphibious Transport Dock

The Amphibious Transport Dock carries Marines, equipment, and amphibious assault vehicles. The Amphibious Transport Dock has a small flight deck capable of managing helicopter operations from the stern. Depending on mission, the Amphibious Transport Dock can carry 800 Marines, 6 helicopters, and 24 amphibious assault vehicles. The amphibious assault vehicles launch from the ship's Well Deck.

Dock Landing Ship

The Dock Landing Ship carries Marines, equipment, and amphibious landing craft. The Dock Landing Ship has a small flight deck capable of managing helicopter operations from the stern. Depending on mission, the Amphibious Transport Dock can carry 330 Marines and 3 Landing Craft Air Cushions in its cavernous Well Deck.

Expeditionary Design

The U.S. Marine Corps is said to be expeditionary because of its capability to rapidly deploy anywhere around the world (if it's not already there), and its capability to sustain combat operations in deployed locations. Marine forces are highly mobile and deployable exactly because they don't carry a lot of heavy equipment. Marines offset their disadvantage in heavy ground forces with airpower.

A Marine Expeditionary Unit is completely self-contained and carries all of its equipment aboard the Amphibious Readiness Group. When put ashore, a Marine Expeditionary Unit carries sufficient supplies to sustain itself for 15 days.

To sustain operations beyond 15 days, or to land a Marine Expeditionary Brigade or Marine Expeditionary Force, the U.S. Marine Corps relies on **Maritime Prepositioned Squadrons** (**MPS**). A Maritime Prepositioned Squadron is a small flotilla of cargo ships stationed at sea close to the hot spots of the world. The flotilla comprises a floating warehouse of military equipment and stores sufficient to land a small force or resupply a large one. The MPS is a means to rapidly mass decisive force against an enemy. An MPS can pull into a port of call and off-load its cargo within 6 days, compared to 30 days if it had to sail from the United States. Marines are

Key Note Term

Maritime Prepositioned Squadron – small flotilla of cargo ships stationed close to hot spots of the world

flown into port and pick up their combat gear. The three MPSs are located in Mediterranean, Indian, and Pacific waters. A single MPS can constitute a MEB and support it for 30 days. All three MPSs together can constitute a MEF.

Special Operations Capable

The U.S. Marine Corps prides itself on being able to conduct special missions and is frequently called on to conduct **Noncombatant Evacuation Operations,** rescuing U.S. citizens and allies from foreign combat zones. A Marine Expeditionary Unit has a large contingent of transport helicopters to safely airlift noncombatants from a foreign combat zone under permissive conditions. A Marine Expeditionary Unit also carries a large contingent of attack aircraft and specialized amphibious vehicles to evacuate noncombatants from a foreign combat zone under hostile or nonpermissive conditions.

Amphibious Specialty

Central to the U.S. Marine Corps mission is the ability to conduct amphibious operations and establish a foothold, or lodgment, in enemy territory. The U.S. Marine Corps conducts a **Vertical Envelopment** flanking or surrounding the enemy using air, ground, and surface assets to strike from multiple directions at once.

Marine forces employ **Operational Maneuver from the Sea** to mask their movements and synchronize attacks. The Amphibious Readiness Group deploys amphibious Marine forces at sea, beyond enemy observation, and then repositions to mislead the enemy and prepare a supporting air assault.

Vertical Envelopment and Operational Maneuver from the Sea enhance Marine combat effectiveness by catching the enemy by surprise and striking at his weakness.

Conclusion

The U.S. Marine Corps is subordinate to the Department of the Navy. The Commandant of the Marine Corps reports directly to the Secretary of the Navy. The Commandant of the Marine Corps directs Supporting Establishments and Marine Operating Forces. The Marine Operating Forces are organized into Marine Forces Atlantic and Marine Forces Pacific. All Marine units are organized into Marine Air Ground Task Forces integrating air and ground combat elements. The MAGTF concept makes the Marines uniquely light and lethal because they use their airpower as flying artillery, relieving them of carrying a lot of heavy equipment. The result is that the Marines can be forward deployed and respond quickly to crises around the globe. Marine Forces are organized into Marine Expeditionary Units, Marine Expeditionary Brigades, and Marine Expeditionary Forces using the MAGTF concept. The largest tactical unit is the MEF. The MEF is composed of a Marine Air Wing and Marine Division. The smallest tactical unit is the MEU. The Marines of a MEU are forward deployed aboard an Amphibious Ready Group. The ships of the ARG can carry Marines and their equipment into battle. A MEU can deploy and sustain itself up to 15 days in battle. To conduct longer operations requires the larger force of the MEB or resupply from Maritime Prepositioned Squadrons. MPSs are floating warehouses of Marine equipment which can pull into nearby ports within six days. The U.S. Marines specialize in amphibious and expeditionary operations. The Marines deploy aboard the ARG and conduct Operational Maneuver From the Sea to surprise the enemy as to the time and location of an attack. The Marines employ the combat power of the ARG to vertically envelop the enemy and attack where he is weakest.

In the following lesson, you will learn about the U.S. Coast Guard and the U.S. Merchant Marine and their places within the U.S. military.

Lesson Review

1. **What is the relation between the Marine Corps and the Department of the Navy?**
2. **What is the mission of the U.S. Marine Corps?**
3. **What is a MAGTF and how does it make the Marines unique?**
4. **What are the three basic tactical units of the Marines?**

Lesson 7

The United States Coast Guard and Merchant Marine

Key Terms

commerce
cutter
ecosystem
flagged
intermodal
logistics
maritime
Operations Plan
sealift
strategic

What You Will Learn to Do

- Explore the organization and mission of the U.S. Coast Guard and Merchant Marine

Linked Core Abilities

- Do your share as a good citizen in your school, community, country, and the world

Skills and Knowledge You Will Gain Along the Way

- Describe the organization of the U.S. Coast Guard
- Explain the five major missions of the U.S. Coast Guard
- Explain how the Coast Guard is unique among the uniform services
- Describe the composition of the U.S. Merchant Marine
- Explain the role of the Merchant Marine in peacetime and war
- Define the key words contained in this lesson

Introduction

Since its start as the Revenue Cutter Service in 1790, the Coast Guard has provided unique benefits to America through its distinctive blend of humanitarian, law enforcement, diplomatic, and military capabilities. Whether equipped with 19th century wooden lifeboats or 20th century high endurance cutters, the Coast Guard has continuously served as America's shield of freedom.

The Merchant Marine is a fleet made up of a nation's commercial ships, both cargo and passenger, and those who operate them. It carries a nation's commerce (imports and exports) during peacetime and becomes a naval auxiliary to deliver troops and material in times of war.

In this lesson, you learn about both the Coast Guard and the Merchant Marine. You also learn about their places in war as well as in times of peace.

The United States Coast Guard

On August 4, 1790, Congress created the Revenue Cutter Service under the Treasury Department to enforce customs laws. In January 1915, Congress combined the Lifesaving Service and Revenue Cutter Service to form the U.S. Coast Guard.

The mission of the U.S. Coast Guard is the safety of lives and property at sea. The Coast Guard's five operating goals include maritime security, maritime safety, protection of natural resources, maritime mobility, and national defense. The official seal of the U.S. Coast Guard is shown in Figure 2.7.1.

Organization

Located within the Department of Homeland Security, the Coast Guard is also one of the nation's five armed services. The Coast Guard is headquartered in Washing-

Figure 2.7.1: The official seal of the U.S. Coast Guard.
Courtesy of the US Coast Guard.

ton, D.C. The Coast Guard's field operating units are divided into two regions: the Atlantic Area, based in Portsmouth, Virginia, and the Pacific Area, in Alameda, California. Each of these Areas is further broken down into Districts, with District headquarters located in nine key cities around the country, as shown in Table 2.7.1.

Table 2.7.1: Coast Guard Field Operating Units	
1st District	Boston, Massachusetts
5th District	Portsmouth, Virginia
7th District	Miami, Florida
8th District	New Orleans, Louisiana
9th District	Cleveland, Ohio
11th District	Alameda, California
13th District	Seattle, Washington
14th District	Honolulu, Hawaii
17th District	Juneau, Alaska

Key Note Term

cutter – small armed vessel in government service

Each District, in turn, includes a wide range of facilities, including Marine Safety Offices, Groups, Air Stations, boat stations, and **cutters**. With 38,000 active duty personnel, supported by 9,000 reservists and 34,000 auxiliaries, the Coast Guard is well positioned to be the first on scene—bringing the right people, equipment, skills, and partnerships—to respond to any local, regional, national, or international crisis. The Coast Guard commissions officers through the Coast Guard Academy in New London, Connecticut (see Figure 2.7.2).

Operations

Key Note Term

maritime – of, relating to, or bordering on the sea

For more than two centuries, the U.S. Coast Guard has protected the American public, the environment, and economic and security interests in U.S. waterways and any **maritime** region in which U.S. interests may be at risk. This wide range of Coast Guard missions can be categorized into five core roles:

- **Maritime security**
- **Maritime safety**
- **Protection of natural resources**
- **Maritime mobility**
- **National defense**

These five core roles are discussed in the following sections.

Figure 2.7.2: The Coast Guard Academy.
Courtesy of US Army JROTC.

Maritime Security

Maritime law enforcement is the oldest of the Coast Guard's numerous responsibilities. As a member of the Department of Homeland Security, the Coast Guard is not subject to *Posse Comitatus* and may conduct law enforcement activities. The Coast Guard's maritime security role consists of seven primary missions: homeland security, drug interdiction, alien migrant and mass migration interdiction, treaty enforcement, domestic fisheries enforcement, and general maritime law enforcement.

Homeland Security

The tragic events of September 11, 2001, highlighted the fact that the Coast Guard is also ideally positioned and equipped for the critical mission area of ports, waterways and coastal security. When America was attacked, Coast Guard National Strike Teams participated in rescue and recovery operations in New York City and Washington, D.C. Additionally, Coast Guard boats, cutters, planes, port security units and reservists were mobilized to protect America's vital ports and waterways. This response signaled the largest homeland port security operation since World War II. Homeland security now stands alongside search and rescue as a priority mission for the Coast Guard.

Drug Interdiction

As the designated lead agency for maritime drug interdiction under the National Drug Control Strategy, the Coast Guard maintains round-the-clock patrols of cutters and aircraft at sea working closely with U.S. and foreign law enforcement agencies and militaries to deny drug traffickers key maritime smuggling routes.

Alien Migrant Interdiction

Alien migrant interdiction operations are an increasingly important area of U.S. national security concern particularly in the post 9-11 environment where control of

America's borders is critical. During the past 20 years, the Coast Guard has interdicted more than 140,000 illegal migrants, primarily from Cuba, Haiti, the Dominican Republic, the Peoples Republic of China, and Ecuador. Far too often, these migration attempts pose safety risks to the undocumented migrants themselves. Smugglers of human cargoes often use ships that are unseaworthy and even ship migrants in sealed cargo containers. Under these conditions, many interdiction missions rapidly evolve to search and rescue and humanitarian aid missions (see Figure 2.7.3).

Mass Migrations

The Coast Guard is always poised to conduct surge operations as crises erupt. In 1994, for example, mass migrations brought migrant interdiction into the national spotlight, when more than 21,000 Haitians and 30,000 Cubans were recovered in four months.

Treaty Enforcement

The Coast Guard faces the daunting challenge of protecting over 3.4 million square miles of Exclusive Economic Zones (Harbors and Commercial ports) and 95,000 miles of coastlines.

Domestic Fisheries Enforcement

The objective of the Coast Guard's fisheries law enforcement program is to provide the on-scene presence necessary to protect America's $52 billion commercial and recreational fishing industry (see Figure 2.7.4). The Coast Guard's priorities are to eliminate illegal encroachment by foreign fishing vessels in Exclusive Economic Zones and to enforce domestic fisheries laws on the 110,000 U.S. commercial vessels harvesting critical fish stocks.

General Maritime Law Enforcement

The Coast Guard is also the primary federal agency responsible for enforcing all maritime laws and treaties. The Coast Guard possesses the unique authority to board any vessel subject to U.S. jurisdiction to make inspections, searches, inquiries, and arrests.

Figure 2.7.3: Search, rescue, and humanitarian aid is part of the mission of the Coast Guard.
Courtesy US Army JROTC.

Figure 2.7.4: The Coast Guard enforces fishery laws.
Courtesy of AP/Wide World Photos.

Maritime Safety

One of the basic responsibilities of the U.S. government is to protect the lives and safety of Americans. On the nation's waterways, the Coast Guard strives to preserve safety at sea through a focused program of prevention, response, and investigation. The Coast Guard's maritime safety role consists of four primary missions: search and rescue, licensing and inspection, recreational boating safety, and the International Ice Patrol.

Search and Rescue

Search and rescue can be broken down into two basic categories: ocean rescue and flood response.

Ocean rescue involves safety on the sea. The sea can be unforgiving and even the most professional mariners can easily find themselves in peril. From its origins as the U.S. Life-Saving Service, the Coast Guard has a long and proud tradition of responding immediately to save lives in peril. The Coast Guard currently responds to more than 40,000 calls for help each year.

Coast Guard search and rescue operations are not limited to the high seas. In coastal and inland areas, it often assists in areas of flooding, as when North Dakota's Red River flooded in 1997, and Hurricane Floyd made landfall along the East Coast in 1999.

Licensing and Inspection

Licensing and inspection includes commercial fishing vessel safety, vessel inspection and prevention, the global merchant fleet, and the Port State Control.

In some areas, such as the Gulf of Alaska, commercial fishing is 10 times more deadly than any other occupation in the country. Through a combination of regulatory, inspection, and education efforts, the Coast Guard strives to prevent tragedies before they occur.

As part of the Coast Guard's inspection efforts, it enforces a wide range of regulations to ensure U.S. and foreign vessels operating in U.S. waters are structurally sound, competently operated, and outfitted with adequate safety systems. Coast Guard safety inspectors track most U.S.-flagged vessels from shipyard construction to final voyage, and emphasize the Prevention through People initiative, which helps mariners to improve safety and decrease the number of accidents and casualties.

In the past, the Coast Guard was primarily concerned with the safety of U.S. vessels. Today, however, the Coast Guard has increasingly shifted its focus to foreign commercial vessels, as 95 percent of passenger ships and 75 percent of cargo ships operating in U.S. waters are foreign flagged. The Coast Guard is also the lead U.S. representative to the International Maritime Organization, an arm of the United Nations. In the wake of 9-11, the Coast Guard spearheaded the United States' efforts to increase international maritime security through IMO, resulting in sweeping changes to international security measures. Domestically, these changes were codified in the Maritime Transportation Security Act of 2002. The Coast Guard is a driving force behind the implementation of measures to improve the training and safety standards of all mariners and vessels plying U.S. waters.

Unfortunately, not every country enforces international standards. To address this reality, the Coast Guard has effective Captain of the Port and Port State Control mechanisms in place that are designed to bring substandard ships into compliance with international standards, or exclude or remove them from U.S. waters.

Recreational Boating Safety

In addition to commercial vessels, nearly 13 million recreational boats cruise American waterways each year (see Figure 2.7.5). Consequently, recreational boating is second only to highway travel in the number of transportation fatalities. As the National Recreational Boating Safety Coordinator, the Coast Guard works to minimize loss of life, personal injury, and property damage through a variety of prevention, education, and enforcement efforts. The all-volunteer Coast Guard Auxiliary plays a central role in this effort.

International Ice Patrol

The Coast Guard is also responsible for the International Ice Patrol. This effort, which primarily takes place in the North Atlantic, is focused on monitoring shipping lanes to warn transiting ships of dangers posed by icebergs.

Protection of Natural Resources

America's marine waters and their **ecosystems** are vital to the health, well being, and economy of the nation. The Coast Guard's protection of natural resources role focuses on two main mission areas: marine environmental protection and marine protected species law and treaty enforcement.

Marine Environmental Protection

There are many diverse and harmful threats and challenges to our environment, including oil and chemical spills, hazardous materials dumping, and marine habitat destruction.

Key Note Term

ecosystem – a community of organisms and its environment functioning as an ecological unit

Figure 2.7.5: Recreational boaters are protected by the Coast Guard.
Courtesy of Corbis Images.

To address shipping regulation challenges, the Coast Guard closely regulates the shipping industry to prevent or minimize the environmental damage caused by oil and chemical spills and the dumping of wastes at sea. The Coast Guard's mandate to do so was significantly strengthened by the Oil Pollution Act of 1990, which was passed in response to the devastating Exxon Valdez oil spill the year before. As a result of these efforts, oil spills have decreased by two-thirds during the past five years.

Marine Protected Species Law Treaty Enforcement

Along with the marine environment, the Coast Guard also protects sensitive marine habitats, marine mammals, and endangered marine species. For example, the Coast Guard is currently working with the marine industry to safeguard the endangered Right whales as they transit the Atlantic shipping lanes, as well as endangered sea turtles in the Gulf of Mexico.

Marine Mobility

The U.S. Coast Guard works to ensure an efficient and effective U.S. Marine Transportation System. The U.S. Marine Transportation System includes all of America's waterways and 361 ports, through which more than two billion tons of foreign and domestic freight and 3.3 billion barrels of oil move each year. The Coast Guard plays a key role in an ongoing initiative aimed at building the public and private partnerships necessary to support a world-class waterway system that improves our global competitiveness and national security.

In today's global economy, the United States remains dependent on ports and waterways for our economic survival. Excluding Mexico and Canada, 95 percent of the nation's foreign trade and 25 percent of its domestic trade depends on maritime transportation. The Coast Guard conducts four maritime mobility-related missions that enhance the effectiveness and efficiency of the U.S. Marine Transportation System: aids to navigation, domestic icebreaking, bridge administration, and waterways/vessel traffic management.

Aids to Navigation

To aid ships transiting congested and complex waterways, the Coast Guard maintains the world's largest system of long- and short-range aids to navigation, with more than 50,000 buoys, fixed markers, and lighthouses. The Coast Guard also maintains the differential global positioning system and Loran C radio navigation systems, enabling mariners to electronically determine their position.

Domestic Icebreaking

Coast Guard domestic icebreakers and buoy tenders ensure that ships carrying essential supplies are able to safely navigate U.S. waterways, especially on the Great Lakes, Chesapeake Bay, Delaware Bay, and rivers of the Northeast, regardless of weather conditions (see Figure 2.7.6).

Bridge Administration

The Coast Guard also is responsible for regulating and ensuring safety and proper operations for approximately 18,000 highway and railroad bridges that span navigable waterways. The Coast Guard routinely issues permits for new bridge construction, orders obstructive bridges to be removed, and oversees drawbridge operations.

Waterways/Vessel Traffic Management

To facilitate the more than $1 trillion worth of domestic and foreign goods that move through U.S. ports and waterways each year, the Coast Guard operates a comprehensive network of precision electronic navigation systems and vessel traffic services aimed at reducing the risk of collision and ensuring the safe, efficient passage of people, ships, and goods.

National Defense

Despite its many roles and missions, the Coast Guard is fully prepared to execute essential military tasks in support of joint and combined forces in peacetime, crisis,

Figure 2.7.6: Icebreakers break ice to facilitate safe U.S. waterway passage. Courtesy of US Army JROTC.

and war. The Coast Guard has five specific national defense missions in addition to its general defense operations and polar icebreaking duties: maritime interception operations; military environmental response operations; port operations, security, and defense; coastal sea control operations; and peacetime military engagement.

General Defense Operations

Like the other U.S. armed services, warfare is one of the Coast Guard's core missions. It commands the U.S. Maritime Defense Zones around the nation and maintains a high state of readiness in order to perform as a specialized branch of the Navy in times of war. Coast Guard forces and capabilities are incorporated in the Unified Combatant Commanders' **Operations Plans**. As part of Operation Iraqi Freedom, the Coast Guard sent 11 cutters and 1250 personnel to secure ports and support coalition forces.

Key Note Term

Operations Plan – military plan of action for future potential crisis or contingencies

Maritime Interception Operations

Coast Guard maritime interception operations leverage its extensive training and expertise in stopping, boarding, searching, and seizing vessels to enforce international sanctions overseas, such as in the Arabian Gulf against Iraq.

Military Environmental Response Operations

Coast Guard military environmental response operations enable the Coast Guard to serve as the tip of the military's spear in responding to environmental disasters. Coast Guard experience with the containment and cleanup of environmental disasters has given its three National Strike Teams the specialized training necessary to respond wherever needed, whether in the burning oil fields of Kuwait or Ground Zero in New York City.

Port Operations, Security, and Defense

The Coast Guard port operations, security, and defense mission leverages unique legal authorities, assets, and expertise to protect U.S. and overseas ports, facilities, and vessels from hostilities. Port security units, manned primarily by reservists, play a prominent role in this effort.

Coastal Sea Control Operations

The Coast Guard coastal sea control operations mission, which was added to the Coast Guard's portfolio in July 2001, is designed to ensure the unimpeded use of designated coastal areas by friendly forces while denying the use of those areas by enemy forces. Specific duties include surveillance and reconnaissance, interdiction of enemy shipping, and protection of friendly forces.

Peacetime Military Engagement

The Coast Guard's peacetime engagement efforts include all activities involving other nations that are intended to shape the security environment in peacetime before military crises can arise. International engagement and training initiatives foster healthy relationships with other countries, thereby promoting peace and stability, democracy, and the rule of law.

Polar Icebreaking

The Coast Guard is also responsible for polar icebreaking operations. This is essential to ensure U.S. scientists in the Arctic and Antarctic have the access, equipment, and supplies they need, while providing them with a floating laboratory from which to conduct vital scientific research.

The United States Merchant Marine

The Merchant Marine is a fleet made up of a nation's commercial ships, both cargo and passenger, and those who operate them. It carries the nation's commerce (imports and exports) during peacetime and becomes a naval auxiliary to deliver troops and material in times of war.

The Merchant Marine has been an important part of the nation since the Revolutionary War period when the government issued letters of marque to privately owned, armed merchant ships and commissions for privateers, which the government outfitted as warships to prey on British merchant ships. The modern Merchant Marine was conceived by Congress with the Merchant Marine Act of 1936.

The mission of the U.S. Merchant Marine is to carry the greater portion of the United States commerce at sea, and serve as a naval or military auxiliary in time of war or national emergency. The official seal of the U.S. Merchant Marine is shown in Figure 2.7.7.

Organization

The U.S. Merchant Marine is an essential component of national defense. It augments the basic sealift capacity necessary to meet defense requirements. Experience gained during previous conflicts has emphasized the importance of Navy coordination with all segments of the maritime industry.

Figure 2.7.7: The official seal of the U.S. Merchant Marine.
Courtesy of US Army JROTC.

The Department of Transportation's Maritime Administration is charged with ensuring a viable U.S. Merchant Marine and maritime industry to meet national security needs. The Maritime Administration, in cooperation with the Navy, supports programs directed toward sustaining the maritime infrastructure, including maritime education and training; national defense features and Title XI loans, operational differential subsidies and maritime security agreements, and the development of technologies and industrial processes.

The U.S. Merchant Marine Academy was established in 1938 as a result of the Merchant Marine Act of 1936. It operates under the Department of Transportation Maritime Administration to graduate qualified mariners.

Operations

In peacetime, the Merchant Marine transacts the nation's **commerce**. In crisis and war, the Merchant Marine supplements the Navy as an arm of the national defense. Merchant vessels become naval cruisers and naval auxiliaries for the transport of troops, munitions, fuel, and supplies necessary to support and maintain military units. The Merchant Marine constitutes a reserve from which a body of trained sea going men are available to augment the personnel of a naval fleet.

The U.S. Merchant Marine provides U.S.-flag civilian-crewed commercial ships and civilian crews to government-owned support ships to deploy U.S. forces overseas and resupply them. These **sealift** assets account for about 95 percent of all the tonnage delivered in support of military requirements in peacetime and during times of crisis. Over 4,800 civilian mariners crew the 200 commercial vessels with military features that are included in the Afloat Preposition Force, Fast Sealift Ships, Ready Reserve Force ships, Maritime Security Fleet, and Navy Fleet Auxiliary Force. Over half of these sealift ships are actively deployed or are in commercial service around the globe.

There are several advantages to using sealift. Unit for unit, ships have a higher hauling capacity than aircraft. Ships can also carry heavy or outsized equipment. Ships can pre-position at sea near a projected threat area. They do not need over-flight rights, and waters more than 12 miles from land are free for navigation.

The Navy's Military Sealift Command (MSC) provides ocean transportation for Department of Defense (DoD) cargo and U.S. forces around the world. More than 70 **strategic** sealift ships transport military equipment, supplies, and petroleum to support U.S. forces overseas. This number is expandable and includes both government and privately owned vessels. In peacetime, more than 95 percent of DoD cargo is transported by U.S.-registered (**flagged**) ships.

MSC ships are noncombatant vessels, operating behind battle lines, and are not considered likely enemy targets. Their noncombatant status enables MSC ships to maintain average crews less than half the size of combatant vessels, therefore they are more economical to operate.

- **MSC ships' merchant mariner crewmembers can also be hired as necessary, while the Navy, even in peacetime, must employ a large number of Navy combatant personnel in case of war**
- **The skill levels of MSC's merchant mariners also enable MSC ships to operate with smaller crews**

MSC is able to provide rapid, sustained response in a changing world with three operational strategies: prepositioning, surge, and sustainment sealift.

Afloat Prepositioning Forces

The Military Sealift Command Prepositioning Program provides operationally ready ships to the military services and the Defense Logistics Agency. MSC's Afloat Prepositioning Force consists of 37 ships, with 35 operating at prepositioning sites in the Mediterranean Sea, Diego Garcia in the Indian Ocean, and Guam in the Western Pacific. The Afloat Prepositioning Force is divided into three parts:

- **Maritime Prepositioning Ships operated for the U.S. Marine Corps**
- **Combat Prepositioning Ships operated for the U.S. Army**
- **Logistics Prepositioning Ships operated for the U.S. Navy, Air Force, and Defense Logistics Agency**

Surge Sealift

Surge includes ships from the U.S. Transportation Command (USTRANSCOM)-controlled fleet; for example, the Fast Sealift Ships (FSS), the Ready Reserve Force (RRF), Large Medium Speed Roll-On/Roll-Off (LMSR) vessels, and the commercial market when contracted by USTRANSOM for support of U.S. forces. Surge shipping delivers the heavy combat power and accompanying supplies in order to facilitate the deployment of predominantly continental U.S. (CONUS) based forces to anywhere in the world.

Sustainment Sealift

To sustain military operations overseas, Military Sealift Command may activate any of three reserve fleets and crew them with mariners from the Merchant Marines: National Defense Reserve Fleet, Ready Reserve Force, Maritime Security Fleet, and Voluntary **Intermodal** Service Agreement program.

National Defense Reserve Fleet (NDRF)

The National Defense Reserve Fleet, under the custody of the Department of Transportation Maritime Administration, is an inactive reserve source of basic Merchant-design-type ships that could be activated within 20 to 120 days to meet the shipping requirements of the United States during national emergencies. This fleet of about 100 ships consists mostly of World War II merchant vessels that are available for use in both military and nonmilitary emergencies, such as a commercial shipping crisis. Ships of the NDRF are located in three fleet sites: James River, Virginia (East Coast); Beaumont, Texas (Gulf Coast); and Suisan Bay, California (West Coast).

Key Note Term

logistics – the aspect of military science dealing with the procurement, maintenance, and transportation of military matériel, facilities, and personnel

---

Key Note Term

intermodal – being or involving transportation by more than one form of carrier during a single journey

---

Ready Reserve Force (RRF)

The Ready Reserve Force (RRF) is a quick response subset of the NDRF. The RRF is a government-owned, inactive fleet of former commercial ships of various types that can respond rapidly in any contingency. RRF ships are maintained in a readiness status such that they can be activated for service within 4 to 20 days. RRF ships are colocated at the same three sites with the NDRF.

Maritime Security Fleet

The Maritime Security Program maintains a U.S.-flag merchant fleet crewed by U.S. mariners to serve both the commercial and national security needs of the United States. In accordance with the Maritime Security Act of 1996, the Department of Transportation's Maritime Administration entered into agreements with 10 shipping companies to participate in a program that would provide the DoD access to U.S.-registered commercial ships, their crews, and other related transportation assets in a time of national emergency. Maritime Security Program payments are paid to vessels operating in U.S. foreign commerce. Vessels include containerships, lighter-aboard ships (LASH) and Roll-on/Roll-off (RO/RO) vessels.

Voluntary Intermodal Shipping (VISA)

The Voluntary Intermodal Shipping Agreement allows U.S.-flag carriers to provide ships and trained crews in three stages depending on the severity and expected duration of the contingency. VISA calls for comprehensive and integrated peacetime planning and exercises by the Maritime Administration, USTRANSCOM, and the Navy's Military Sealift Command. After activation, the commercial carrier is to proceed to the nearest port and disembark their civilian cargo, then proceed to the nearest military port to pick up its designated government cargo. Commercial carriers are paid a subsidy to participate in the VISA program.

Conclusion

The U.S. Coast Guard operates as part of the Department of Homeland Security to fulfill peacetime missions in maritime security, maritime safety, protection of national resources, and maritime mobility. The Coast Guard also fulfills roles vital to national defense throughout peacetime, crisis, and war: general defense operations; maritime interception operations, military environmental response operations; Port operations, security, defense; coastal sea control operations; peacetime military engagement; and polar icebreaking. In times of crisis and war, the Coast Guard will be given over to the U.S. Navy and work at the direction of the Unified Combatant Commands.

The Merchant Marine is a fleet made up of a nation's commercial ships, both cargo and passenger, and those who operate them. It carries the nation's commerce (imports and exports) during peacetime and becomes a naval auxiliary to deliver troops and material in times of war. The Merchant Marine augments the basic sealift capacity necessary to meet defense requirements. The Department of Transportation's Maritime Administration is charged with ensuring a viable Merchant Marine and maritime industry to meet national security needs. Toward this end, the Merchant Marine plays a vital role with respect to Military Sealift Command's requirement to support military operations overseas with Afloat Prepositioning Forces, Surge Forces, and Sustainment Forces. The Merchant Marine crew Navy ships of the Afloat Prepositioning Forces and Fast Sealift Ships are forward deployed around the world. The Merchant Marine stands ready to reactivate and crew ships of the National Defense Reserve Fleet and the Ready Reserve Fleet. The Merchant Marine serves aboard the Maritime Security Fleet and commercial vessels participating in the Voluntary Intermodal Service Agreement, ready to come to the service of their country when called on by the president.

In the following lesson, you will learn about the opportunities you can find in the Peace Corps. You will learn about the origins of the Peace Corps as well as its many divisions, one of which might appeal to you.

Lesson Review

1. **To which executive department does the Coast Guard report?**
2. **What are the five major missions of the Coast Guard?**
3. **Why is the Coast Guard able to conduct law enforcement activity?**
4. **What is the Merchant Marine?**

Lesson 8

The Peace Corps

Key Terms

partnership
service-learning
volunteer

What You Will Learn to Do

- Explore the purpose and structure of the Peace Corps

Linked Core Abilities

- Do your share as a good citizen in your school, community, country, and the world
- Communicate using verbal, nonverbal, visual, and written techniques

Skills and Knowledge You Will Gain Along the Way

- Explain the mission and goals of the Peace Corps
- Describe the backgrounds and requirements of Peace Corps volunteers
- Identify the types and locations of projects performed by Peace Corps volunteers
- Describe how other countries benefit from Peace Corps projects
- Explain the educational benefits available to Peace Corps volunteers
- Define the key words contained in this lesson

Chapter 2

Introduction

The Peace Corps was born from a challenge that then-Senator John F. Kennedy issued to students at the University of Michigan to serve their country by living and working in developing countries. Since then, the Peace Corps has placed over 178,000 **volunteers** in 136 host countries to work on projects from agriculture and AIDS education to information technology and environmental preservation. In this lesson you will explore the role of the Peace Corps as an agency of the federal government dedicated to world peace and friendship.

The Origins of the Peace Corp

After a day of campaigning for the presidency, John F. Kennedy (see Figure 2.8.1) arrived at the University of Michigan in Ann Arbor on October 14, 1960, at 2:00 a.m., to get some sleep, not to propose the establishment of an international volunteer organization. Members of the press had retired for the night, believing that nothing interesting would happen. But 10,000 students at the University were waiting to hear the presidential candidate speak, and it was there on the steps of the Michigan Union that a bold new experiment in public **service-learning** was launched.

The assembled students heard the future president issue a challenge: how many of them, he asked, would be willing to serve their country and the cause of peace by living and working in the developing world? The reaction was both swift and enthusiastic, and since 1961, more than 178,000 Americans have responded to this enduring challenge. Since then, the Peace Corps has demonstrated how the power of an idea can capture the imagination of an entire nation.

On March 1, 1961, President Kennedy signed an executive order establishing the Peace Corps. Three days later, R. Sargent Shriver was appointed its first director. In

Figure 2.8.1: The Peace Corps was established by John F. Kennedy.
Courtesy of Bettman/Corbis Images.

July, Peace Corps assignments were planned for Ghana, Tanzania, Colombia, the Philippines, Chile, and St. Lucia. More than 5,000 applicants took the first exams to enter the Peace Corps.

On August 28, 1961, President Kennedy hosted a ceremony at the White House Rose Garden to honor the inaugural group of volunteers who would serve in Ghana and Tanzania. The 51 Americans who landed in Accra, Ghana, made an immediate impression on their hosts: they formed a chorus on the airport's tarmac in front of the minister of education and other officials and sang the Ghanaian national anthem in Twi, the local language.

On September 22, 1961, Congress approved legislation formally authorizing the Peace Corps, giving it the mandate to "promote world peace and friendship" through three goals:

- **To help the people of interested countries and areas in meeting their needs for trained workers**
- **To help promote a better understanding of Americans on the part of the peoples served**
- **To help promote a better understanding of other peoples on the part of Americans**

By the end of 1963, 7,300 volunteers were in the field, serving in 44 countries from Afghanistan to Uruguay. More than half of the volunteers worked in education; one-fourth in community development; and the remainder in agriculture, health care, and public works. By June 1966, more than 15,000 volunteers were working in the field, the largest number in Peace Corps' history.

Since 1960, when then-Senator John F. Kennedy challenged students at the University of Michigan to serve their country in the cause of peace by living and working in developing countries, more than 178,000 Peace Corps volunteers have served in 136 countries all over the globe. They've been teachers and mentors to countless children. They've helped farmers grow crops, worked with small businesses to market products, and shown women how to care for their babies. More recently, they've helped schools develop computer skills and educated entire communities about the threat of HIV/AIDS.

Throughout its history, the Peace Corps has adapted and responded to the issues of the times. In an ever-changing world, Peace Corps volunteers meet new challenges with innovation, creativity, determination, and compassion. These are the qualities that have allowed the Peace Corps to achieve its mission since 1961, and they remain the keys to achieving that mission today.

Organization

The Peace Corps is an independent agency within the executive branch of the U.S. government. The president of the United States appoints the Peace Corps director and deputy director, and the appointments must be confirmed by the U.S. Senate. The Senate Foreign Relations Committee is charged with general oversight of the activities and programs of the Peace Corps, and the House Committee on International Relations serves a similar function. The Peace Corps annual budget is determined each year by the congressional budget and appropriations process and is part of the foreign operations budget. Generally, the Peace Corps budget is about 1 percent of the foreign operations budget.

Operations

The world has changed since 1961, and the Peace Corps has changed with it. With 7,733 volunteers in 72 countries, today's Peace Corps is more relevant than ever. Think of the Peace Corps and you might imagine teaching in a one-room schoolhouse or farming in a remote area of the world, as shown in Figure 2.8.2.

Although education and agriculture are still an important part of what the Peace Corps does, today's volunteers are just as likely to be working on HIV/AIDS awareness, helping to establish computer learning centers, or working on small business development. Peace Corps volunteers work in the following areas:

- **Education, youth outreach, and community development**
- **Business development**
- **Environmental awareness**
- **Agriculture development**
- **Health and HIV/AIDS**
- **Information technology**

Education, Youth Outreach, and Community Development

Education is fundamental to human progress, enabling individuals and communities to acquire skills and knowledge essential for improving their quality of life. Yet in much of the developing world, access to basic education is limited. Education is the Peace Corps largest program area, with volunteers serving as teachers of En-

Figure 2.8.2: The Peace Corps offers many opportunities in agriculture.
Courtesy of James Leynse/Corbis Images.

glish, math, science, and business (see Figure 2.8.3). Education volunteers introduce innovative teaching methodologies; encourage critical thinking in the classroom; and integrate issues like health education and environmental awareness into English, math, science, and other subjects. Many also work in curriculum or materials development and train teachers informally or formally in conversational English, academic subjects, or methodology, thus achieving a truly sustainable impact.

Education volunteers are uniquely positioned to be highly effective community development workers. Through the strong relationships they forge with students, parents, and other community members, volunteers engage in a wide variety of outreach projects concerning at-risk children or youth, adult literacy, health or HIV/AIDS education, environmental awareness, development of libraries and resource centers, and information technology.

Primary Education Teacher Training

Volunteers act as resources for elementary school teachers and occasionally provide classroom instruction. They work with one or more schools, including teachers colleges, modeling participatory methodologies, conducting workshops, and providing ongoing support to local teachers. Some primary education projects focus specifically on health, HIV/AIDS, the environment, childhood development, English as a Second Language (ESL), remedial education, science, language arts, or a foreign language.

Secondary Education English Teaching

Volunteers teach conversational English, English as a second language, or content-based English in middle and high schools, creating opportunities for students and local teachers to contribute to their country's development. In addition to classroom teaching, Volunteers share resources, develop teaching materials with local teachers, and become involved in community- and school-based projects.

Figure 2.8.3: Volunteers can use their teaching skills and become instructors.
Courtesy of Philip Gould/Corbis Images.

Secondary Education Math or Science Teaching

Volunteers in math teach basic concepts, including remedial math, geometry, algebra, statistics, probability, and calculus (see Figure 2.8.4). They also work in after-school programs, youth clubs, and library development. Volunteers in science teach general science, biology, chemistry, and physics. They also integrate health and environmental education into the curriculum and engage in other school and community activities.

Secondary Education English Teacher Training

Teacher trainers work with new and experienced English teachers, training student teachers at teachers colleges or providing in-service training to experienced teachers in current methodologies, subject content, and resource development, thus creating sustainable improvements in teaching that will affect generations of future students. Projects include increasing local teachers' English language competency and conversational skills and organizing teacher associations or training seminars.

Secondary Education Teacher Training

Volunteers work with education offices, schools, and local teachers, focusing on methodology, individualized instruction, classroom management, and resource development for teachers of students with special needs. Volunteers also counsel parents and the community to raise public awareness and understanding of people with disabilities.

University English Teaching

Volunteers work with university-level students who need enhanced English language skills to make use of academic and technical resources published in English in their study of languages, literature, business, medicine, engineering, or other fields. Volunteers teach English grammar, conversation, phonetics, American literature and culture, creative writing, and linguistics; establish English language clubs and resource centers; share ideas and develop materials with fellow teachers; and integrate communicative teaching techniques into the classroom.

Figure 2.8.4: Math and science are just two of the education areas covered by the Peace Corps.
Courtesy of LWA-Dann Tardif/Corbis Images.

Construction and Skilled Trades Education

Volunteers teach vocational education in schools, technical institutes, and training centers (see Figure 2.8.5). They also work with communities and local governments to facilitate the construction of schools, health centers, markets, and other projects while transferring their skills to tradespeople and students in their communities. Their activities include estimating costs and quantities of materials, determining types of tools required, conducting inventory control, working with industrial equipment, and teaching building techniques.

Business Development

In many countries where volunteers serve, governments and local communities face impediments to economic growth, such as high unemployment, rapidly increasing populations, unskilled workforces, and a lack of private sector investment. Peace Corps volunteers have a long history of working with individuals and communities to promote economic opportunities at the grassroots level.

Business volunteers focus on increasing family income, improving the environment for businesses, educating young people, and helping businesses find markets for traditional or value-added products. They participate at many levels, whether helping artisan cooperatives in rural Africa market their handmade goods or training people in eastern Europe to take advantage of new free-market opportunities.

Often, business volunteers begin in a classroom setting, which gives them a position in the community as respected leaders and makes other projects possible. These projects include training entrepreneurs in the basic skills of small business development and working with women to help them expand their access to credit and find new markets for their products. Some volunteers work with development banks, nongovernmental organizations, and municipalities to support local development projects. Most business volunteers have business or public administration degrees or experience; others have degrees in other disciplines and a strong interest in business and nonprofit organizations.

Figure 2.8.5: Construction education is essential in emerging nations.
Courtesy of LWA-JDC/Corbis Images.

Business Advising

Volunteers work in a variety of settings, assisting both private and public businesses, local and regional governments, nonprofit organizations, women's groups and youth groups, and educational institutions. They train and advise entrepreneurs and managers in business planning, marketing, financial management (see Figure 2.8.6), and product design; advise agricultural cooperatives, agribusinesses, and farmers; develop and write project funding proposals; and work with community and business support groups. Other projects include assisting with credit programs; facilitating business-training workshops; and teaching business courses, English, and Junior Achievement programs.

Business Development

Volunteers work in a wide variety of projects in secondary schools, technical institutes, universities, nongovernmental organizations, and business centers. They consult with businesses and conduct seminars on starting a business, strategic planning, marketing, merchandising, organizational development, and tourism development. They also advise Junior Achievement organizations, teach basic business subjects and English, develop business education curricula, and design training materials; work with women and minority groups to strengthen their participation in the economic system; and assist local and regional governments in planning and implementing economic development strategies.

Nongovernmental Organization Development

Volunteers work with local, national, or international nongovernmental organizations (NGOs) that deal with youth, social services, small business development, or the environment. Typical projects include increasing an NGO's organizational capacity and sustainability; creating strategic and funding plans; raising public awareness of an NGO's mission; conducting community outreach; recruiting, training, and motivating NGO volunteers; developing mission statements, bylaws, and

Figure 2.8.6: Volunteers can use their expertise to counsel businessmen and entrepreneurs.
Courtesy of Peter Beck/Corbis Images.

other documentation; working with boards of directors; mentoring and skill building of staff; and increasing the quality and effectiveness of an NGO's services.

Urban and Regional Planning

Volunteers work with municipalities and communities, as well as with regional or national governments. Projects include assessing the impact of planned activities or economic and environmental development on communities, planning infrastructure for primary and secondary cities, planning and controlling budgets, and coordinating activities between governmental organizations and communities.

Environmental Awareness

In many developing countries, environmental problems are magnified by communities' direct dependence on their local environment for drinking water, fuel wood, or land for farming. Environmental damage can have enormous consequences on a community's livelihood; likewise, meeting a growing community's needs can have important implications for the environment.

Peace Corps volunteers are leaders in grassroots efforts to protect the environment, working on projects such as establishing forest conservation plans and developing alternatives to wood as a fuel source. They collaborate with various organizations to promote environmental education through projects like recycling, wildlife protection, and park management (see Figure 2.8.7).

Volunteers also work to provide potable water to rural and urban communities and to alleviate waterborne diseases.

Volunteers have degrees and experience in a variety of areas, from forestry, biology, and environmental science to recreation and park administration, education, and engineering. Among the qualities sought is a strong interest in the environment.

Figure 2.8.7: Peace Corps volunteers can assist local residents in establishing good environmental management.
Courtesy of Dave G. Hauser/Corbis Images.

Environmental Education or Awareness

Volunteers assist communities where environmental issues are in conflict with basic needs for farming and income generation. Their activities are limited only by their own creativity and that of the community. Activities include teaching in elementary and secondary schools; providing environmental education to youth groups and individuals outside school settings; helping environmental groups organize and develop, often in newly emerging democracies; promoting sustainable use of forest or marine resources by communities; developing income-generating activities for communities living near protected areas; and managing sanitation in urban areas.

Forestry

Volunteers help communities conserve natural resources by working on projects such as soil conservation; watershed management and flood control; production of sustainable fuels; improvement of agroforestry practices such as fruit production; building live fences and alley cropping; and preservation of biodiversity, sometimes near national parks or other reserves.

Parks and Wildlife

Volunteers provide technical assistance and training in natural resource conservation, generally in close affiliation with national parks or other reserves. Their activities include technical training of park managers, working with park staff on wildlife surveys, conducting community-based conservation such as sustainable use of forest or marine resources, and promoting income-generating activities for communities living near protected areas.

Environmental and Water Resources Engineering

Volunteers work with local governments and communities to improve water and sanitation facilities. They train people in facilities operation and maintenance, help communities access resources and form management committees to sustain facilities, design and build potable-water sources and supply systems, construct sewage and irrigation systems, design and build garbage collection facilities, and build earthen dams and concrete spillways.

Agriculture Development

Agriculture is the primary economic activity of most of the world's people, and yet many countries cannot produce adequate supplies of healthy food. Deficiencies in quantity and quality of food can cause serious health and economic problems.

Peace Corps volunteers help farmers improve local diets and increase income through farming techniques consistent with environmental conservation. They work with communities and farmers on projects such as implementing agroforestry techniques to improve soil quality and conserve water, fisheries, beekeeping and honey production (see Figure 2.8.8), organic vegetable gardening, and nutrition education.

Agriculture volunteers also work with farmer cooperatives, nongovernmental organizations, and agribusinesses on basic business practices, crop and livestock production, organizing networks of farmers, and conducting production cost-and-price analyses.

Figure 2.8.8: Beekeeping and honey production can bring food and economic development to a community.
Courtesy of David Barnes/Getty Images.

The Peace Corps agriculture programs attract volunteers with a variety of backgrounds. Many have a bachelor's degree (in any discipline) and a strong interest in agriculture and gardening, while others have specialized degrees and experience in agricultural and animal sciences and agribusiness. Volunteers without degrees have relevant experience from jobs or personal endeavors.

Agriculture and Forestry Extension

Volunteers' projects include establishing and maintaining soil and water conservation structures and practices; fruit tree production, live fences, and other agriculture-related forestry practices; fish cultivation; raising trees in small nurseries; apiculture and honey production; livestock health; meat and wool production; range management; vegetable gardening; and nutrition education.

Applied Agricultural Science

Volunteers encourage sustainable crop production through promotion of organic farming techniques and better farm management. Activities include conducting workshops on integrated pest management; introducing composting, green manures, and other soil improvement techniques; testing new varieties of seeds and demonstrating post-harvest management methods; and teaching agriculture and extension methodologies in formal training institutions.

Farm Management and Agribusiness

Volunteers work with small-scale farmers, farmers' cooperatives, agribusinesses, and nongovernmental organizations. They teach basic business practices such as marketing, credit price determination, and general business planning; work on crop and livestock production and preservation; assist in organizing networks of local farmers; identify market structures and channels; and perform production cost-and-price analysis.

Animal Husbandry

Volunteers work to enhance farm families' nutrition and household income through improved livestock management techniques (see Figure 2.8.9). Activities include promoting vaccination against common diseases; teaching farmers better production techniques; improving marketing techniques for products like meat, wool, and eggs; developing land-use plans for pastoral farmers; and projects such as vegetable gardening, range management, and beekeeping.

Health and HIV/AIDS

One of the most serious worldwide threats to public health and development is the spread of HIV/AIDS. Volunteers in HIV/AIDS education and prevention train youth as peer educators, collaborate with religious leaders to develop appropriate education strategies, provide support to children orphaned by HIV/AIDS, and develop programs that provide support to families and communities affected by the disease. In May 2003, the Peace Corps committed 1,000 new volunteers to work on HIV/AIDS-related activities, as part of President George W. Bush's Global AIDS Relief Package.

In addition to HIV/AIDS prevention, volunteers also work on basic health care issues. By focusing on prevention, human capacity building, and education, Peace Corps volunteers help improve basic health care at the grassroots level, where their impact can be the most significant and where health needs are most pressing. In helping communities take more responsibility for their own health care, volunteers work to ensure the sustainability of their projects (see Figure 2.8.10).

The majority of Peace Corps volunteers serving in health and HIV/AIDS programs have a bachelor's degree (which can be in any discipline) and a strong interest in health, while some volunteers have degrees only in a health-related area.

Figure 2.8.9: Livestock management can help a community's nutritional and income value.
Courtesy of Tim Flach/Getty Images.

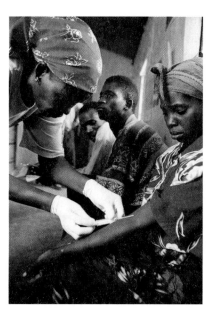

Figure 2.8.10: Prevention of disease and education of health-related issues makes a community stronger.
Courtesy of The International HIV/AIDS Alliance/Corbis Images.

Health Extension

Volunteers raise awareness in communities about the need for health education. They act as catalysts for a wide range of activities, limited only by the creativity of the community and the volunteer. Activities include identifying local leaders to teach families about maternal and child health, basic nutrition, or sanitation; setting up training on nutrition, sanitation, or oral rehydration therapy; organizing groups to raise money for needed health-care materials; and training of trainers for peer education about AIDS and other sexually transmitted diseases.

Public Health Education

Volunteers teach public health in classrooms and model methodologies and subjects for primary and secondary school teachers. Projects include undertaking "knowledge, attitude, and practice" surveys in communities; assisting clinics or government planning offices in identifying health education needs; devising educational programs to address local health conditions; assisting in marketing messages aimed at improving local health practices; performing epidemiological studies; and serving as backup professionals for other health volunteers.

Water and Sanitation Extension

Volunteers serve in a broad range of projects, including organizing and mobilizing communities to provide hygiene education; tapping springs, constructing wells, and building latrines; improving potable-water storage facilities; and doing community outreach to heighten awareness of water and sanitation issues.

Information Technology

Due to a lack of resources and education, many of the world's developing countries have been unable to take advantage of the advances in technology. Today, however, Peace Corps volunteers are working to help people in these communities take part in the information technology revolution.

Information technology volunteers help communities and organizations capitalize on available and appropriate information technology, helping to bridge the divide between those who can afford access to technology and those who cannot (see Figure 2.8.11). They identify innovative approaches that enable resource-poor communities to use information and communications technology for their own development purposes.

Information technology volunteers typically have backgrounds and degrees in computer science or information systems, or knowledge of or experience in basic computer applications such as word processing, spreadsheets, and databases, along with strong leadership and organizational skills.

Technology Work Area

Volunteers provide technical training and support to school systems, health ministries, municipal government offices, and nongovernmental organizations. By teaching computer skills and data processing, helping to develop regional databases, and implementing networks for businesses and government offices, volunteers link entrepreneurs to new business opportunities (including e-commerce), expand farmers' access to information on market prices, bring the Internet into classrooms, and provide forums for communities to share ideas about development activities.

Peace Corps Benefits

You give and you get. The chance to make a real difference in other people's lives is the reason most volunteers serve in the Peace Corps. But that is not the only benefit of Peace Corps service. Volunteers also have the chance to learn a new language, live in another culture, and develop career and leadership skills. The Peace Corps experience can enhance long-term career prospects whether you want to work for a corporation, a nonprofit organization, or a government agency. The Peace Corps can even open doors to graduate school.

Figure 2.8.11: Peace Corps volunteers help developing nations become more technologically savvy.
Courtesy of James L. Amos/Corbis Images.

From practical benefits such as student loan deferment, career benefits like fluency in a foreign language, and the intangible benefits that come with making a difference in people's lives, there are a variety of rewards for the dedicated service of volunteers.

Professional and Career Benefits

The benefits of serving as a Peace Corps volunteer go beyond making a difference in other people's lives. Peace Corps volunteers gain valuable cross-cultural experience and improve their foreign language skills, providing a foundation for successful careers in today's global marketplace. And Peace Corps support doesn't stop when your service is completed.

Through the Peace Corps Office of Returned Volunteer Services, volunteers also have access to a variety of job search resources and enjoy an advantage in applying for certain federal jobs.

Skills for the Global Marketplace

Fluency in foreign languages, international experience, and cross-cultural understanding are highly sought-after assets in today's global economy. The Peace Corps provides three months of intensive training before service begins and offers continued training throughout a term of service. These new skills can help you achieve long-term career goals by enhancing your marketability to employers. Volunteers returning from abroad have used their Peace Corps experience as the foundation for successful careers in a variety of areas, from government to business to education.

Job Placement Support

The Peace Corps provides transition assistance related to jobs and education through our 11 regional recruitment offices. In addition, a directory of former volunteers and others who are willing to offer career advice is maintained, providing a ready-made job network in a wide variety of fields. The Peace Corps also publishes a biweekly newsletter with job announcements, graduate school information, and industry overviews. The Peace Corps also sponsors career workshops throughout the year.

Advantages in Federal Employment

Volunteers who complete two years of service receive one year of noncompetitive eligibility for employment in the federal government. This means that if you meet the minimum qualifications for a position, you can be hired without going through the standard competitive process.

Education Benefits

Peace Corps or graduate school? Two unique programs offer the best of both worlds. The Peace Corps has established **partnerships** with colleges and universities across the United States that offer academic credit and financial incentives to volunteers during or after Peace Corps service. The Master's International Program allows you to incorporate Peace Corps service into a master's degree program at more than 40 colleges and universities. And the Fellows/USA program offers former volunteers scholarships or reduced tuition at more than 30 participating schools.

Key Note Term

partnership – a legal relation existing between two or more entities contractually associated as joint principals in a business

Master's International Program

The Master's International Program offers the unique opportunity to combine Peace Corps service with a master's degree program. Prospective students apply separately to Peace Corps and to a participating graduate school. After acceptance by both, students will study on campus, usually for one year, and then spend the next two years earning academic credit while working overseas in a related Peace Corps project. Most schools provide students in this program with opportunities for research or teaching assistantships, scholarships, or tuition waivers for the credits earned while serving in the Peace Corps.

Fellows/USA

Fellows/USA offers volunteers who have returned home scholarships or reduced tuition in advanced degree programs. Some also receive housing allowances, paid employment, or health benefits. In return for these benefits, Fellows make a commitment to work in an underserved U.S. community as they pursue an advance degree in a variety of disciplines. Fellows teach in public schools, work in public health facilities, and contribute to community development projects at nonprofit organizations. Volunteers can apply for the Fellows/USA any time after they complete their Peace Corps service.

Financial Benefits and Loan Deferment

While no one considers joining the Peace Corps for the money, you might be surprised at some of the financial benefits of Peace Corps service.

During Service: Pay and Living Expenses

Peace Corps provides volunteers with a living allowance that enables them to live in a manner similar to the local people in their community. It also provides complete medical and dental care and covers the cost of transportation to and from the country of service.

After Service: Funds for Transition

Peace Corps recognizes that returning from overseas requires some adjustment, so when you complete your service, volunteers receive over $6,000 toward transitioning to life back home. The money is yours to use as you wish: for travel, a vacation, making a move, or securing housing.

Deferment of Student Loans

Volunteers may defer repayment on student loans under several federal programs, such as Stafford (formerly known as guaranteed student loans), Perkins, direct, and consolidation loans. Volunteers with Perkins loans are eligible for a 15 percent cancellation of their outstanding balance for each year of Peace Corps service. Because the rules that authorize deferment are complicated and subject to change, it is best to contact your financial lending institution to see how this benefit applies to your situation.

> ### Rewards That Last a Lifetime
>
> The benefits of Peace Corps service don't end with overseas service. It's an experience to draw on for the rest of your life. As is often said, the Peace Corps isn't simply something great. It's the beginning of something great.

Qualifications

There are some specific requirements that need to be met before you can become a Peace Corp volunteer. These qualifications are as follows:

- **All Peace Corps volunteers must be U.S. citizens of at least 18 years of age.**
- **There is no upper age limit. In fact, the oldest volunteer ever to serve in the Peace Corps was 83.**
- **You don't have to know another language.**
- **Having a four-year college degree by the time you're ready to leave for the Peace Corps will help your chances of acceptance. But it isn't absolutely necessary, and for some programs work experience, relevant skills, and/or a community college degree can qualify you.**

Application Process

Applying to become a Peace Corps volunteer is a simple process. The following sections give you all the information that you need to get your application started and how the Peace Corps proceeds after your application is submitted.

Where to Apply

You can apply to become a volunteer by visiting the Peace Corps Web site at http://www.peacecorps.gov/. There you will find information about the Peace Corps as well as the correct application.

You Submit the Application

What's in the application? Well, there are the usual questions about your education, your work and volunteer experience, your interests and hobbies, and so on. There are also a few essay questions to give you a chance to tell us why you want to join the Peace Corps and what you're expecting to get out of the experience. The second part of the application, the Health Status Review, is designed to help us understand your medical situation so we can determine what countries and regions will allow you the best access to the health care you need.

We Contact You for an Interview

You've sent in your application, submitted any additional requests from your regional recruitment office, and now it's time for your Peace Corps interview. The Peace Corps interview generally takes place after you have returned all application materials to your regional recruitment office. The interview will last about an hour and may be conducted in person or over the phone. Here are some topics you and the recruiter will most likely discuss:

- **Your reasons for considering Peace Corps volunteer service**
- **Your expectations and concerns about working overseas for two years**
- **Your past work experiences, including volunteer service, paid employment, and campus or community involvement**
- **Your experiences living and working with people who are different from you**
- **Your preferences and flexibility about Peace Corps volunteer assignments and geographic placement**
- **Personal life issues such as vegetarianism, current romantic relationships, and current financial or legal obligations**

You're Nominated for a Position

After your interview, your recruiter will match your skills with a program that needs those skills and nominate you to that program. When deciding on your nomination, your recruiter is most concerned with finding a fit between your skills and a country's needs. You'll need to be flexible and trust that we will match you up with the program that is best for both you and the community you'll be serving. Nomination means that you will know the general program you will work in, the geographic region, and your approximate departure date.

You Get Medical and Legal Clearance

After you've been nominated, a member of the Peace Corps medical screening team will review your Health Status Review form. You will then be mailed a packet with instructions about your next steps—your physical, dental, and eye exams (see Figure 2.8.12). You'll then see a doctor and dentist and have your eyes checked. You can do all of this locally, through your regular doctors.

Why all the personal questions? We need to have complete and accurate information about your health to place you in a country that has adequate medical facilities to accommodate your health care needs. So answer all the questions honestly and be sure not to leave anything out. The information you provide will be kept confidential.

Many applicants worry that if they have any existing health conditions, they will be automatically disqualified for Peace Corps service. This is not true—in fact, the majority of applicants are medically cleared with no problems, and our medical facilities are capable of handling a range of health conditions. We can also work with you to ensure that you have the prescriptions you need, if this is an issue.

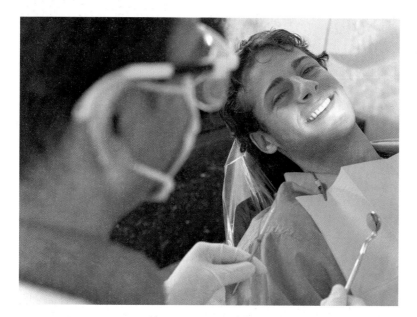

Figure 2.8.12: You are medically assessed before you are sent out into the field.
Courtesy of Brand X/Foto-search.

You Qualify Based on Skills and Suitability

The Peace Corps has established legal standards of eligibility for all applicants. Most legal documentation will be collected before your nomination, but you may be asked for more information during the placement phase of the process about your marital status, dependents, financial obligations, or other circumstances that could affect your eligibility. The final step in legal clearance is a background check through the Federal Bureau of Investigation.

We Contact You with a Placement

The application process is done, but the adventure is just beginning. You've finished your application and interview and sent in all of your medical and legal forms. You're officially cleared and ready to go. At this stage, you'll receive a formal invitation packet in the mail. You'll have 10 days to review it and decide whether you want to accept your invitation to serve as a Peace Corps volunteer. Contact your placement officer within this 10-day window to let him or her know your decision. The invitation packet will include your volunteer job description, the date when you'll depart, passport and visa applications, a pretraining questionnaire, and a volunteer handbook to guide you in preparing for departure. After you've accepted your invitation, we'll send you another packet containing information specific to your destination—resources about the country where you'll be going, what to bring, and a description of the training you'll receive when you arrive. You'll also receive information about your predeparture orientation in the United States Soon you and the other volunteers in your training group will be on your way to your country of service.

Conclusion

Today's Peace Corps is more vital than ever, stepping into new countries such as East Timor, working in emerging and essential areas such as information technology and business development, and committing more than 1,000 new volunteers as a part of President Bush's HIV/AIDS Act of 2003. Peace Corps volunteers continue to help countless individuals who want to build a better life for themselves, their children, and their communities.

From building your professional expertise to gaining a greater understanding of the big picture, the Peace Corps will sharpen your skills, expand your experience, and increase your understanding.

The following lesson introduces you to AmeriCorps and the opportunities you can find through this service organization.

Lesson Review

1. What are the three goals of the Peace Corps?

2. Identify the six operational areas for Peace Corps volunteers.

3. What kinds of qualifications are necessary to become a Peace Corps volunteer?

4. Identify two education benefits available to Peace Corps volunteers.

Lesson 9

AmeriCorps

Key Terms

community service
financial grant
nonprofit group

What You Will Learn to Do

- Explore the purpose and structure of AmeriCorps

Linked Core Abilities

- Do your share as a good citizen in your school, community, country, and the world
- Communicate using verbal, nonverbal, visual, and written techniques

Skills and Knowledge You Will Gain Along the Way

- Explain the mission and goals of AmeriCorps
- Explain how AmeriCorps projects are funded
- Identify groups and organizations supported by AmeriCorps
- Identify the types of programs sponsored by AmeriCorps
- Describe the personal and community benefits of an AmeriCorps project
- Define the key words contained in this lesson

Introduction

Key Note Term

nonprofit group – a group or organization designed not to make or intended to make a profit

AmeriCorps is a network of national service programs that engage more than 50,000 Americans each year in intensive service to meet critical needs in education, public safety, health, and the environment. AmeriCorps members serve through more than 2,100 **nonprofit groups**, public agencies, and faith-based organizations. They tutor and mentor youth, build affordable housing, teach computer skills, clean parks and streams, run after-school programs, and help communities respond to disasters. In this lesson, you learn what opportunities are available to you in the AmeriCorps program.

Origins

Key Note Term

community service – any form of service provided for the community or common good

AmeriCorps was created by the National and **Community Service** Trust Act signed into law by President William Clinton (see Figure 2.9.1) on September 21, 1993. The legislation created the Corporation for National and Community Service to administer AmeriCorps and the other national service programs.

Mission

AmeriCorps has set and defined precise missions:

- **Getting Things Done.** AmeriCorps helps communities meet their education, public safety, human or environmental needs through service. Every AmeriCorps program becomes a powerful model for communities to apply in all of their problem-solving.

- **Strengthening Communities.** AmeriCorps unites individuals from different backgrounds and institutions of all kinds in the common effort to improve our communities.

Figure 2.9.1: President Clinton signed into law the act that created AmeriCorps.
Courtesy of Joyce Naltcha-jan/Getty Images.

- **Encouraging Responsibility.** AmeriCorps encourages members to explore and exercise their responsibilities to their communities, their families, and themselves in their service experience and throughout their lives.

- **Expanding Opportunity.** AmeriCorps helps those who help America. AmeriCorps members receive awards to further their education or pay back their student loans as well as invaluable job experience, specialized training, and life skills.

Organization

AmeriCorps is part of the Corporation for National and Community Service, which in turn is part of USA Freedom Corps, a White House initiative to foster a culture of citizenship, service, and responsibility. President George W. Bush created USA Freedom Corps to coordinate citizen volunteer efforts both domestically and abroad. As part of that initiative, the president called on all Americans to devote the equivalent of at least two years of their lives (4,000 hours) to service and volunteerism. The USA Freedom Corps is working to help every American answer the president's call to service by coordinating various volunteer programs including Citizen Corps, Learn and Serve America, Peace Corps, National Senior Service Corps, and AmeriCorps.

Operations

Fifty thousand Americans are serving their communities 20 to 40 hours a week through AmeriCorps. Most AmeriCorps members are selected by and serve with local and national nonprofit organizations such as Habitat for Humanity (see Figure 2.9.2), the American Red Cross, City Year, Teach for America, and Boys and Girls Clubs of America, as well as with a host of smaller community organizations, both secular and faith-based.

Figure 2.9.2: Habitat for Humanity is one AmeriCorps agency.
Courtesy of Erik S. Lesser/Getty Images.

In exchange for a year of service, AmeriCorps members earn an education award of $4,725 that can be used to pay for college or graduate school or to pay back qualified student loans. About half the members also receive a modest annual living allowance of $9,300 and health benefits.

Programs

AmeriCorps is composed of several different programs. The following sections list and describe these. Does one interest you?

AmeriCorps*State and National

AmeriCorps operates in a decentralized manner that gives a significant amount of responsibility to states and local nonprofit groups. Roughly three-fourths of all AmeriCorps' **financial grant** funding goes to governor-appointed state service commissions, which award grants to nonprofit groups to respond to local needs. Most of the remainder of the grant funding is distributed by the Corporation for National and Community Service directly to multistate and national organizations through a competitive grants process. The organizations that receive grants are responsible for recruiting, selecting, and supervising AmeriCorps members. AmeriCorps grantees include national groups such as the U.S. Veterans Initiative, National Council of La Raza, Catholic Network of Volunteer Service, and Boys and Girls Clubs of America (see Figure 2.9.3), as well as hundreds of smaller faith-based and local community organizations.

AmeriCorps*VISTA

For more than 35 years, AmeriCorps*VISTA (Volunteers in Service to America) members have helped impoverished individuals and communities attain self sufficiency (see Figure 2.9.4). Members serve full-time for a year with nonprofit groups, public agencies, and faith-based organizations throughout the country, working to fight illiteracy, improve health services, create and expand businesses, increase housing opportunities, and bridge the digital divide. Approximately 6,000

Figure 2.9.3: The Boys and Girls Clubs of America are part of AmeriCorps.
Courtesy of Boys & Girls Club of America, © 2001.

Figure 2.9.4: VISTA volunteers help impoverished and disadvantaged Americans.
Courtesy of Anton Vengo/Superstock.

AmeriCorps*VISTA members serve in more than 1,100 local programs; nearly 15 percent of AmeriCorps*VISTA members are assigned to projects that support the work of faith-based organizations.

AmeriCorps*NCCC

AmeriCorps*NCCC (National Civilian Community Corps) is a 10-month, team-based, full-time residential program for men and women between the ages of 18 and 24. It combines the best practices of civilian service with the best aspects of military service, including leadership training and team building. Members serve in diverse teams of 10 to 14 individuals. Priority is given to projects in homeland security and disaster relief. Teams are based at five campuses across the country and are assigned to projects in their respective regions. Approximately 1,200 members serve in AmeriCorps*NCCC.

Initiatives

The Corporation for National and Community Service sponsors AmeriCorps initiatives to teach computer skills, tutor and mentor youth, build new homes, clean the environment, and help communities respond to disasters

National Service Bridging the Digital Divide

Our country is in the middle of a technology revolution, yet too many citizens are being left behind. Studies show that many lower-income families, minorities, and those who live in rural areas lack critical access to technology. You can help close the digital divide. As an AmeriCorps member, you can spend the next year bringing technology to people who need it (see Figure 2.9.5). You can work one-on-one with young people, introducing them to computers and the wonders of the Internet; help a local nonprofit build a Web site; connect a Native American community to the information superhighway; help adult learners; assist teachers; or organize volunteers.

Figure 2.9.5: Introduce young people to the Internet and teach them how to use computers.
Courtesy of Gideon Mendel/Corbis Images.

National Service and Literacy

The Corporation for National and Community Service, through AmeriCorps, National Senior Service Corps, and Learn and Serve America, is making national service a vehicle to mobilize and increase the numbers of tutors to support the literacy development of young children. All children must learn to read well and independently and master the fundamentals of mathematics to get on track to college and a good job. To accomplish this, the Corporation for National and Community Service supports the following types of activities:

- **AmeriCorps*State and National has 439 programs that have literacy as a component of their service with a total of more than 13,500 full- and part-time members.**
- **AmeriCorps*VISTA has more than 332 projects with a total of 2,375 members. Members recruit volunteers and help manage local literacy programs.**
- **AmeriCorps*NCCC has worked on over 20 literacy projects around the country. Members have tutored children, planned education programs, and conducted outreach to parents.**

National Service and Math

AmeriCorps offers funding and resources to improve math skills, including the following:

- **MathPARTNERS.** This is a project that developed a mentoring curriculum to accompany the America Counts mathematics initiative. The project is no longer active, but the mentoring curriculum and the mentor training materials are still available at no cost.
- **Eisenhower Regional Consortia and Clearinghouse.** This National Network works collaboratively to improve and strengthen K–12 mathematics and science education for all. It is a unique regional and national system that provides professional development, fosters collaboration, and disseminates exemplary products and resources.

National Service and Faith-Based Organizations

Across the country, faith-based organizations are on the front lines, working to improve lives in some of the hardest pressed communities in America. Giving vital help to these efforts are the volunteers supported by the Corporation for National and Community Service. Created by Congress in 1993, the Corporation for National and Community Service provides opportunities for 1.5 million Americans of all ages to engage in service to address the nation's pressing unmet needs through three programs: AmeriCorps, Learn and Serve America, and the National Senior Service Corps. Tens of thousands of these volunteers serve with faith-based organizations.

AmeriCorps gives citizens the opportunity to engage in full-time service to their community. Working through more than 1,000 national and local nonprofit and faith-based organizations, AmeriCorps members tutor and mentor at-risk children; make schools and neighborhoods safer; build homes; and do other tasks that make communities stronger. Of the 50,000 AmeriCorps positions this year, more than 6,000 are in faith-based organizations.

National Service and Homeland Security

The 9-11 attacks and the possibility of future terrorist actions have created daunting new challenges in the area of homeland security. New threats and increased demands face our nation's public safety, health and emergency preparedness officials. Meeting this demand will require action on many fronts, including tapping the nation's volunteer and national service resources. The Corporation for National and Community Service engages more than 2 million citizens in AmeriCorps, The National Senior Service Corps, and Learn and Serve America. Many of these citizens now provide services in public safety, public health and disaster relief.

Public Safety

Public safety is one of the four primary service activities for AmeriCorps and The National Senior Service Corps. Thousands of volunteers serve with and for police departments and land management agencies. They are not armed, nor can they make arrests, but they carry out vital tasks including organizing neighborhood watch groups (see Figure 2.9.6), community policing, victim assistance, fingerprinting and other administrative tasks that free officers to do frontline work. In five years, AmeriCorps has organized 46,000 safety patrols, and last year alone senior volunteers carried out 131,000 patrols that freed up 540,000 hours of police time.

Public Health

AmeriCorps members and National Senior Service Corps volunteers provide a variety of public health services including immunizing children and adults, serving as case managers, distributing health information, and providing health screenings. Last year alone, AmeriCorps members distributed health information to 500,000 people and conducted health screenings of 181,000 individuals; while National Senior Service Corps volunteers assisted in immunizing 270,000 children and adults.

Figure 2.9.6: Community neighborhood watch groups help make neighborhoods safer.
Courtesy of David Cummins
Eye Uniquitous/Corbis
Images.

Disaster Preparedness and Relief

From hurricanes and tornadoes to forest fires and floods, AmeriCorps members and National Senior Service Corps volunteers specially trained in disaster relief have responded to disasters in more than 30 states (see Figure 2.9.7). Volunteers have a long track record of working with FEMA and other relief agencies in helping run emergency shelters, assisting law enforcement, providing food and shelter, managing donations, and helping families and communities rebuild. Hundreds of national service volunteers have directly assisted victims of the 9-11 terrorist attacks by providing family services, organizing blood drives, and raising funds and counseling victim's families.

Figure 2.9.7: AmeriCorps and National Senior Service Corps volunteers performed invaluable services after the hurricanes ravaged Florida in 2004.
Courtesy of AP/Wide World
Photos.

Joining AmeriCorps

There are three different ways to receive an AmeriCorps application and apply to the program(s) of your choice:

- **Apply on-line directly at http://www.americorps.org/. Complete the application one time and send it electronically to up to 10 programs at a time.**

- **Download the AmeriCorps application, complete it, and send it by mail to each program (requires Acrobat Reader).**

- **Contact 1-800-942-2677 or e-mail questions @americorps.org to request an application kit.**

Conclusion

AmeriCorps strengthens communities through projects that address education, public safety, the environment, and other unmet human needs. AmeriCorps members develop and implement projects to address these needs and learn new skills in the process. In exchange for their service with AmeriCorps, members earn money for college. If your community has a need that you think could benefit from AmeriCorps support, take a look at the different programs within AmeriCorps.

This lesson concludes the Service to the Nation chapter. You have learned about the various arms of the military as well as about the Peace Corps and AmeriCorps. Each entity offers a wide variety of opportunities to you.

Chapter 2

Lesson Review

Lesson Review

1. **List the four missions of AmeriCorps.**
2. **Identify the three major programs of AmeriCorps.**
3. **What is the purpose of AmeriCorps*State and National?**
4. **Describe at least one way AmeriCorps supports homeland security.**

Leadership Theory and Application

Being a Leader

Leadership Defined

Key Terms

behavior
direction
leadership
motivation
purpose

What You Will Learn to Do

- Identify your leadership strengths and opportunities for improvement

Linked Core Abilities

- Communicate using verbal, nonverbal, visual, and written techniques
- Take responsibility for your actions and choices
- Treat self and others with respect

Skills and Knowledge You Will Gain Along the Way

- Describe leader behaviors that create the desire to follow
- Explore leader behaviors related to purpose, direction, and motivation
- Identify ways to develop leadership behaviors
- Define the key words contained in this lesson

Introduction

It is important to have a clear definition of leadership and a precise vision of what it takes to lead. This lesson covers leadership behavior and how those actions relate to purpose, direction, and motivation. You learn how to identify way to develop your own personal leadership behaviors.

Defining Leadership

One definition of **leadership** is the ability to influence others to accomplish a mission in the manner desired by providing purpose, direction, and motivation.

Purpose is the reason for doing what has been requested. **Direction** gives the knowledge to do what has been requested. **Motivation** gives others the will to do what has been requested.

The interaction between purpose, direction, and motivation create a variety of situations that require specific leader and follower **behaviors** to accomplish the mission; therefore, the BE, KNOW, DO leadership framework can be applied to both leader and follower. The role of the leader and follower in a specific situation is seen in Figure 1.1.1.

Peter Drucker, a highly regarded researcher of management and organizations, defines a leader as someone who has followers, gets followers to do the "right thing," sets examples, takes responsibility, asks what needs to be done, is tolerant of diversity, and is a "doer."

Within organizations, people are assigned to positions of authority and responsibility. They have others reporting to them for whom they are responsible. This is called the chain of command and is an important part of organizational structure. In team sports, the coach is the leader and gives direction to team members. A similar structure exists in scouts, churches, schools, and government.

Drucker's definition of leadership, however, is not confined to a leader assigned to a position within a chain of command. If you have no followers, there is no one to lead and therefore no leader exists. If you have followers, assigned or otherwise, that you are influencing to accomplish something, Drucker would identify you as a leader.

Key Note Terms

leadership – the ability to influence, lead, or guide others to accomplish a mission in the manner desired

purpose – something set up as an object or end to be attained

direction – an explicit instruction

motivation – provide a need or a purpose which causes a person to want to do something

behavior – the manner of conducting oneself

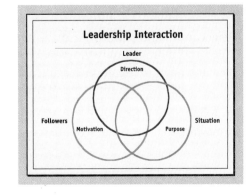

Figure 1.1.1: Leadership interaction.
Courtesy of US Army JROTC.

As a high school student do you think of yourself as a leader? Do you influence others? Your friends ? Your brother or sister? Do you influence members of a team in your school? Your church? Scouts? JROTC? Sure you do!

You may not have the chain of command positional authority, but you lead by setting the example for your brothers and sisters. You persuade your friends to do something they had not thought possible. You even lead yourself. In fact, that is where leadership begins—WITHIN YOU!

Being a leader is an awesome responsibility. Are you leading others to do the right thing? Take a look at a few case studies. After you have read all three cases, make a list of the leader behaviors in each and identify if they were used effectively, ineffectively, or not at all; then, add any leader behaviors you think would be important to you. Finally, ask yourself, which leader behaviors do I possess right now? And, which behaviors do I need to improve to become a good leader?

Case Studies

Which leader behaviors do you possess right now? Which behaviors do you need to improve to become a good leader? Think about these two questions as you read the following case studies. They will give you the opportunity to see how three very different people effectively used some leadership behaviors, failed to use others effectively, or did not apply some of them at all. Read each case study carefully.

Case #1

Jon is normally an average student; however, when he takes charge of a group to complete a project, his work and the finished effort of the group are always outstanding.

When asked about his group's results, his teammates proudly answered, "Jon makes it easy for us to complete our tasks. He helps us and makes suggestions when we need help, but he lets us do the work. If we have a problem, he always listens to our ideas on how to fix it.

"Because he is always excited about what he is doing, we get excited, too. He seems to know all he can about a task before we get started on it. While we are doing the task, he respects our views about how to complete it. He effectively uses the talents of everyone on the team, and he makes smart decisions. He is always there for us if we need him and, somehow, he still finds the time to do his share of the project. Because of his effective work habits, he instills good works habits in us also.

"He accepts responsibility for the outcome of our tasks, whether good or bad. None of us wants a project to be done poorly, but he does not blame others for any mistakes that he or the team may have made. After finishing one task, we are always glad to begin the next project under his direction."

Would you like to be a member of Jon's team? What are his desirable characteristics? What are his undesirable characteristics?

Case #2

Maria knows exactly what her position is all about. She gets excited whenever an instructor assigns her a project because she knows that she can get it done. Sometimes, she even suggests projects to her instructor. Based on her ideas, the instructor usually assigns them to her and her team.

Maria is highly motivated and has very structured work habits. She likes to map out a project in which everything is her decision. She then tells her team members how to do each step of their tasks according to her direction. She watches everything that her team members do, and if they appear to be doing a task differently from her plan, she criticizes them.

Maria got upset once when a teammate was caught cheating. At first, she was afraid to talk to that person about the incident, and she did not know what to say to her peers who had also heard about it. Finally, after asking herself how she would like to be treated if she were the one involved, she called a team meeting.

At the meeting, Maria informed everyone that all team members make mistakes, not only as a team but also as individuals. She hoped that if they ever had any problems, they would turn to her and/or to another team member for help. They agreed.

Would you like to be a member of Maria's team? What are her desirable characteristics? What are her undesirable characteristics?

Case #3

Brian is an easygoing person. He wants to complete projects with plenty of time left so that he and his friends on the team can relax. After he assigns tasks to each of his team members, he lets them figure out the best way to complete the tasks—without giving them any help, direction, or supervision. Plus, he rarely makes any decisions.

Then, when the time comes to complete the project, he still turns it in even though parts of it are not finished. When the final grade comes back, his group makes the lowest mark in the class, prompting an instructor to ask, "Why wasn't your project done?"

Brian passes the blame on to his team members by saying, "They didn't complete their parts like they should have. I don't believe that I should have to be responsible for or to receive a bad grade because of their sloppy efforts."

When the other team members find out their grades, they approach Brian, "Why didn't you tell us everything that we were supposed to do? We could have worked harder and did it better if we had just known."

Would you like to be a member of Brian's team? What are his desirable characteristics? What are his undesirable characteristics?

Reflection Questions

These three case studies illustrate the positive and negative application of leader behaviors. Do you possess any of them? What do you appreciate most about your leader behaviors? Can you identify which behaviors you need to work on to become an effective leader? Would you like to change or add any of them? Can you identify any positive behaviors in other people that you would like to adopt? In the next case study, see if you can pick up ways to add new leadership behaviors to your character.

Case #4

Jason North had an opportunity one day to visit his father at work. He noticed that his dad's employees worked very hard for him. However, Peter, a mechanic who had worked on the assembly line for many years, seemed to resist all friendliness or help from the others. He also avoided speaking to Mr. North most of the time.

That afternoon, while the other employees and Jason were present, Mr. North approached Peter. He asked him, "What do you think of us purchasing the MXR-78 to help increase the production of the assembly line?"

Peter answered, "Why are you asking me? I really don't know much about it."

Mr. North responded, "You have a lot of experience here, and I would like you to find out if the MXR-78 would make the line run more efficiently. So, will you do this for me?" With urging from the others, Peter accepted.

Later that evening, Jason asked his dad, "Why did you ask Peter to do that job?" Mr. North replied, "Peter is a reliable and experienced employee. He just needed some individual recognition. So, I gave him that assignment to make him feel more a part of this team."

Note

Although the previous story is just one example that pertains to only several leadership behaviors, Jason can definitely learn from his father's approach in dealing with Peter. A positive role model like Mr. North can be a powerful influence in one's desire to adopt another person's positive leadership behaviors.

Making the Change

After you identify behaviors that you want to have, then what? Think of ways to fit the behavior into your personality and into the way you want to lead. Use that skill whenever it is appropriate—practice will make it a part of your style.

On the other hand, changing a negative behavior into a positive one is not easy. It may be similar to breaking an old habit. Use the following steps to change a negative behavior:

1. **Realize the need for change.**
2. **Have a positive attitude toward the change.**
3. **Follow through.**

Change is never easy, so keep trying. Just like other tasks, change requires dedication and perseverance.

Conclusion

Now is the time to begin identifying the leadership behaviors that you would like to possess. By adding new behaviors and/or changing negative ones, you can have a major influence on the development of your leadership potential. If you can perform a task a certain way and can see it through to completion, this positive behavior can become a lifetime habit.

The next lesson covers leadership traits, behaviors, and contingencies. You will continue to study what makes an effective leader, and how you can hone your leadership skills.

Lesson Review

1. **What did you learn about how you influence others?**
2. **How effective do you think you are in influencing others?**
3. **Are there some leadership characteristics you would like to adopt? Why?**
4. **Define the term *motivation*.**

Chapter 1

Leadership Reshuffled

Key Term

approach

What You Will Learn to Do

- Compare leadership styles

Linked Core Abilities

- Take responsibility for your actions and choices
- Treat self and others with respect

Skills and Knowledge You Will Gain Along the Way

- Describe how leadership has evolved
- Compare different approaches to leadership
- Discuss what leadership styles work best in different situations
- Define the key word contained in this lesson

Introduction

History shows that there has been a great interest in determining what makes a good leader. In fact, studies can be traced back as far as the end of the nineteenth century during the industrial revolution. As a result, leadership studies have been categorized into three general eras:

- **Traits—1800s to 1940s**
- **Behaviors—1940s to 1970s**
- **Contingency—1960s to present**

In this lesson, you learn what it takes to be a leader, and examine different leadership styles.

Traits Approach

During the late nineteenth century and early twentieth century, it was believed that leaders were born. It was a man's heritage that provided this innate ability to lead. One was born with special characteristics or traits to enable him to lead others effectively.

To prove this philosophy, spanning some 40 years, researchers studied existing political, industrial, and religious leaders. They expected to find that these leaders would possess certain characteristics that would distinguish them from their followers (see Figure 1.2.1).

The researchers were unable to provide evidence to support their belief that leaders are born. Their findings identified a number of traits that were common to those in leadership positions; traits such as intelligence, dependability, sociability,

Figure 1.2.1: Are humans born with the ability to lead or is this a developed trait?
Courtesy of Bettman/Corbis Images.

aggressiveness, originality, popularity, and humor. However, they also found different situations required the use of different traits. Others concluded there was no evidence to support that just having those traits would help one become a leader, much less an effective leader.

These inconsistent findings led others to continue the search for predictions and understanding of how effective leaders lead. There was an accepted belief that a combination of traits was one element of the equation. Personality alone, however, was not proven to be the only or even the dominant factor in leading others.

Behavior Approach

At the advent of World War II, researchers began to expand their search for the source of leader effectiveness. They began to look at and categorize the "behaviors" of effective leaders. They felt this was a more positive research **approach** because behaviors can be observed much more objectively, they can be measured more precisely, and they can be taught.

A researcher by the name of Kurt Lewin (1938) provided the foundation for the behavior approach of leadership. He identified a continuum of leadership behaviors that included the following:

- **Democratic style of consulting with their followers and allowing them to participate in decision making**
- **Autocratic style of making the decisions alone**
- **Laissez-faire style of providing no direction at all**

> **Note**
>
> Kurt Lewin, born in Germany in 1890, was considered by some to be the most charismatic psychologist of his time. His formal training in psychology began in 1910 in Berlin and led to a Ph.D. in the experimental study of associative learning. To learn more about Lewin, go to http://www.utexas.edu/coc/journalism/SOURCE/j363/lewin.html.

Although very different behaviors were identified, there was no evidence as to which style was most effective and which style to use in what situation. Additionally, each style created different reactions from different followers; therefore, the researchers could not clearly articulate the best way to lead effectively.

The Ohio State Leadership Studies, held at Ohio State University starting in 1945 and continuing through the 1960s, continued the search for leader behaviors. Almost 2,000 behaviors were identified and subsequently reduced to a more manageable number; however, two primary leadership behaviors stood out among the many: relationship and structure.

Relationship behaviors dealt with the concern for people and included behaviors such as treating team members as equals, being friendly and approachable, making work pleasant, listening to other's ideas, and looking out for the personal well-being of others.

Structure behaviors dealt with the concern for task and included such behaviors as setting and communicating expectations, establishing work schedules, sharing work procedures, and making work assignments.

There was some evidence coming forth that people-oriented leaders were linked with follower satisfaction levels and that effective leadership required both task and relationship behaviors. However, a few questions remained. Does effective leadership come from just the traits and behaviors of the leader? How are traits and behaviors influenced by the type of task and the type of work group?

Contingency Approach

Even though there was the desire to include situational factors in leadership effectiveness studies, this inclusion did not happen until the 1960s. This approach assumes that the effectiveness of the leader's personality, style, and behavior is contingent upon the requirements of the situation and further supports the belief that

- **There is no one best way to lead**
- **The situational factors will determine the most effective style and behaviors**
- **You can teach leadership behaviors**
- **The leader does have an impact on group or organization effectiveness**
- **Leadership effectiveness is affected by the interaction between situational factors and personal characteristics**

Modern approaches to leadership effectiveness have a somewhat integrated view of traits, behavioral, and contingency approaches. Historically, researchers have studied leader behaviors by observing executives in a variety of organizations. If the definition of leadership is agreed as "the ability to influence, lead, or guide others to accomplish a mission in the manner desired by providing purpose, direction and motivation," should the behaviors of anyone who influences others be examined? Are *all* humans, leaders in families, schools, communities, and life?

As a result of these historical perspectives, several approaches to leadership style have been identified. Those most common are the trait approach, the situational approach, the follower approach and the contingency model.

- **The trait approach maintains that a person either does or does not possess the specific traits that are considered to be the essentials of leadership.**
- **The situational approach assumes that certain situations call for specific types of leadership behaviors and that the leaders will be those who best fit the requirements of the situation.**
- **The follower approach holds that the needs of group members determine who will lead. Leadership, then, is a coincidence between the needs of the group and the abilities a person happens to have.**
- **The contingency model maintains that personal styles and situational characteristics combine to determine leadership. A proper match between styles and situations is essential.**

What does all this mean to you? To answer that, return to the definition of leadership:

Leadership is the ability (or process) to influence, lead, or guide others so as to accomplish a mission in the manner desired by providing purpose, direction, and motivation.

There have been studies over a number of years directed at gaining more understanding about effective leadership. The desire to assist people in the behaviors that effectively influence, lead, and guide others remains a highly regarded search. The more you understand the behaviors that create the desire to follow, the more you will be able to determine the leadership behaviors that will work best for you; more importantly, the ones that do not.

Have you ever wondered how some leaders influence, excite, stimulate, and energize others? When you were influenced, excited, stimulated, or energized by someone else to do something you thought impossible, did you reflect on those times so you could copy the behaviors you liked? Think of those teachers you remember most. What was it they did that made you remember them?

Conclusion

As researchers continue to study the characteristics of leaders, and as the world continues to change through technology and human growth, one common key ingredient to leading others successfully is the ability to successfully lead oneself. Leading from the inside out is the foundation to building successful relationships in your family, church, community, and school. Your relationships with others are the foundation of trust, and trust is the foundation to empowerment and alignment of the mission you are leading others to accomplish.

The following lesson takes a look at leadership from the inside out. You will examine what it takes to be an effective leader by looking inward.

Lesson Review

1. **What are the three general eras into which leadership studies have been categorized?**

2. **Compare and contrast the traits, behavior, and contingency approaches to leadership.**

3. **Give a definition of leadership.**

4. **Which two behaviors stood out from the rest in the Ohio State Leadership Studies?**

Leadership from the Inside Out

Key Terms

beliefs
bribery
coercion
dilemma
ethics
favoritism
norms
prejudices
selfless service
tenets
tunnel vision
unethical
values

What You Will Learn to Do

- Develop a personal code of ethics, comparing the values it represents with the Army values

Linked Core Abilities

- Communicate using verbal, nonverbal, visual, and written techniques
- Take responsibility for your actions and choices
- Apply critical thinking techniques

Skills and Knowledge You Will Gain Along the Way

- Describe the values that leaders possess
- Assess how attitudes affect a person's actions
- Explore how life experiences affect a person's values
- Describe how the similarities and differences in people's values can impact how they interact with others

- **Relate your values to the seven Army values**
- **Define the key words contained in this lesson**

Introduction

Values are the driving force behind an action. When a leader gives his or her unit a particular mission, it is usually based on what that leader believes to be right. The leader's decisions and actions as well as the followers' actions must be motivated by their inherent values whether they are strong feelings of right vs. wrong, ethical vs. unethical, or important for the majority vs. important just for personal gain.

America needs leaders who possess character and competence. They must be willing and able to live up to a defined set of values, possess the required attributes, and develop the required skills. This lesson covers how to take an inventory of your values and how those values can help you as a leader of others.

Defining Values

Values are ideas about the worth or importance of things, concepts, and people. They come from your **beliefs** or attitudes, and they influence your behavior because you use them to decide between alternatives. You may, for example, place value on such things as truth, money, friendship, justice, or selflessness.

Your values can influence your priorities. Because they are the basis for beliefs and attitudes, you may become emotional regarding certain issues. These values begin early in life and develop throughout your adulthood. You develop, process, evaluate, and prioritize beliefs or values in an order of importance that helps guide your daily existence in society. Strong values are what you put first, what you will defend most, and what you want to give up least.

There are seven individual values that all leaders and followers possess: *loyalty, duty, respect, selfless service, honor, integrity,* and *personal courage*. By listing these values in this order, note that they spell out the acronym: LDRSHIP, pronounced *leadership*. When used correctly, these values are the basis for building trust in relationships. They should be at the core of your character. The more you develop these values in yourself, the more successful you will be in life.

> **Loyalty.** To bear true faith and allegiance to the U.S. Constitution . . . and your peers.
>
> **Duty.** To fulfill your obligations.
>
> **Respect.** To treat people as they should be treated.
>
> **Selfless service.** To put the welfare of the nation . . . before your own.
>
> **Honor.** To live up to all values.
>
> **Integrity.** To do what is right, legally and morally.
>
> **Personal courage.** To face fear, danger, or adversity.

Key Note Terms

values – a principle, standard, or quality considered worthwhile or desirable in a person or group; an ideal

beliefs – a personal truth; mental acceptance or conviction of particular truths of someone or something

Sometimes values will conflict. Suppose your value of *loyalty* conflicts with your value of *integrity*. For example, if your supervisor wants you to write up a report on an incident in a manner that does not reflect the truth, you still have the moral responsibility to prepare it honestly. Whatever you decide in this example, the quality that you value most will guide your actions. The following sections discuss each of these values.

Loyalty

Loyalty establishes the correct ordering of your obligations and commitments. Traditional American values place loyalty in order of family, God, and country. Loyalty to family means providing for the safety, security, health, and well-being of those you depend on and those who depend on you. Placing family first will free you to take care of other obligations. Loyalty to God means building your moral character to maintain strength in the face of adversity. And loyalty to country means upholding the laws and Constitution of the United States and participating as a good citizen to sustain our democracy. Members of the US Armed Forces demonstrate ultimate loyalty to country by offering to give their lives in defense of the Constitution. To exhibit the value of loyalty, you must

- **Respect the U.S. Constitution and its laws**
- **Demonstrate strong moral character and virtue**
- **Show faithfulness to your family, friends, and peers**

Duty

Duty is a commitment to fulfilling obligations. Everybody has obligations to self, family, friends, society, and humanity (see Figure 1.3.1). Performing one's duty is complicated by the fact some obligations are difficult, time consuming, unpleasant, and dangerous. Members of the US Armed Forces are expected to demonstrate continual devotion to duty. Devotion to duty means always fulfilling your expected obligations without fail. Leaders are expected to perform "above and beyond" the call of duty, always doing more than expected. And finally, the military's highest award, the Medal of Honor, is reserved for those who demonstrate selfless duty in conditions of extreme danger.

To exhibit the value of duty, you must

- **Carry out the requirements of your job**
- **Meet professional standards**
- **Fulfill your legal, civic, and moral obligations**

Respect

Respect is recognition of the positive value a person represents to another person or organization. Respect is reciprocal; it must be both given and received to be properly recognized. Respect is earned by deeds and accomplishment. Respect can be lost by misdeeds and incompetence. Once lost, respect is difficult to regain. Respect is an important element of trust, which is a critical component of teamwork, which is the foundation of leadership. People won't follow leaders they don't respect. To exhibit this value, you must

Figure 1.3.1: Duty can be anything from loyalty to country to honoring family commitments.
Courtesy of Brian Leng/Corbis Images.

- **Treat all people with dignity**
- **Demonstrate consideration for others**
- **Create a climate of fairness**

Selfless Service

Key Note Term

selfless service – a willingness to put the welfare of others first; to sacrifice, if need be, even to the point of giving up one's own life, in service to the nation

Selfless service, placing the concerns of others before your own, is another essential element of teamwork and trust. People won't follow leaders they don't trust. Selfless service builds the bonds of trust by ensuring followers their leaders will always do what is right with the best interests of their people uppermost in mind.

To exhibit the value of selfless service, you must

- **Focus your priorities on service to your community or to the nation**
- **Place the needs of the organization above personal gain**

Honor

Honor represents the set of all values (courage, duty, integrity, loyalty, respect, and selfless service) that make up the public code for Army JROTC.

Honor and moral identity stand together because individuals identify with group values and norms. Significantly, the value of honor provides the motive for action. Honor demands adherence to a public moral code, not the protection of an individual's reputation. To exhibit the value of honor, you must

- **Adhere to and identify with a public code of professional values**
- **Employ honor as your motive for action**

Integrity

Integrity, coming from the Latin root of *integritas*—which is also the same root for the word *integer*—refers to a notion of completeness, wholeness, and uniqueness.

From this foundation, the meaning of integrity encompasses the sum total of a person's set of values: *it is that person's private moral code.* A breach of any of these values will damage the integrity of that individual. To exhibit the value of integrity, you must

- **Possess a high standard of moral values and principles**
- **Show good moral judgment**
- **Demonstrate consistent moral behavior**

Doing the Right Thing

The commanding officer and staff of doctors and nurses of a Mobile Army Surgical Hospital (MASH) worked on the wounded Americans who poured in from the latest fire fight. The medics also brought in a Vietnamese soldier with a live, unexploded grenade embedded in his flesh. Ordnance experts informed the commander that the slightest movement of the firing pin could set off the device, killing everyone in the area.

Acting quickly, the commander directed the hospital staff to use available materials and equipment to build a sandbag barricade around the operating table; then, performing the operation alone, he delicately removed the grenade. He wrapped it carefully in a flak jacket and handed it to the demolition team. The operation was successful, and the patient lived. His integrity and commitment to save the life of another human being made this commander an excellent doctor, leader, and role model.

Personal Courage

Personal courage comes in two forms. *Physical courage* is overcoming fears of bodily harm and doing your duty. *Moral courage* is overcoming fears of other than bodily harm while doing what needs to be done (see Figure 1.3.2). Personal courage involves the ability to perform critical self-assessment, to confront new ideas, and to change. To exhibit this value, you must

- **Conquer fear in physical and moral contexts**
- **Take responsibility for decisions and actions**
- **Demonstrate a capacity to learn and grow**

Key Note Term

tenets – a principle, belief, or doctrine generally held to be true

Personal courage is rooted in believing in yourself, your fellow teammates, your unit, and your devotion to the mission of the organization. Throughout history, courageous people have accomplished the seemingly impossible and followed the basic **tenets** of a Code of Conduct (a set of guidelines that in the US Armed Forces specifies how service members are to conduct themselves in combat and in the event they are taken prisoner by the enemy).

Moral courage is standing up for your values, moral principles, and convictions. You show moral courage when you do something based on one of your values or moral principles, knowing that the action may not be in your best interest. It takes special courage to support unpopular decisions and to make it difficult for others to do the wrong thing.

Others may encourage you to choose the course of action that is less ethical, the easiest, or the most convenient; however, do not make it easy for others to do

Figure 1.3.2: New York firefighters displayed both physical and moral courage on 9-11.
Courtesy of Bernd Obermann/Corbis Images.

wrong. Stand up for your beliefs and for what you know is right. Do not compromise your individual values or moral principles. In the end, by following your principles, you will be earning the respect and trust of the team.

Colin Powell: A Study in Leadership

From his early days at City College of New York, to his stint as a White House Fellow, to National Security Advisor for President Reagan, Chairman of the Joint Chiefs of Staff for President George H. W. Bush, to Secretary of State for President George W. Bush, Colin Powell rose through the ranks of military and political power. Leadership played a large part in the evolution of such a stellar career. At a crucial point in the career of any leader, the ability to influence others to make the right decision can be a great challenge. All leaders must have advocates, be aware of their adversaries, convince peers, subordinates, and superiors, to support their decisions and recommendations. Such is the case of Colin Powell (see Figure 1.3.3).

The son of Jamaican immigrants, Powell was raised in the South Bronx. He was educated in the New York City public schools and at City College of New York (CCNY). He participated in ROTC at CCNY and received a commission as an Army second lieutenant upon graduation. He subsequently received a Master of Business Administration degree from George Washington University.

Powell served two tours of duty in Vietnam and as a battalion commander in Korea. He later commanded the 2nd Brigade, 101st Airborne Division (Air Assault) and V Corps, US Army, Europe. Prior to being named as Chairman of the Joint Chiefs of Staff, he served as the Commander in Chief, Forces Command, headquartered at Fort McPherson, Georgia.

General Powell has been the recipient of numerous U.S. military decorations, including the Defense Distinguished Service Medal, Bronze Star Medal, and the Purple Heart. His civilian awards include the Presidential Medal of Freedom, the Congressional Gold Medal, and an honorary knighthood (Knight Commander of the Bath) from the Queen of England. He retired from the US Army in 1993.

Powell left his position as Secretary of State in 2005 with the admiration and respect of people around the world. Powell has been a shining example of values and integrity throughout his career, which he continues in his retirement.

Figure 1.3.3: General (Retired) Colin Powell.
Courtesy of Reuters/Corbis Images.

Norms

To live together in harmony, people must agree on certain beliefs and values that lead to group **norms** or rules of conduct. Norms can be formal; they can also be informal or unwritten rules or standards of conduct that govern behavior of group members.

Formal norms are generally policies or regulations, such as traffic signals, laws, or safety codes. They dictate actions that are required or forbidden. For example, your school could have a formal norm that allows you to make up tests after you have been sick.

On the other hand, students may have an informal norm between them where they agree to lend each other notes so that they can copy the classwork they missed when absent. This norm comes from a shared value about the importance of helping out a fellow classmate.

An informal norm can also run against a group's goal. For example, students who want to be accepted by their peers may feel pressure to follow destructive informal norms, such as using drugs or cutting classes.

Importance of Beliefs, Values, and Norms

Beliefs, values, and norms guide the actions of individuals and groups. They are like a traffic control system—signals giving direction, meaning, and purpose to our lives. They are powerful. Past experiences involving such things as family, school, church, work, and social relationships shape your individual values, beliefs, and attitudes. Understand the importance of nurturing and shaping these qualities in your followers because they are fundamental motivating factors.

> ### Key Note Term
>
> **norms** – a principle of right action binding upon members of a group and serving to guide, control, or regulate proper and acceptable behavior; a pattern or trait taken to be typical in the behavior of a social group

Mutual respect between you and your team members motivates them to follow your orders. Make it a general rule to think through situations and choose the course of action that will gain you the long-term respect of your followers, seniors, and peers. By earning their respect, you will be exerting your influence on their beliefs, values, and norms.

Character

Character is a person's inner strength; it is not only a major factor that determines how a person behaves, it is also the link (or interaction) between values and behaviors. For example, a person of character does what he or she believes is right, regardless of the dangers or circumstances involved, whereas a person's behavior shows his or her character. The three interacting parts that make up a person's character and competence are values, attributes, and skills. Each one of these parts must interact to have a complete and well-balanced character.

There is no simple formula for success in the situations that you may face, either as a leader or in life. The key is to remain flexible and attempt to gather as many facts as the circumstances will allow before you must make a decision. When dealing with others, every situation has two sides; listen to both. The way you handle challenges depends on how you interact with the factors of leadership (followers, the leader, the situation, and communications).

Character can be strong or weak. People with strong character recognize what they want and have the drive, energy, self-discipline, willpower, and courage to get it; people with weak character do not know what is needed and lack purpose, willpower, self-discipline, and courage.

Furthermore, people who can admit when they are wrong are exhibiting strong character, but people who place blame on someone or something else are indicating a weak character, which their followers will readily recognize.

People want to be led by leaders who provide strength, inspiration, and guidance and will help them to become winners. How much they are willing to trust a leader depends on their assessment of that leader's courage, competence, and commitment.

Character Building

You build strong and honorable character over time by hard work, study, and challenging experiences. You must also understand yourself—your strengths and weaknesses. Be open to feedback and advice from others; however, you must take the responsibility for continually building and strengthening your character. Others can help, but they cannot do it for you. To build strong and honorable character, you should

- **Assess the present strength of your values and character**
- **Determine what values you want to promote**
- **Seek out tasks and situations that support developing such character**
- **Select a role model who demonstrates the values and character you want to develop**

Ethics

Ethics are principles or standards that guide professionals to do the moral or right thing—that is, what ought to be done. Because leaders are decision makers, they must make choices based on values and beliefs; however, sometimes it takes more than beliefs and values to come to a wise decision. A leader must also employ those principles or standards that guide them to do the moral and right thing. It is your responsibility as a leader to do the right thing.

> **Note**
>
> The difference between a manager and a leader is that a manager always does things right; a leader always does the right thing.

Sometimes leaders are put in situations where two or more values conflict, otherwise known as a **dilemma**. You may have to choose between two or more undesirable alternatives. Perhaps you are faced with a simple dilemma, such as when you choose between going hungry or eating something you really dislike.

An ethical dilemma, on the other hand, is more complicated because an individual must decide between two or more values that are at odds. When you find yourself in an ethical dilemma, you must search for the morally right thing to do (see Figure 1.3.4). The right thing to do is the moral action that best serves the ideals of your organization or group. The "highest moral good" is what professional ethics are all about.

If you make the right decisions when faced with an ethical problem, you will continually build your character and leadership. If you fall into the trap of taking the easy way once or twice, however, you will tend to justify your actions and then begin to erode your character. Your followers will sense this over a period of time and gradually lose respect for you. You will then be forced to use **coercion** to motivate them and will eventually lose the necessary foundation for positive, inspired leadership.

Key Note Terms

ethics – rules, principles, or standards that guide individuals or groups to do the moral or right thing in accordance with accepted principles of right and wrong

dilemma – an argument presenting two or more equally conclusive alternatives against an opponent

Key Note Term

coercion – the act, process, or power of forcing someone to act or think in a given manner, such as by using force or threats as a form of control

Figure 1.3.4: At one point or another, everyone encounters an ethical dilemma.
Courtesy of Corbis Images.

Pressures to Be Unethical

Anyone can be ethical when there are no pressures to be **unethical**. At times, however, there are certain things such as personal ambition, convenience, greed, and **prejudices** that get in the way of ethical behavior. After all, leaders have human desires and motivations.

Sometimes there is pressure to bend or break the rules a little to get a promotion, gain popularity, or make it easier on a subordinate. The saying *the end justifies the means* could provide every leader with an easy excuse for doing something questionable. Leaders must be aware of these temptations and guard against them by maintaining a professional code of ethics.

A principle, a belief, or a value is but a concept until it is tested under pressure. The following are a few examples of some temptations that can get you into trouble.

Setting Impossible Goals

There are times when leaders demand too much from the team or from individuals. Perhaps they have no idea of what the task entails, or maybe they want to make themselves look good. Whatever their reasoning, they are behaving unethically toward the group.

Leaders must realize that doing a good job takes time, ability, and careful attention to detail. When you lead, ensure that you do not practice **tunnel vision** by getting so absorbed in the end result that you neglect to consider what your team is capable of doing. Being too ambitious or setting impossible goals can result in negative effects. If you ask too much of your team members, they could lose respect and confidence in you as their leader and experience a loss of morale. The following story illustrates these points.

Steve was excited about starting his job at Hamburger Alley. Working a few hours after school and on weekends would give him some extra cash. Although he had never worked at a fast-food restaurant, he felt semiqualified. After all, he and his friends had eaten at Hamburger Alley many times, but besides that, he had used his parents' grill on several occasions.

Steve's excitement began to fade after his second day on the job. This was because of Joe, the young assistant manager. Joe was so caught up with impressing the manager that he expected too much from his kitchen crew.

Before he had hired Steve, Joe employed a grill operator who had five years of experience. His name was Larry. With all the experience Larry had, he was very quick. He could handle the dinner crowd all by himself, grilling several hamburgers and steaks in a matter of minutes.

When Joe hired Steve, he expected the same performance. Although Steve needed to be trained, Joe assumed that he could catch on and be up to speed in a few days. That is what he expected because he did not want to hire another employee to help with the dinner crowd. If he could keep costs down by having a small kitchen crew, he could look good in the eyes of his boss.

Steve's disappointment grew, and he began to lose respect for Joe. Steve finally did receive some training on the grill, but it would take time for him to improve his speed. Joe just could not seem to realize this fact. "Larry can handle the dinner crowd. Why can't you? You've been here for three weeks already." Steve tried to explain to Joe that, as with anything, he would improve with practice. But despite Steve's explanations, Joe did not realize what being a grill operator involved.

One day, after Steve called in sick and Joe could not find a replacement, Joe was forced to substitute as grill operator. That was all it took. By performing the job himself, Joe developed an understanding of the job. He immediately realized that he was asking too much of his rookie employee.

When Steve returned to work, Joe had a talk with him. "You're a good employee, Steve. I'm sorry I didn't really understand your point of view. I do, in fact, need someone with experience for that dinner crowd. But because you have potential," Joe explained, "I'm going to keep you on so you can work a lighter shift and gain experience."

Placing Self-Interest Ahead of Ethical Norms

Self-interest is probably the most common cause of unethical acts. When leaders do things to improve their personal situation or to avoid criticism or punishment, they often lose sight of accomplishing the mission and of what is really important. Instead, they may be doing extra favors intentionally to please their supervisors so that they "look good." As a result, team members lose trust, respect, and confidence in them. Plus, team morale and spirit also drops because followers feel that their leader put his or her own recognition ahead of their well-being.

In your quest to "look good," have you noticed that temptation is often close at hand? For example, you are wrestling with a tricky multiple-choice question that you feel will make the difference between receiving an A or B on a test. After deliberating between responses B and C, you decide to circle C. When you are almost finished with the test, you happen to hear some students in the hall discussing the answers. You learn that B was the correct answer for that question. What do you do? You did not intentionally cheat. You just happened to overhear the correct answer.

The student in this case decided to leave the answer as C, knowing that it was incorrect. Some people would argue that such an action is stupid. Rather, it shows that the person values honesty and has the integrity and character to act on that value in the face of temptation. Remember, the habit of being ethical on little things tends to carry over to the big things.

Doing What You Think Other People Want You to Do

All human beings have the need to be accepted. That is why you have to guard against the pressures that other people can put on you to behave unethically. Such temptations can come from many sources—your peers, your followers, or your supervisor.

If you encounter pressure from team members or from a supervisor, do not give into it; that would be a violation of professional ethics because it involves misrepresenting the truth. Leaders must be honest with themselves as well as with others. Remember, as a leader, you are setting an example for your team. Doing what you think other people want you to do contributes to an unethical climate. It also destroys the real respect for the people in charge and ruins their power as a leader. Keep in mind there is a difference between being popular and being respected.

A platoon leader gave Bill's squad the project to clean up an old shed behind the JROTC classroom. On the Saturday morning the squad arrived to do the work, the weather was rainy and miserable. Bill did not want the project any more than his teammates did, but he knew it was an important and necessary project.

Shortly after starting, one of the team leaders and several other members of the squad came up to the squad leader. The team leader said, "Bill, we don't think we should have gotten this project. We're getting more than our share of the hard jobs. Besides, it's too dangerous out here. Someone could easily get hurt picking up broken glass or falling on a loose board and landing on a rusty nail.

"I pitch in tomorrow's game and I don't want to hurt my arm doing this stuff. We feel that you didn't stick up for us when the platoon leader gave you this project. We think you care more about a promotion than you do about us."

The team leader continued, "I'll tell you what you could do to let us know how wrong we are and that you really do care about us. We could move a few things around and pick up some of the glass, then we could fake a few injuries—you know, a few cuts and some torn clothes. You can then call the project off and tell the platoon leader that it just wasn't safe out here. You could even recommend that this is a project for the school maintenance staff. That way, we can all go home and get out of this rain. No one will ever know the difference. So, what do you say, Bill?"

As you read this, the answer seems so obvious. But, when it occurs in reality, the temptation to give in to this kind of peer pressure can be great.

Using Your Position to Threaten or Harass Subordinates

Respect is a two-way street. How can you respect your team if you do not treat them with respect? It is impossible. You should not motivate your followers through fear or threats. A leadership environment that is full of fear and criticism is not healthy. Remember, you are supposed to lead by example and foster the development of subordinate leaders so eventually they can assume more responsibilities.

Leading with **favoritism** ("why can't your people get as much accomplished as Tom does?") is just as damaging as using criticism that is not constructive. They both chip away at the confidence and morale of team members.

Likewise, you should refrain from using **bribery** ("if you help me write this report, I'll promote you to my assistant"). This temptation is extremely destructive. Team members may feel like they can never truly please their leader, so why try. It shows poor judgment, moral principle, and integrity on the part of the person in charge. Obviously, a team will not have much respect or confidence in this leader.

Key Note Terms

favoritism – the showing of special favor

bribery – the act of giving or offering to, or accepting money, property, or a favor from someone in a position of trust to persuade or influence that person to act dishonestly

Maintaining Your Ethics

In your heart, you usually know the right thing to do. The real question is whether you have the character to live by sound professional values when under pressure. If you have the right beliefs and values, the thing to do in most situations will be clear and you will do it. Just think through the problem, sort out the facts, and weigh the alternatives.

Developing an Ethical Climate

To develop and maintain the proper ethical climate, leaders should reach out to their organizations, know the details of their job, trust their people, and take risks on their behalf. Recognizing that actions speak more powerfully than words, leaders encourage openness and even criticism, they listen and support followers who show initiative, and they forgive honest mistakes made in the process of learning. Leaders have three ethical responsibilities that promote a healthy environment:

- **Be a good role model**
- **Develop followers ethically**
- **Lead in such a way that you avoid putting your teammates into ethical dilemmas**

Understanding Your Self-Image

Leading from the inside out means to set examples and model the behavior that you want others to do. If you know what is important to you, you can make sure your actions are supporting the things you value most. You need to lead yourself before you can lead others.

Self-image is how you see yourself. It is what you think about your characteristics, your physical body, your morals and values, your needs and goals, and your dreams. Having a good self-image is being satisfied with and accepting what you see in yourself.

When you become a leader, you need to constantly be aware of how you see yourself. Be honest with yourself and try not to have illusions about what you are or what you would like to be. If you believe that you cannot do a task, or if you are not consistent with the values that you think you have, you may begin to have doubts about yourself. Leaders who openly display doubt, hesitation, or uncertainty in their own abilities will likely cause their followers to also have doubt in them and in their leadership.

If what you see is not what you want to be, you can make changes. You can become the person you want to be. The change will require you to practice those mental, physical, and emotional attributes discussed earlier in this lesson. You will need to determine what is important to you and what you value most. If you begin to think positively about yourself, others will see your confidence and will want to follow you. The following are some points to remember as you begin to develop your self-image.

- **Focus on the positive.** One way to improve your self-image is to identify all of the positive qualities that you possess. A certain amount of emphasizing the positive is necessary to boost your own self-image. What do you like *most* about yourself? How can you do *more* of what you like most?

- **Self-disclosure.** Self-disclosure is talking to others about yourself. As you talk to others, you will realize that your problems and shortcomings are no different from theirs. What do they like *most* about you? How can you do *more* of what they like most about you?

- **Reflection.** Think back over the choices you made and the things you did during the day. What were these behaviors saying about you? Were they displaying the values that you want to incorporate into your life? Did you practice the mental, physical, and emotional attributes you want to possess? Did they change your self-image? Would you do things differently if you had another chance to?

Conclusion

As a leader, you are responsible for making decisions; however, do not decide on a course of action without thinking over the consequences. The choice you make should be based on your values. Apply these values to every leadership situation to build the trust and confidence of your followers. Beware of temptations and pressures that can affect a leadership situation. Remember, anyone can make a decision, but effective leaders base their decisions on the highest moral good. Let your personal and professional codes of ethics guide you to do what is morally right.

In the next lesson, you will learn about principles and leadership.

Lesson Review

1. List the seven values that all leaders and followers possess.

2. Why is it important to treat all people with respect?

3. Choose one of the three ethical responsibilities in this lesson and explain it.

4. Define the term *tunnel vision*.

Chapter 1

Lesson Review

Principles and Leadership

Key Terms

attributes
censure
convictions
diversified
doctrine
philosophy
recrimination
self-evaluation

What You Will Learn to Do

- Draft a plan for using the 11 principles of leadership to improve your leadership abilities

Linked Core Abilities

- Communicate using verbal, nonverbal, visual, and written techniques
- Take responsibility for your actions and choices
- Apply critical thinking techniques

Skills and Knowledge You Will Gain Along the Way

- Describe 11 principles of leadership
- Describe the BE, KNOW, and DO attributes of a leader
- Identify how a cadet can demonstrate leadership character and competence
- Define the key words contained in this lesson

Introduction

When you think of a leader, you think of someone who is in charge or someone with authority. To be an effective leader, one must possess certain traits, abide by certain principles, and have an appropriate style. This lesson introduces the 11 principles of leadership. Being an effective leader requires more than possessing certain traits; you must also follow these principles, which are basic tools of a successful leader. Use them to evaluate yourself and then to develop a plan to improve your ability to lead.

Leadership is the process of influencing others to accomplish a mission. The leadership skills that you use to accomplish a mission are the same whether you are in a classroom, your neighborhood, church, home, or JROTC. To be a good leader, you must provide teammates with purpose, direction, and motivation. Purpose helps them to understand why they are performing a project; direction shows what they must do; and motivation gives them the desire or initiative to do everything they are capable of doing to accomplish their mission.

Origins of Principles

The 11 principles of leadership have long been the foundation of military leadership **doctrine**. They have stood the test of time and have guided the conduct and action of successful leaders of both past and present.

The US Army tested their validity in 1970 when the Army War College and the Continental Army Command Leadership Board did a study on leadership effectiveness. The results dramatically demonstrated that these guidelines are appropriate today and in the future for leaders and followers at every level. The findings of these studies also indicated that most leadership mistakes resulted simply from the failure to apply these principles properly.

Knowledge of these principles— and of basic human nature—will help you to be an effective leader in any situation. As you study them over the next several pages, keep in mind your strengths and weaknesses. Think about how you can best apply these principles to improve your leadership ability.

The Principles of Leadership

To know yourself, you must understand who you are. Where do your interests lie? Do you have a special talent? What are your weaknesses? Do you have a least favorite subject? What are some of your faults? Answering these questions is part of **self-evaluation** (see Figure 1.4.1). Through the process of self-evaluation, leaders determine their capabilities and limitations.

> **Key Note Term**
>
> doctrine – a principle (or creed of principles) relating to a specific belief, subject, theory, or branch of knowledge; the fundamental policy or standard for a principle or set of principles on a specific subject, theory, or branch of knowledge; something that is taught

> **Key Note Term**
>
> self-evaluation – to, with, for, or toward oneself or itself

Figure 1.4.1: Taking an honest look at yourself can help you perform a self-evaluation.
Courtesy of US Army JROTC.

By knowing themselves, leaders can take advantage of their strengths and work to overcome their weaknesses. Seeking self-improvement means continually strengthening your **attributes**. This desire to improve increases your competence and adds to the confidence your followers have in your ability to train and lead them.

Some techniques for applying this principle are as follows:

- **Analyze yourself objectively to determine your weak and strong qualities. Strive to overcome the weak ones and further strengthen those in which you are strong.**

- **Ask for honest opinions from your team members and instructors as to how you can improve your leadership ability.**

- **Profit by studying the causes for the success or failure of other leaders, past and present.**

- **Develop a genuine interest in people; acquire the "human touch."**

- **Master the art of effective writing and speaking.**

- **Develop a philosophy of life and work.**

- **Have a definite goal and plan to attain it.**

Read the following story and see how Patty identified and then overcame her weaknesses, thereby strengthening her attributes as a leader.

Patty was a drum major for the school marching band. She had just inherited the position from Tom, a graduating senior. Tom, who was very well liked and respected, led the band to their first state championship last year.

"What type of drum major will I be?" she thought to herself. "I cannot compete or compare myself with Tom. It's true that he was good, but I have certain strengths of my own," she reassured herself.

> **Key Note Term**
>
> **attributes** – qualities or characteristics (such as a belief, value, ethic, character trait, knowledge, or skill) that belong to a person or thing; a distinctive personal feature

> **Key Note Term**
>
> **philosophy** – discipline comprising as its core logic, aesthetics, ethics, metaphysics, and epistemology

She then began to review her good qualities. She was very enthusiastic, which always seemed to motivate people. She was a good musician who understood the principles of conducting. And she had a good ear for rhythm, enabling her to detect when the band's tempo was off.

After Patty's first week as drum major, she realized that although she was good, there was definite room for improvement. She would make changes that the band would not pick up on right away, and the percussion section always seemed to be a beat behind her.

Fortunately, it did not take her long to find out why these mistakes were occurring. A friend of hers videotaped the band practice one day so that Patty could see some of her weaknesses. Plus, some of the band members told her they had a hard time understanding what she wanted them to do because she did not explain it well.

Although Patty knew the sound, tempo, and rhythm that she wanted to hear, she needed to explain it better to the band members so that they knew exactly what she expected. Additionally, she realized that she needed to point out their mistakes and to give them an example of how she wanted them to play the new songs.

The percussion section's problem was that they had a hard time seeing her. They were at the very back of the field and she was at the front. To correct this problem, she decided to stand on a platform.

After Patty discovered her weaknesses, she tried to improve them. She thanked the band members for their suggestions and, letting her excitement show, she told them she wanted it to be another great year—maybe another state championship year.

Patty immediately knew her strengths, but she did not actually become aware of her weaknesses until she was in a leadership position. This is not uncommon. The important thing is that once she knew what qualities she needed to change, she made an effort to do so.

> **Note**
>
> Know yourself and seek self-improvement.

Be Technically Proficient

Your team members expect you to be proficient at your job; therefore, leaders must demonstrate to their teammates that they are qualified to lead. Technical competence requires a leader to be able to perform all tasks associated with the job or assignment as well as to train team members to do their jobs.

Use the following techniques to enhance your application of this principle:

- **Seek a well-rounded education. Supplement school with independent reading, research, and study.**
- **Seek out and foster associations with capable leaders or mentors. Observe and study their actions.**
- **Broaden your knowledge in other areas whenever possible; keep abreast of current events (see Figure 1.4.2).**
- **Seek opportunities to apply knowledge through the exercise of authority. You acquire good leadership only through practice.**

Figure 1.4.2: Read newspapers and magazines to stay on top of current events.
Courtesy of Jose Luis Pelaez, Inc/Corbis Images.

- **Familiarize yourself with the capabilities and limitations of all elements of your authority.**

- **Always prepare yourself for the job of a leader at the next higher level.**

- **Learn and apply sound leadership and management techniques.**

By seeking Army JROTC education and training and taking advantage of the leadership opportunities it has to offer, you have already started developing your technical proficiency.

Seek and Take Responsibility for Your Actions

Leading always involves responsibility. With the knowledge you gained from an honest self-evaluation and with a sound technical foundation required to do your job, you must take the initiative to accomplish your mission. You also want people on your team who can handle responsibility and who will help you to perform the mission.

By seeking responsibility, you develop professionally and increase your leadership ability. Accepting responsibility for all that a unit does or fails to do is part of a leader's job.

Use these techniques to assist you in applying this principle:

- **Seek diversified leadership positions that will give you experience in accepting responsibility.**

- **Take every opportunity that offers increased responsibility.**

- **Perform every act, large or small, to the best of your ability.**

- **Accept just criticism.**

- **Admit mistakes when you make them and take corrective action; avoid evading responsibility by placing the blame on someone else; ensure that any mistakes by team members are not due to an error on your part.**

- **Adhere to what you think is right; have the courage of your convictions.**

- **Possess the competence necessary to make sound and timely decisions.**

- **In the absence of orders or guidance, seize the initiative and take the necessary action based on personal judgment, training, and experience.**

> **Key Note Term**
>
> **diversified** – to produce variety

> **Key Note Term**
>
> **convictions** – a strong persuasion or belief

Lesson 4 Principles and Leadership   **225**

Make Sound and Timely Decisions

Leaders must be able to reason under the most critical conditions and decide quickly what action to take. If they delay or avoid making a decision, their indecisiveness may create hesitancy, loss of confidence, and confusion within the unit, and it may cause the project to fail. Because leaders are frequently faced with unexpected circumstances, it is important to be flexible. Leaders must be able to react promptly to each situation; then, when circumstances dictate a change in plans, prompt reaction builds confidence in them.

The following techniques will help you apply this principle:

- **Develop (through constant practice) a logical and orderly thought process**
- **Consider the effects of your decisions**
- **Ensure that team members are familiar with your policies and plans**
- **When you have time, plan for every possible unforeseen event that may arise**
- **Encourage team members to participate in the planning process; consider their advice and suggestions before making decisions**
- **Give team members sufficient time to make necessary plans**

Set the Example

A leader must set a good example. This is a heavy responsibility, but you, as a leader, have no choice. No aspect of leadership is more powerful. If you expect honor, integrity, courage, loyalty, respect, selfless service, and duty from your followers, you must demonstrate them. Because your followers will imitate your behavior, you must set high, but attainable standards, be willing to do what you require of your followers, and share their hardships. Your personal example affects people more than any amount of instruction or form of discipline. You are their role model.

The following are some techniques for applying this principle.

- **Be physically fit, well groomed, and correctly dressed**
- **Master your emotions as the leader who is subject to uncontrolled bursts of anger or to periods of depression will be less effective as a leader**
- **Maintain an optimistic outlook and a will to succeed; the more difficult the situation, the more you must display an attitude of calmness and confidence**
- **Conduct yourself so that your personal habits are not open to censure**
- **Exercise initiative and promote the spirit of initiative in your followers**
- **Be loyal; support the policies of superiors**
- **Avoid being partial to any follower**
- **Be morally courageous; establish principles and stand by them**
- **Develop conviction within your followers that you are the best person for the position you hold**
- **Delegate responsibility and authority and avoid oversupervision to develop leadership among your teammates**
- **Strive for professional competence**

Key Note Term

censure – an opinion or judgment that criticizes or condemns sternly

Try to identify how Sylvia used the previous techniques to set an example for her team in the following story.

Bob Peters was proud of his mother, Sylvia. Her sales company just promoted her to regional product manager from district supervisor. She was definitely good at what she did.

Because Bob was studying leadership in JROTC, he wanted to analyze the reasons for his mother's success. So, one day while he waited at her office after school, he had an opportunity to talk with members of her sales team.

Mike, who had worked for Sylvia for two years, said that she was really an inspiration to the team. "Selling a product can be tough, but Sylvia guides us in a way that makes the job easier. She sets realistic goals and gives us our own territories. But the main reason that we respect her so much is because she does so much more than just plan and organize. She's right there beside us selling, too. And, if we run into a problem with a client, we know that we can go to her for advice.

"I guess that you could say your mom is a great salesperson who's really committed to the success of the company. That shows in what she does and in the way she does it. She is a good role model for our sales team."

Know Your Personnel and Look Out for Their Welfare

Leaders must know and understand the members of their unit. It is not enough just to know a team member's name. As a leader, you need to understand them as individuals—their interests, values, and attitudes. In short, you must know why they act the way they do. Commit time and effort to listen to and learn about them. Try to observe, become personally acquainted with, and recognize them as individuals with different backgrounds and different personalities. To be successful in this principle, you must have knowledge of individual and group behavior; without this knowledge, you cannot understand the "why" of your follower's actions.

The behavior of team members is often driven by their desire to satisfy certain physical and safety needs. Whether or not they put their best effort in the performance of their duty and achieving the unit's goal depends on the satisfaction of those needs. By showing that you care, you can earn their trust and respect. If they trust you, they will willingly work to help you accomplish the mission.

Use the following techniques to improve your application of this principle:

- **See and be seen; be available; be friendly and approachable**
- **Develop a knowledge and understanding of your followers**
- **Concern yourself with what makes your teammates "tick"**
- **Help your personnel out when they ask for or are in need of it**
- **Administer discipline timely, fairly, and impartially; ensure fair and equitable distribution of awards**
- **Encourage individual development**
- **Share hardships to better understand your followers' behaviors and reactions**

Read the following story and identify the actions that John took to apply this principle.

Summer was approaching, and John's goal was to work and make money during the three-month break. He wanted to save his money for a CD player. His friends in the neighborhood also wanted to earn some money. One day, four of them got together and came up with an idea. They would offer a lawn maintenance and pool cleaning service to several neighborhoods for the summer. John was appointed manager of the business because he was the one who had the van to haul the equipment.

John thought about what was motivating his three friends to work. He also considered what they could each contribute to the business. Derek, whose father was recently laid off, needed to help his family. Derek had a lawn mower and could cut the grass. Jim didn't really need the money but wanted to have a productive summer. He had an electric hedge clipper and could trim bushes. Matt was working to save his money for college. With a pool at home, it was obvious that he would be responsible for cleaning the pools. John also had a lawnmower and could help Derek.

All four boys worked at getting customers. As manager, John did the scheduling and supervised loading the equipment into his van. He was also responsible for bringing a first aid kit and a large jug of water.

Business was off to a great start. Before long, one month had passed and the boys were working hard and making money. John began to notice that every so often Jim would call the night before and say that he could not work the next day. John took it in stride for a while. Because John knew that Derek really needed the money, John asked him if he would also trim the bushes. Derek did not object. He was glad to have the opportunity to earn the extra money and did not mind taking over Jim's work when asked to do so.

After Jim missed three days in one week, John decided to speak to him. "I know that you're not in this for the money, but this is a business and we all depend on each other," John explained. Jim apologized, saying that he just wanted to have some time to enjoy the summer. The two of them talked until they came to an agreement. Jim would work four days a week, allowing Derek to substitute for him for one day. Jim was happy with his day off, Derek was happy to earn a little extra money, and John was pleased that he could help meet the needs of his friends and still keep the business going.

Keep Your Followers Informed

We live in a society where mass media constantly keeps us informed of what goes on around us. We are taught in school to look for the logic in things, to think for ourselves, and to question things which do not make sense to us. It is only natural that followers look for logic in the orders of a leader. They expect their leaders to keep them informed and, whenever possible, to explain the reasons behind each requirement.

People do their best when they know why they are doing something. Keeping followers informed not only helps them to execute orders, but it also encourages initiative, improves teamwork, and enhances morale. Although it is natural for people to fear the unknown, keeping them informed also reduces fear and rumors. Techniques to apply this principle are as follows:

- Use the chain of command

- When explaining why tasks must be done, inform team members of your intent (see Figure 1.4.3)

- Be alert to detect the spread of rumors

- Build morale by informing team members of their successes; be quick to recognize their accomplishments

- Let team members know that you will accept honest errors without **recrimination**; be prompt and fair in backing them

- Keep your team informed about current rules and regulations

- Give advice and assistance freely when your followers request it

Develop a Sense of Responsibility in Your Followers

The members of your team will feel a sense of pride and responsibility when they successfully accomplish a new task you have given them. When you delegate responsibility to followers, you are indicating that you trust them. This trust that you place in them will make them want even more responsibility.

As a leader, you are a teacher and are responsible for developing your followers. Help them meet their potential by giving challenges and opportunities that you feel they can handle. Give them more responsibility when they show that they are ready. Encourage them to take the initiative and work toward completing a task. Some techniques for applying this principle are as follows:

- When explaining why tasks must be done, tell your team members what to do, not how to do it; hold them responsible for results

- Assign your team members to positions commensurate with their demonstrated or potential ability; give them frequent opportunities to perform duties at a higher level

- Insist that your personnel live by the standard to accept responsibility willingly

Figure 1.4.3: Keep your team members informed so they understand why they need to perform certain tasks.
Courtesy of US Army JROTC.

Ensure Each Task Is Understood, Supervised, and Accomplished

Your followers must understand what you expect from them. They need to know what you want done, what the standard is, and when you want it done. If you have a specific way you want a task accomplished, they need to know what it is.

Supervising lets you know if your followers understood your orders, and it shows your interest in them and in the accomplishment of the task; however, you should not oversupervise (which can cause resentment) or undersupervise (which can cause frustration).

When followers are learning new tasks, tell them what you want done, show them how you want it done, and then let them try it. Watch their performance and be available to answer questions. Accept performance that meets your standards; reward performance that exceeds your standards; correct performance that does not meet your standards.

Determine the cause of the poor performance and take appropriate action. By holding subordinates accountable for their performance, they realize they are responsible for accomplishing tasks as individuals and as teams.

Apply this principle using these techniques:

- **Ensure the need for an order exists**
- **Again, use the chain of command**
- **Through study and practice, develop the ability to think and communicate clearly, and to issue clear, concise, and positive orders**
- **Encourage followers to seek immediate clarification of any misunderstanding as to the task you want them to accomplish; question them to determine if there is any doubt or misunderstanding**
- **Correct errors in such a way as to encourage your followers; avoid public criticism**
- **Exercise care and thought in the supervision of your orders**

Build a Team

Leaders must have well-trained team members if they are to accomplish any project or mission. A leader must develop a team spirit that motivates members to work confidently.

Because task accomplishment is based on teamwork, it is evident that the better the teamwork, the better the team will perform the task. In addition, members of a group will perform better if they have a sense of belonging and team spirit. Team spirit is a two-way street, The group as a whole gives its members a feeling of accomplishment, security, and recognition; then each team member gives his or her best back to the team. Teamwork starts in the smallest unit and carries through to the largest organization. All team members must understand that their contribution to the unit is important and recognized.

Your teammates need confidence in your abilities to lead them and in their abilities to perform as members of the team. Your group becomes a team only when the members can trust and respect you and each other as trained professionals, and can see how their contributions to the team's goals are important.

Techniques to apply this principle are as follows:

- **Ensure that all training is meaningful and its purpose is clear to all members of the team**
- **Develop mutual trust and understanding**
- **Develop subordinate leaders; ensure they know and understand their personnel**
- **Explain to all members their responsibilities and the importance of their role in the effectiveness of the team**

Employ Your Team in Accordance with its Capabilities

Your group has capabilities and limitations—know them. Your team members will get satisfaction from performing tasks that are reasonable and challenging, but they will become dissatisfied if you give them tasks that are too easy or too difficult to accomplish. You must use sound judgment when employing the team because each time it fails, the members lose confidence in their abilities and in your competence as their leader. In time, this lowers morale, esprit de corps, discipline, and proficiency.

Here are some techniques for applying this principle:

- **Analyze all tasks that your supervisor assigns to you. If the means at your disposal are inadequate, inform your supervisor and request the necessary support. However, use the full capabilities of your team before requesting assistance.**
- **Keep yourself informed as to the effectiveness of your team.**
- **Ensure that the tasks you assign to subordinates are reasonable.**
- **Assign tasks fairly among the members of the group.**
- **Make decisions based on sound leadership principles.**

Use these 11 principles of leadership whenever you are put in charge of a group situation. They will help you to accomplish tasks and to care for your team. Think of them as a guide for leadership action.

The BE, KNOW, DO Attributes

For leadership to be effective, all leaders must learn, understand, and apply sound techniques. Among these techniques, leaders must have a thorough understanding of how to apply the *BE, KNOW, DO* attributes to real-life situations. Regardless of the circumstances of the situation, leaders must concentrate on what they *are* (their beliefs and character), what they *know* (human nature and their job), and what they *do* (provide purpose, direction, and motivation).

At this early stage in your leadership development, the intention is to introduce the *BE, KNOW, DO* attributes and show how they interrelate to other leadership techniques. This information will help to clarify these relationships.

Complete mastery of your leadership skills will not come naturally. Instead, you must acquire them through study and application. The key is to understand how the various leadership fundamentals can work best for you; therefore, use the *BE, KNOW, DO* attributes to the degree with which you feel most comfortable when developing a leadership style that best suits your beliefs, character, and abilities.

What a Leader Must BE

You must be a person of strong character committed to professional moral standards. You must set the correct example of individual values and be able to resolve complex problems. You must understand that you are transmitting your beliefs and values to your followers by the behavior you display. You inform them of the norms and behavior that you will accept from them by your personal conduct and behavior. Leadership traits are shown in Table 1.4.1.

Table 1.4.1: BE Leadership Traits

AS A LEADER, YOU MUST	EXAMPLES
BE a person of strong and honorable character	Compassion, consistency, determination, flexibility, initiative*, role modeling, and self-discipline
BE an example of individual values and committed to professional moral standards	Honor, integrity*, courage*, loyalty*, respect, selfless service, and duty
BE able to resolve complex problems.	Interpret the situation, analyze all factors/forces that apply and choose the best course of action.

In addition to the leadership traits shown by an asterisk in Table 1.4.1, other *BE* traits include

- **Bearing**
- **Dependability**
- **Endurance**
- **Enthusiasm**

Several examples of the leadership principles that reflect what a leader must *BE* are as follows:

- **Seek responsibility and take responsibility for your actions**
- **Set the example**

What a Leader Must KNOW

Leaders must learn before they can lead. You need to know (understand) standards, yourself, your job, and your unit to be an effective leader. Knowledge is far more important than memorization; it is understanding. Your subordinates expect you to be the most knowledgeable person in the unit. You, as a leader, owe it to your followers to meet these expectations.

Four examples of leadership traits that a leader must *KNOW* are as follows:

- **Judgment**
- **Knowledge**
- **Tact**
- **Unselfishness (selflessness)**

Examples of leadership principles that reflect what a leader must *KNOW* are as follows:

- **Know yourself and seek self-improvement**
- **Be technically proficient**
- **Know your personnel and look out for their welfare**

Table 1.4.2 shows you what a leader must *KNOW* to be successful.

Table 1.4.2: KNOW Leadership Traits

AS A LEADER, YOU MUST:	EXAMPLES
KNOW the four factors of leadership and how they affect each other.	The leader, the follower, the situation, the communication
KNOW yourself.	Personality and performance; strengths and weaknesses; knowledge, skills, and attitudes
KNOW human nature.	Potential for good and bad behavior, how depression and sadness contribute to fear and panic, and how fear affects performance
KNOW your job.	Plan and communicate effectively; supervise and counsel; display competence; develop subordinates; Make good, sound, and timely decisions; and use available resources.
KNOW your unit.	Know how to develop individual and team skills, cohesion, and discipline.

What a Leader Must DO

Action is the key. You can be all that a leader is supposed to be and know everything there is to know about being a leader, but unless you do those things that a leader must do, you are doomed to failure. Ultimately, it is what a leader does that is most important. A leader must provide the following:

- **Purpose.** You must explain the "why" in communicating your intent so that your followers clearly understand the desired outcome.
- **Direction.** You must listen to your superior, then support him or her by providing assistance in keeping the task on track and providing guidance and supervision to your team members.
- **Motivation.** Motivation is the cause of action, the required incentive; it is what gives you and your followers the will to accomplish the mission.

Here are two examples of leadership traits that a leader must *DO*:

- **Decisiveness**
- **Justice**

Examples of leadership principles that reflect "what a leader must *DO*" are as follows:

- **Make sound and timely decisions**
- **Keep your followers informed**
- **Develop a sense of responsibility in your followers**
- **Ensure each task is understood, supervised, and accomplished**
- **Build a team**
- **Employ your team in accordance with its capabilities**

Table 1.4.3 shows what a leader must *DO* to be successful.

Table 1.4.3: DO Leadership Traits

AS A LEADER, YOU MUST:	EXAMPLES
DO (PROVIDE) purpose.	Explain the "why" of missions and clearly communicate your intent.
DO (PROVIDE) direction.	Plan; maintain standards; set goals; make decisions and solve problems; supervise; evaluate, and counsel; and build (train and develop) teams.
DO (PROVIDE) motivation.	Take care of followers, be fair and consistent in your standards, develop cohesive teams, make training meaningful, reward performance that exceeds standards, and correct performance that does not meet standards.

Conclusion

The education of a leader is continuous, building on past experiences and training. The traits and principles of leadership as well as the *BE, KNOW, DO* attributes provide a framework for the development and self-evaluation of a leader. Use them in conjunction with other leadership techniques to assess yourself and to develop a plan of action to add to your leadership skills and abilities.

In the next lesson, you will learn about sexual harassment and assault. You will learn the difference between sexual harassment and good-natured kidding, and see that assault can take many forms.

Lesson Review

1. Why is it important for a leader to perform a self-evaluation?

2. Choose one technique you can use to develop sound decision making and explain it.

3. In what ways can you keep your followers informed?

4. Compare and contrast each element of the *BE, KNOW, DO* concept.

Chapter 1

Lesson Review

Sexual Harassment/Assault

Chapter 1

Key Terms

date rape
perpetrator
sexism
sexual harassment
vulnerable

What You Will Learn to Do

- Take action to prevent and/or stop sexual harassment and assault

Linked Core Abilities

- Communicate using verbal, nonverbal, visual, and written techniques
- Take responsibility for your actions and choices
- Treat self and others with respect

Skills and Knowledge You Will Gain Along the Way

- Determine the potential consequences of sexual harassment/assault for the individuals involved
- Assess the role of individual point of view in determining what is sexual harassment
- Locate resources for assisting victims of sexual harassment or assault
- Define the key words contained in this lesson

Introduction

Sexual harassment is not a joke. It's demeaning, degrading, disrespectful, and potentially damaging to another human being. What might seem like harmless fun to you might be very hurtful to another. This lesson looks at sexual harassment and assault. You learn what is considered unacceptable and possibly illegal behavior, and what to do if you feel you have been the target of sexual harassment.

Sexual Harassment

Sexual harassment covers a wide range of behavior that has been divided into two types:

- **Quid pro quo harassment. This refers to a request for some kind of sexual favor or activity in exchange for something else. It is a kind of bribe or threat, such as "If you don't do X for me, I will fail you/fire you/make your life miserable."**
- **Hostile environment harassment. This indicates any situation where sexually charged remarks, behavior, or displayed items cause discomfort. Harassment of this type ranges from lewd conversation or jokes to display of pornography.**

Both men and women can be victims of sexual harassment, though it is far more common for women to be subjected to harassment by men. Unfortunately, even as women continue to gain equality, **sexism** remains alive. Male sexist attitudes can create an environment where men feel they have the right to use words, ideas, and attitudes that degrade women. Even though physical violence is not involved, the fear and trauma that such harassment can cause are extremely harmful.

Peer **sexual harassment** is a problem for both girls and boys, and the effects from this experience can affect students' lives negatively well past their high school days. School performance can suffer as students exhibit absenteeism, a decrease in the quality of schoolwork, skipped or dropped classes, lower grades, loss of friends, tardiness, and truancy. These symptoms can ruin chances for college admission or merit scholarships, and can lead to fewer career choices and lost opportunities for a bright future.

Figure 1.5.1: Comments and looks can be considered sexual harassment.
Courtesy of Richard Hutchings/ Corbis images.

Physical symptoms of sexual harassment include sleep disturbance and appetite changes. Students feel angry, upset, and threatened by sexual harassment, all of which contributes to lowered self-esteem and confidence.

Some types of sexual harassment that are happening in schools across the nation are as follows:

- **Inappropriate comments, jokes, gestures, or looks (see Figure 1.5.1)**
- **Sexual pictures, photographs, illustrations, messages, or notes**
- **Sexual messages/graffiti about someone on bathroom walls, in locker rooms, and so on**
- **Sexual rumors about someone**
- **Calling students gay or lesbian**
- **Spying on students in dressing rooms or showers**
- **Flashing or "mooning" others**
- **Touching, grabbing, or pinching others in a sexual way**
- **Pulling at clothing in a sexual way**
- **Intentionally brushing against someone in an inappropriate way**
- **Pulling someone's clothing off or down**
- **Blocking someone's way or cornering him or her in a sexual way**
- **Forcing someone to kiss you**
- **Forcing someone to do something sexual**

Many students have reported sexual harassment as the norm in their school. Aside from inappropriate language, rumors, and inappropriate touching, sexual assaults and rapes have also been reported on some school campuses and in school buildings. When this happens, everyone is a victim. Students begin to see school as an intimidating, hostile, and unsafe place. They feel **vulnerable** and may even alter their own behavior in attempt to decrease that sense of vulnerability.

Most of the literature on sexual harassment indicates that over 90 percent of the time males are the **perpetrators** of sexual harassment against females. Recent studies, however, have documented a high level of sexual harassment experienced by boys as well as girls.

Sexual harassment is a specific type of sex discrimination that has been defined by the courts over the past 30 years. Sexual harassment is defined as *uninvited and unwelcome verbal or physical conduct directed at an individual because of his or her sex*. Schools are required to maintain a grievance procedure that allows for prompt and equitable resolution of all sex discrimination, including sexual harassment. The procedures must clearly prohibit sexual harassment of students by faculty and staff. It must also prohibit harassment of students by students.

Key Note Terms

vulnerable – capable of being wounded or injured; susceptible to being hurt

perpetrator – one who carries out a crime or a deception

Sample Sexual Harassment Policy

Many schools and places of employment have clearly defined policies on sexual harassment, procedures to follow if sexual harassment occurs, and set penalties for those who commit sexual harassment. The following is a sample policy:

[*Company name*] believes that you should be afforded the opportunity to work in an environment free of sexual harassment. Sexual harassment is a form of misconduct that undermines the employment relationship. No employee, either male or female, should be subjected verbally or physically to unsolicited and unwelcomed sexual overtures or conduct.

Sexual harassment refers to behavior that is not welcome, that is personally offensive, that debilitates morale and, therefore, interferes with work effectiveness.

Behavior that amounts to sexual harassment may result in disciplinary action, up to and including dismissal.

Definition

[*Company name*] has adopted, and its policy is based on, the definition of sexual harassment set forth by the Equal Employment Opportunity Commission (EEOC). The EEOC defines sexual harassment as unwelcome sexual advances, requests for sexual favors, and other verbal or physical conduct of a sexual nature when:

- Submission to such conduct is made either explicitly or implicitly a term or condition of your employment

- Submission to or rejection of such conduct by you is used as the basis for employment decisions affecting you

- Such conduct has the purpose or effect of unreasonably interfering with your work performance or creating an intimidating, hostile or offensive working environment

Employer's Responsibility

[*Company name*] wants you to have a work environment free of sexual harassment by management personnel, by your coworkers, and by others with whom you must interact in the course of your work as a [company name] employee. Sexual harassment is specifically prohibited as unlawful and as a violation of [*company name*]'s policy. [*Company name*] is responsible for preventing sexual harassment in the workplace, for taking immediate corrective action to stop sexual harassment in the workplace and for promptly investigating any allegation of work-related sexual harassment.

Complaint Procedure

If you experience or witness sexual harassment in the workplace, report it immediately to _____. You may also report harassment to any other member of [*company name*]'s management or ownership. All allegations of sexual harassment will be quickly investigated. To the extent possible, your confidentiality and that of any witnesses and the alleged harasser will be protected against unnecessary disclosure. When the investigation is completed, you will be informed of the outcome of that investigation.

Retaliation Prohibited

[*Company name*] will permit no employment-based retaliation against anyone who brings a complaint of sexual harassment or who speaks as a witness in the investigation of a complaint of sexual harassment.

Written Policy

You will receive a copy of [*company name*]'s sexual harassment policy when you begin working for [*company name*]. If at any time you would like another copy of that policy, please contact _____ . If [*company name*] should amend or modify its sexual harassment policy, you will receive an individual copy of the amended or modified policy.

Reproduced with permission from CCH Business Owner's Toolkit™ (www.toolkit.cch.com) published and copyrighted by CCH Tax & Accounting.

Hostile Hallways Statistics

One sexual harassment study, called Hostile Hallways, documented that the majority of sexual harassment that occurs in American high schools is between peers. Eighty-seven percent of the girls and 71 percent of the boys reported being sexually harassed by a current or former student at school. Adult school employees reportedly had targeted one in four girls and one in ten boys.

In this study, 66 percent of all boys and 52 percent of all girls surveyed admitted they had sexually harassed someone in the school setting. Of the 59 percent of students who said they had sexually harassed someone in the school setting, 94 percent claimed they themselves had been harassed.

The Hostile Hallways study identified who was being sexually harassed, when they were being harassed, and where. Students were asked why they engaged in sexual harassment and which of the following six reasons applied to their behavior:

- **It's just a part of school life/a lot of people do it/it's no big deal**
- **I thought the person liked it**
- **I wanted a date with the person**
- **My friends encouraged/pushed me into doing it**
- **I wanted something from that person**
- **I wanted the person to think I had some sort of power over them**

Clearly, sexual harassment is wrong and YOU are responsible to help create and foster a positive school climate that does not tolerate behaviors associated with discrimination and sexual harassment.

Take Action

You can refer back to the *BE, KNOW, DO* attributes model, profiled in the previous lesson. Sexual harassment behaviors are not part of who you want to *BE*. You *KNOW* what sexual harassment is and why it is harmful. When you see it happening to others, or when you experience it yourself, take action and *DO* something about it. Tell a teacher, a counselor, your parents, or a police officer immediately.

The best way you can help in creating a safe school environment is to believe in and act according to the lessons discussed in the Lesson 3, Leadership from the Inside Out, and live to the values of loyalty, duty, respect, selfless service, honor, integrity, and personal courage.

Sexual Harassment and Assault

Your sexuality is a private matter for you to express when, where, and to whom you choose. Sexual abuse occurs when someone violates that privacy or tries to interfere with or take away your choices. It can range from an offensive sexual comment or display to spousal abuse and rape. This section describes the different types of sexual abuse and presents strategies for coping and prevention.

Assault includes a wide range of victimizations, distinct from rape or attempted rape. Assaults may or may not involve force and can include actions such as being beaten, grabbed or fondled. Assault also includes verbal threats. Sexual assault includes completed or attempted attacks generally involving unwanted sexual contact between the victim and offender.

How to Cope

Every victim of assault should receive immediate medical attention. If possible, go to a trauma center or a hospital emergency room. If you were sexually assaulted be sure to wait until after you are examined by medical personnel before you shower, bathe, drink, eat, smoke, or change clothing. This is important so that any evidence can be collected from your body or your clothing.

If you become the victim of verbal, physical or sexual assault, get to a safe place. Then contact someone you trust and who can help you.

Assault is a crime. It is your decision whether or not to file a police report. If you decide to report the assault, the report should be filed with the police department in the city/town where the assault occurred, or with the State Police

The Impact on Health

In the case of sexual assault, you should consider being tested for pregnancy, sexually transmitted diseases, and AIDS. Medical evidence can be collected up to 72 hours after an assault. There is no cost to the victim who has no insurance for the rape exam.

Nine out of ten incidents of violence have an emotional effect on the victim. The most commonly reported effects are anger, fear, and becoming more cautious and less trusting, but can also include depression, confusion, sleep disturbances, including nightmares, erratic mood swings, eating disorders, anxiety, and flashbacks.

Although it is important to receive medical attention after an assault, it is just as important to get emotional help. A therapist, psychiatrist, minister, rabbi, school counselor, or crisis counselor can provide the emotional and psychological support you need. Talk with friends and family members, too.

The Internet can also be a wonderful resource for information and references. Websites such as Promote Truth (http://www.promotetruth.org/) offer ideas and suggestions for continuing on an emotionally healthy path after an assault.

Rape and Date Rape

Any sexual act by a person against another person's will is defined as rape. It is an expression of power and control. Here are some rape statistics:

- **An estimated 868 rapes or attempted rapes are committed every day. This means 36 per hour, or 1 rape or attempted rape every 1.6 minutes.**

- **Nearly three-fourths of rape and sexual assault survivors know their attackers.**

- **It is estimated that 68 percent of rape survivors do not report the crime to the police. The most common reason given for not reporting is that the attack was a "personal matter."**

- **More than half of rape or sexual assault incidents are reported to have occurred either within one mile of the victim's home or at the home.**

Rape is a problem, especially acquaintance rape. This is also called **date rape**. Any sexual activity during a date that is against one partner's will constitutes date rape, including situations where one partner is too drunk or drugged to give consent. Most date rape victims do not report the incidents. Victims may believe that they can't prove it, that they might have asked for it, that she should be ashamed if drugs or alcohol were involved, or that their assailants may seek revenge if accused.

Beyond the initial harm, rape has serious effects on mental and physical health. According to http://familydoctor.org, approximately 31 percent of all rape victims develop rape-related post-traumatic stress disorder and can experience short-term, intermediate, and long-term effects.

Short-term effects (from 3 to 4 months) are as follows:

- **Generalized anxiety and fear**
- **Disturbance of eating, sleeping, thoughts, relationships**
- **A need to create safety such as changing one's phone number**
- **Impaired social functioning**
- **Difficulty in maintaining/establishing relationships**
- **Guilt for not preventing assault**
- **Sudden, unpredictable changes of residences and disappearances**

Intermediate effects (up to 1 year) are as follows:

- **Disruption and change in lifestyle such as a change of residence or change of job**
- **Increased dependence on family**
- **Sleep disturbance, often nightmares**
- **Fear and phobias, such as going out in public or being alone or obsessive cleanliness**
- **Sexuality issues such as poor body image, flashbacks, or loss of enjoyment**
- **Poor self-esteem thinks in terms of "damaged goods"; thinks others can tell**

Key Note Term

date rape – sexual assault perpetrated by the victim's escort during an arranged social encounter

Figure 1.5.2: Always go with a buddy when you're exercising outdoors.
Courtesy of Jim Craigmyle/Corbis Images.

Long-term reactions (up to 4 years) are as follows:

- **Anger toward offender, legal system, family, or friends**
- **Diminished capacity to enjoy life**
- **Hyper-vigilance to danger such as being fearful of new and risky situations**
- **Continued sexual dysfunction**

Remember that "no" means "no!" Any sexual activity against another person's will is rape.

Staying Safe

No matter how safe you feel in any situation, you can never be too sure. Take steps to prevent incidents, sexual or otherwise, from occurring. The following are some possible steps to take:

- **Avoid situations that present clear dangers.** Don't walk or exercise alone at night or in unsafe areas (see Figure 1.5.2) and always travel with at least one other person. Don't work or study alone in a building. If someone looks suspicious to you, contact security or someone else who can help you.
- **Avoid the use of drugs or alcohol.** Anything that reduces or obliterates your judgment will make you more vulnerable to any kind of assault.
- **Watch your belongings.** Keep your keys with you at all times but don't attach them to anything that could identify them as yours, such as your ID or credit cards. Carry bags or backpacks close to your body. If someone tries to grab your purse or bag, let it go rather than risk injury.
- **Avoid people who make you feel uneasy.** If there is a fellow student or coworker who puts you on your guard, avoid situations in which you need to spend time alone with them. Speak to an instructor or supervisor if you feel threatened.

- **Communicate.** Be clear about what you want from people with whom you associate either personally or professionally. Don't assume that others want what you want, or even know what you want. If you have a request, make it respectful and invite a response.

Staying Safe on the Internet

One of the attractions of the Internet is the anonymity of the user, and this is why it can be so dangerous. You don't always know with whom you are interacting. You may think you know, but unless it's a school friend or a relative, you really can't be sure. Because of the way the Internet works, you can actually be interacting with a pedophile or sexual predator and not know it until it's too late. With the explosion of the Internet into a powerful, worldwide medium, the danger to young people has drastically increased.

The most common means by which sexual predators contact children over the Internet is through chat rooms, instant messages, and e-mail. In fact, 89 percent of sexual solicitations were made in either chat rooms or instant messages and 1 in 5 youth (ages 10–17 years) has been sexually solicited online (*Journal of American Medical Association*, 2001). Considering that 25 percent of kids online participate in real-time chat and 13 million use instant messaging, the risks of such children, either knowingly or unknowingly, interacting with a predator is alarming.

To Report Illegal Online Activity

The National Center for Missing and Exploited Children (NCMEC) provides excellent resources concerning sexual exploitation of children and related issues for the lay public, counseling community, and law enforcement agencies. NCMEC has created an extensive Web presence for its Exploited Child Unit: http://www.missingkids.com. These Web pages provide background information on laws and legislation, tips and pointers for parents and children, and lists of preventive resources on the various aspects of child sexual exploitation.

In addition to its Web pages, NCMEC, in partnership with the U.S. Postal Inspection Service, the U.S. Customs Service, and the Federal Bureau of Investigation, serves as the National CyberTipline. To report possible illegal online activity related to child pornography, predation, or any other type of child sexual exploitation, call the CyberTipline: 800-843-5678 (800-TheLost) or visit their Web site: http://www.missingkids.com.

If you have been sexually exploited online, or you want more information about this activity, check out www.katiesplace.org.

Adapted from www.protectkids.com

Seeking Help

What should you do if you've been raped? If you're raped, you should first get to a safe place, away from your attacker. You should then go to a hospital emergency room to be checked. You can call the police from the hospital. Don't bathe or change your clothes before you go to the hospital. Just get there as fast as you can.

Being raped can have a huge effect on your life. You may feel disbelief, fear, anxiety, and possibly even guilt. You may have an upset stomach or feel nervous. About half of all people who are raped say they are depressed the first year after the attack. It's important that you keep appointments with your doctor. Be sure to tell him or her about any physical, emotional or sexual problems you have during this time, even if you don't think they're related to the rape.

Be sure to visit your doctor one or two weeks after the rape to review the results of the tests done in the emergency room. Your doctor will give you information and tell you more about other support services, too. Some of these services include hospital social workers, local rape crisis services, your local public health department and the state attorney general's office.

Remember, sexual assault is a terrible crime. But it's not your fault, and you didn't cause it to happen. Rape is against the law. You have the right to report this crime to the police, and you have the right to be treated fairly during the justice process.

Conclusion

Sexual harassment is never appropriate in any setting, whether at school or at work. Sexual harassment is demeaning, cruel, demoralizing, and humiliating as well as illegal. It shows a lack of respect for others and can create a climate of fear that could lead to more potentially serious violations such as rape and date rape. Sexual harassment should never be tolerated. If you or someone you know is experiencing sexual harassment, challenge the individual, notify an authority, do something to eliminate the problem before it spins out of control. Assault includes verbal threats or any attempt to do violence to another.

This lesson concludes the chapter, "Being a Leader." Practice what you have learned in these lessons and continue to sharpen your leadership skills. These skills will help you be the kind of person you want to be as you go through your life.

Lesson Review

1. Define the term *sexual harassment*.
2. List four types of sexual harassment.
3. What are three symptoms that might be exhibited by someone experiencing sexual harassment?
4. If you or a friend were being sexually harassed, who would you talk to about it?
5. What is the difference between sexual harassment and assault?

Leadership Skills

Lesson 1

Steps from the Past

Key Terms

discipline
drill
maneuver
precision
unison

What You Will Learn to Do

- Explain the importance of drill in military discipline

Linked Core Abilities

- Communicate using verbal, nonverbal, visual, and written techniques

Skills and Knowledge You Will Gain Along the Way

- Describe the origin of drill dating back to the Continental Army of the United States

- Identify five purposes of drill in times of war and peace

- Explain civilian control over the military

- Compare the qualities of discipline instilled in the Continental Army to what military drill develops today

- Define the key words contained in this lesson

Chapter 2

Introduction

This lesson introduces you to the importance of **drill** and ceremonies, their history and purpose. The **precision** and timing of drill promotes skill, teamwork, and **discipline**. In later lessons, you will understand the roles of leaders and followers in drill, and practice individual drill movements.

The History of Drills

In 1775, when this country was striving for independence and existence, the nation's leaders were confronted with the problem of not only establishing a government but also organizing an army that was already engaged in war. From the "shot heard around the world" on April 19, 1775, until Valley Forge in 1778, revolutionary forces were little more than a group of civilians fighting Indian-style against well-trained, highly disciplined British forces (see Figure 2.1.1).

For three years General Washington's troops endured many hardships, including lacking funds, rations, proper clothing, and equipment. Additionally, they suffered loss after loss to the superior British troops. These hardships and losses mostly stemmed from the lack of a military atmosphere in this country.

Recognizing the crisis, General Washington (through Benjamin Franklin, the American Ambassador to France) enlisted the aid of a Prussian officer, Baron Friedrich von Steuben. Upon his arrival at Valley Forge on February 23, 1778, Baron von Steuben, a former staff officer with Frederick the Great, met an army of several thousand half-starved, wretched men in rags. His first comment was, "No European army could be kept together in such a state." To correct these conditions, he set to work immediately, writing drill movements and regulations at night and teaching a model company of 120 men during the day.

Key Note Terms

drill – the execution of certain movements by which individuals or units are moved in a uniform manner from one formation to another, or from one place to another; movements are executed in unison and with precision

precision – Being precise, accurate, or exact

discipline – orderly, obedient, or restrained conduct

Figure 2.1.1: The unskilled Americans were at a disadvantage against the organized and trained British.
Courtesy of Time Life Pictures/Getty Images.

Chapter 2   Leadership Skills

Discipline became a part of military life for these selected individuals, and they learned to respond to commands without hesitation (see Figure 2.1.2). This new discipline instilled in these soldiers a sense of alertness, urgency, and attention to detail. Confidence in themselves and in their weapons grew as each man perfected the movements. As they mastered the art of drill, they began to work as a team, and they developed a sense of pride in their unit.

Observers were amazed to see how quickly and orderly von Steuben could form and **maneuver** the troops into different battle formations. Officers observed that organization, chain of command, and control were improved as each man had a specific place and task within the formation.

Later, General Washington dispersed the members of the model company throughout the Army to teach drill. From this drill instruction, they improved the overall effectiveness and efficiency of the Army.

To ensure this uniformity and overall effectiveness continued, von Steuben wrote the first field manual for the US Army in 1779, "The Regulations for the Order and Discipline of the Troops of the United States" (commonly referred to as the "Blue Book"). The Army did not change the drill procedures initiated at Valley Forge for 85 years, until the American Civil War. In fact, many of those original drill terms and procedures still remain in effect today.

Purposes and Objectives of Drill

Throughout history armies have practiced drill. In times of war, leaders used drill to move troops and equipment quickly from one location to another in an orderly manner. Drills also show how many can move as one in a flawlessly timed effort. These **unison** movements are still important on the battlefield where mistakes can

Key Note Term

maneuver – to perform a movement in military tactics (or in drill) normally to secure an advantage

Figure 2.1.2: Discipline and drills gave soldiers a sense of alertness and attention to detail.
Courtesy of Ted Spiegel/Corbis Images.

cost lives. In peacetime, drill provides a means of enhancing morale, developing a spirit of cohesion, and presenting traditional and well-executed ceremonies.

When individuals react to commands rather than thought, the result is more than just a good-looking ceremony or parade—it's discipline. Drill has been and will continue to be the backbone of military discipline. In addition to discipline, military drill teaches and develops

- **Self-confidence**
- **Personal pride**
- **Esprit de corps**
- **Teamwork**
- **Attention to detail**
- **Unit pride**

Conclusion

Through hard work and discipline, you can learn and develop the leadership skills and abilities necessary to become an effective leader in drill as well as in many other situations. An individual with pride and discipline will respond on command to produce the finest drill maneuvers in all of JROTC. Make your first step a good one and follow it through with other steps towards a successful future.

In the next lesson you will learn about the roles of leaders and followers when performing drills. Both leaders and followers have important places in these exercises.

Key Note Term

unison – in complete or perfect agreement; at the same time

Chapter 2

Lesson Review

1. What was the name of the first field manual?
2. List three advantages to learning and participating in drills.
3. What are the purposes of drills?
4. Define the term *unison*.

Lesson 2

Roles of Leaders and Followers in Drill

Key Terms

cadence
column
command of execution
inflection
interval
preparatory command
rhythmic
selfless
snap
supplementary command
tone

What You Will Learn to Do

- Demonstrate effectual command voice in drill

Linked Core Abilities

- Take responsibility for your actions and choices

Skills and Knowledge You Will Gain Along the Way

- Describe the responsibilities of a follower and leader in drill
- Identify the types of drill commands
- Describe the elements of a proper command voice
- Define the key words contained in this lesson

Introduction

This lesson introduces you to the roles of leaders and followers in drill. It discusses the different types of commands and the importance of command voice. It also prepares you for the practical application of drill by explaining the responsibilities of a small unit (team or squad) drill leader.

One of the fundamental purposes of *Leadership Lab* is to reinforce and let you practice the leadership style and skills that you are trying to develop. In *Leadership Lab*, you will have the opportunity to demonstrate the traits of leadership, concepts of teamwork, pride in your unit, and the chain of command.

The remainder of this unit is an explanation and practical application of drill which is designed to strengthen your character, knowledge, and skills as an Army JROTC cadet. Drill and the application of basic leadership techniques will help you to develop in these areas.

Responsibilities of a Follower

The role you play and your responsibilities as a follower in drill are of great importance to the unit. By your obedience to unit leaders, your appearance, and your willingness to contribute to the unit's mission, you are showing the team spirit of a follower, helping to make the unit what it is and contributing to its success.

As a follower, you share the same responsibilities of your leaders to uphold the basic values of loyalty to your unit, personal responsibility, and **selfless** service. It is your duty to complete your job to the best of your ability and to put the needs and goals of the unit before your own.

Responsibilities of a Leader

In your role as leader, your responsibilities include setting a good example, knowing your job, and being concerned about the welfare of your followers. You must also show your obedience to your leaders and, at the same time, demonstrate the initiative of a follower. Finally, you must show ability and willingness to contribute to the success of your unit's missions.

You must show your leaders and followers that you uphold the same basic values of unit loyalty, personal responsibility, and selfless service. If you rise to the challenge of these responsibilities, you can make your followers feel confident in you, in themselves, and in the unit.

Commands and the Command Voice

The responsibilities of a leader include the proper use of command voice. When leaders give commands properly and with a good command voice, they help ensure that subordinates carry out their orders immediately and correctly.

How often have you heard a command given that demands immediate action? Your mom or dad may have given you that command about something as simple as mowing the lawn or cleaning up your room. Their authority came through loud and clear; the voice said, "Do what I say, NOW!"

The same thing happens in *Leadership Lab* except the commands come from drill leaders. If you are a leader, learn to give commands so that your followers clearly understand you and respond with immediate action.

Commands

A drill command is an oral order of a commander or leader. The precision with which personnel execute a movement is affected by the manner in which the commander or leader gives the command. Most drills have two parts: the **preparatory command** and the **command of execution**. Neither part is a command by itself.

The preparatory command states the movement that the leader wants subordinates to perform and it mentally prepares them for its execution. The command of execution signals when subordinates are to execute the movement. For example, in the command "forward, march," "forward" is the preparatory command and "march" is the command of execution.

> **Note**
>
> The command "ready, aim, fire" is an example of a two-part command that contains two preparatory commands.

After leaders give a preparatory command, they may command "as you were" to revoke that command. However, after they give the command of execution, any revocation is improper, and personnel should execute the movement in the best possible manner.

Some commands require the use of a **supplementary command** to reinforce other commands and to ensure proper understanding and execution of a movement. Supplementary commands, given by subordinate leaders, may be a preparatory command, a part of a preparatory command, or a two-part command. These commands extend to the lowest subordinate leader who has control over another element of the command within the same formation. The leader giving the initial preparatory command must allow sufficient time for subordinate leaders to give the supplementary commands before giving the command of execution.

Use the following basic rules to help you when giving commands. These rules and accompanying examples may seem difficult to understand, but they show the complexity of commands in drill.

- **Give all commands from the position of attention**
- **While at the halt, face the unit when giving commands**
- **For marching commands, move simultaneously with the unit to maintain correct position**
- **When marching, give commands in the direction of the troops**

Key Note Terms

preparatory command – the part of a drill command that states the movement to be carried out and mentally prepares personnel for its execution

command of execution – the part of a drill command that tells when the movement is to be executed (carried out)

Key Note Term

supplementary command – an oral order given by a subordinate leader that reinforces and complements a higher order to ensure proper understanding and execution of a movement

Subordinate leaders normally give supplementary commands over their right shoulder; however, you will learn several exceptions to this rule in later drill instruction.

- If a company is in formation, platoon leaders give supplementary commands following all preparatory commands of the commander. For example, when the preparatory command is "company," platoon leaders immediately come to attention and command "platoon." The company commander then commands "attention." Squad leaders do not participate in these commands. Also, if the company commander gives the preparatory command "parade," platoon leaders repeat it, but the squad leaders do not. The company commander then gives the command of execution "*rest.*"

- To change the direction of a unit when marching, leaders give the preparatory command and the command of execution for each movement so they begin and end on the same foot in the direction of the turn. For example, give the preparatory command "column right" and the command of execution "march" as the right foot strikes the ground. The **interval** between the preparatory command and command of execution is normally one count or one step.

- When a command requires the execution of a movement different from the other elements within the same formation, or at a different time, subordinate leaders give their supplementary commands at the time set by the procedures covering the movement. For example, your platoon is in a **column** formation. After the platoon leader commands "column of twos from the left," the first and second squad leaders command "forward" and the third and fourth squad leaders command "stand fast." On the command of execution "march," the first and second squads execute the movement. At the appropriate time, the third squad leader commands, "column half left, march" for both the third and the fourth squads.

- The only commands that use unit designations such as company or platoon are "attention" and "halt."

- Combined commands, such as "fall in," "fall out," "rest," and "at ease" combine preparatory and execution commands and do not require a supplementary command. Leaders give these commands with **inflection** and at a uniformly high pitch and loudness comparable to that of a normal command of execution.

Directives

In contrast to commands, directives are oral orders given by commanders to direct or cause subordinate leaders or a lead element to take action. Commanders give directives rather than commands when it is more appropriate for subordinate elements to execute a movement or to perform a task as independent elements of the same formation.

Commanders give directives in sentence form, normally prefixed by the phrases "have your units" or "bring your units." For example, "have your units open ranks and stack arms" or "bring your units to present arms." "Take charge of your units" is the only directive on which a commander relinquishes a command and salutes are exchanged.

Command Voice

A properly given command should be understood by everyone in the unit. Correct commands have three important elements: **tone**, **cadence**, and **snap**, and they demand a willing, accurate, and immediate response by everyone in the unit.

Key Note Terms

interval – the lateral space between personnel in a formation, measured from right to left with close, double, or normal spacing

column – a formation in which people or elements are arranged one behind the other

---

Key Note Terms

inflection – the rise and fall in the pitch and the tone changes of the voice

tone – a sound of distinct pitch, loudness, vibration, quality, and/or duration; the particular or relative pitch of a word or phrase

cadence – the uniform rhythm in which a movement is executed, or the number of steps or counts per minute at which a movement is executed

snap – an immediate, sharp, precise response to a drill command

The Proper Tone of Command Voice

The way you deliver commands has a direct bearing on how those commands are understood and carried out. One way to help your unit be the best is to learn to control the tone of your voice. This section shows you how, with a little practice, you can give the best commands possible.

Voice Control

Loudness is the key factor in tone control. The command must be loud enough so that subordinates can hear it and there is no doubt as to the action that the leader requires. To do this, you must project your voice without raising your hand to your mouth.

In most cases, the leader stands at the front and center of the unit. He or she then speaks while facing the unit so that his or her voice reaches everyone. The command voice should come from the diaphragm (the large muscle that separates the chest cavity from the abdominal cavity). The throat, mouth, and nose act as amplifiers to give fullness and to project the voice.

It is necessary for the voice to have carrying power, but excessive exertion is unnecessary and harmful. A typical result of trying too hard is the almost unconscious tightening of the neck muscles to force sound out. This produces strain, hoarseness, sore throat, and, worst of all, indistinct and jumbled sounds instead of clear commands. You can achieve good voice control through good posture, proper breathing, correct adjustment of throat and mouth muscles, and confidence. The best posture for giving commands is the position of attention.

Distinctiveness

Distinctiveness depends on the correct use of the tongue, lips, and teeth to form the separate sounds of a word or group of sounds into syllables. Distinct commands are effective; indistinct commands cause confusion. Leaders can pronounce all commands correctly without loss of effect if they speak their words correctly. To develop the ability to give clear, distinct commands, practice them slowly and carefully, prolonging the syllables; then gradually increase the rate of delivery to develop proper cadence but still pronounce each syllable distinctly.

Inflection

Inflection is the rise and fall in pitch and the tone changes of the voice. Pronounce each preparatory command with a rising inflection. As described on the preceding page, the most desirable pitch when beginning a preparatory command is near the level of the natural speaking voice.

A common fault with beginners is to start the preparatory command in a pitch so high that, after employing a rising inflection, it is impossible to give the command of execution with clarity or without strain. When giving the command of execution, use a sharper tone and a slightly higher pitch than the last syllable of the preparatory command. Remember, the best way to develop a command voice is to practice.

In combined commands such as "fall in" or "fall out," give them without inflection and with the uniform high pitch and loudness of a normal command of execution.

The Proper Cadence of Command Voice

When giving commands, cadence is the uniform and **rhythmic** flow of words. Intervals between the words make the preparatory command understandable and signal when to expect the command of execution. These intervals also allow time for subordinate leaders to give any supplementary commands.

When supplementary commands are necessary, the commander or leader should allow one count between the preparatory command and the supplementary command. The leader should also leave a count between the supplementary command and the command of execution.

The Snap of Command Voice and Movement

After the leader gives a command, there is a brief time between the end of the command of execution and the time when subordinates actually execute the move. The inflection of the command voice at the end of the command of execution should draw an immediate, sharp, and precise movement (or snap) to this command. If done properly, everyone in the unit moves at the same time, creating an impressive, well-drilled, and uniform appearance. Remember, effective leaders depend on the command voice to show confidence in their ability to command.

Conclusion

Proper execution of commands and command voice takes practice. But when leaders know their responsibilities and prepare for drill, they will discover that being a drill leader is a lot easier.

You learn how to use your leadership skills and take charge in the following lesson. You will draw on what you've already learned about leadership as you work through the next lesson.

Key Note Term

rhythmic – regular or orderly repetition of sounds or movements; steady; recurring with measured regularity

Chapter 2

Lesson Review

1. **Explain how selfless service benefits your unit.**
2. **Compare the preparatory command and the command of execution. Give two examples.**
3. **What is the difference between a directive and a command?**
4. **Compare and contrast tone, cadence, and snap.**

Lesson Review

Lesson 3

Using Your Leadership Skills/Taking Charge

Key Terms

command of execution
command voice
preparation
procedure

What You Will Learn to Do

- Analyze personal strengths and weaknesses as a drill leader

Linked Core Abilities

- Take responsibility for your actions and choices

Skills and Knowledge You Will Gain Along the Way

- Describe the preparation of a drill leader before a drill
- Describe the procedure a drill leader takes to teach a drill
- Identify five characteristics of a capable drill leader
- Define the key words contained in this lesson

Introduction

This lesson introduces you to how leaders use their leadership skills to prepare themselves for taking charge during drills.

Learning to Lead

For leaders to command respect and obedience from their subordinates, they must be prepared to lead as well as be ready for any situation. Their attitude and appearance must set a good example for others to follow.

Taking charge is not as easy as it sounds. It is not just having a neat and correct appearance, knowing drill commands, or using proper **command voice**; it is being a good follower, a good leader, and knowing how and when to use proven leadership techniques (such as the traits and principles of leadership).

Read the following story and see if you can personally identify with any of the mistakes that Mark made after he took charge of a squad as its new drill leader.

Mark usually arrives late to his JROTC class. As he joins the formation, he always greets several of his buddies. He hardly ever has a straight gigline or a pressed uniform; his hair is usually uncombed; and his shoes look like he never polishes them. Day after day, he goes through the process of trying to call his squad to attention. They barely listen to him, continuing to talk and laugh.

He finally gets their attention and begins drill practice. During the drill, he consistently gives a few wrong commands and makes several timing errors, but his squad members usually execute the drills correctly anyway. Seeing them get ahead of him frustrates Mark, but by that time the class is over and he does nothing about it.

One day, Mark finally asks a senior cadet, "Why is my squad so hard to keep in line? I can't get them to shape up. I don't get angry, I ask them nicely, and I still can't get any discipline or respect."

The senior cadet replies, "If you really want an honest answer . . . I think they don't see you as a leader. You give them the wrong commands; you don't know correct timing or cadence; and your appearance . . . well, it needs a lot of work. Learn the drills and look like a leader. You can't inspire respect if you don't have any for yourself. By the way, when was the last time you polished those shoes?"

In the next few weeks, Mark's leadership skills and appearance improved. Soon, the squad saw a difference—Mark was becoming a better leader. He knew the drills, looked the part of a leader, and did not tolerate any slackening off once the class period began.

The mistakes that Mark made as a drill leader include having a poor appearance, not knowing the drills or using the proper command voice, and not being able to discipline his friends. Instead of immediately taking the initiative of a leader or setting the proper examples, he waited until the squad got out of control. Then he had to make changes. Being a consistent leader may appear to be difficult, but it will make your job easier. How did **procedure** and **preparation** play a role in Mark's situation?

Drill leaders are also instructors; therefore, they must know how to teach drill movements to their subordinates and to provide remediation. If you become a drill leader, one of the most commonly accepted ways to teach and remediate drill is from a position centered in front of your team where you can provide **commands of execution**. From this position, you can

Key Note Term

command of execution – a part of a drill command that tells when the movement is to be executed (carried out)

Figure 2.3.1: Demonstrate to your cadets the proper way to execute a drill movement.
Courtesy of US Army JROTC

- **Explain and demonstrate each new drill movement before your team members practice it and then have them execute it. Remember to require snap in every movement. Ensure the movement is understood and done correctly by each subordinate before trying another movement. Drill periods are short, so make the most of available time.**

- **Observe team members carefully to ensure everyone executes the movement correctly.**

- **Remediate by making on-the-spot corrections as necessary. Be prepared to give individual instruction to those personnel who need it. This means knowing exactly what a subordinate did wrong and being able to demonstrate the correct way. Teach your unit the correct movements the first time and they will make fewer mistakes.**

Be prepared to use discipline as necessary. Junior leaders often find this difficult because the people they discipline are their peers and friends. Do not give discipline for any other reason than to improve the unit. Leaders do not have to feel wrong about enforcing discipline: it should not be personal; it must be purely professional. Never discipline someone in front of others; instead, take that person someplace private to discuss and correct the behavior.

Note

Praise in public; criticize in private. You will receive more instruction on how to properly conduct a counseling session in other leadership levels.

Conclusion

When leaders know their responsibilities and prepare for drill, they discover that being a drill leader is easier and more rewarding than they expected. Followers respect and obey leaders more if the leaders are competent and confident. Keep in mind the leadership traits and other fundamentals presented in this lesson. The following list summarizes the responsibilities that good drill leaders should understand and implement:

- **Be consistent**
- **Be sincere; show respect and care about the well-being of your subordinates**
- **Have energy, patience, and spirit**
- **Have military neatness and bearing**
- **Follow regulations precisely, as an example for others to follow**
- **Be knowledgeable of drill procedures and commands**
- **Provide feedback or on-the-spot corrections when mistakes are noted**
- **Be fair and use judgment when applying discipline**

This list is not all inclusive. The *Leadership* instruction in subsequent years will expand on this list as your understanding of leadership and your leadership potential grows and develops. For now, however, remember that when leaders know and apply drill commands and leadership techniques properly, their confidence and motivation build confidence and motivation in their followers.

In the following lesson, you will learn about stationary movements. This is part of the drill that you will do as a squad.

Lesson Review

1. **List three responsibilities that a good drill leader should understand.**
2. **Why is it important to have a good appearance and understand the drills?**
3. **What is a command voice?**
4. **Define the term** *command of execution*.

Lesson 4

Stationary Movements

Key Terms

at ease
attention
facing
parade rest
rest
salute

What You Will Learn to Do

- Demonstrate correct stationary movements on command

Linked Core Abilities

- Communicate using verbal, nonverbal, and written techniques

Skills and Knowledge You Will Gain Along the Way

- Describe the position of attention
- Describe how to respond to positions of rest commands
- Describe how to respond to facing commands
- Describe the correct way to salute in a variety of situations
- Define the key words contained in this lesson

Chapter 2

Introduction

The basic skills covered in this lesson are necessary to master because they are building blocks for other movements used during *Leadership Lab*. Additionally, they are important for you in developing discipline and self-confidence and for your unit in ensuring uniformity of movement and improving its overall effectiveness and efficiency. This lesson examines stationary movement skills from the position of attention to how to salute correctly in various situations.

Stationary Movements

Stationary movements include attention and rest positions, facing, and saluting. These movements, along with marching techniques, make up the squad and platoon movements. In drill, you start most of your movements from the position of attention; however, you will discover that in some instances, you execute certain rest movements from other rest positions.

Position of Attention

You assume the position of attention on the command "fall in" or "squad (platoon, and so on), attention."

To assume the position of **attention**, as shown in Figure 2.4.1, bring your heels together sharply on line, with your toes pointing out equally, in a 45-degree angle. Rest the weight of your body evenly on the heels and balls of both your feet. Keep your legs straight without locking your knees. Hold your body straight, chest lifted and arched, and shoulders square. Keep your head and face straight to the front, with your chin drawn in so that your head and neck are on a vertical line.

Let your arms hang straight without being stiff. Curl your fingers so that the tips of your thumbs are alongside and touching the first joint of your forefingers. Keep your thumbs straight along the seams of your trouser leg, with the first joint of your fingers touching your trousers. While you are in this position, stand still and remain silent unless otherwise directed.

Figure 2.4.1: Standing at attention.
Courtesy of US Army JROTC.

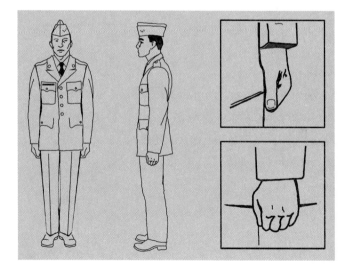

Positions of Rest

Positions of rest allow troops to relax while maintaining formation to conserve their strength and energy for extended movements.

Parade Rest

A drill leader can only give the command for this rest position from the position of attention. The command for it is **parade rest**. This is shown in Figure 2.4.2.

On the command of execution "rest," move your left foot about 10 inches to the left of the right foot. Keep your legs straight without locking your knees, and rest the weight of your body equally on the heels and balls of both feet.

At the same time, center your hands at the small of your back on your belt. Keep the fingers of both hands extended and joined, interlocking your thumbs so that the palm of your right hand is outward. Keep your head erect as you would in the position of attention. Remember to remain silent and do not move unless otherwise directed.

From the position of parade rest, you may execute "stand at ease," "at ease," and "rest."

Stand At Ease

The command for this movement is "stand at ease." On the command of execution "ease," execute parade rest, but turn your head and eyes directly toward the leader of the formation. You may execute "at ease" or "rest" from this position.

The command for this movement is **at ease**. On this command, you may move; however, you must remain standing and silent with your right foot in place. You may execute **rest** from this position.

Rest

The command for this movement is "**rest**." On this command, you may move and talk unless otherwise directed. However, you must remain standing with your right foot in place. You may execute "at ease" from this position.

Key Note Term

parade rest – command to place feet apart, knees unlocked, and clasp hands behind the back in a somewhat relaxed position

Key Note Terms

at ease – command to relax the body while remaining silent in place and not assuming any particular position

rest – a position where you remain standing with your right foot in place; in certain situaions, you may move or talk in this position unless otherwise directed

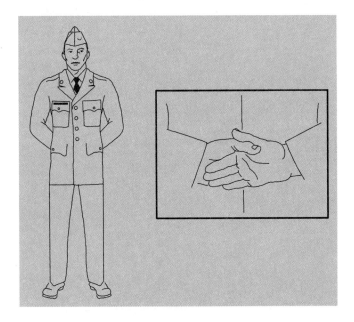

Figure 2.4.2: Standing at parade rest.
Courtesy of US Army JROTC.

Facing

Key Note Term

facing – pivoting movement executed while stationary to orient the body left, right, or opposite current position

Facing, left or right, is a two-count movement. The command is "left (right), face." See Figure 2.4.3 for an example of executing a left face. On the command of execution "face," slightly raise your right heel and left toe and turn 90 degrees to the left on your left heel, assisted by a slight pressure on the ball of the right foot. Keep your left leg straight without stiffness and allow your right leg to bend naturally. On the second count, place your right foot beside the left foot, resuming the position of "attention." Your arms remain at your sides, as in the position of attention, throughout this movement.

Facing to the rear is also a two-count movement. The command is "about, face" (see Figure 2.4.4). On the command of execution "face," move the toe of your right foot to a point touching the marching surface about half the length of your foot behind you. Rest most of your body weight on the heel of your left foot, and allow your right knee to bend naturally. On the second count, turn to the right 180 degrees on the left heel and ball of your right foot, resuming the position of attention. Again, your arms remain at your sides throughout this movement.

> **Note**
>
> The individual positions and stationary movements are the basic skills required in drill. You will learn these positions and the correct execution of them before proceeding to other drill movements, such as facing and marching and squad drill.

The Hand Salute

The hand **salute** is a one-count movement. The command is "present, arms."

When a drill leader commands "order, arms," you may release the salute. "Order, arms" is a one-count movement. On the command of execution "arms," return

Key Note Term

salute – act of raising right hand to eyebrow, fingers straight, hand slightly cupped and tilted forward, as a gesture of courtesy

Figure 2.4.3: Executing a left face.
Courtesy of US Army JROTC.

Figure 2.4.4: Executing an about face.
Courtesy of US Army JROTC.

your hand sharply to your side, resuming the position of attention. You execute the hand salute while marching alone; however, if you are a member of a unit, the leader salutes for the entire unit. If you are alone and at a double time, you must first come to quick time before you can execute the salute.

When reporting or showing courtesy to an individual, turn your head and eyes toward the person and salute at the same time. Subordinates initiate the salute at the appropriate time and terminate it upon acknowledgment.

Conclusion

This lesson covered the basics to completing stationary movements in drill. The stationary movements include the positions of attention, rest, facing, and the hand salute.

Next you will learn about steps and marching. You will build on the stationary movements to you learn in this lesson and add movement to the skills you already know.

Lesson Review

1. What is the proper position of attention?
2. What is the difference between parade rest and standing at ease?
3. What is the command for presenting a salute?
4. Define the term *rest*.

Lesson 5

Steps and Marching

Key Terms

double time
halt
quick time
rest
steps

What You Will Learn to Do

- Demonstrate correct marching technique on command

Linked Core Abilities

- Communicate using verbal, nonverbal, visual, and written techniques

Skills and Knowledge You Will Gain Along the Way

- Describe how to execute marching movements from various commands
- Describe how to respond to halt commands
- Define the key words contained in this lesson

Introduction

This lesson builds on the instruction regarding stationary movements. It describes the different **steps** used during drill. The two basic steps used in marching are the 30-inch step and the 15-inch step. Use combinations of these steps, facing movements, and rests to march alone or in groups.

Key Note Term

steps – a step is the prescribed distance from one heel to the other heel of a marching soldier

Basic Marching Information

The following basic marching information pertains to all marching movements, including the 30- and 15-inch steps.

- All marching movements executed from the "halt" are initiated from the "position of attention".

- Except for "route step march" and "at ease march", all marching movements are executed while marching at "attention". Marching at "attention" is the combination of the "position of attention" and the procedures for the prescribed step executed simultaneously.

- When executed from the "halt", all steps except "right step" begin with the left foot.

- For short-distance marching movements, the commander may designate the number of steps forward, backward, or sideward by giving the appropriate command: "**One step to the right (left), MARCH**" or "**Two steps backward (forward), MARCH**". On the command of execution "**MARCH**", step off with the appropriate foot, and halt automatically after completing the number of steps designated. Unless otherwise specified, when directed to execute steps forward, the steps will be 30-inch steps.

- All marching movements are executed in the cadence of "Quick Time" (120 steps per minute), except the 30-inch step, which may be executed in the cadence of 180 steps per minute on the command "**Double Time, MARCH**".

- A step is the prescribed distance from one heel to the other heel of a marching soldier.

- All 15-inch steps are executed for a short distance only.

The 30-inch Step

Historically, marching has been an essential infantry skill to efficiently move troops and effectively mass force on the battlefield. As an important part of drill and ceremony, marching remains pertinent today as an effective means of instilling order and discipline among the ranks. The 30-inch step is the standard stride for marching. The standard pace of march is 120-steps per minute, otherwise called "quick time."

Quick Time

The command to march forward from the halt is "forward, march." This command automatically instructs you to use the 30-inch step. On the preparatory command "forward," shift the weight of your body to your right foot, without noticeable movement. Then, on the command of execution "march," step forward 30 inches with the left foot and continue marching with 30-inch steps. Keep your eyes and head forward, as shown in Figure 2.5.1.

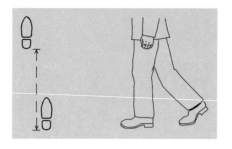

Swing your arms in a natural motion, without exaggeration, approximately nine inches to the front and six inches to the rear of the trouser seams. Keep your elbows straight, thumbs forward, and fingers curled in the same position as at attention so that the fingers just clear the trousers.

The Halt

The command to **halt** marching is "squad (platoon, etc.), halt." Your leader gives the preparatory command "squad (platoon, etc.)," as either foot strikes the marching surface as long as the drill leader gives the command of execution "halt" the next time that foot strikes the marching surface.

The halt requires two counts. After your leader commands "halt," move the additional step (required after the command of execution) to bring the trailing foot alongside the lead foot. Then, assume the position of attention—this ends the movement.

Rest Movements in Marching

Rest movements allow troops to conserve energy and revive while maintaining the momentum of the march.

At Ease, March

The drill leader gives the command "at ease, march" as either foot strikes the marching surface. On the command of execution "march," you are no longer required to retain cadence; however, you must still remain silent and maintain the approximate interval and distance. You can only resume "**quick time,** march" or "route step, march" from this rest movement.

Route Step, March

You execute "route step, march" in exactly the same manner as you did "at ease, march" except that you may drink and/or talk. From this rest movement, you can only resume marching at attention on the command "**quick time**, march."

Double Time

At the command "**double time, march,**" march in the cadence of 180 counts or steps per minute with a 30-inch step. You can respond to this command from the halt or while marching at quick time with a 30-inch step.

When at the halt, and your leader gives the preparatory command "double time," shift the weight of your body to the right foot without noticeable movement. On the command of execution "march," raise your forearms to a horizontal position,

---

Key Note Term

halt – command to bring moving formation to standstill

Key Note Terms

rest – relaxed form of march without a set cadence to conserve troops' energy

quick time – standard marching pace at 120 steps per minute

Key Note Term

double time –fast marching pace at 180 steps per minute

with fingers and thumbs closed, palm down, and knuckles out. At the same time, step out with your left foot. March with 30-inch steps at the cadence of double time. Swing your arms to the front and rear, keeping your forearms horizontal.

When marching with a 30-inch step in the cadence of quick time (120 counts or steps per minute), a drill leader can give the command "double time, march," when either foot strikes the marching surface. Then, on the command of execution "march," take one more 30-inch step at quick time and step off with your trailing foot, double timing as previously described.

To resume marching with a 30-inch step at the quick time cadence, your leader gives the command "quick time, march." The leader gives this command as either foot strikes the marching surface. On the command of execution "march," take two more 30-inch steps at double time, lower your arms to your sides, and resume marching with a 30-inch step at the quick time cadence.

The 15-inch Step (Half Step)

The 15-inch step was designed to slow a formation's advance to facilitate positioning on the battlefield as well as the parade field. The 15-inch step facilitates corrective maneuvers to keep a formation together in the advent of uneven terrain or a turn. Historically, tight formations were the primary means for concentrating force. Today, a tight formation is another demonstration of effective leadership and discipline

Forward Step

To march with a 15-inch step from the halt, the command is "half step, march." On the preparatory command "half step," shift the weight of your body to your right foot without noticeable movement. Then, on the command of execution "march," step forward 15 inches with your left foot and continue marching with 15-inch steps, as shown in Figure 2.5.2. Your arms should swing as they do when you march with a 30-inch step.

To change from a 30-inch step to a 15-inch step while marching, the command is "half step, march." Your leader may give this command as either foot strikes the marching surface. Then, on the command of execution "march," take one more 30-inch step and begin marching with a 15-inch step. Your arms should swing as they do when you march with a 30-inch step.

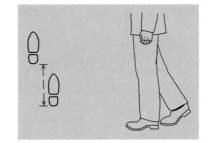

Figure 2.5.2: The 15-inch step.
Courtesy of US Army JROTC.

To direct you to resume marching with a 30-inch step, the leader commands, "forward, march" as either foot strikes the marching surface. Then, on the command of execution "march," take one more 15-inch step and begin marching with a 30-inch step.

To halt while marching at the half step, use the same procedures described in the 30-inch step. This step again has two counts.

It is important to note that while marching forward using the half step, the basic commands that your leader can give are "mark time, march," "forward, march," and "halt."

Right/Left Step

To march to the right or left with a 15-inch step, the command is "right (left) step, march." You perform the command only while at the halt. On the preparatory command "right (left) step," shift the weight of your body, without noticeable movement, onto the left (right) foot.

To execute right-step march, on the command of execution "march," bend your right knee slightly and raise your right foot only high enough to allow freedom of movement. Place your right foot 15 inches to the right of your left foot, and then move your left foot (keeping the left leg straight) alongside your right foot as in the position of attention. Continue this movement, keeping your arms as they are in the position of attention. Reverse this procedure to perform left-step march.

To halt when executing right- or left-step march, your leader commands "squad (platoon, etc.), halt." This movement has two counts. The leader gives the preparatory command when both heels are together. On the command of execution "halt," take one more step with your lead foot, then place the trailing foot alongside it, resuming the position of attention.

Backward Step

To direct you to march backward with a 15-inch step, your leader gives the command "backward, march." You perform the command only while you are at the halt. On the preparatory command "backward," shift the weight of your body, without noticeable movement, onto your right foot. Then, on the command of execution "march," take a 15-inch step backward with your left foot and continue marching backward with 15-inch steps. Let your arms swing naturally. To halt from backward march is a two count movement. This halt is basically the same as from the 30-inch step.

Changing Step in Marching

Your drill leader may command "change step, march" when the right foot strikes the marching surface. On the command of execution "march," take one more step with the left foot, then in one count place the right toe near the heel of the left foot and step off with the left foot. Let your arms swing naturally.

If you are marching in a formation and you notice that you are not leading with the correct foot, you should change step on your own automatically.

Marching in Place

The command for marching in place is "mark time, march." Your leader gives this command as either foot strikes the marching surface, from a 30-inch or 15-inch forward marching step. On the command of execution "march," take one more step, bring the trailing foot alongside the lead foot, and begin to march in place.

To begin marching in a 30-inch step from marching in place, your leader commands "forward, march." On the command of execution "march," take one more step in place then step off with a 30-inch step. Follow these same procedures if your leader commands "half step, march" except step off with a 15-inch step.

Drill Tips

The following tips can help you when you're commanding or performing drills.

- When at a halt, start all marching movements from the position of attention.

- Except for "route step, march" and "at ease, march," execute all marching movements while "marching at attention." Marching at attention is the combination of the position of attention and the procedures for the prescribed step executed simultaneously.

- When executed from the halt, all steps except "close interval, march," "right step march," and "about face" begin with your left foot.

- Unless otherwise specified, use 30-inch steps for marching forward.

- Execute all marching movements in the quick time cadence except for the command "double time, march."

- Execute all 15-inch step movements for a short distance only.

Keep in mind that marching is a five-step process:

1. Preparatory command step.

2. Intermediate or thinking step.

3. Command of execution step.

4. Additional step after the command of execution.

5. Execution of movement.

Conclusion

This lesson covered the basic steps and marching. You learned about the 30-inch step, the 15-inch step, changing step in marching, and marching in place.

The following lesson covers squad drills. In this lesson, you will learn the basics of squad formations and how to march the squad, with tips for conducting a proper drill.

Lesson Review

1. What is the standard size march step?
2. What is the advantage of rest moves while marching?
3. What is the difference between a quick-time and double-time march?
4. What is the correct command sequence for calling a formation to halt?

Lesson 6

Squad Drill

Key Terms

close interval
column
double interval
file
flank
formation
line
normal interval
pivot
rank

What You Will Learn to Do

• Demonstrate correct response to squad drill commands

Linked Core Abilities

• Communicate using verbal, nonverbal, visual, and written techniques
• Do your share as a good citizen in your school, community, country, and the world

Skills and Knowledge You Will Gain Along the Way

• Describe how to respond to commands when forming and marching the squad
• Identify the different types of squad formations and their related drill commands
• Identify the locations of key squad personnel in squad formation
• Define the key words contained in this lesson

Introduction

This lesson introduces you to the basics of practicing squad drill. It covers squad formations and teaches you how to march the squad, with tips for conducting a proper drill. To execute squad drill, you must first know how a squad forms and what your responsibilities are when it forms, such as knowing how to fall in, line up, and align yourself. After you have mastered these techniques, learning how to march uniformly with others is important in becoming a part of a sharp drill squad.

> ### General information about squad drill
>
> - Perform individual drill movements as described in the last lesson while executing drill as a squad member
> - The squad has two prescribed formations: **line** (or **rank**) and **column** (or **file**); however, your squad leader may form the squad in a column of twos from a column formation
> - When a squad forms in a line, its members are numbered from right to left; when in a column, from front to rear
> - When the squad drills as a separate unit and is in a line formation, the squad leader takes a position three steps in front of and centered on the squad
> - When it drills as a separate unit and is in a column or column of twos, the squad leader's position is three steps to the left and centered on the squad
> - When the squad drills as part of a larger formation, the squad leader occupies the number one (base) position of the squad

Key Note Terms

line – to form up in ranks, facing forward the length of the formation.

rank – to form up line abreast.

column – to form up in files, facing forward the width of the formation.

file – to form up in a column.

formation – patterned arrangement of troops

Squad Formations

The squad has two prescribed **formations**—line and column, as shown in Figure 2.6.1. The squad, however, may be formed into a column of twos from a column formation. When the squad is in line, squad members are numbered from right to left; when in column, form front to rear. The squad normally marches in column, but it may march in line for short distances.

When the squad is in a line formation, the squad leader assumes a post three steps in front of and centered on the squad; when in a column or a column of twos, three steps to the left and centered on the squad. When the squad drills as part of a larger unit, the squad leader occupies the number one (base) position of the squad and carries a weapon in the same manner as prescribed for other riflemen in the squad.

Forming the Squad

The squad normally forms in a line formation; however, it may re-form in column when each member can identify his exact position (equipment grounded) in the formation.

To form at normal interval, the squad leader comes to the position of attention and commands "fall in." On the command "fall in," the following actions occur simultaneously.

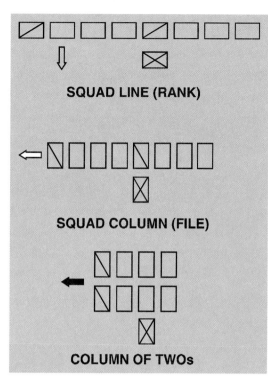

Figure 2.6.1: Squad formations.
Courtesy of US Army JROTC.

Each cadet double-times to their position in the formation.

The right-**flank** cadet positions themselves so that when the squad is formed it is three steps in front of and centered on the squad leader.

The right-flank cadet comes to the position of attention and raises their left arm laterally at shoulder level, elbow locked, fingers and thumb extended and joined, and palm facing down. They ensure that the left arm is in line with the body.

The cadet to the immediate left of the right-flank cadet comes to the position of attention, turns their head and eyes to the right, and raises their left arm in the same manner as the right flank cadet. They obtain proper alignment by taking short steps forward or backward until they are on line with the right-flank cadet. They then obtain exact interval by taking short steps left or right until their shoulder touches the extended fingertips of the right-flank cadet. As soon as the cadet to the left has obtained normal interval, each cadet individually lowers their arm to their side, sharply turn their head and eyes to the front, and assume the position of attention.

The right-flank cadet then sharply returns to the position of attention.

All other members of the squad form in the same manner except that the left flank cadet does not raise their left arm.

> **Key Note Term**
>
> **flank** – the side of the formation, either left or right

> **Note**
>
> The right-flank cadet raises their arm and looks straight to the front unless the squad is to align on an element to its right. If they align on an element to the right, they turn their head and eyes to the right and align themselves with that element.

Intervals

When the squad "falls in" for formation, it may be commanded to assume different spacing intervals between troops. Interval types include normal, close, and double.

Normal Interval

Normal interval spacing is a single arm's distance between troops. When the leader commands "Dress Right, **DRESS**" and "Ready, **FRONT**," the right-flank cadet stands fast. On the command of execution "**DRESS**," all cadets except the right-flank cadet turn their heads and eyes to the right and align themselves on the cadet to their right.

Each cadet, except the left-flank cadet, extends their left arms out to the side at shoulder level with elbows locked, fingers together, and palms down. They position themselves with short steps right or left so that their right shoulder touches the fingertips of the cadet to their right. On the command of execution "**FRONT**," each cadet sharply returns to the position of attention. Proper aligning in normal interval is shown in Figure 2.6.2.

If the squad leader wants to check the alignment, on the command of execution "**DRESS**," squad leader faces to the "half left" in marching and marches by the most direct route to a position on line with the squad, halts one step from the right flank cadet, and faces down the line. From this position, the squad leader verifies the alignment of the squad, directing the cadets to move forward or backward as necessary, calling them by name or number: "Cadet Jones, forward two inches; number eight, backward four inches."

The squad leader remains at attention, taking short steps to the right or left as necessary to see down the squad. Having aligned the squad he centers himself on the

Key Note Term

normal interval – single arm's distance between troops in rank

Figure 2.6.2: Aligning in normal interval.
Courtesy of US Army JROTC.

right-flank cadet by taking short steps left or right. The squad leader then faces to the half right in marching, returns to his position (center of the squad), halts perpendicular to the formation, faces to the left, and commands "Ready, **FRONT**." These procedures also apply when aligning the squad at close or Double Interval.

Close Interval

Close interval spacing is a single elbow's distance between troops. To have a squad form at close interval, the command is "At Close Interval, Fall In," To obtain close interval, place the heel of your left hand on your left hip even with your waist, your fingers and thumb together and extended downward. As shown in Figure 2.6.3, keep your elbow in line with your body, touching the right arm of the cadet to your left.

To align the squad at close interval, the leader commands "At Close Interval, Dress Right, **DRESS**" and "Ready, **FRONT**." The procedure is the same for aligning at normal interval, except that the cadets obtain close interval.

Double Interval

Double interval spacing is two arms' distance between troops. To have a squad form at a double interval, the leader commands "At Double Interval, Dress Right, **DRESS**" and "Ready, **FRONT**." On the command of execution DRESS, each cadet (except the right flank man) turn their head and eyes to the right, align themselves on the cadet on the right. At the same time each cadet (except the right and left flank man) raises both arms out to their sides at shoulder level so that their fingertips touch the fingertips of the cadets on their right and left. The left-flank cadet only raises the right arm to shoulder level.

Counting Off

Your squad may count off in line or column formation. The command is "Count, **OFF**." When in a line formation, the squad counts from right to left. On the command of execution "**OFF**" all cadets except the right-flank cadet turn their heads and eyes to the right. The right-flank cadet counts "one"; the next cadet to the left turns his or her head and eyes to the front and counts "two." Each remaining cadet follows in the same manner, counting with the next higher number.

Figure 2.6.3: Aligning in Close Interval.
Courtesy of US Army JROTC.

When in a column formation, execute counting off from front to rear. Then, on the command of execution "**OFF**," the cadet at the head of the column turns his or her head and eyes to the right, counts "**ONE**" over the right shoulder, and sharply returns to the position of attention. Each remaining cadet in the column counts off in the same manner, using the next higher number each time. The last cadet in the column does not turn his or her head and eyes to the right.

Changing Intervals

To ensure that each squad member understands the number of steps to take, the squad leader should command "Count, OFF" prior to changing intervals. Additionally, squad members do not raise their arms to measure distance (as they did to fall in) when changing intervals.

To change from normal interval to close interval, the command is "Close Interval, **MARCH**," On the command of execution "**MARCH**," the right-flank cadet stands fast. All cadets to that cadet's left execute "Right Step, **MARCH**," take one step less than the number of their position in line, and halt. For example, the fourth cadet in line would take three steps then "**HALT**."

To change from close interval to normal interval, the leader gives the command "Normal Interval, **MARCH**." The right-flank cadet stands fast on the command of execution "**MARCH**." All cadets to the left of the right-flank cadet execute "Left Step **MARCH**," take one step less than their number of their position in line (for example number nine man takes eight steps), and "**HALT**."

To change from normal to double Interval, the command is "Double Interval, **MARCH**." On the command of execution " **MARCH**," the right-flank cadet stands fast. The cadets to the left of that cadet face to the left as in marching, take one 30-inch step less than the number of their position in line(for example number seven takes six steps), "**HALT**," and execute "Right Face."

To change from double to normal interval, the command is "Normal Interval, **MARCH**." On the command of execution "**MARCH**," the right-flank cadet stands fast. The remaining cadets face to the right as in marching, take one 30-inch step less than the number of their position in line, "**HALT**," and execute "Left Face."

> **Note**
>
> The squad leader takes the correct number of steps to maintain his position of three steps in front of and centered on the squad. To review the 30-inch step, refer to Chapter 2, Lesson 5.

Rest and Dismissal

Rest movements are the same for a squad as they are for individuals. Your squad leader may command "**FALL OUT**" if a more relaxed position than rest is appropriate. If the squad leader commands "**FALL OUT**," you may move out of the formation, but you must stay in the immediate area.

Your drill leader dismisses the squad from the position of attention. The command is "**Dissmissed**." Upon hearing that command, all members of the squad may then leave the area.

Marching the Squad

To march the squad, use the following procedures:

- **For short distances only, the squad may be marched forward while in a line formation.**

- **When marching long distances, the squad is marched in column.**

- **To form a column formation from a line formation, the command is "Right, Face."**

- **When a column formation is originated from a line formation at close interval, the squad may be marched for short distances at the half step with less than correct distance. To obtain correct distance while marching with less than correct distance, the command is "Extend, MARCH." On the command of execution "MARCH," the number one man takes one more 15-inch step and then steps off with a 30-inch step. Each squad member begins marching with a 30-inch step at the approximate point where the number one man stepped off, or as soon as correct distance has been obtained.**

More Drill Tips

- The squad normally marches in a column, but for short distances it may march in a line formation

- To form a column formation from a line formation, the command is "right, face"

- When a column formation is at close interval, the squad may march for short distances at the half step

Changing Direction

From the halt, the command to start the squad in motion and simultaneously change the direction of march 90 or 45 degrees is "**Column Right (Left), MARCH**" or "**Column Half Right (Left), MARCH**." On the command of execution " **MARCH**," the lead cadet faces to the right (left) as in marching by pivoting to the right (left) on the ball of the right foot and steps off in the indicated direction taking a 30-inch step with the left foot and continues to march. The number two cadet adjusts his step by lengthening or shortening as necessary to reach the approximate pivot point of the lead cadet. When he reaches the approximate pivot point of the lead cadet, he pivots to the right (left) on the ball of the lead foot taking a 30-inch step with the trail foot in the new direction. All other cadets step off with the left foot and continue to march forward taking 30-inch steps and execute in the same manner as the number two cadet in approximately the same place until the entire squad has executed the column movement.

To change the direction of march 90 or 45 degrees when marching, the squad leader gives the preparatory command "**Column Right (Left) or Column Half Right (Half Left)**" as the foot in the desired direction strikes the marching surface. The squad leader then gives the command "**MARCH**" the next time that foot strikes the marching surface. On " **MARCH**," the lead cadet takes one additional step, pivots in the commanded direction as the pivot foot strikes the surface, and continues to march in the new direction. Other cadets continue to march forward and execute the pivot as previously described (see Figure 2.6.4).

Key Note Term

pivot – to turn in position

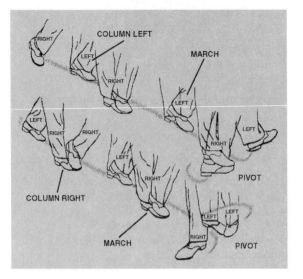

Figure 2.6.4: Changing marching direction.
Courtesy of US Army JROTC.

To march in the opposite direction, the command is "**(Rear, MARCH)**." The squad leader gives the preparatory command "to the Rear" as the right foot strikes the marching surface and commands "**MARCH**" the next time the right foot strikes the surface. On "**MARCH**," all cadets take one more step with their left foot, pivot on the balls of both feet, turn 180 degrees to the right, and step off in the new direction. Do not swing your arms when you make the pivot.

To avoid an obstacle in the line of march, the squad leader commands, "INCLINE AROUND LEFT (RIGHT)." The lead cadet inclines around the obstacle and resumes the original direction. All other cadets follow the lead cadet.

Marching to the Flank

When your squad marches to the flank, it does so only for short distances, and always in a column formation. The command is "**Right (Left) Flank, MARCH**." Your squad leader gives the preparatory command "**Right (Left) Flank**" when the foot in the desired direction strikes the marching surface, and the command of execution "**MARCH**" when that foot strikes the marching surface the next time.

On the command "**MARCH**," all cadets take one more step, pivot 90 degrees in the indicated direction on the ball of the lead foot, and step off in the new direction with the trailing foot. As your squad begins marching in the new direction, they should glance out of the corner of their right eye and dress to the right.

Forming a Column of Twos and Re-Forming

When marching in a squad, you march in a column (one long line) most of the time. A variation of this formation is the column of twos, as shown in Figure 2.6.5. The column of twos is always formed from a file formation when the squad is at the halt. The command is "**Column of Twos to the Right (Left), MARCH**." On the preparatory command by the squad leader, the lead team leader commands "**STAND FAST**."

280 *Chapter 2   Leadership Skills*

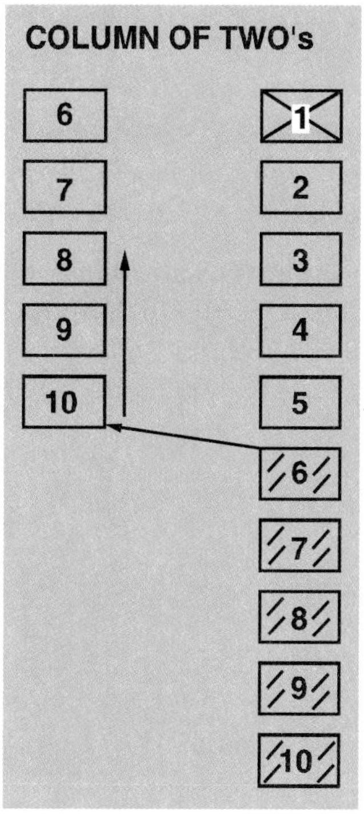

COLUMN OF TWO's

6	1
7	2
8	3
9	4
10	5
	6
	7
	8
	9
	10

Figure 2.6.5: Forming a column of twos.
Courtesy of US Army JROTC.

The trailing team leader commands "Column Half Right (Left), **MARCH**." On the command of execution "**MARCH**," the trailing team leader executes a column half right (half left) and inclines to the right (left) around the lead column. The cadets in the trailing team follow their leader.

When the trailing team leader reaches a point even with the lead team leader, he or she commands "**Mark time, MARCH**." As the cadets behind the trailing team leader align themselves with the cadets in the lead column, they continue to march in place. When they are in position, the trailing team leader commands, "**Team, HALT**."

Re-forming a single file from a column of twos is only done from the halt. The command is "**File from the Left (Right), MARCH**." On the preparatory command by the squad leader, the lead team leader commands, "**FORWARD**" and the trailing team leader commands "**STAND FAST**."

On the command of execution "**MARCH**," the lead team begins marching forward. When the second cadet from the rear of the lead team is abreast of the trailing team leader, that team leader commands "Column Half Right (Left)." Then, when the last cadet of the lead team is abreast (of the trailing team leader) and the last cadet's right foot strikes the marching surface, the trailing team leader commands "**MARCH**." The trailing team leader then inclines right (left) to follow the lead team at the appropriate distance.

Conclusion

This lesson explained the basics so you can begin practicing squad drill. It takes concentration and diligence to master the squad drill techniques. Properly executed, a smooth squad march reflects on the professionalism of your JROTC team.

This lesson concludes Unit 2, "Leadership Theory and Application." In the following unit, "Foundations for Success," you will learn how to better yourself through self awareness, personal growth, sharpening your learning, study, and communication skills, and understanding what causes and how to handle conflict.

Lesson Review

1. What is standard spacing when falling into formation?

2. What is the difference between "Falling Out" and being "Dismissed?"

3. With which foot do you always begin marching?

4. What is the difference between a flanking movement and a column movement?

Leadership Planning

Development

Key Terms

assess
conceptual skills
executing
interpersonal skills
technical skills

What You Will Learn to Do

- Create a plan of action to develop leadership skills through the Leadership Development Program

Linked Core Abilities

- Build your capacity for lifelong learning
- Take responsibility for your actions and choices

Skills and Knowledge You Will Gain Along the Way

- Describe the components of the Leadership Development Program
- Describe the seven values of leadership
- Describe the 15 dimensions of leadership
- Define the key words contained in this lesson

Introduction

This lesson introduces and explains the Cadet Command's Leadership Development Program as it applies to JROTC and to *you*. The focus of this program is to **assess** *your* leadership ability and potential; therefore, the effort that *you* put into it will directly benefit *you* and will help the instructors and others involved in *your* growth and development to better predict *your* success and potential to be a cadet leader.

Having an assessment and development process of some kind is a fundamental component of teaching and learning. The study of leadership is no different. Such a process lets those who teach and those who study leadership know when and to what degree they have been successful.

Key Note Term

assess – to pass judgment or assign value

Leadership Opportunities

The instructor staff will plan for a variety of leadership opportunities to meet the quantity and variety of objectives you encounter in JROTC. Over time, these different assignments will provide a wide variety of long- and short-term opportunities. Some typical opportunities include the following:

- **A senior position in the cadet chain of command other than what you currently hold for a designated period of time**
- **Leader during a ceremony, inspection, and so on**
- **Trainer or coach during a *Leadership Lab* class**
- **Assistant instructor for a *First Aid* or *Map Reading* Class**
- **Team leader for a color guard performance**
- **Team leader for a drill event**
- **Community service project leader**
- **Class trainer or instructor for a specific task or presentation**

Why Seek Leadership Opportunities?

There are many reasons why you might want to seek out leadership opportunities. You can build your confidence and develop your skill at guiding and influencing others to accomplish specific tasks. You can also work on your overall ability to accomplish missions while caring for people and expanding your capabilities for the future.

Note

Good individual *character* is a prerequisite for good leadership.

Leadership Development Program

The Leadership Development Program (LDP) is based on the principle that cadets be "trained to standards." Cadet standards are expressed in terms of both the seven values and the 15 dimensions of leadership. The Leadership Development Program is a continuous process of training, evaluating, counseling, retraining, and re-evaluating. Evaluation is a fundamental part of training; it lets both you and your instructors know when and to what degree they have been successful.

Components of the Leadership Development Program include the following:

- **Train**
- **Evaluate**
- **Counsel**
- **Retrain**
- **Reevaluate**

You will be counseled, developed, and your progress assessed throughout the remainder of your cadet experiences in JROTC. You will be involved in instruction that will provide you with progressive experiences that will challenge you mentally and physically. As you progress, and the expectation of your performance increases, the instructor staff will assess and counsel your growth and development.

Leadership Assessment Process

The focus of the Leadership Development Program is to assess your leadership ability and potential; its aim is to develop you to the maximum extent possible. Your instructors will carefully assess you each time they place you in a leadership

Figure 3.1.1: Leaders will evaluate your performance.
Courtesy of US Army JROTC.

position. When you are not leading, you will be assessed as a follower. The Leadership Assessment Process provides a formal method of evaluation by offering leadership opportunities, assessing leadership performance, and providing effective feedback.

Leadership opportunities provide practical applications in the exercise of leading and caring. It is under these conditions that your growth and development are maximized. The instructor staff document and measure your growth and development against established standards, not in terms of cadet against peer. You also receive timely feedback and have the opportunity to write self-assessments.

Assessing Leadership Performance

The goal of leadership assessment is to develop competent and confident leaders. It should be a positive and useful experience. To do an assessment, the instructors will make judgments about how well you act and cause others to act in terms of the seven leadership values and the 15 leadership dimensions. Therefore, they will make judgments regarding

- **Your values**
- **The attributes and skills that you appear to have, based on how well you reflect them in your actions and behavior**

> ### Note
> In this case, the term *skills* refers to abilities or competencies and *behavior* refers to performance or the application of those skills consistent with or influenced by your character.

Providing Effective Assessments

One key to your growth in technical and leadership skills and abilities is in offering positive assessments. Each time instructors assess your performance, they address notable strengths and weaknesses as well as specific means for making improvement. Common means of providing feedback may include written test scores, performance results, counseling sessions, and coaching.

To promote development of an individual, instructors counsel and coach you on how to improve your values, attributes, skills, and/or actions. A fundamental belief is that a person can learn and develop all of these qualities.

The goal, then, is to develop better cadet leaders now so they will continue to use their leadership skills and abilities throughout their lives. Instructors can influence this goal by the success of their leadership assessment and development efforts.

Leadership Assessment Criteria: Values and Dimensions

In the Leadership Development Program, the foundation for assessment of your leadership potential and development are the seven leadership values and the 15 leadership dimensions. With these values and dimensions, there are performance indicators and standards that help the instructors to define what your minimum acceptable performance should be. Essentially, these indicators guide their judgment process and aid in the overall consistency in making assessments about your growth and development.

The Seven Leadership Values

The aspects required for leaders to have character and competence are the seven leadership values. Understanding these values is only the first step. As a leader, you must not only understand them, you must believe in them, model them in your own actions, and teach others to accept and live by them. They are listed in order to form the acronym LDRSHIP.

- **Loyalty:** Bear true faith and allegiance to the *U.S. Constitution*, your unit, and friends
- **Duty:** Fulfill your obligations
- **Respect:** Promote dignity, consideration, fairness, and equal opportunity; treat people as they should be treated
- **Selfless service:** Place the welfare of the nation, your community, your unit, and your subordinates before your own
- **Honor:** Adhere to the code of values
- **Integrity:** Exhibit high personal moral standards
- **Personal courage:** Face physical and moral adversity

The Fifteen Leadership Dimensions

The aspects of character and competence of leaders and their actions to achieve excellence are the basis for 15 leadership dimensions. Do you recall the *BE, KNOW, DO* attributes? Character describes what leaders must *BE*; competence refers to what they must *KNOW*; and actions are what leaders must *DO*. Along these same lines, the 15 dimensions are broken down into the three categories of attributes (*BE*), skills (*KNOW*), and actions (*DO*).

> **Note**
>
> As you study these 15 dimensions, notice the similarities between them and other leadership concepts that have been presented.

Attributes (What Leaders Must BE)

Values tell us part of what the leader must *BE*; the other side of what a leader must *BE* are the leader attributes. Leader attributes influence leader actions; leader actions in turn always influence the unit. Attributes are a person's fundamental qualities and characteristics. They are more or less permanent, yet you can develop them over time through correct and habitual practices. The attributes are as follows:

- **Mental:** Possess will, initiative, and discipline, self-judgment, self-confidence, intelligence, and cultural awareness
- **Physical:** Maintain appropriate level of physical fitness and professional bearing
- **Emotional:** Display self-control, balance, and stability; be calm under pressure

Skills (What Leaders Must KNOW)

Skill development is a part of self-development and is a prerequisite to action. Values and leader attributes form the foundation of character, which in turn serves as the basis of knowing (competence) and doing (leadership). The self-discipline that leads to teamwork is rooted in character. Teamwork depends on the actions of competent leaders of proven character who know their profession and act to improve their units. The best leaders constantly strive to improve and to get better at what they do. Their self-discipline focuses on learning more about their profession and continually getting the team to perform better. They build competence in themselves and in their subordinates. Leaders develop competence by developing at least three types of skills.

- **Conceptual skills** (*skills with ideas*): Demonstrate sound judgment, problem-solving, critical/creative thinking, and moral reasoning
- **Interpersonal skills** (*people skills*): Coach, teach, counsel, motivate, and develop subordinate leaders
- **Technical skills** (*job skills*): Possess the necessary expertise to accomplish all tasks

Actions (What Leaders Must DO)

Leaders act. They bring together everything they are, everything they believe, and everything they know how to do to provide purpose, direction, and motivation. Leaders work to influence people, operate to accomplish the mission, and act to improve their unit.

Developing the right values, attributes, and skills is the only preparation to lead. Leadership does not begin until you act. Leaders who live up to values, who display attributes, who are competent, who act at all times as they would have their subordinates act, will succeed. Leaders who talk a good game but cannot back their words always fail in the long run.

Leader actions fall into the three categories of influencing, operating, and improving. Influencing is the method of reaching goals while operating and improving. It consists of the following dimensions:

Key Note Terms

conceptual skills – capacity for sound judgment, problem-solving, critical/creative thinking, and moral reasoning

interpersonal skills – ability to work with and positively relate to other people

technical skills – understanding and ability needed to perform assigned tasks

- **Communicating:** Display good oral, written, and listening skills
- **Decision making:** Employ sound judgment and logical reasoning; use resources wisely
- **Motivating:** Inspire, motivate, and guide others toward mission accomplishment

Operating is what you do to accomplish the mission in the short-term, to get the job done on time and to standard. It consists of the following dimensions:

- **Planning and preparing:** Develop detailed executable plans that are feasible, acceptable, and executable
- **Executing:** Meet mission standards, take care of subordinates, and efficiently manage resources (time, people, and material)
- **Assessing:** Efficiently and effectively evaluate plans in terms of their purpose and mission to facilitate consistent improvement

Improving is ensuring the long-term improvement in the organization and its members. It consists of the following dimensions:

- **Developing:** Invest adequate time and effort to develop individual subordinates as leaders; this includes mentoring
- **Building:** Spend time to improve individuals, teams, groups, and the unit; this includes fostering an ethical climate
- **Learning:** Seek self-improvement/growth; envision and adapt to change

Because people act based on their values, attributes, and skills, supervisors can effectively make assessments of those character qualities. Ultimately, however, whether an individual improves in leadership ability (and self-confidence) is up to that person.

Key Note Term

executing – to carry out or put into effect; to do what is required

Conclusion

The Leadership Development Program can help you to learn more about your own leadership strengths, weaknesses, and potential; predict your success as a cadet leader; and evaluate how well you can handle certain leadership situations and responsibilities. Your ability to further develop these skills and your leadership potential is up to you. Your growth does not end with this lesson. You must continue to self-develop these skills by applying them to all types of situations—in school, at work, and throughout your life.

Knowing yourself and making self-assessments are important elements of being a leader. Because the instructors will be evaluating you on the 7 leadership values and the 15 dimensions, do a self-assessment to determine what you believe are your strongest and weakest values and dimensions. Identify at least one strategy that you plan to take to improve on your weak values and dimensions.

The following lesson examines the importance of goal setting. You will learn how to set challenging yet attainable goals for yourself and for those whom you lead.

Lesson Review

1. What are the five components of the Leadership Development Program?
2. What are the three elements of the Leadership Assessment Process?
3. List the seven leadership values.
4. List three of your strongest and weakest leadership attributes and discuss how you might improve.

Lesson 2

Goal Setting

Key Terms

goals
priority
tangible

What You Will Learn to Do

- Establish performance goals related to the JROTC program

Linked Core Abilities

- Build your capacity for lifelong learning
- Take responsibility for your actions and choices

Skills and Knowledge You Will Gain Along the Way

- Explain the value of goal setting for task achievement
- Discuss how a positive leadership role motivates others
- Discuss how goal setting affects achievements and motivation
- Describe feelings and outcomes of winning and losing
- Define the key words contained in this lesson

Introduction

Setting goals for yourself is an important step in becoming who you want to be and what you want to accomplish. It has been proven that specific and difficult goals, with feedback, lead to higher performance. So often we are told to "do our best." That can be in the accomplishment of a cross-country race, a basketball game, an English test or anything we want to accomplish. But what is "your best?" What if the cross-country coach said he wanted you to increase your speed so you could take two minutes off your best time? How about striving for 85 percent or higher on the English test? When someone has been given goals that are specific and challenging and they are given continuous feedback the impact on the accomplishment is impressive.

In this lesson, you will learn the importance of setting reasonable goals that you can achieve and adding more challenges as you go along.

Understanding the Importance of Goals

Goals tell you what needs to be done. Difficult goals are an internal stimulus to push hard to accomplish. And feedback tells you how you are doing. It points out the gap between what you have done and what you want to do. Additionally, self-generated feedback is a stronger motivator than external feedback. That means if you can establish a feedback process for yourself, you will be more motivated than if someone else provides that feedback.

It has also been proven that if the person involved has the opportunity to participate in the goal setting process, they will try harder.

Important to the goal-setting process is that the individual or team is committed to the goal and will not lower or abandon it; they feel capable of attaining the goal; the goal has been made public; and it has been self-set rather than assigned.

Setting Goals

Setting clear and specific goals offers purpose and direction for both leaders and followers. When you are in a leadership position, you and your followers should ensure that you have a set of clearly written and defined goals and priorities and that, everyone must understand and support them.

There are several key points or guidelines that you should consider when setting goals for your team. These guidelines include the following:

- **Make goals realistic and attainable**
- **Ensure that goals lead to improved individual and team performance**
- **Involve team members in the goal setting process**
- **As a minimum, establish goals for training, maintenance (of appearance and personal property), discipline, morale, cohesion, and development of followers**
- **Develop a program or set of policies to achieve each goal**

Developing Plans to Achieve Goals

After you have analyzed a situation, you can begin setting goals based on what you want the team to accomplish. For each goal you set, you need a well-defined plan that explains how you intend to achieve it. Develop plans by identifying the task or tasks that your team must accomplish, putting them in **priority**, and establishing all the conditions necessary to carry out each task. Remember to consider the capabilities of your team members when assigning tasks.

Write the plan down on paper (see Figure 3.2.1). This helps you to organize the details of how to reach the goal. By having something **tangible**, such as a written version of the plan, you can see exactly what you want to accomplish, when, how, and with what resources. A properly written plan can help you to remain focused on the results.

It is also important to have a method to monitor and evaluate your team's progress (see Figure 3.2.2). This helps you and the other team members stay on schedule and it gives you a basis to make changes to your plan as necessary. Use a checklist or some other document that spells out exactly what the standards are that you must accomplish. Post those standards for everyone to see. Another good method of evaluation is to seek feedback from instructors or others.

Remember, as a leader, you influence your teammates by what you say, write, and most important, do. Every leadership situation is unique; therefore, every goal you set and every plan you develop must be flexible and adapted to each situation. You must be able to look at every situation, analyze it, and then determine exactly what actions you should take to accomplish the mission.

Figure 3.2.1: Writing down goals can help you organize your plan to achieve them.
Courtesy of Corbis Images.

Figure 3.2.2: When goals are achieved, check them off and go on to the next task.
Courtesy of Paul Edmondson/Corbis Images.

Conclusion

As you learned in this lesson, goals are critical to motivation. You reviewed the guidelines for goal setting, learned how to set your own performance goals, and established a mechanism for tracking and evaluating progress.

Lesson Review

1. What is the purpose of goals?

2. Why are evaluation and feedback important to attaining goals?

3. Describe some important attributes of good goals?

4. What is the purpose of plans?

Chapter 4

Leadership Strategies

Lesson 1

Celebrating Differences— Culture and Individual Diversity

Key Terms

culture
discrimination
ethnic
impartial
inclusionary
minority
stereotypes
synergy

What You Will Learn to Do

- Employ strategies for neutralizing the impact of personal prejudices and stereotypes on your relationships with others

Linked Core Abilities

- Take responsibility for your actions and choices
- Treat self and others with respect

Skills and Knowledge You Will Gain Along the Way

- Identify how people display prejudice toward others
- Identify reasons for discrimination and stereotyping
- Describe ways a leader can guide diverse groups to work together as a team
- Define the key words contained in this lesson

Introduction

Captain Kirk, Lieutenant Uhura, Lieutenant Sulu, Ensign Chekhov, Mr. Spock, Worf, Data, and Geordi La Forge—what a cast of characters! The crew members were international, interplanetary, half-human and half-vulcan, and humanoid and blind with a visor for seeing. Yes, *Star Trek* and *Star Trek: The Next Generation* raised some issues about diversity.

Synergy is when you and your team members cooperate together and create better results than they could get working alone. Each individual is unique and you must value that uniqueness, just like Captain Kirk and his crew did. Real synergy is celebrating differences, teamwork, open-mindedness, and finding new and better ways of doing things.

On July 26, 1948, President Harry S. Truman signed Executive Order 9981. This order called for the integration of the armed forces and an end to discrimination against soldiers because of race, color, or creed. Although the Army completed its desegregation in the 1950s, the assignment of whites and members of **minority** groups to the same units did not ensure total equality, racial harmony, or a fully integrated Army. The Army, similar to society at large, began to address the questions and challenges of the race issue seriously in the 1960s. Today, every Army element is expected to have an active race relations and equal opportunity program. Laws and regulations provide guidelines to ensure the execution of these programs.

Employees of private organizations as well as members of the military come from all walks of life, different geographical areas, and numerous racial and **ethnic** backgrounds. They bring with them their own challenges and prejudices. The leader's challenge is to direct members of these diverse groups in a way that will cause them to work together as a team. It is not an easy task, but is one that can be accomplished through informed, fair, and impartial leadership and educational awareness.

Key Note Terms

synergy – a joint action or force

minority – a racial, religious, or ethnic group different from the dominant group

Key Note Term

ethnic – of, pertaining to, or characteristic of the basic groups of people with a common history, language, culture, and identity

Values and Attitudes

Values and attitudes are important to the daily functioning of our lives. They help form the basis of how you see yourself and those around you as individuals, how you see others, and how you interpret the world in general. As a leader, you will often be involved with individuals who have different values and attitudes from your own; you have probably already experienced many of these differences. Some may have been due to religious or cultural backgrounds; others may have stemmed from racial or ethnic backgrounds.

In your role as a leader, you will also be a counselor and a helper. To communicate well with others, it is necessary for you to understand the dynamics involved with the value and attitude differences that occur within each human being and that can come between people.

There are cultural differences and similarities in assigning levels of importance to values. In a study that evaluated the levels of importance 29 values in 5 cultures, none of them were shared by all five cultures as *primary values* (values that are most important to an individual and worth dying for, such as one's country, patriotism, freedom, or religion) or *secondary values* (values that are important but not worth dying for, such as money). Other values evaluated by the study were respect for youth, human dignity, hierarchy, authoritarianism, education, and frankness.

As a member of society, you are involved daily with attitudes and behavior and must understand how one affects the other. As you can see in the following, there is a continuous chain relationship between them:

- **My attitudes affect my behavior**

- **My behavior affects your attitudes**

- **Your attitudes affect your behavior**

- **Your behavior affects my attitudes**

Attitudes can have positive or negative implications. Although they can help make sense out of life experiences, individuals cannot change them easily. Furthermore, you may not always be aware of the extensive influences that your attitudes have on other people, jobs, and situations or how they can affect a person's learning, personality, prejudices, and productivity.

Self-Concept

As a leader, you will constantly be dealing with people. It will make your job a lot easier if you know and have an idea of who you are and how you relate to others. You need to know how you are perceived by others.

The most important single factor affecting people's communication with others is their self-concept, that is, how they see themselves and their situations. Although situations may change from moment-to-moment or place-to-place, people's beliefs about themselves are always determining factors in their communicative behavior. People have literally thousands of concepts about themselves: who they are, what they stand for, where they live, what they do and do not do, what they value, and what they believe.

Self-concept is the picture you have of yourself as seen through your own thoughts, development, perceptions, and feelings.

- *Development* is the way you feel about yourself, which has a direct relationship to your upbringing; it includes values and attitudes
- *Perception* refers to the interpretation and the amount of "emotional charge" attributed to past events and present situations
- *Feelings* refer to the positive or negative, good or bad, indifference or intensity, of emotions or interpretation of oneself

Contrary to what you would like, you cannot buy self-concept/personality attributes from a store. Your personality is a combination of heredity and life experiences. To gain a better understanding of self-concept, where it comes from, and how it develops, look at the main ingredients: heritage and needs fulfillment/emotional development.

Heritage

As soon as you came into this world, society classified you in terms of the following:

- **Gender**, such as male, female
- **Race**, such as White, Black, Hispanic, Asian
- **Nationality**, such as American, German, Irish, Swedish
- **Religion**, such as Catholic, Jewish, Muslim
- **Family** status, such as lower, middle, upper class
- **Legal status**, such as foreign or native citizen
- **Environment**, such as from country, suburbs, inner city
- **Physical status**, such as a cute or ugly baby
- **Parentage**, such as married, single, divorced

Needs Fulfillment/Emotional Development

Your personal, psychological, emotional, and physical needs define your self-concept. As you grow older, you define your own needs (what is important to you). How you feel about yourself has a direct relationship on others around you. Examine Table 4.1.1. If you do not have a positive self-image, how will you project yourself, especially if you are a leader?

Remember, how you view yourself impacts not only how you view others, but how they view you. Some differences exist because each person places a different importance on different needs. People would like to be better than they are. You can change if you want. The most important thing to consider is that no one else can make you change. You have the right to fight to remove inappropriate or incorrect perceptions, prejudices, and discriminatory attitudes and behavior.

Table 4.1.1: Positive vs. Negative Self-Image

Positive Self-Image	Negative Self-Image
Love of self and others	Hate of self and others
Excited about reaching out for the adventure of life	Hide from life and its miseries
Experience serenity, joy, hope, and trust	Experience anxiety, despair, distrust, and anger
Develop your intelligence	Blind to your potential
Decisive, assertive	Indecisive, defensive, aggressive
Enjoy your physical abilities	Deny or exaggerate physical abilities
Create	Destroy
Tolerant, accepting	Bigoted, prejudiced
Self-actualizing	Suicidal/homicidal
Open	Closed
Trusting	Hidden agendas
Assertive	Defensive

Prejudice and Discrimination

You live in America, the most democratic (and free) country in the world. Why, then, is there still prejudice and discrimination in this land of opportunity?

You might ask yourself, "Am I prejudiced?" It has often been said that everyone is prejudiced to a certain degree. Everyone operates on prejudgments and makes discriminating distinctions every day. For example, if you had good luck with one type of car, you can be expected to be prejudiced in favor of that model; when voting, many people discriminate between Republican, Democrat, or another party's candidates.

These examples illustrate the frequency in everyday life that people make decisions based on their prejudices or discriminatory practices. However, the negative forms of prejudice and discrimination have adverse impacts on leadership and unit cohesion.

Prejudice

Prejudice is defined as a feeling, favorable or unfavorable, toward a person, object, or group that may or may not be based on actual experience(s). It is generally agreed that a racial prejudice is a negative attitude toward a racial or ethnic group that is maintained through **stereotypes**.

Key Note Term

stereotypes – an uncritical or formalized conception, notion, or attitude

In looking at the norms, values, beliefs, and attitudes developed through socialization, you may have said to yourself that each of those concepts may impact positively or negatively on how you view the world around you. Indeed, these concepts are the sources of bias or prejudice that unquestionably can distort how you make "sense" of reality.

If you agree with the idea that norms, values, beliefs, and attitudes do exist within each of us (and that they do influence our ability to perceive, and that influence can also be called prejudice), it would seem then that all humans are capable of being prejudiced.

Another factor that is closely related, if not interwoven, with the norms, values, beliefs, and attitudes is one's culture. A **culture** is the total of the learned behaviors of a group of people that are generally considered to be the tradition of that people and are transmitted from generation to generation. These learned behaviors include language and nonverbal norms, such as body language, facial expressions, and color consciousness.

Key Note Term

culture – civilization

Many people confuse color with culture. You can share aspects of a culture, but not color. Color is genetic; culture is learned. In many cultures, skin color differences take on a measure of importance, status, or value. The color of one's skin in certain cultures may dictate how that individual is treated within that culture. Color has a tremendous impact on perceptions in the United States because most Americans respond to color by making assumptions and treating people based on skin color.

Not convinced? Here is a question to ask yourself. *Do you behave differently around people who are of a different color?* You may not want to behave differently, but you may recognize that you do from time to time. Your behavior largely depends on the environment that you are in. If you are in control, or think you are, your behavior is pretty constant. After you become the minority, so to speak, you may become suspicious, feel threatened, distrust may set in, and your behavior may change.

The following highlights some of the explanations for prejudice:

- **A dominant group avoids the feelings of sympathy for "dominated people" through over-exaggerations of negative qualities. A dominant group is the one in control of the major positions in a society and that sets the standards for the whole society.**

- **The belief that one's own family and society are unique and correct. You might feel that your group is the natural one and judge others based on this standard.**

> **Note**
>
> Every human group seems to do this, serving as a positive reinforcement within each society.

- **Prejudice is a natural outgrowth of the "we-they" contrast.** After an opponent is present, prejudice can be expected. Loosely scattered members of a group then come together to face a common opponent.

- **The transfer of internal personal problems to external objects.** People who have a distorted need to feel superior to others use scapegoats in this way.

- **A particularly negative experience with a member of a particular racial or ethnic group in the past** might bring up memories that can cloud your judgment in the present. You may also tend to judge the whole society by your own experiences. If you have not been a victim of prejudice, you may not see it in others.

- **The "earned reputation" approach** means that members of society shift the justification for prejudice to a target group: "if only they would mend their ways, prejudice would go away."

Unfortunately, people with negative attitudes generally tend to express themselves with action, and they act out their prejudices in various way. The most common ways are as follows:

- **Openly talking about their prejudices with like-minded friends and expressing their dislikes freely.**

- **Avoiding members of the disliked group, even at the cost of considerable inconvenience.**

- **Actively making detrimental distinctions about a group, to the extent of excluding all members of that group from certain types of employment, educational opportunities, politics, and so on.**

- **Committing acts of violence, especially when under conditions of heightened emotions.**

Now that you have explored prejudice and learned explanations for its existence, turn your attention to discrimination.

Discrimination

Discrimination is defined as the actions or practices carried out by members of dominant groups, or their representatives, that have a differential and harmful impact on members of subordinate groups. The actions may be open or hidden, direct or indirect, intentional or unintentional. The actors in these events may be individuals, groups, or organizations.

It is crucial to understand that there is a direct link between discrimination and power. Without power, discrimination is passive and ineffective. With power, discrimination maintains the dominance of one group over another. The term *power* in this context means the expenditure of energy to get things done. The groups in power are those that can effectively discriminate: they can pass laws, make rules, and decide who belongs in and who remains on the outside.

Causes for discrimination include the following:

- **Group size.** This may be the simplest explanation for discriminatory behavior among dominant group members. They fear they will be overwhelmed by the sheer number of the subordinated "masses." Racial groups that continually increase in size have always been the targets for some form of control. On the other hand, the smaller the ethnic minority group, the less threatening it is.

> **Key Note Term**
>
> **discrimination** – to show preference for or prejudice against

- **Social distance.** The attempt by a dominate group to keep a distance between it and a subordinate group by limiting access and intimacy. For example, you cannot join a specific club unless you earn $250,000 a year.

- **Competition.** It always serves the dominant group's best interests to limit competition with a subordinate group, from competing for scarce economic resources to other forms such as athletic competition.

- **Status consciousness.** Minority groups occupy a generally low status in American society. For example, status-conscious whites avoid lower-status people due to their prejudicial perceptions.

Stereotyping

Stereotyping is related to just about all of the factors discussed above. A stereotype, whether favorable or unfavorable, is an exaggerated belief associated with a category. Its function is to justify (or rationalize) our conduct in relation to that category. People naturally seek to understand or make sense of their environment. Because you cannot possibly analyze or respond to all of the information that you receive, you may tend to narrow your focus on subsets of that information. You will usually select the subset that you believe to be most important. People then categorize (stereotype) this information to serve a useful function, depending on their group (religious, racial, ethnic, cultural, and so on) affiliation.

- **Categorization simplifies your environment.** It enables you to generate expectations and guides your behavior toward a person or an object based on those expectations.

- **When you categorize a person as a member of a group, you may assume that he or she has a variety of characteristics that you believe members of that category have. You then look at people as a group based on a variety of factors (such as age, religion, gender, race) and whether they are part of the in-group (most like you) or the out-group (most different from you). The people that you tend to categorize (stereotype) most are the out-group.**

- **Stereotypes are fixed, rigid ideas associated with a category. They are not identical with the category, but are overgeneralizations or oversimplifications about a category.**

- **Because stereotypes can be either favorable or unfavorable, they can lead to love-prejudice or hate-prejudice relationships.**

- **Stereotypes are the rationalizers that allow you to justify behavior to categorically accept or reject a group and to selectively maintain your perception and thinking about a group.**

- **There may be examples of behavior by members of a group that support the belief offered in an expressed stereotype of a given group. For example, one can find a few people in groups who are dishonest, but those examples do not warrant that all within the group are dishonest.**

There are also a number of sources that not only develop but support and sustain stereotypes. In fact, there is very little chance of anyone not being exposed to at least one of these sources of stereotypes.

The very socialization process discussed earlier in this lesson is a powerful source in the development of stereotypes.

- Hearing and/or telling ethnic, racist, or sexist jokes
- Reading the literature of a culture or society, whether fact or fiction, has a powerful influence on our thinking and behavioral processes
- The coverage of news on radio and television plus movies all carry powerful messages that create and support stereotyping

Racial Tension

Racial tension within an organization is often the result of poor leadership. The major reasons for racial tension include the following:

- **Insensitive leadership. Leaders must realize the effect that their actions and comments have on subordinates and on their attitudes, behaviors, and perceptions**
- **Racial prejudice and discrimination**
- **Unfair administration of rewards and punishment, promotions, and duties**
- **Limited recognition and awareness of minorities**

Up to this point, you have looked at some of the factors that impact on perceptions and attitudes and their relation to prejudicial and discriminatory behavior. You saw that when you judge a person's worth based on a perception or an attitude, your effectiveness as a leader is degraded. You will not communicate as well and trust will not be nourished to its fullest potential within an organization.

Strategies for Creating Change

So, now that you have some awareness about factors and causes that impact negatively on race relations and equal opportunity, what can you do about it? How can you remove or change some of the negative attitudes, behaviors, perceptions, or stereotypes? This section offers some strategies for change that will require lots of work and some risk on your part.

Leaders Can Create Change

As a leader, you need to be aware of discrimination and prejudices before they can begin to impact on minority groups, and more important, on people's feelings within those groups. Failure to take these strategies for change to heart can severely hamper a unit's mission accomplishment, cohesion, and trust.

- **Overcome prejudices by learning the facts and applying sound reasoning processes.**
- **Be prepared to detect and evaluate warning signs of possible unrest that may stem from racial issues in units and take immediate action to eliminate the causes.**
- **Know all you can about your subordinates—their values, attitudes, how they came to be the way they are, and what they want to be. This means knowing more about subordinates than just their names. Do not base this knowledge on unfounded opinions about the race or ethnic origin of a subordinate but on the facts about each individual.**

- Promote mutual understanding through effective communication. Realize that there will always be difficulties in the communication process and deal with the filters, barriers, and breakdowns as they occur. Although the difficulties may be complicated, when minorities lose trust in their leaders, the situation is out of control. Make communication effective by fostering an understanding that reduces racial tensions.

- Give fair and **impartial** treatment to all.

Lessening Prejudice, Adverse Perceptions, and Stereotyping

It has been suggested that if members of society can accomplish the following conditions, the causes and effects of prejudice will be lessened:

- Make contacts with people on an equal status and under a spirit of cooperation.

- Share goals.

- Encourage people to work on common problems.

- Create appropriate educational activities.

- Sanction contacts by law.

- Accept differences. Disagreement is okay, but rather than using statements such as "you are wrong" or "that's your opinion," do not deny others their experiences. Be willing to explore other's experiences as you explore your own thoughts, feelings, and experiences that brought you to your conclusion.

- Listen actively. Listen for understanding instead of agreement. Paraphrase back to the speaker the message you received. Listen with the same intensity to everyone.

- Provide feedback. Be behavior specific. Let others know what impact they have on you. Learn to separate intent and effect. Avoid using labels.

- Share behaviors/feelings. Honestly share with the group where you stand on subjects, and be willing to explore how you got there.

- Encourage feedback. Do not defend or rationalize your behavior; accept what others have to say. This is where active listening is imperative. Remember, agreement is not necessary.

- Use **inclusionary** language. Use terms such as "we" and "us"; do not use "they," "he," or "she."

- Avoid stereotypes. Learn to distinguish between characteristics based on factual evidence and characteristics based on overgeneralizations.

Recognize that thinking in terms of categories is a normal human function and be aware when you are doing it. Recognize also that people consciously and unconsciously hold stereotypes as a result of their social conditioning. Because people distinguish by recognizing their existence and by gathering factual information about different individuals, learn to look at people as individuals rather than not groups. Interacting with people who are different than you can help you to see people as they really are.

Creating Change from a Personal Level

There are three ways that you personally can create change. The most readily available tactic for change is *dialogue*. This tactic is particularly effective to change people who are on the fence, who need support for new thought, or who are seriously

Key Note Term

impartial – fair and unprejudiced

Key Note Term

inclusionary – to invite or include

Figure 4.1.1: Accepting others' ideas is a positive step toward ending stereotypes.
Courtesy of Digital Vision, Ltd.

trying to make sense out of their deepest commitments. It is less effective for those whose minds are strongly made up in an opposite direction. Dialogue has available to it various methods for effectively presenting information: conversation, debates, and panel discussions are all common.

Another tactic designed to be stronger than dialogue is *confrontation*. This involves using the skills of effective feedback and active listening in a nonthreatening way. For example, consider the following response to a statement "you" made to a group of people:

> When you made that statement, I perceived it as being racist and it made me feel uncomfortable because I sense a feeling of superiority on your part.

At this point, renegotiation is in order. Confrontation involves no longer being silent. The silent majority of Americans—those who have never committed themselves either to overt racism or to active involvement in the cause of civil rights—will now have to stand up and be counted.

The final tactic is *education*, from which comes understanding. Educate other people. Do not close your ears when you hear bigoted remarks. Racism becomes more respectable when it goes unchallenged. Most people are simply ignorant of the facts.

The education necessary to change existing perceptions will never work if it consists mainly of the same people lecturing to others. It must involve active participation by all types of people at all levels. Advice from well-informed members of other groups also helps.

Everyone must work to perform—or at least process information—on three levels at once (if need be). These levels are as follows:

- **Understand yourself and how you see the situation around you**
- **Understand others because they will not be like you in many cases; use intercultural communication**
- **Understand your environment, where it is coming from, and the direction it is headed**

Conclusion

Although all minorities and other groups are interwoven throughout every fiber of our society, racist, prejudiced, and discriminatory attitudes and behaviors still exist. Unless you have a firm grip on some of the "whys" behind these challenges, you may be prone to repeat them. It is illegal to discriminate or tolerate discrimination in any form. As a leader, it is important to promote trust, respect, and cooperation to accomplish assigned missions. As a leader, you set the tone by your own example. Understand the causes of discrimination, be alert to its presence, and actively work to eliminate it wherever it's found.

The following lesson discusses the performance indicators of leadership and developmental skills as well as mentoring. You will learn mentoring and counseling skills, such as active listening, responding, and questioning. These are all skills crucial to becoming a good leader.

Lesson Review

1. **What did Executive Order 9981 accomplish?**

2. **How can your self-concept influence the way you see others?**

3. **What would cause you to behave differently around individuals of another color, culture, or religion?**

4. **Define the term *stereotype*.**

Performance Indicators

Key Terms

communication
counseling
development
evaluation
flexibility
purpose
support

What You Will Learn to Do

- Outline a developmental counseling plan

Linked Core Abilities

- Communicate using verbal, nonverbal, visual, and written techniques
- Treat self and others with respect

Skills and Knowledge You Will Gain Along the Way

- Describe performance indicators used to assess leadership skills
- Describe the qualities and skills of an effective counselor
- Identify assessment and counseling strategies
- Define the key words contained in this lesson

Chapter 4

Introduction

This lesson focuses on and lists the performance indicators used to assess the leadership of yourself and others based on the leadership dimensions. Use the performance indicators as assessment and counseling tools. When you prepare an evaluation, make comments that apply specifically to the individual you are evaluating. Do not limit yourself to the general indicators listed here. Be specific; be precise; be objective; be fair.

Performance Indicators

This section is organized around the leadership dimensions shown in Figure 4.2.1.

Values

Values include loyalty, duty, respect, selfless service, honor, integrity, and personal courage. This section covers what to look for when determining these specific values.

Leaders of character and competence . .			act to achieve excellence by providing purpose, direction and motivation.		
Values "Be"	Attributes "Be"	Skills[4] "Know"	Actions[5] "Do"		
Loyalty Duty Respect Selfless Service Honor Integrity Personal Courage	Mental[1] Physical[2] Emotional[3]	Interpersonal Conceptual Technical Tactical	**Influencing** Communicating Decision Making Motivating	**Operating** Planning/ Preparing Executing Assessing	**Improving** Developing Building Learning

Figure 4.2.1: Leadership dimensions.
Courtesy of US Army JROTC.

[1]The mental attributes of an Army leader are will, self-discipline, initiative, judgment, self-confidence, intelligence, and cultural awareness.

[2]The physical attributes of an Army leader are health fitness, physical fitness, and military and professional bearing.

[3]The emotional attributes of an Army leader are self-control, balance, and stability.

[4]The interpersonal, conceptual, technical, and tactical skills are different for direct, organizational, and strategic leaders.

[5]The influencing, operating, and improving actions are different for direct, organizational, and strategic leaders.

Loyalty

Leaders who demonstrate loyalty

- Bear true faith and allegiance in the correct order to the Constitution, the Army, and the organization
- Observe higher headquarters' priorities
- Work within the system without manipulating it for personal gain

Duty

Leaders who demonstrate devotion to duty

- Fulfill obligations—professional, legal, and moral
- Carry out mission requirements
- Meet professional standards
- Set the example
- Comply with policies and directives
- Continually pursue excellence

Respect

Leaders who demonstrate respect

- Treat people as they should be treated
- Create a climate of fairness and equal opportunity
- Are discreet and tactful when correcting or questioning others
- Show concern for and make an effort to check on the safety and well-being of others
- Are courteous
- Don't take advantage of positions of authority

Courtesy of Digital Vision, Ltd.

Selfless Service

Leaders who demonstrate selfless service

- Put the welfare of the nation, the Army, and subordinates before their own
- Sustain team morale
- Share subordinates' hardships
- Give credit for success to others and accept responsibility for failure themselves

Honor

Leaders who demonstrate honor

- Live up to Army values
- Don't lie, cheat, steal, or tolerate those actions by others

Integrity

Leaders who demonstrate integrity

- **Do what is right legally and morally**
- **Possess high personal moral standards**
- **Are honest in word and deed**
- **Show consistently good moral judgment and behavior**
- **Put being right ahead of being popular**

Personal Courage

Leaders who demonstrate personal courage

- **Show physical and moral bravery**
- **Take responsibility for decisions and actions**
- **Accept responsibility for mistakes and shortcomings**

Attributes

Attributes are positive qualities, traits, and characteristics. The attributes covered in this section include mental, physical, and emotional.

Mental Attributes

Courtesy of US Army JROTC.

Leaders who demonstrate desirable mental attributes

- **Possess and display will, self-discipline, initiative, judgment, self-confidence, intelligence, common sense, and cultural awareness**
- **Think and act quickly and logically, even when there are no clear instructions or the plan falls apart**
- **Analyze situations**
- **Combine complex ideas to generate feasible courses of action.**
- **Balance resolve and flexibility**
- **Show a desire to succeed; do not quit in the face of adversity**
- **Do their fair share**
- **Balance competing demands**
- **Embrace and use the talents of all members to build team cohesion**

Key Note Term

flexibility – adaptable to change

Physical Attributes

Leaders who demonstrate desirable physical attributes

- **Maintain an appropriate level of physical fitness and military bearing**
- **Present a neat and professional appearance (see Figure 4.2.2)**
- **Meet established norms of personal hygiene, grooming, and cleanliness**
- **Maintain Army height and weight standards**
- **Render appropriate military and civilian courtesies**

Figure 4.2.2: Pride in your appearance is a desirable attribute.
Courtesy of US Army JROTC.

- **Demonstrate nonverbal expressions and gestures appropriate to the situation**
- **Are personally energetic**
- **Cope with hardship**
- **Complete physically demanding endeavors**
- **Continue to function under adverse conditions**
- **Lead by example in performance, fitness, and appearance**

Emotional Attributes

Leaders who demonstrate appropriate emotional attributes

- **Show self-confidence**
- **Remain calm during conditions of stress, chaos, and rapid change**
- **Exercise self-control, balance, and stability**
- **Maintain a positive attitude**
- **Demonstrate mature, responsible behavior that inspires trust and earns respect**

Skills

Specific skills should be examined when reviewing performance. These include interpersonal, conceptual, technical, and tactical skills. Obviously, not every skill is applicable to every individual.

Interpersonal Skills

Leaders who demonstrate interpersonal skills

- **Coach, teach, counsel, motivate, and empower subordinates (see Figure 4.2.3)**
- **Readily interact with others**
- **Earn trust and respect**

Figure 4.2.3: Coaching is one way to demonstrate interpersonal skills.
Courtesy of Pete Saloutas/Corbis Images.

- **Actively contribute to problem solving and decision making**
- **Are sought out by peers for expertise and counsel**

Conceptual Skills

Leaders who demonstrate conceptual skills

- **Reason critically and ethically**
- **Think creatively**
- **Anticipate requirements and contingencies**
- **Improvise within the commander's intent**
- **Use appropriate reference materials**
- **Pay attention to details**

Technical Skills

Leaders who demonstrate technical skills

- **Possess or develop the expertise necessary to accomplish all assigned tasks and functions**
- **Know standards for task accomplishment**
- **Know the small unit tactics, techniques, and procedures that support the organization's mission**
- **Know the drills that support the organization's mission**
- **Prepare clear and concise operation orders**
- **Understand how to apply the factors of mission, enemy, terrain and weather, troops, time available, and civil considerations (METT-TC) to mission analysis**

Key Note Term

support – to encourage or help

- **Master basic soldier skills**
- **Know how to use and maintain equipment**
- **Know how and what to inspect or check**
- **Use technology, especially information technology, to enhance communication**

Actions

When assessing action performance, look for those qualities that include influencing, communicating (both oral and written), decision making, motivating, operating, planning and preparing, executing, assessing, improving, developing, building, and learning. This section covers these specific actions.

Influencing

Leaders who influence

- **Use appropriate methods to reach goals while operating and improving**
- **Motivate subordinates to accomplish tasks and missions**
- **Set the example by demonstrating enthusiasm for and, if necessary, methods for accomplishing assigned tasks**
- **Make themselves available to assist peers and subordinates**
- **Share information with subordinates**
- **Encourage subordinates and peers to express candid opinions**
- **Actively listen to feedback and act appropriately based on it**
- **Mediate peer conflicts and disagreements**
- **Tactfully confront and correct others when necessary**
- **Earn respect and obtain willing cooperation of peers, subordinates, and superiors**
- **Challenge others to match their example**
- **Take care of subordinates and their families, providing for their health, welfare, morale, and training**
- **Are persuasive in peer discussions and prudently rally peer pressure against peers when required**

Key Note Term

communication – the sharing of information

- Provide a team vision for the future
- Shape the organizational climate by setting, sustaining, and ensuring a values-based environment

Communicating

Leaders who communicate effectively

- Display good oral, written, and listening skills
- Know how to persuade others
- Express thoughts and ideas clearly to individuals and groups (see Figure 2.4.4)

Oral Communication

Leaders who effectively communicate orally

- Speak clearly and concisely
- Speak enthusiastically and maintain listeners' interest and involvement
- Make appropriate eye contact when speaking
- Use gestures that are appropriate but not distracting
- Convey ideas, feelings, sincerity, and conviction
- Express well-thought-out and well-organized ideas
- Use grammatically and doctrinally correct terms and phrases
- Use appropriate visual aids
- Act to determine, recognize, and resolve misunderstandings
- Listen and watch attentively; make appropriate notes; convey the essence of what was said or done to others
- Respond appropriately to verbal and nonverbal feedback
- Keep conversations on track

Figure 4.2.4: Good communication skills help you get your message across to others.
Courtesy of US Army JROTC.

Chapter 4 Leadership Strategies

Written Communication

Leaders who effectively communicate in writing

- **Are understood in a single rapid reading by the intended audience**
- **Use correct grammar, spelling, and punctuation**
- **Have legible handwriting**
- **Put the "bottom line up front"**
- **Use the active voice**
- **Use an appropriate format, a clear organization, and a reasonably simple style**
- **Use only essential acronyms and spell out those used**
- **Stay on topic**
- **Correctly use facts and data**

> **Note**
>
> DA Pam 600-67 discusses techniques for writing effectively.

Decision Making

Leaders who make effective, timely decisions

- **Employ sound judgment and logical reasoning**
- **Gather and analyze relevant information about changing situations to recognize and define emerging problems**
- **Make logical assumptions in the absence of facts**
- **Uncover critical issues to use as a guide in both making decisions and taking advantage of opportunities**
- **Keep informed about developments and policy changes inside and outside the organization**
- **Recognize and generate innovative solutions**
- **Develop alternative courses of action and choose the best course of action based on analysis of their relative costs and benefits**
- **Anticipate needs for action**
- **Relate and compare information from different sources to identify possible cause-and-effect relationships**
- **Consider the impact and implications of decisions on others and on situations**
- **Involve others in decisions and keep them informed of consequences that affect them**
- **Take charge when in charge**
- **Define intent**
- **Consider contingencies and their consequences**
- **Remain decisive after discovering a mistake**

- **Act in the absence of guidance**
- **Improvise within the commander's intent; handle a fluid environment**

Motivating

Leaders who effectively motivate

- **Inspire, encourage, and guide others toward mission accomplishment**
- **Don't show discouragement when facing setbacks**
- **Attempt to satisfy subordinates' needs**
- **Give subordinates the reason for tasks**
- **Provide accurate, timely, and (where appropriate) positive feedback**
- **Actively listen for feedback from subordinates**
- **Use feedback to modify duties, tasks, requirements, and goals when appropriate**
- **Recognize individual and team accomplishments and reward them appropriately**
- **Recognize poor performance and address it appropriately**
- **Justly apply disciplinary measures**
- **Keep subordinates informed (see Figure 2.4.5)**
- **Clearly articulate expectations**
- **Consider duty positions, capabilities, and developmental needs when assigning tasks**
- **Provide early warning to subordinate leaders of tasks they will be responsible for**
- **Define requirements by issuing clear and concise orders or guidance**
- **Allocate as much time as possible for task completion**
- **Accept responsibility for organizational performance**
- **Credit subordinates for good performance**
- **Take responsibility for and correct poor performance**

Figure 4.2.5: Give information as you get it to keep everyone in the loop.
Courtesy of US Army JROTC.

Operating

Leaders who effectively operate

- **Accomplish short-term missions**
- **Demonstrate tactical and technical competency appropriate to their rank and position**
- **Complete individual and unit tasks to standard, on time, and within the commanders intent**

Planning and Preparing

Leaders who effectively plan

- **Develop feasible and acceptable plans for themselves and others that accomplish the mission while expending minimum resources and positioning the organization for future missions**
- **Use forward planning to ensure each course of action achieves the desired outcome**
- **Use reverse planning to ensure that all tasks can be executed in the time available and that tasks depending on other tasks are executed in the correct sequence**
- **Determine specified and implied tasks and restate the higher headquarters' mission in terms appropriate to the organization**
- **Incorporate adequate controls such as time phasing; ensure others understand when actions should begin or end**
- **Adhere to the "⅓–⅔ Rule"; give subordinates time to plan ⅓ time for notice and ⅔ time for execution**
- **Allocate time to prepare and conduct rehearsals**
- **Ensure all courses of action accomplish the mission within the commander's intent**
- **Allocate available resources to competing demands by setting task priorities based on the relative importance of each task**
- **Address likely contingencies**
- **Remain flexible**
- **Consider Standard Operating Procedures (SOPs), the factors of METT-TC, and the military aspects of terrain (OCOKA)**

Another Acronym

What does OCOKA mean?

- O—Observation
- C—Cover and concealment
- O—Obstacles
- K—Key terrain
- A—Avenues of approach

- Coordinate plans with higher, lower, adjacent, and affected organizations
- Personally arrive on time and meet deadlines; require subordinates and their organizations to accomplish tasks on time
- Delegate all tasks except those they are required to do personally
- Schedule activities so the organization meets all commitments in critical performance areas
- Recognize and resolve scheduling conflicts
- Notify peers and subordinates as far in advance as possible when their support is required
- Use some form of a personal planning calendar to organize requirements

Executing

Leaders who effectively execute

- Use technical and tactical skills to meet mission standards, take care of people, and accomplish the mission with available resources
- Perform individual and collective tasks to standard
- Execute plans, adjusting when necessary, to accomplish the mission
- Encourage initiative
- Keep higher and lower headquarters, superiors, and subordinates informed
- Keep track of people and equipment
- Make necessary on-the-spot corrections
- Adapt to and handle fluid environments
- Work through obstacles, difficulties, and hardships to accomplish the mission
- Keep track of task assignments and suspense's; adjust assignments, if necessary; follow up

Assessing

Leaders who effectively assess

Key Note Term

evaluation – to appraise or find the value of

- Use assessment techniques and **evaluation** tools, especially After Action Reviews (AARs), to identify lessons learned and facilitate consistent improvement
- Establish and employ procedures for monitoring, coordinating, and regulating subordinates' actions and activities
- Conduct initial assessments when beginning a new task or assuming a new position
- Conduct In=Progress Reviews (IPRs)
- Analyze activities to determine how desired end states are achieved or affected
- Seek sustainment in areas when the organization meets the standard
- Observe and assess actions in progress without oversupervising
- Judge results based on standards
- Sort out important actual and potential problems
- Conduct and facilitate AARs; identify lessons

- Determine causes, effects, and contributing factors for problems
- Analyze activities to determine how desired end states can be achieved ethically

Improving

Leaders who effectively improve the organization

- Sustain skills and actions that benefit themselves and each of their people for the future
- Sustain and renew the organization for the future by managing change and exploiting individual and institutional learning capabilities
- Create and sustain an environment where all leaders, subordinates, and organizations can reach their full potential

Developing

Leaders who effectively develop

- Strive to improve themselves, subordinates, and the organization
- Mentor by investing adequate time and effort in **counseling**, coaching, and teaching their individual subordinates and subordinate leaders
- Create a climate that expects good performance, recognizes superior performance, and doesn't accept poor performance
- Design tasks to provide practice in areas of subordinate leaders' weaknesses
- Clearly articulate tasks and expectations and set realistic standards
- Guide subordinate leaders in thinking through problems for themselves
- Anticipate mistakes and freely offer assistance without being overbearing (see Figure 2.4.6)
- Observe, assess, counsel, coach, and evaluate subordinate leaders
- Motivate subordinates to develop themselves

> **Key Note Term**
>
> **counseling** – an interchange of opinions, perceptions, and ideas

Figure 4.2.6: To err is human.
Courtesy of Jon Feingersh/Corbis Images.

- Arrange training opportunities that help subordinates achieve insight, self-awareness, self-esteem, and effectiveness

- Balance the organization's tasks, goals, and objectives with subordinates' personal and professional needs

- Develop subordinate leaders who demonstrate respect for natural resources and the environment

- Act to expand and enhance subordinates' competence and self-confidence

- Encourage initiative

- Create and contribute to a positive organizational climate

- Build on successes

- Improve weaknesses

Building

Leaders who effectively build

- Spend time and resources improving the organization

- Foster a healthy ethical climate

- Act to improve the organization's collective performance

- Comply with and support organizational goals

- Encourage people to work effectively with each other

- Promote teamwork and team achievement

- Exemplify good team players

- Offer suggestions, but properly execute decisions of the chain of command and NCO (Noncommissioned Officer) support channel—even unpopular ones—as if they were their own

- Accept and act on assigned tasks

- Volunteer in useful ways (see Figure 2.4.7)

Figure 4.2.7: Volunteer to help make your community strong.
Courtesy of Ariel Skelley/Corbis Images.

- Remain positive when the situation becomes confused or changes
- Use the chain of command and NCO support channel to solve problems
- Support equal opportunity
- Prevent sexual harassment
- Participate in organizational activities and functions
- Participate in team tasks and missions without being requested to do so
- Establish an organizational climate that demonstrates respect for the environment and stewards natural resources

Learning

Leaders who effectively learn

- Seek self-improvement in weak areas
- Encourage organizational growth
- Envision, adapt, and lead change
- Act to expand and enhance personal and organizational knowledge and capabilities
- Apply lessons learned
- Ask incisive questions
- Envision ways to improve
- Design ways to practice
- Endeavor to broaden their understanding
- Transform experience into knowledge and use it to improve future performance
- Make knowledge accessible to the entire organization
- Exhibit reasonable self-awareness
- Take time off to grow and recreate
- Embrace and manage change; adopt a future orientation
- Use experience to improve themselves and the organization

Developmental Counseling

Leadership **development** is one of the most important responsibilities. Developing your leadership abilities should be one of your highest priorities.

Just as training includes AARs and training strategies to fix shortcomings, leadership development includes performance reviews. These reviews result in agreements between leader and subordinate on a development strategy or plan of action that builds on the subordinate's strengths and establishes goals to improve on weaknesses. Leaders conduct performance reviews and create plans of action during developmental counseling.

Key Note Term

development – to get gradually stronger and better; to make known in detail

The Leader's Responsibilities

Organizational readiness and mission accomplishment depend on every member's ability to perform to established standards. Leaders must mentor their subordinates through teaching, coaching, and counseling.

People often perceive counseling as an adverse action. Effective leaders who counsel properly can change that perception. Leaders conduct counseling to help subordinates become better members of the team, maintain or improve performance, and prepare for the future. Just as no easy answers exist for exactly what to do in all leadership situations, no easy answers exist for exactly what to do in all counseling situations. To conduct effective counseling, however, you should develop a counseling style with the characteristics as follows:

- **Respect.** View subordinates as unique, complex individuals, each with a distinct set of values, beliefs, and attitudes.
- **Communication.** Establish open, two-way communication with subordinates using spoken language, nonverbal actions, gestures, and body language. Effective counselors listen more than they speak.
- **Support.** Encourage subordinates through actions while guiding them through their problems.

Leader Counseling Skills

One challenging aspect of counseling is selecting the proper approach to a specific situation. To counsel effectively, the technique you use must fit the situation, your capabilities, and your subordinate's expectations.

All leaders should seek to develop and improve their own counseling abilities. The techniques needed to provide effective counseling will vary from person to person and session to session; however, general skills that you'll need in almost every situation include active listening, responding, and questioning.

Active Listening

During counseling, you must actively listen to your subordinate. When you're actively listening, you communicate verbally and nonverbally that you've received the subordinate's message. To fully understand a subordinate's message, you must listen to the words and observe the subordinate's manners. Elements of active listening you should use include the following:

- **Eye contact.** Maintaining eye contact without staring helps show sincere interest. Occasional breaks of contact are normal and acceptable. Subordinates may perceive excessive breaks of eye contact, paper shuffling, and clock-watching as a lack of interest or concern. These are guidelines only. Based on cultural background, participants in a particular counseling session may have different ideas about what proper eye contact is.
- **Body posture.** Being relaxed and comfortable will help put the subordinate at ease. However, a too-relaxed position or slouching may be interpreted as a lack of interest.
- **Head nods.** Occasionally nodding your head shows you're paying attention and encourages the subordinate to continue.

- **Facial expressions.** Keep your facial expressions natural and relaxed. A blank look or fixed expression may disturb the subordinate. Smiling too much or frowning may discourage the subordinate from continuing.

- **Verbal expressions.** Refrain from talking too much and avoid interrupting. Let the subordinate do the talking while keeping the discussion on the counseling subject. Speaking only when necessary reinforces the importance of what the subordinate is saying and encourages the subordinate to continue. Silence can also do this but be careful. Occasional silence may indicate to the subordinate that it's okay to continue talking, but a long silence can sometimes be distracting and make the subordinate feel uncomfortable.

Active listening also means listening thoughtfully and deliberately to the way a subordinate says things. Stay alert for common themes. A subordinate's opening and closing statements as well as recurring references may indicate the subordinate's priorities. Inconsistencies and gaps may indicate a subordinate's avoidance of the real issue. This confusion and uncertainty may suggest additional questions.

While listening to subordinates, pay attention to their gestures. These actions complete the total message. By watching a subordinate's actions, you can "see" the feelings behind the words. Not all actions are proof of a subordinate's feelings, but they should be taken into consideration. Note differences between what the subordinate says and does. Nonverbal indicators of a subordinate's attitude include the following:

- **Boredom.** Drumming on the table, doodling, clicking a ballpoint pen, or resting the head in the palm of the hand.

- **Self-confidence.** Standing tall, leaning back with hands behind the head, and maintaining steady eye contact.

- **Defensiveness.** Pushing deeply into a chair, glaring at the leader, and making sarcastic comments as well as crossing or folding arms in front of the chest.

- **Frustration.** Rubbing eyes, pulling on an ear, taking short breaths, wringing the hands, or frequently changing total body position.

- **Interest, friendliness, and openness.** Moving toward the leader while sitting.

- **Openness or anxiety.** Sitting on the edge of the chair with arms uncrossed and hands open.

Consider these indicators carefully. Although each indicator may show something about the subordinate, don't assume a particular behavior absolutely means something. Ask the subordinate about the indicator so you can better understand the behavior and allow the subordinate to take responsibility for it.

Responding

Responding skills follow up on active listening skills. A leader responds to communicate that the leader understands the subordinate. From time to time, check your understanding: clarify and confirm what has been said. Respond to subordinates both verbally and nonverbally. Verbal responses consist of summarizing, interpreting, and clarifying the subordinate's message. Nonverbal responses include eye contact and occasional gestures such as a head nod.

Questioning

Although questioning is a necessary skill, you must use it with caution. Too many questions can aggravate the power differential between a leader and a subordinate and place the subordinate in a passive mode. The subordinate may also react to excessive questioning as an intrusion of privacy and become defensive. During a leadership development review, ask questions to obtain information or to get the subordinate to think about a particular situation. Generally, the questions should be open-ended so as to evoke more than a yes or no answer. Well-posed questions may help to verify understanding, encourage further explanation, or help the subordinate move through the stages of the counseling session.

Counseling Errors

Effective leaders avoid common counseling mistakes. Dominating the counseling by talking too much; giving unnecessary or inappropriate "advice"; not truly listening; and projecting personal likes, dislikes, biases, and prejudices interfere with effective counseling. You should also avoid other common mistakes such as rash judgments, stereotypes, loss of emotional control, and inflexible methods of counseling and improper follow-up. To improve your counseling skills, refer to the following guidelines.

- **Determine the subordinate's role in the situation and what the subordinate has done to resolve the problem or improve performance**
- **Draw conclusions based on more than the subordinate's statement**
- **Try to understand what the subordinate says and feels; listen to what the subordinate says and how the subordinate says it**
- **Show empathy when discussing the problem**
- **When asking questions, be sure that you need the information**
- **Keep the conversation open-ended; avoid interrupting**
- **Give the subordinate your full attention**
- **Be receptive to the subordinate's feelings without feeling responsible to save the subordinate from hurting**
- **Encourage the subordinate to take the initiative and to say what the subordinate wants to say**
- **Avoid interrogating**
- **Keep your personal experiences out of the counseling session unless you believe your experiences will really help**
- **Listen more; talk less**
- **Remain objective**
- **Avoid confirming a subordinate's prejudices**
- **Help the subordinate help himself**
- **Know what information to keep confidential and what to present to the chain of command**

The Leader's Limitations

Leaders can't help everyone in every situation. Even professional counselors can't provide all the help that a person might need. You must recognize your limitations and, when the situation calls for it, refer a subordinate to a person or agency more qualified to help.

The Counseling Process

Effective leaders use the counseling process. It consists of four stages: identify the need for counseling, prepare for counseling, conduct counseling, and follow up.

Identify the Need for Counseling

Quite often organizational policies, such as counseling associated with an evaluation or counseling required by the command, focus a counseling session. You may, however, conduct developmental counseling whenever the need arises for focused, two-way communication aimed at subordinate development. Developing subordinates consists of observing the subordinate's performance, comparing it to the standard, and then providing feedback to the subordinate in the form of counseling.

Prepare for Counseling

Successful counseling requires preparation. To prepare for counseling, do the following:

- **Select a suitable place**
- **Schedule the time**
- **Notify the subordinate well in advance**
- **Organize information**
- **Outline the counseling session components**
- **Plan your counseling strategy**
- **Establish the right atmosphere**

Select a Suitable Place

Schedule counseling in an environment that minimizes interruptions and is free from distracting sights and sounds as shown in Figure 4.2.8.

Schedule the Time

When possible, counsel a subordinate during the duty day. Counseling after duty hours may be rushed or perceived as unfavorable. The length of time required for counseling depends on the complexity of the issue. Generally a counseling session should last less than an hour. If you need more time, schedule a second session. Additionally, select a time free from competition with other activities and consider what has been planned after the counseling session. Important events can distract a subordinate from concentrating on the counseling.

Figure 4.2.8: Find a quiet and comfortable place for counseling.
Courtesy of Tom Stewart/Corbis Images.

Notify the Subordinate Well in Advance

For a counseling session to be a subordinate-centered, two-person effort, the subordinate must have time to prepare for it. The subordinate should know why, where, and when the counseling will take place. Counseling following a specific event should happen as close to the event as possible; however, for performance or professional development counseling, subordinates may need a week or more to prepare or review specific products such as support forms or counseling records.

Organize Information

Solid preparation is essential to effective counseling. Review all pertinent information. This includes the **purpose** of the counseling, facts and observations about the subordinate, identification of possible problems, main points of discussion, and the development of a plan of action. Focus on specific and objective behaviors that the subordinate must maintain or improve as well as a plan of action with clear, obtainable goals.

Outline the Components of the Counseling Session

Using the information obtained, determine what to discuss during the counseling session. Note what prompted the counseling, what you aim to achieve, and what your role as a counselor is. Identify possible comments or questions to help you keep the counseling session subordinate-centered and help the subordinate progress through its stages. Although you never know what a subordinate will say or do during counseling, a written outline helps organize the session and enhances the chance of positive results.

Plan Counseling Strategy

As many approaches to counseling exist as there are leaders. The directive, nondirective, and combined approaches to counseling were addressed earlier. Use a strategy that suits your subordinates and the situation.

Key Note Term

purpose – a desirable end or aim

Establish the Right Atmosphere

The right atmosphere promotes two-way communication between a leader and subordinate. To establish a relaxed atmosphere, you may offer the subordinate a seat or something to drink. You may want to sit in a chair facing the subordinate because a desk can act as a barrier.

Some situations make an informal atmosphere inappropriate. For example, during counseling to correct substandard performance, you may direct the subordinate to remain standing while you remain seated behind a desk. This formal atmosphere, normally used to give specific guidance, reinforces the leader's rank, position in the chain of command, and authority.

Conduct the Counseling Session

Be flexible when conducting a counseling session. Often counseling for a specific incident occurs spontaneously as leaders encounter subordinates in their daily activities. Good leaders take advantage of naturally occurring events to provide subordinates with feedback.

Even when you haven't prepared for formal counseling, you should address the four basic components of a counseling session. Their purpose is to guide effective counseling rather than mandate a series of rigid steps. Counseling sessions consist of

- **Opening the session**
- **Developing the plan of action**
- **Recording the session**
- **Closing the session**

Ideally, a counseling session results in a subordinate's commitment to a plan of action. Assessment of the plan of action becomes the starting point for follow-up counseling.

Open the Session

In the session opening, state the purpose of the session and establish a subordinate-centered setting. Establish the preferred setting early in the session by inviting the subordinate to speak. The best way to open a counseling session is to clearly state its purpose. For example, an appropriate purpose statement might be: "The purpose of this counseling is to discuss your duty performance over the past month and to create a plan to enhance performance and attain performance goals." If applicable, start the counseling session by reviewing the status of the previous plan of action.

You and the subordinate should attempt to develop a mutual understanding of the issues. You can best develop this by letting the subordinate do most of the talking. Use active listening; respond and question without dominating the conversation. Aim to help the subordinate better understand the subject of the counseling, for example, duty performance, a problem situation and its impact, or potential areas for growth.

Both you and the subordinate should provide examples or cite specific observations to reduce the perception that either is unnecessarily biased or judgmental; however, when the issue is substandard performance, you should the standard. The conversation, which should be two-way, then addresses what the subordinate needs to do to meet the standard. It's important that you define the issue as substandard performance and don't allow the subordinate to define the issue as an unreasonable standard, unless you consider the standard negotiable or are willing to alter the conditions under which the subordinate

Develop a Plan of Action

A plan of action identifies a method for achieving a desired result. It specifies what the subordinate must do to reach the goals set during dimensions that were discussed earlier; it should show the subordinate how to modify or maintain his behavior. It should avoid vague intentions such as "Next month I want you to improve your land navigation skills." The plan must use concrete and direct terms. For example, you might say: "Next week you'll attend the Map Reading class with cadets from North Central High School's drill team. After the class, Cadet 1st Lieutenant Dixon will coach you through the land navigation course. He will help you develop your skill with the compass. I will observe you going through the course with Cadet 1st Lieutenant Dixon, and then I will talk to you again and determine if your plan of action sets the stage for successful development.

Record the Session

Although requirements to record counseling sessions vary, a leader always benefits by documenting the main points of a counseling session. Documentation serves as a reference to the agreed upon plan of action and the subordinate's accomplishments, improvements, personal preferences, or problems. A complete record of counseling aids in making recommendations for professional development, schools, promotions, and evaluation reports.

Close the Session

To close the session, summarize its key points and ask if the subordinate understands the plan of action. Invite the subordinate to review the plan of action and what is expected of you, the leader. With the subordinate, establish any follow-up measures necessary to support the successful implementation of the plan of action. These may include providing the subordinate with resources and time, periodically assessing the plan, and following through on referrals. Schedule any future meetings, at least tentatively, before dismissing the subordinate.

Follow Up

The counseling process doesn't end with the counseling session. It continues through implementation of the plan of action and evaluation of results. After counseling, you must support subordinates as they implement their plans of action. Support may include teaching, coaching, or providing time and resources. You must observe and assess this process and possibly modify the plan to meet its goals. Appropriate measures after counseling include follow-up counseling, making referrals, informing the chain of command, and taking corrective measures.

Assess the Plan of Action

The purpose of counseling is to develop subordinates who are better able to achieve personal, professional, and organizational goals. During the assessment, review the plan of action with the subordinate to determine if the desired results were achieved. You and the subordinate should determine the date for this assessment during the initial counseling session. The assessment of the plan of action provides useful information for future follow-up counseling sessions.

Conclusion

This lesson covered performance indicators as well as developmental counseling. Developmental counseling is subordinate-centered communication that outlines actions necessary for subordinates to achieve individual and organizational goals and objectives. It can be either event-oriented or focused on personal and professional development.

In the next lesson, you will be introduced to the valuable skill of negotiating. Through negotiation, you can work with others to accomplish just about any task.

Lesson Review

1. What are the values on which you base your performance review?

2. Choose two planning and preparing actions on which performance reviews are based and discuss them.

3. What are the different skills needed in oral and written communication?

4. What are the characteristics on which you should develop your counseling style?

Negotiating

Chapter 4

Key Terms

negotiation
principled negotiation

What You Will Learn to Do

- Negotiate a win/win solution for a given situation

Linked Core Abilities

- Communicate using verbal, nonverbal, visual, and written techniques
- Treat self and others with respect
- Apply critical thinking techniques

Skills and Knowledge You Will Gain Along the Way

- Explain how trust and betrayal affects relationships
- Discuss the effects of competition and collaboration in relationships
- Explore the effects of win-lose, win-win, and lose-lose strategies in negotiations
- Define the key words contained in this lesson

Introduction

Negotiation is a way of life; you are involved in it every day—when you negotiate with your parents on how late you can stay out, with your teachers for a makeup test, with your boss for a raise, or with your friends when deciding which movie to go to. Earlier in your JROTC classes, communication and working out conflict were discussed. They are important elements to the negotiating process. This lesson covers an effective way to negotiate to a win-win solution.

Key Note Term

negotiation – an attempt to reach a win=win agreement

Using Winning Colors®

In *Foundations for Success*, Chapter 1, Lessons 1 and 2, you were introduced to the Winning Colors® assessment tool. As you learned, Winning Colors® can be an invaluable asset to

- Improve understanding of how to cooperate and communicate with others
- Provide clues to motivation
- Clarify learning styles
- Offer insight to conflict resolution style
- Uncover essential aspects of communication

Refer back to those lessons to see how Winning Colors® can help you in your negotiation skills. You can use each of the four behaviors to achieve a win-win for all parties involved in negotiations.

Fair Negotiations

Most often as two people begin to discuss their differences, they begin with their position: what they believe in and what they want from the discussion. After you have determined what your position is, you go about arguing for it—even demand it. It is from that point you begin to compromise and barter away at your demands and walk away unsatisfied, angry, and feeling like a loser. On the other side, if you yelled loud enough and long enough and you were able to beat down your opponent, you might walk away with all your demands and feel successful in the process. However, you notice your relationship with this person has degenerated and you feel sad about having lost a friend or classmate (see Figure 4.3.1).

When you negotiate, you want to be fair. The criteria for fair negotiations include producing a wise agreement, being efficient, and improving or at least not damaging the relationship.

When you argue over positions, you usually have not taken the time to explore other alternatives; therefore, the decision you come up with may not be the best available solution. When you argue over positions you are not being efficient because you are not listening to each other and most likely repeating your position over and over. You are not moving forward to solutions. When you argue over positions, the relationship can be damaged. Anger sets in and words are said and often not forgotten. You might win this battle, but you also might lose the war.

Principled negotiation is neither soft (giving in) or hard (controlling). It is based on the criteria for fair negotiations and focused on a win-win for all parties. If a win-win is not possible at the time of negotiations, you can agree to have a win-win or no deal, set aside the negotiations, and return at a time that the parties can search for the third alternative.

When using soft negotiations the participants are usually friends, seeking agreement, making concessions, trusting others, changing positions easily, accepting, giving things up to reach an agreement, and yielding to pressure. When using hard negotiations the participants are adversaries, both maintaining the goal of victory, demanding concessions, distrusting others, trying to win a contest of will and applying pressure.

Principled centered negotiations are neither soft nor hard. They are the third alternative to negotiations and are focused on win-win situations.

Principled centered negotiations have four basic points:

- **People.** Separate the people from the problem
- **Interests.** Focus on interests, not positions
- **Options.** Generate as many as you can
- **Criteria.** Results are based on an agreed-on set of objectives or standards

Some ways to keep focused on win-win principled center negotiations are as follows:

- Have clear goals, understood and agreed on. Use the goals to test whether issues are relevant or not.
- Be on the lookout for win-lose. It can develop subtly. If you feel under attack, or feel yourself lining up support, you are likely in a win-lose contest.
- Listen empathetically to others. Stop yourself from working on counter arguments while another person is speaking. Take the risk of being persuaded. Try the other person's reasoning on for size (see Figure 4.3.2).

Figure 4.3.2: The only way to learn anything is to listen.
Courtesy of Corbis Images.

- **Avoid absolute statements that leave no room for modification.** "I think this is the way . . ." is better than "This is *the only* way . . ."

- **If you are planning for others, provide some means for their involvement.** The doers should feel that they can have influence on decisions that affect them.

- **Try to make decisions by consensus rather than by victory of the majority.**

- **Test to see that trade-offs and compromises are truly accepted by all.**

- **Draw a continuum line and have members place themselves on it regarding the issue.** It often occurs that the different "sides" are not far apart.

- **Be alert to selling or winning strategies in others and avoid using them yourself.** "Any intelligent person can see the advantages . . ." would be a danger signal.

When the parties involved in the negotiation first identify the outcome, discuss interests, begin to generate possibilities to reach the outcome, and ensure the interests of each party are met, then the relationships will either be maintained or increased. Additionally, there will be a wise agreement and the parties would have used their time efficiently.

What would you do?

You and your friends are planning for the weekend. There has been discussion around going to the movies, or renting a movie and watching it at someone's home with popcorn and soda, or going ice-skating or even attending the football team's practice game. You and your friends have been discussing these options all week. It is now Friday and time to decide what you will do. You really want to go to the practice game because your younger brother is on the team and you want to support him. Your best friend wants to watch a movie at someone's home because he does not have enough money to go out to a movie or ice skate. There is a long awaited movie on at the theater that your other friend has been waiting to see. Although everyone likes to ice skate, none of your friends are pushing hard for that.

How would you negotiate a win-win situation with your friends?

Conclusion

This lesson showed that negotiation is a way of life. You are involved in it every day. As discussed in previous JROTC classes, communication and working out conflict are important elements to the negotiating process. The key concepts to put into practice from this lesson are the effective ways to negotiate to a win-win solution.

The next lesson deals with decision making and problem solving. In this lesson, you will learn how to use specific steps to make the best choices possible.

Lesson Review

1. What are the four basic points for principled, centered negotiations?

2. What are the criteria for fair negotiations?

3. Discuss how you have participated in a negotiation with family or friends. What was the outcome?

4. What are the differences between hard and soft negotiations?

Lesson 4

Decision Making and Problem Solving

Key Terms

cohesive
contingencies
improving
influencing
intuitions
non-judgement
objectively
operating

What You Will Learn to Do

- Solve a problem using the seven-step problem-solving process

Linked Core Abilities

- Communicate using verbal, nonverbal, visual, and written techniques
- Apply critical thinking techniques

Skills and Knowledge You Will Gain Along the Way

- Describe the seven-step problem-solving process
- Describe the decision-making process
- Describe behaviors that contribute to or block efforts to solve a group problem
- Define the key words contained in this lesson

Introduction—Putting Your Leadership Skills in Perspective

Key Note Terms

influencing – to exercise or have physical or moral influence on

operating – to work, function; to conduct or manage

improving – to make better

As defined in previous JROTC lessons in this chapter, leadership is the process of **influencing** others by providing purpose, direction, and motivation while **operating** to accomplish the mission and **improving** the organization. Purpose gives subordinates a reason why they should do different things, sometimes under stressful circumstances. Direction shows what must be done. Through motivation, leaders give subordinates the will to do everything they are capable of doing to accomplish a mission.

Leadership Framework

Recall the fundamentals of *BE, KNOW,* and *DO.* As you can clearly see in Figure 4.4.1, they are deeply embedded throughout the leadership framework. The top of this framework shows the four categories of things that leaders must *BE, KNOW,* and *DO.* They are values, attributes, skills, and actions. The bottom lists the dimensions of leadership, grouped under these four categories. The dimensions consist of the 7 values and 15 subcategories under attributes, skills, and actions.

Leadership starts at the top, with the character of the leader, with your character. To lead others, you must first ensure your own house is in order.

The leadership framework is a tool that will allow you to think about leadership as a whole. The dimensions each contain components that are all interrelated; none stand alone. This framework will help you to put your job, your followers, and your unit into perspective. Think about it in this manner:

Be, Know, Do

BE a leader of character. Embrace the values and demonstrate the leader attributes. Study and practice so that you will have the skills to *KNOW* your job. Then act. *DO* what is right to achieve excellence.

Figure 4.4.1: Values and subcatagories.
Courtesy of US Army JROTC.

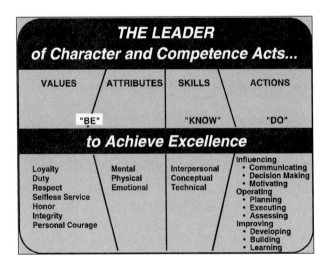

Approaches to Decision Making and Problem Solving

A leader is expected to get the job done. To do so, he or she must learn to plan, analyze situations, identify and solve problems (or potential problems), make decisions, and set realistic and attainable goals for the unit. These are the thinking or creative requirements of leadership and they set direction. These actions provide vision, purpose, and goal definition. They are your eyes to the future, and they are crucial to developing a disciplined, **cohesive**, and effective organization.

Decision making and problem solving are basic ingredients of leadership. More than anything else, the ability to make sound, timely decisions separates a leader from a nonleader. It is the responsibility of leaders to make high-quality decisions that are accepted and executed in a timely fashion.

Leaders must be able to reason under the most critical conditions and decide quickly what action to take. If they delay or avoid making a decision, this indecisiveness may create hesitancy, loss of confidence, and confusion within the unit and may cause the task to fail. Because leaders are frequently faced with unexpected circumstances, it is important to be flexible. Leaders must be able to react promptly to each situation; then, when circumstances dictate a change in plans, prompt reaction builds confidence in them.

Within business and the military today, leaders at all levels use some form of a decision-making and problem-solving process. There are at least several different approaches (or models) for decision making and problem solving. The most common is the seven-step problem-solving and decision-making process.

> **Key Note Term**
>
> **cohesive** – sticking together

The Seven-Step Problem-Solving and Decision-Making Process

Having a logical thought process helps ensure that you will not neglect key factors that could influence the problem and ultimately your decision. In fact, you should always apply a clear, logical thought process to all leadership situations that you encounter. The seven-step process is an excellent tool that can guide you in solving problems and making those sound and timely decisions. The seven steps are as follows:

1. **Identify (recognize/define) the problem.**
2. **Gather information (facts/assumptions).**
3. **Develop courses of action (solutions).**
4. **Analyze and compare courses of action (alternatives/solutions).**
5. **Make a decision; select the best course of action (solution).**
6. **Make a plan.**
7. **Implement the plan (assess the results).**

The following sections describe each of these steps in detail.

Step 1: Identify the Problem

Being able to accurately identify the nature of a problem is a crucial undertaking. All leadership problems, whether they involve a work-related situation or a counseling session, are exploratory in nature; that is, leaders do not always identify the correct cause of a problem or develop the best plan. In fact, two of the most common errors leaders make are identifying the wrong problem and identifying the wrong causes of a problem. Plus, the tendency for leaders to make mental errors increases as their levels of stress increase. Everyone makes mistakes. If leaders are given false information, it may lead them to incorrect problem identification and to incorrect assumptions about the causes of a problem. If leaders then fail to determine the true source of a problem, they may develop an inadequate plan.

Learn to identify the real problems. Consider all angles. Learn to seek only accurate information that leads to the real causes of a problem. To ensure that information is accurate, question its validity. In other words, leaders must take what accurate information they have, use their best judgment, and make educated assumptions about the causes of a problem. They then must consider the courses of action that will be most likely to succeed.

Step 2: Gather Information

In this step, leaders must gather all available information that pertains to or can influence the situation (identified problem) from sources such as higher, lateral, and subordinate levels of command as well as from applicable outside agencies. Although some of the information may not bear on the problem at hand, it must be available for leaders to consider when developing and analyzing courses of action.

The amount of available time in a leadership situation can be a limiting factor on how much time a leader spends performing the various steps of the problem-solving and decision-making process. If time is extremely limited, this is the only step that leaders may omit so they can quickly think through the remaining steps.

Step 3: Develop Courses of Action

With the problem identified and available information gathered, you are now ready to develop possible courses of action. Keep an open mind throughout this step and be prepared to anticipate change. "Sixty percent (of good problem solving) is the ability to anticipate; 40 percent . . . is the ability to improvise, to reject a preconceived idea . . . , and to rule by action instead of acting by rules" (S.L.A. Marshall).

Think of as many "what-ifs" as you can and prepare for them; do not be surprised. The laws of probability are strongly in favor of surprise. Develop courses of actions to counteract events that might hinder accomplishment of your mission. Conducting brainstorming sessions is a good technique to use when there is difficulty in developing courses of action. Brainstorming is a creative technique that encourages several people to suggest as many solutions to a problem as possible. Generally, you want to have at least two or three possible courses of action—more if the situation dictates and time permits.

Step 4: Analyze and Compare Courses of Action

The next step is to determine which course of action will best solve the problem. Therefore, leaders should develop as many advantages and disadvantages for each course of action as possible. Then they must **objectively** and logically analyze the advantages and disadvantages of each one against the advantages and disadvantages of the others.

Up to this point in the problem-solving and decision-making process, leaders should have involved subordinates to research the problem, gather information, and develop and analyze the various courses of action. *Subordinates are more likely to support a plan or decision if they took part in its development.* This technique will pay off in terms of increased interest, higher morale, and better efficiency by team members.

Step 5: Make a Decision

After you have carefully analyzed the possible courses of action using all available information, consider your **intuitions** and emotions. The decision-making process is not a purely objective, mathematical formula. The human mind does not work that way, especially under stress. Instead, the mind is both rational and intuitive, and because the decision-making process is a thought process, it is also both rational and intuitive. Your intuition is that aspect of your mind that tells you what "feels" right or wrong. Your intuition flows from your instincts and experience.

However, never make the mistake of making decisions guided totally by emotions or intuitions and immediately doing what "feels" right. *This is a prescription for disaster.* Follow the problem-solving process as rationally and objectively as possible. Gather information; then develop, analyze, and compare courses of action. Consider your intuition or hunches, emotions, and values. Try to identify a "best" course of action that is logical and likely to succeed and that also "feels" right in terms of your intuition, values, and character. Finally, make your decision, make a plan, and take action.

Step 6: Make a Plan

Make a plan that includes who would do what, when, where, how, and why. Be as specific as time permits but do not leave out vital information that could prevent mission accomplishment. Plus, ensure that you specify the what, when, where, how and why for all personnel or elements under your authority. Finally, include **contingencies** in your plan that address possible unexpected situations or actions. Develop these contingencies based on the assumptions made when you identified the problem and gathered available information.

As you did when developing the courses of action, be prepared to anticipate change. The ability to make appropriate changes in decisions and plans requires a certain flexibility of mind, which is a crucial trait of a good problem solver, decision maker, and planner.

Key Note Term

objectively – without prejudice

Key Note Term

intuitions – instinctive knowledge or feeling; immediate perceptions

Key Note Term

contingencies – chances or possible occurrences

Step 7: Implement the Plan

After the decision and plan are made, it is time to act. In this final step, you must put the plan into action and then evaluate it to ensure that the desired results are being achieved. Evaluation is often a neglected step in the decision-making process.

> **Note**
>
> President Harry S. Truman kept a plaque on his desk with the inscription "The buck stops here." Truman was one of America's most honest and ethical presidents. He never flinched from accepting responsibility for his decisions, however unpopular or controversial.

Approaches to the Planning Process

Planning is the cornerstone of all other functions: What goes on in planning affects what is done in the remaining functions. There is an old saying that has proven itself time and time again: "If you fail to plan, you plan to fail; plan your work, then work your plan."

Planning is also the basis for the problem-solving, decision-making process. Leaders spend many hours planning the activities of their organization. In doing so, they must consider the missions and objectives of their unit and how they are going to best accomplish them.

Every activity in which you take part during the day requires some degree of planning and at least one person to do that planning. Naturally, depending on the activity, some aspects of it may require more planning (and more people) than other aspects. Therefore, performing detailed, careful planning should be like a habit. It should be automatic and continuous throughout the activity. Just like in the problem-solving and decision-making process, there are specific steps that you should follow when planning. Likewise, there is more than one planning process. This part of the lesson presents the four-step planning process.

Four-Step Planning Process

When planning, leaders must visualize, consider, and examine all the factors involved in accomplishing a mission. Planning is not an easy process and it requires a lot of work. The first approach to planning consists of four basic steps that can help leaders focus on the essential information when planning an activity. These four steps are as follows:

1. **Define the objective.**
2. **Study the current situation.**
3. **List and examine possible courses of action.**
4. **Select the course of action that will best help to achieve the objective.**

Simply stated, there are two primary purposes of planning: selecting an objective and deciding on how to accomplish it. In the four-step planning process, step one addresses the first purpose; the remaining steps show how you can use planning to reach your objective.

Step 1: Define the Objective

In this step, leaders begin to define or break down their primary objective by determining the various *tasks*, *conditions*, and *standards* that are necessary to complete it.

Defining the objective sounds easy; everybody knows what they want to do. If you are in business, you might say, "I want to make a profit." That is a good objective, but there is more to it than that. How much profit do you want to make? When do you want to make it?

There is more to setting an objective than just saying what you want (or would like) to do or what a supervisor wants you to do. Be specific. Ensure that subordinates have a clear understanding of the objective so that everyone will be working to accomplish the same thing.

Defining the objective so that it indicates what action is required is the first part of clearly identifying the *task*. Everyone involved must know exactly what they must do to accomplish the objective. Additionally, use words that describe the action that must be done, for example, to "sell" so many items, "fill out" so many forms, or "build" a bridge.

Next, identify any *conditions* that describe the circumstances under which you must perform the objective. For example, say you are a member of a junior band and the group wants to meet 95 percent of the requirements (*standard*) necessary to become senior-band members (*task*). The circumstances or conditions are those factors that you must plan for to ensure task accomplishment (such as obtaining sheet music, having the correct mix of instruments, rehearsing for our example).

Finally, state the objective in a way that makes it measurable. If an objective does not have a measurable *standard*, how will you know when you have accomplished it? Think back to the objective of "making a profit." When have you achieved this objective? Is it when you make $1? . . . $50? . . . $100? By stating your objective in measurable terms, you will know when you have reached it.

Defining the objective is a critical step. Without a well-defined objective, it would be difficult to complete the remaining steps of the planning process. After you are satisfied with the objective, proceed to the next step.

> **Note**
>
> A good objective is clearly defined and measurable.

Step 2: Study the Current Situation

You are now ready to study the situation that can affect or influence your ability to accomplish the objective. Stop and look at what you have to work with: How much *time* do you have? How many *people* will help you? What kind of *supplies* do you have? What other *resources* are available to help you?

Next, identify any barriers or obstacles that may stand between you and your goal. Some of these barriers may be a lack of time, people, supplies, and/or other resources.

As you can see, studying the current situation involves a systematic process of defining tasks and arranging resources with respect to mission accomplishment. You should consider five factors when performing this step: effective use of time; identification of subtasks, people, and resources; and setting priorities.

Time

Time is an important factor. You must consider time when you plan events, meet deadlines, and set goals; then you must make plans and execute tasks according to an established time schedule. Effective leaders will schedule their time and the activities of their team to meet these events, deadlines, and goals. You must also ensure that your team members can do all of the tasks within the specified time frame.

Tasks

Identify all the tasks and subtasks that your team must do to accomplish the objective. Be specific. Develop detailed lists to record them and, just as you did in defining the objective, set measurable standards for each task and subtask.

People

After you have a detailed list of tasks/subtasks, determine if you have enough people to do the job. Tentatively match someone to each task/subtask. Base your selection on what each task/subtask requires versus the capabilities of your team members and on how many people (work hours) you will need to accomplish the objective.

Set Priorities

You will always have some tasks that are more important than others or you must start them before others because of how difficult they are. In these situations, plan a "to-do" list in terms of priority for every task and subtask you have identified. Determine which ones your team must do first, second, and so on until you have included everything necessary to carry out the plan. Establish priorities in categories (priority A, priority B, priority C, and so on) for each item on the "to-do" list. Do the A priorities first, then the Bs, the Cs, and so on.

Resources

Identify all resources that are necessary to complete the objective. Determine what is and what is not available; then, before you begin work, set aside what is on hand for later use and make arrangements to obtain the items that you do not have but will need. While completing the task, periodically check the status of your resources and follow up on the availability of those items that you are still trying to obtain.

Steps 3 and 4: Examining and Selecting the Best Courses of Action

You must now list all of the different ways you can think of to accomplish the objective and to decide on the best course of action. First, list all the different courses of action; then eliminate all that can't be accomplished within the given resource constraints (such as not enough time, knowledge, material, or people). Finally, choose between the remaining viable courses of action. The most common method is to list the advantages and disadvantages of each course of action separately, then choose the one that is most advantageous. Often, however, there is no single best solution, in which case the decision will require a tradeoff analysis. A tradeoff analysis begins by defining a set of selection criteria and assigning a numeric value to each according to its level of importance. Each course of action is then compared with the selection criteria and assigned matching values. The assigned values are summed and each course of action accorded a separate weight. The best course of action is the one with the highest or lowest weighted value, depending on the selection criteria. For example, if you're buying a car and need to choose between vehicles of approximately the same cost, you could make a list of features you consider important. Assign each feature a priority, 1 (low); 2 (medium); and 3 (high); then match features to assign each vehicle a weighted value. Finally choose the car with the highest value corresponding to the vehicle with the most features you feel are important.

Leadership Case Study

Jack Wilson, Cindy Spencer, Craig Summers, Alicia Benson, Jacob Walker, and Abdul Al-Kahtani have been assigned to do a group project for their class in U.S. history. They are required to meet outside of class to identify a significant historical document in U.S. history other than the Constitution and Declaration of Independence and work together to research and report on the events that led to the creation of the document. The report is to be 10 to 15 typed pages. They are also required to make a 30-minute, creative presentation to the class that communicates their findings. They have six weeks to conduct the research, write the paper, and prepare their in-class presentation.

Jack and Cindy have been designated to be the team leaders. Their responsibility is to organize the team, assign roles and responsibilities, and assure that the assignment is done well and completed on time. The project grade accounts for 30 percent of the course grade. Half of the grade is based on individual contribution and half of the grade is a team grade awarded to each team member alike. As team leaders, Jack and Cindy can earn up to 10 extra credit points on the project depending on how well the team performs.

The team met for the first time in class on the day the assignment was given. Jack made a quick list of what needed to be done and was eager to make assignments. Cindy wanted to talk with the group to develop a list of assignments together. Craig announced his disdain for history and suggested that all he cared to study was math and science. Alicia sat silently, drew pictures on a piece of paper, and said nothing the entire meeting. Jacob noted that he was an avid student of history and offered several examples of U.S. historical documents that the team could research. Abdul voiced his doubts about Jacob's knowledge and expertise and questioned how much historical data would be available for the documents Jacob suggested. After 15 minutes of talking, the team had made no progress in determining a course of action. All they could decide was that they would need to meet again some day after school to figure out what to do. But they could not agree on a time or place to meet. They considered six different dates and times, but at least one person had a conflict with every time that was suggested.

Cindy and Jack walked to their next class together. "I'm worried about this, Jack," Cindy began. "This team is a mess. We don't agree on anything. Craig doesn't even want to do this. Alicia just sits there. And Jacob and Abdul don't exactly get along. We can't even schedule a meeting together. How are we going to put all this together?"

Jack and Cindy decided that they would meet together to lay out some possible solutions to the challenges they faced on this project. During their meeting they made a list of problems to be addressed:

- Find an agreeable time and place to meet as a team
- Agree on a U.S. historical document for their project
- Assign roles for the project
- Set deadlines for what will be due when
- Put together a project plan

Jack and Cindy looked at their list. "This is a good start, Cindy," Jack noted, "But I think we need more detail."

"I think you're right, Jack." Cindy added. "So what do you think we should do to fill in the blanks in our plan?"

"Why don't we try the seven-step problem-solving method we have talked about in JROTC?" Jack suggested.

"Sounds reasonable," Cindy said. "We may as well try to do it instead of just talking about it. What were those steps again?"

Jack and Cindy looked back over their notes of the problem-solving steps.

- Identify the problem
- Identify facts and assumptions
- Generate alternatives
- Analyze alternatives
- Compare alternatives
- Make and execute your decision
- Assess the results

Put yourself in the place of Jack and Cindy. As with most problems, there are multiple dimensions to this problem. Based on what you know of their situation, identify what you think are the three most important dimensions of the problem to address and work through the seven-step problem-solving process. Here are some facts that you can assume:

Jack Wilson is a JROTC student who knows Cindy Spencer and has worked well with her on past projects. He is a good student and is an active cadet in the JROTC program.

Cindy Spencer is also a JROTC student. She is also a good student, who is active in student government, and plays on the school soccer team.

Craig Summers is an exceptionally bright person who loves math and science but is not interested in English and history. He is cooperative, but "tells it like it is."

Alicia Benson is a quiet individual who no one knows very well. She is artistic and keeps to herself. Although she does not say much, she will voice her opinion when you ask.

Jacob Walker is a talker who always has an opinion about any given topic. He is very active in the social scene at school. Although he projects an image of having it all together, no one really knows how well he does in school. He is there all the time and talks a good deal, but the people around him have the feeling he is "all talk and no action."

Abdul Al-Kahtani is a new student in the school, whose parents have recently moved to the United States from Saudi Arabia. He is very bright and speaks English well, but he seems to have trouble understanding when people are joking and when they are being serious. He likes the United States and works very hard to get along with people, but it is obvious that Jacob rubs him the wrong way.

Conclusion

Successful leaders are energetic. They exert a great deal of effort to communicate effectively, solve problems, make decisions, set goals, plan, execute plans, and supervise/evaluate. These are a leader's directional (or thinking) and implementing skills. As a leader, you cannot expect positive results from your subordinates unless you work equally hard at solving problems, making plans, and putting plans and decisions into action. Successful leaders also work hard at accomplishing their missions and objectives while maintaining only the highest possible standards of performance.

In your professional and leadership development you should strive to exercise the same degree of effort and excellence.

In the following lesson, you will learn how to lead meetings. This lesson will give you the skills that you need to take control of a meeting and get the most out of the time you have and the people in attendance.

Lesson Review

1. List the seven steps to the problem-solving and decision-making process.
2. Choose one of the seven steps and explain it.
3. List and explain the four-step planning process.
4. Explain behaviors that can disrupt your ability to solve a problem.

Leading Meetings

Chapter 4

Key Terms

agenda
attendee
conclude
facilitate

What You Will Learn to Do

- Prepare for a meeting

Linked Core Abilities

- Take responsibility for your actions and choices

Skills and Knowledge You Will Gain Along the Way

- Describe how to plan for a meeting
- Explain the general rules for leading and participating in effective meetings
- Define the key words contained in this lesson

Introduction

This lesson looks at five keys to leading meetings, the nine steps to planning a meeting, the general rules of leading effective meetings, and the skills to facilitate the process efficiently and effectively.

Many people dislike meetings. They are typically unorganized, and the purpose for the meeting is many times unclear. Attendees are unaware of their roles and their responsibilities. It does not need to be like that. This lesson provides you with the right information to conduct productive meetings. You are also given some sample tools that you can use when you are leading a project and expect to lead regular meetings with your project team.

Five Keys to Leading Meetings

In today's busy world, people just don't have time to sit in meetings that are unproductive and ineffective. It is important that the leader does not just call a meeting and then sit back to see what happens. He or she must do some preparation to determine the purpose and the outcome for the meeting. The following are the key elements of leading meetings. Each one of these elements is critical to the success of a meeting:

- **Planning.** Things that must be done to prepare for a meeting
- **Starting.** How you set the tone and create the climate for the meeting
- **Focusing.** How you keep the meeting on track
- **Facilitating.** Things a leader can do to involve participants, be supportive, resolve conflict, and manage differences
- **Concluding.** Way in which the leader ends the meeting and assures that the participants are satisfied with the outcome and they understand what is expected of them for follow-up actions

Planning the Meeting

How do you typically plan for a meeting? Thorough planning is critical to leading a successful meeting. There are nine sequential steps that can help you plan effectively:

1. **Clarify purpose**
2. **Define outcomes**
3. **Sequence activities**
4. **Invite attendees**
5. **Schedule meeting**
6. **Prepare presentations**
7. **Create agenda**
8. **Communicate agenda**
9. **Prepare meeting room**

These nine steps are covered in the following sections.

Clarify the Purpose of the Meeting

This is a short statement describing the primary purpose of the meeting. It should start with a verb (to decide, to solve, to view, to hear, to inform, to negotiate, to listen, to review).

Define the Outcome

The desired outcome describes the expected results of the meeting; the product that participants will take away with them when the meeting is over. It can be a written plan or new knowledge. It may include both task and process outcomes. It is written with nouns and phrases, not verbs (an action plan, a solution, a decision, clarity, an informed staff are task outcomes; a cooperative attitude, commitment, motivated team members are process outcomes).

Sequence the Meeting Activities

It's important to design the sequence of meeting activities. Always plan an introduction and a summary to the meetings. Sequence the topics in order of priority, in logical sequence where information is needed to come to conclusions, alternate high-energy and low energy topics whenever possible, and allow sufficient time for closing.

Invite Meeting Attendees

Determine who should attend, their roles, and ground rules. Essential **attendees** are those with relevant information or expertise, those that will make the final decision, people who are affected by the decision, and anyone who might be a barrier to implementation. Group roles are those tasks that can be shared by several people at the meeting. Some suggested roles are the designated leader responsible for managing the meeting; timekeeper for keeping track of time and reminding group of planned start and stop times; recorder to keep minutes of the proceedings; process observer to observe behavior and make comments about how the meeting is proceeding and staying true to the ground rules; and a facilitator who may simultaneously fill the roles of timekeeper, chart person, and process observer. Ground rules are guidelines for desired behavior that will enhance the process of the meeting. Good ground rule examples include only one person at a time talks, listen to the person who is talking, no side conversations, communicate directly and honestly, and limit contributions to five minutes.

Schedule the Meeting

Decide what time the meeting is to begin and what time it is to end. Set meeting length according to the agenda items, energy needed, time, and logistical constraints. Energy usually drops after two hours. Schedule ten-minute breaks every two hours. Determine logistics, equipment and supplies required, and administrative matters. Administrative matters include meeting location, room layout, equipment usage, refreshments, and notification.

Prepare the Meeting Presentation

Select the appropriate military briefing format: information, decision, mission, or staff briefing. Research the topic. Obtain all available information, write detailed notes, and organize your thoughts. Determine the purpose of your briefing. Analyze your audience, evaluate your setting, and determine any time constraints. Plan the briefing. Refine your thesis statement, plan your major parts and sort them. Write a draft introduction and a draft conclusion. Rehearse your briefing as many times as possible. Revise the briefing. Focus on your audience's perspective. How will they receive your message? Do your facts validate your introduction, body, and conclusion? Review your style. Revise everything as necessary. Prepare your audiovisuals. Develop an effective method for answering questions. Be prepared to handle any problems which may surface during your briefing. Make printed copies of your presentation to give to all meeting participants.

Create the Agenda

Construct an agenda that can be accomplished within the scheduled time period. Prioritize topics and annotate any expected decisions. Establish timeframes for each topic. If possible, allow time for new business or unexpected topics toward the end of the meeting. Conclude each meeting by summarizing major decisions and reviewing assigned taskings.

Communicate the Agenda

Deliver copies of the agenda to meeting participants in advance. Allow sufficient time for participants to prepare for the meeting. Review the agenda at the outset of the meeting and reprioritize items as necessary. Follow the agenda and keep participants on time and on topic.

Prepare Meeting Room

Prepare the meeting room in advance (see Figure 4.5.1). Coordinate with protocol officers to ensure the room is properly prepared for high-ranking dignitaries. Check and verify all audiovisual equipment is functioning properly. Obtain presentation copies in advance and verify compatibility with audiovisual equipment. Assign seating positions and placename placards. Distribute printed materials around the table. Adjust the lighting and queue the presentations.

Initially these steps might seem like a lot of work and somewhat tedious; however, when you become comfortable with the steps you will find they will become automatic. When you see the positive results of leading effective meetings and reaching your desired outcomes, you will be admired by others because you will be showing you respect them by not wasting their time.

Starting the Meeting

How you start the meeting can set the tone for success. The following are activities that should be included in starting the meeting:

- **Welcome and introductions**
- **Statement of the task**
- **Statement and display of the desired outcomes**
- **Background**
- **Review or develop the agenda and display it**
- **Clarify expectations**
- **List or set ground rules and display them**
- **Clarify roles**

Focusing the Meeting

One of the major problems in leading a meeting is keeping the meeting focused on the task. There are many ways to assure that the meeting adheres to the agenda and to deal with interruptions. Here are some guidelines you can use to keep the meeting on task.

Lead the meeting through the agenda. Take charge. Use a style of leadership appropriate to the task, the situation, and the willingness and ability of the participants. Introduce each agenda item. Cover time and desired results. Keep the discussion on track by referring to the following structures:

- **Task**
- **Desired outcomes**
- **Agenda items**
- **Ground rules**
- **Roles**
- **Time limit**

Focus attention by using a chart pad and easel or other visual aid. Maintain a "parking lot" of important items not relevant to the present discussion. At the end of the agenda item, briefly summarize what was accomplished and/or decided; identify unfinished business and what to do; and check for clarity and agreement.

Facilitating the Meeting

A meeting leader is responsible to **facilitate** participant involvement, deal with conflict, manage differences, make sure that everyone is heard, and keep communications open. The following are tips on how to encourage participation:

- **Get input from lower-level people first**
- **Ask open-ended questions**
- **Use active listening, paraphrase, and be attentive**
- **Acknowledge positive participation**
- **Allow opportunities for everyone to speak**
- **Be supportive of new ideas and minority views; seek first to understand before agreement or disagreement**
- **Distinguish the differences between assumptions and facts**

> **Key Note Term**
>
> **facilitate** – to encourage participation

Concluding the Meeting

When the agenda has been completed it is time to put closure to the meeting. **Conclude** by first summarizing what has been accomplished during the meeting; then compare the accomplishments with the desired outcomes; identify unfinished business and suggest ways to address those issues; complete the action plan for agreed-on actions; evaluate the meeting for things you can do better at the next meeting.

> **Key Note Term**
>
> **conclude** – close the meeting by summarizing what was discussed and agreed

General Meeting Rules

Conducting meetings is a process—a process of setting an agenda that will lead to a specific outcome. Like any process it can be improved through understanding the skills and rules of conducting an effective meeting. The best way to lead orderly, productive meetings is to follow these guidelines.

Meeting Agendas

Each meeting must have an **agenda**. It would be helpful if it was drafted at the previous meeting by one or two members. Putting detail in it prior to the actual meeting and, if possible, send it to the participants in advance; however, this would not occur at an initial meeting or a onetime meeting. If the agenda was not developed before a meeting, spend the first five or ten minutes to do so with the attendees.

Agendas should have the following information (following the what, where, when, who, and how method):

> **Key Note Term**
>
> **agenda** – schedule of items to be discussed at meeting addressing who, what, when, where, and how

- **Agenda topics (include a sentence that would define each item and why it is being discussed)**
- **Presenters for each topic**
- **Time allocation for each topic**
- **Type of action required (discussion, decision, announcement)**

The flow of the agenda will typically be as follows:

- **Warm-ups: short activities used to free the attendees minds of the things they left behind to attend this meeting**
- **Review of agenda so the team can add, delete, modify as needed**
- **Scheduling breaks if longer than one hour**
- **Meeting evaluation so the team can discuss their feelings about the topics covered; if a follow-up meeting is to occur, draft the next agenda**

Meeting Facilitator

Each meeting should have a facilitator who is responsible for keeping the meeting focused on its purpose and moving in accordance to the time allocations. The team leader normally takes this role; however, it can be assigned to any team member and rotated when several meetings are expected. The chief responsibilities of the facilitator are as follows:

- **Keep the discussion on topic and within the time allocated. When the time allocation is drawing near, inform the group so they can either adjust the time allocation at the expense of other items, postpone the discussion for another meeting or move on as scheduled.**
- **Intervene if there are sidebars or when there are multiple discussions going on at the same time.**
- **Ensure everyone is heard and no one person dominates the discussions.**
- **Bring discussion to a close with summary statements.**
- **Act as a scribe to record key subjects, decisions made, potential agenda items for subsequent meetings, and action items (who has agreed to do what and by when).**

At the end of the meeting, the facilitator will draft the agenda for the next meeting with the assistance by the team. Ensure the meeting evaluation takes place. This should include decisions on what will be done to improve the next meeting.

Keep the attendees in the "here and now." Once the meeting begins, everyone is expected to give their full attention. Often meetings are held away from the everyday work place to ensure members are not distracted. Because this is not always possible, the "100-mile rule" is established (each member is to behave as if they were 100 miles away from their daily routine). If members continue to disrupt the meeting by receiving messages, making phone calls, and/or not returning on time from breaks, the facilitator may need to remind them of this rule.

Effective Discussions

Your meeting now has an agenda and a facilitator, and the meeting is underway. Another aspect of effective meetings is to facilitate effective discussions. Every meeting should include mechanisms that allow for open discussion. The following techniques are provided and can be used in meetings or whenever an effective discussion is desired:

- **If you are unclear about a topic, the comments of a participant, or the argument provided from another team member, ask for clarification. Ask them to repeat the information using examples, pictures, diagrams, data, or just other words.**

- **Don't let dominators take over the discussions. Make sure you ask those who have not had the opportunity to speak for their input. Be a gatekeeper and make opportunities for everyone to be heard.**

- **Before debating or defending each idea that is discussed, actively explore the idea and search for understanding before agreement or disagreement. Listening is not an easy thing to do.**

- **While listening, compile what has been said and then summarize and restate it to the group; ask if what was said was captured correctly.**

- **If the time allocation given to a topic seems to be taking longer, remind the team of the deadlines and either accelerate or postpone the time allocations.**

- **Learn to listen for when the topic has been "talked out." If there is silence, it could be just an opportunity for thinking about what was said. If someone repeats their point more than once, it could be that they felt they were not heard. Do not assume the discussion is over, but do not assume it is not. Intervene with questions like, "do we have anything else to add to this topic?" or "are we ready to move on?"**

- **Periodically check to how the team is feeling about the decision making process. Check to see if the team agrees with the position, decision, or summary of discussions.**

- **Throughout the meeting check the "pulse" for the outcome. Ask: "Are we getting what we want from this discussion? What can we do differently?"**

Record Keeping

The next step in the meeting process is to establish the record-keeping system for your meetings so you can refer back to decisions and agreements generated from the meetings. Such record keeping can prevent the rehashing of issues previously discussed. Agendas, minutes, and the actions are included in your record-keeping system.

Table 4.5.1 is a sample agenda for your use if you are leading a project and expect to have regular meetings with the project team. It is a good tool to use when you lead a service project. The agenda incorporates several elements useful in documenting the purpose for the meetings as well as action and future lists.

Table 4.5.1: Sample meeting agenda

Agenda for Project Team

Project Team:

Goals:

Meeting Date:

Icebreaker.

Review the agenda: add or delete items as necessary. Estimate the amount of time for each item. Rank the item: must do today/should do today.

Status reports on individual assignments.
(List individual assignments and responsible person here.)

Other reports, presentations, activities or discussions.
(List them here identifying the item type, e.g., decision, discussion, action.)

Review of the status of the project: Where are we now relative to our plan?

Assignments for follow-up activities (What? By whom? Due date?)

Upcoming events, presentations, special meetings, etc.

Review of items on the action list.

Review of items of the future list.

Agenda items for the next regular meeting.

Special activity schedule for this meeting.

The meeting minutes remind members of the topics discussed, the decisions made on those topics, the actions and responsible persons and due dates for those actions, and the list of future items to be included in subsequent agendas.

A sample of a two-part team meeting record is provided in Table 4.5.2 and can be used to capture the minutes of the meeting.

Table 4.5.2: Team Meeting Record

Project Team Meeting Record, Part 1

Meeting Number   Date
Location

Project name

Mission Statement:

To indicate "present"	Future list: items for future consideration.
Member	
Member	
Member	
Member	
Member	
Member	
Member	
Member	
Others attending:	Meeting review
	Pluses Minuses
Agenda: Enter key words indicating the agenda topics. Check off an item when it is completed. Items not completed will be incorporated into the next meeting.	

( ) 1. Warm-up

( ) 2. Agenda review

( ) 3.

( ) 4.   Next Meeting

( ) 5.

( ) 6.   Date

( ) 7.   Time

( ) 8. Set agenda for next   Location
meeting

( ) 9. Meeting evaluation

Project Team Meeting Record, Part 2

Topic 1: (brief description)

Decisions/Conclusions:

Next Steps:

Topic 2: (brief description)

Decisions/Conclusions:

Next Steps:

Topic 3: (brief description)

Decisions/Conclusions:

Next Steps:

Conclusion

In this lesson, you learned the five keys to leading meetings, the nine steps to planning a meeting, the general rules of leading effective meetings and the skills to facilitate the process efficiently and effectively.

In the following lesson, you will learn some important techniques for supervising others.

Lesson Review

1. List the five keys to leading effective meetings.

2. List the nine steps to planning an effective meeting.

3. What are some methods for facilitating effective discussions?

4. Consider the last meeting you attended. Was it effective? What would you do different?

Lesson 6

Supervising

Key Terms

correction
discipline
motivation
supervising
teaching

What You Will Learn to Do

- Understand the components of leadership and explain how learning styles and preferences impact learning

Linked Core Abilities

- Take responsibility for your actions and choices
- Treat yourself and others with respect

Skills and Knowledge You Will Gain Along the Way

- Explain the role of discipline in leadership
- Describe examples of effective supervisory skills
- Define the key words contained in this lesson

Chapter 4

Introduction

Effective leaders empower people, and empowered people achieve desired outcomes. Through clear communication, praise, and correction, effective leaders enable people to meet and exceed standards.

A good leader must be a teacher, coach, and counselor. Leaders must also be alert and aware of what's going on around them. By attending to details, a leader determines which standards are and aren't being met.

This lesson shows you how to become the best possible leader. It presents examples of effective supervision through direct leadership and considers the role of discipline.

Direct Leadership

When you think of a leader, you might imagine a person seated behind a big desk. Effective leaders, however, do much more than sit at a desk and sign documents. This lesson discusses direct leadership —a face-to-face, hands-on type of leadership style.

For an example of a leader, consider a school principal. A principal might have to wade through a fair amount of paperwork, but a vital part of his or her day is spent interacting with staff and students, parents, and members of the school board. To be an effective leader, he or she must have strong interpersonal skills and be able to communicate clearly. This principal must also listen well to gather clear data about the school and then analyze the data to determine what is and isn't working. By practicing direct leadership, the principal is involved, visible, and aware of what is happening in the school and with the student body.

Effective leaders also pay close attention to details. A leader must be alert and able to multitask to move fluidly and quickly from one task to another. Imagine a high school senior overseeing the yearbook staff. Some on his staff are graphic artists, working hard to develop a cohesive "look" for that yearbook. Other members are organizing the hundreds of portraits and ensuring that each yearbook picture coincides with the correct name. If these students are to produce a yearbook that doesn't leave out a single student and is visually attractive as well as consistent, the yearbook supervisor must maximize group performance. This requires attending to very different details, from the creative artwork to the names and pictures. When a leader sees what is or isn't being done well, he or she can provide praise or **correction**. Direct leadership involves coaching people to perform tasks on their own so they understand what is needed to achieve a specific outcome.

Remember that the ultimate goal of leadership is to produce independence. Too much supervision can undercut confidence; not enough supervision and the goal will likely not be met. An effective leader recognizes when someone is sufficiently skilled to attempt a task. Furthermore, an effective leader can fine-tune the amount of feedback that an individual needs and recognize when less supervision is required.

Consider this example: Your mother asks you to teach your seven-year-old brother to walk to his friend's house by himself. Your direct leadership task is to help him

Key Note Term

correction – to make or set right

develop the skills he'll need, such as crossing the street safely, and also instill the confidence in him to accomplish this goal. If you follow him to his friend's house every time, you would undercut his confidence and, consequently, might impede his independence. If you just send him off without showing him the way, however, he might become lost and frightened and lose even more confidence. Obviously, effective direct leadership requires presence so that corrections can be tendered, such as "Don't just step into the street. Stop and look both ways." Being present also allows a leader to tender praise, such as "Hey, you remembered to stop and look. Great job!" Perhaps most important, effective leadership requires recognition of when someone is ready to attempt a task on their own.

Checking enables correction, and correction improves performance. Those improvements in performance promote independence. But how much checking serves learning? And when does checking undercut confidence? These are questions that only an aware leader can answer.

Learning Styles and Preferences

A leader's task is to lead team members to a state of mastery and independence. That way, standards of performance will be met regardless of conditions. This requires teaching and learning; however, because individuals learn in different ways, a leader must adjust to various learning styles. One person might prefer a detailed verbal explanation of what is expected; another person might learn best by simply seeing what is expected. Some people require more feedback than others. Some are comfortable making mistakes and learning from them. For others, learning is slowed by too many mistakes and too much criticism. To maximize learning, a leader must attend to the learning preferences of each student.

Here's an example: The captain of the volleyball team recognizes that the team will not achieve its full potential unless the freshmen fill vital roles. By working with her young teammates, she discovers that one girl performs best when she is pushed to excel. That girl responds to high expectations and firm coaching; however, a patient approach accelerates the learning of another player. A third girl learns best when the captain physically demonstrates appropriate form, and a fourth girl's learning is helped along by the captain taking the time to explain why one jumps and moves in a certain way.

In this example, the captain took the time to note the effects of different teaching techniques. After each practice, she analyzed the effectiveness of each technique and made changes as needed. By adapting to various learning styles, she maximized learning . . . and success.

Role of Discipline and Standards

As discussed earlier in this lesson, effective leaders develop confidence in those they supervise. Leaders also develop the skills that enable a group to achieve its mission, whether it's winning a football game or planning a vacation. Within a group, each person has a task, whether it's catching a football or ensuring there is enough bottled water for the group. By supervising and teaching, leaders enhance performances, but leaders can't always be present because the diverse duties of leaders keep them from being everywhere they might like to be.

For example, the captain of a football team can't see everything on the field. If his team is to achieve its potential, the players must have **discipline**. Discipline is the desire and the will to do what one is expected to do, which serves as cohesion for the group and the group's mission. Discipline trumps selfishness, and compels a person to act in the best interest of the group and the group's goal.

> ### Note
>
> General Dwight D. Eisenhower, quoting Lieutenant General Leslie J. McNair in 1941, said: "Our troops are capable of the best discipline. If they lack it, leadership is faulty."

> ### Setting a Disciplined Example
>
> As a leader, it is important that you learn self-discipline and be an example to your followers.
>
> - Make certain that you arrive to appointments on time
> - Always look your best and be well-groomed
> - Stand straight and tall
> - Accomplish your goals to the best of your ability and in a timely manner
> - Take that extra step to ensure every detail is attended to and covered
>
> By adopting discipline in your own life, you set the standard and give your followers something to emulate.

Discipline empowers every member of a group. It also keeps a leader focused on details and delivering the supervision, correction, and instruction that people need to maximize their performance. Discipline within each member of a group develops independence and elevates effort.

Leaders insist on set standards. When leaders clearly convey what is needed and then offer feedback, the members of the group can ratchet up their performance until it meets or exceeds standards. Consider again the student overseeing his yearbook staff. When he sees that one of his graphic artists has produced a page that is not up to the standard of the others, he must not let that page pass his approval. To do so undercuts cohesion and lowers the standard for future work. That student must correct and teach—and then praise when the standard is met.

Discipline is developed in the little things. A football captain who arrives on time, is well conditioned, and is ready to play is an example to the rest of the team. A football captain who arrives late and out of shape undercuts success, not only in his own performance but in the performance of the players that emulate him. Cohesion is served when each member of a team develops discipline. That discipline allows a linebacker to keep working out in the weight room when he'd rather be outside, hanging with his friends. Discipline throughout a group also develops confidence in each other. The linebacker will understand that even if he's alone in the weight room, his teammates are running or drilling, and that all members of the team will come to a game prepared to play.

> **Note**
>
> General George S. Patton said, "Discipline is based on pride in the profession of arms, on meticulous attention to details and on mutual respect and confidence. Discipline must be a habit so ingrained that it is stronger than the excitement of battle or the fear of death."

Supervising to Achieve Desired Results

Supervision is a vital aspect of communication. It means keeping a grasp on the situation by ensuring that subordinates properly perform their duties and implement unit plans and policies. Supervision includes the following:

- **Setting the example**
- **Specifying the goal, objective, or standard**
- **Delegating authority/fixing responsibilities**
- **Coordinating efforts and activities**
- **Resolving conflicts with peers/subordinates**
- **Inspecting and evaluating**
- **Providing feedback**

Oversupervision versus Undersupervision

There is a narrow line that determines the levels of adequate supervision. On one side of the line is oversupervision; on the other side is undersupervision.

Figure 4.6.1: Discipline includes the concept that everyone performs the same task in unison.
Courtesy of US Army JROTC.

Oversupervision can stifle initiative, make subordinates resentful, undermine trust, or undermine delegation of authority. On the other hand, undersupervision can lead to mission failure, especially in cases where the leader's intent was not fully understood, or where there was disorganization or a lack of coordination between units. Undersupervision can also make leaders look as though they do not care. Both extremes can lead to resentment and low morale.

Evaluating

Evaluating is a part of supervising that means judging the worth, quality, value, or significance of people, ideas, or things. Evaluation includes the following:

- **Looking at the way subordinates accomplish a task**
- **Performing all types of firsthand checks and inspections**
- **Assessing, gathering information, and asking subordinates questions**
- **Obtaining feedback on how well something is being done**
- **Interpreting feedback by asking: "Does the feedback indicate the plan will succeed?" or "Does it indicate the need for a modification or a major change in plans or policies?"**

Supervising Techniques

Supervising is the key to enforcing discipline. One of the most effective supervising techniques is on-the-spot correction. Very simply put, correction accelerates learning. It pinpoints where standards are not being met. A leader with strong interpersonal skills can correct learners in a way that maintains a strong self-concept, and strong self-concept promotes self-confidence.

To develop effective correction, you must subject yourself to analysis. At the end of a day you must ask, "Did my correction enhance performance? Did it promote independence?" If not, you should develop alternative forms of correction. Focus on acquiring those approaches that best serve the individual learning of those you oversee. Self-analysis is one way of taking responsibility for the choices you made that day. Self-analysis also improves your citizenship skills because it makes you more effective in a group, school, and community. Self-analysis also enables you to be a lifelong learner and, therefore, an ever more effective leader.

The following are positive steps in correcting:

- **Correct where it is needed**
- **Focus on the performance, never the person**
- **Give one correction at a time; do not overload**
- **Don't keep bringing it up; when the correction is over, it is over**

Key Note Term

supervising – to have the charge and direction of; to oversee and direct; keep tabs on; keep and eye on; keep under surveillance

Motivation

People who don't perform up to standards need correction. That correction should be precise and focus on what is wrong with the person's attempt to achieve a task, not what is wrong with the person.

People who achieve at or above standards should be praised; praise fosters **motivation** and confirms that a task has been completed according to standards. Praise also supports morale, cohesion, and discipline, and keeps a group focused and motivated.

When giving praise, always be precise and communicate exactly what is correct about a specific performance. Consider this example: A coach at a basketball practice shouts, "Good job out there! Keep it up!" That vague praise can confuse players. They might try to recall what they were doing right before the coach praised them, and they might even wonder if the coach was talking to them. But if the coach yells, "Good job of blocking out for rebounds, Katie and Leah," all the players understand what the coach wants, as well as who is meeting the standard and who isn't. Katie and Leah can acquire pride and further motivation from the coach's precise praise, and the other players can aspire to the coach's clear standard.

Key Note Term

motivation – something that incites or has a tendency to incite to determination and action

Teaching

As a leader, you also serve as a teacher, and you transfer knowledge through clear communication. An effective leader teaches in logical sequences, notes successes and failures, and provides feedback and praise. Effective leaders also teach by example through nonverbal cues. Because demonstration is an essential element of

Figure 4.6.2: Let your group know when they've performed well.
Courtesy of US Army JROTC.

teaching, you must be competent. Competency furthers the effectiveness of teaching because it demonstrates not only that you are entitled to teach, but you provide a role model for the members of the group.

The people that you lead need your guidance to achieve their potential. Ironically, achieving that potential means that one day, to a large degree, your learners will no longer need you. The end goal of leadership is to develop enough skill and confidence in individuals so they can operate largely without supervision. They will do so empowered with the tool of discipline and the precise understanding of what is expected of them.

Conclusion

If you hoard too much authority, the members of your group will never attain the competence and confidence that serve success. The measure of supervision will vary from person to person, but the desired outcome remains the same: to develop proficiency, pride, and confidence so that your team, whatever the circumstances, can achieve its goal through discipline, motivation, and cohesion.

The next lesson covers team development and additional leadership concepts. These concepts serve effective leadership. They also support group success.

Chapter 4

Lesson Review

Lesson Review

1. **What is discipline and why is it important?**
2. **What are the roles of teaching and correction in leadership?**
3. **Why is praise effective?**
4. **Why is motivation important to a group?**

Team Development

Key Terms

actions
beliefs
constructive criticism
cooperate
cultivate
dedication
followership
professionalism
self-discipline
self-reliance
staff study
teamwork

What You Will Learn to Do

- Assess personal qualities as a team member

Linked Core Abilities

- Take responsibility for your actions and choices
- Treat yourself and others with respect

Skills and Knowledge You Will Gain Along the Way

- Identify the characteristics of individual responsibility, self-reliance, followership, and teamwork
- Explain the importance of individual responsibility, self-reliance, and followership to teamwork
- Describe the responsibilities of a team leader and the leadership factors that affect teamwork
- Define the key words contained in this lesson

Introduction

This lesson covers several fundamental leadership concepts: individual responsibility to yourself and to others on a team, the benefits of self-reliance, the traits of good followership, and the importance of a team and teamwork. All of these concepts are part of becoming a leader and all are equally important to the successful completion of a mission.

Individual Responsibility

Key Note Term

cultivate – to foster the growth of

Do you believe you are a good follower or team member? Being a good follower is one of the first steps to becoming a good leader. To be successful at both, know your individual responsibilities and then **cultivate** your self-reliance and self-image. Know how to apply the traits of followership and the role that you play in a team will be more rewarding and challenging. You will have many opportunities throughout JROTC to develop your leadership skills and abilities, be a follower and a team member, and lead a team, squad, and higher.

Your individual responsibilities include respecting yourself, being honest with yourself, and developing confidence and a winning attitude (see Figure 4.7.1). By respecting yourself, you will know how to respect others. Treating others as you want to be treated is an important quality in good human relations.

If you always strive to do your best, you will become a better follower and a better leader.

Key Note Term

constructive criticism – a comment that is meant to improve or help

A part of being honest with yourself and treating others as you wish to be treated is learning to accept criticism. Accepting criticism is not easy to do, but receiving **constructive criticism** can help you to improve yourself. As you continue to develop your desirable personality traits and leadership skills and abilities, you will become more confident of yourself and of your ideas.

Figure 4.7.1: Self-respect and confidence are essential to being a good team member.
Courtesy of US Army JROTC.

Additionally, by showing respect, honesty, fairness, and responsibility to others, you are being a good follower and a good leader. Make these qualities and the ones discussed previously, a part of your own personal leadership style. When you do, the changes you see in others will be a reflection of the changes in you.

Self-Reliance

Self-reliance means being able to depend on your own efforts and abilities; it is also having confidence in and exercising your own powers of judgment. To improve your self-reliance, you must be honest in acknowledging areas where you need change.

When you are a member of a team and you are self-reliant, your entire team benefits. By doing your part of a task to the best of your abilities (the leadership trait of dependability), your team members do not have to pick up the slack. Then, if every member of the team does their part, the team is more apt to finish its task on schedule and to meet or exceed the expected standards.

Self-reliance can also benefit you. When you can rely on yourself to do something, it gives you a feeling of pride. Self-reliance demonstrates your competence and commitment to other team members. Your team members will be confident that you are committed and, as a result of your **actions**, you can instill confidence in them.

Followership

Followership is knowing how to act as a member of a team. Good followership is essential to good team performance. There are certain qualities or traits of followership that all team members must display to ensure their team is capable of accomplishing its missions. They include competence, **dedication**, **professionalism**, and **self-discipline**.

Additionally, followership requires every member of a team to conscientiously apply their **beliefs** and knowledge about a task or situation before they act. Then, the direction of their actions should be governed by:

- **Established standards and priorities**
- **Rules of conduct**
- **The best interests of the team**

By using a commonsense approach and taking only the actions that are appropriate and necessary for each situation, the team and all its members will be able to successfully accomplish any assigned task.

The Team and Teamwork

Similar to all leaders, team leaders have responsibilities to their subordinates and to their superiors. Striving to keep their team productive is one of the team leader's most important goals. A team that can work well together, as shown in Figure 4.7.2, can effectively accomplish its assigned missions.

Key Note Term

self-reliance – the ability to make your own decisions confidently and independently

Key Note Terms

action – behavior or conduct

followership – accepting the guidance or leadership of another; the capacity or willingness to follow a leader

dedication – loyalty to a cause, ideal, or system; to commit oneself to a particular course of thought or action

professionalism – the ability to do and to take pride in doing a job well; the conduct, aims, or qualities that characterize a profession or professional person

self-discipline – training, regulating, or controlling oneself (or one's conduct, personality, performance, and so on) for the sake of personal improvement

beliefs – a personal truth; mental acceptance or conviction of particular truths of someone or something

Figure 4.7.2: Teams that work well together can accomplish just about anything.
Courtesy of US Army JROTC.

Responsibilities of a Team Leader to Team Members

Leaders at all levels of the chain of command must set the example for their subordinates to follow. Team members need and expect from their leaders guidance, trust, loyalty, respect, and understanding. To accomplish this, the team leader must:

- **Be a decisive leader.** Make accurate and timely decisions to prevent subordinates from wasting their time waiting for instructions, making the decisions themselves, or losing their respect in the unit's leadership.

- **Be an appreciative leader.** Respect and value the ideas, positive work efforts, skills, and abilities of subordinates. Reward and/or recognize them appropriately.

- **Develop initiative in subordinates.** Give them responsibilities that are commensurate with their skills and abilities.

- **Be a caring, sensitive, and compassionate leader.** Sensitive leaders are not weak, nor do they back down. They listen well. They avoid rejecting ideas and work toward compromise. Caring and compassionate leaders sympathize with the problems of their team members and they help to solve them.

- **Communicate effectively with subordinates.** Make all communications (written and oral) clear and concise. Do not expect them to read your mind. This leads to frustration and disappointment, and the assigned task may not be completed to standards.

Responsibilities to the Chain of Command

Team leaders are at the level where most decisions are made above them, yet they are responsible for accomplishing the tasks resulting from those decisions. Therefore, team leaders must be responsible (by showing loyalty, dependability, and integrity—just to name a few of the leadership traits) to authorities as well as to their teammates.

Team leaders owe their superiors a completed task: finished on time, to the best of their ability, and at the least expense possible. They are in a leadership position because superiors believe they can do the job; team leaders must prove it to them that they can!

How Effective Leadership Affects the Team

Two of the most important affects that can come from effective leadership are the successful completion of a task and a sense of pride for a job well done. To obtain these results, team leaders must motivate their team members to produce high quality work. This means that assigned tasks are completed to the supervisor's satisfaction and on time. Team leaders can be effective, responsible leaders by:

- **Applying as many of the leadership traits as possible.** Leaders who possess many positive leadership traits can by their actions create an environment where team members work harder, accomplish more, enjoy the task, and act as a cohesive unit.

- **Pitching in and getting their hands dirty.** The team will realize you are there to help them.

- **Listening to, understanding, and supporting their teammates.** Although team members realize that leaders have responsibilities to their chain of command, they also want assurances that their immediate supervisor is there to support them and not to take advantage of them. If subordinates know that personal gain and recognition are not their leader's goal, but that doing the job is, they will show the degree of respect and trust that produces high quality work.

Teamwork

Teamwork is the effort of a group to complete a task or mission. Successful teamwork requires each team member to **cooperate** with other members of the group to complete the effort as directed.

Importance of Teamwork

Learning about teamwork is an important part of JROTC. It is a team spirit where all members work together to achieve the same goals. It is a willingness to give other team members a friendly push when they need it or a pat on the back when they deserve it. In teamwork, each member of the team expects the same degree of effort from the other. Then, when one teammate does it right, the whole team wins and when cooperation coexists with teamwork, the mission moves more quickly.

If a situation should ever arise where someone calls on you to complete a job, task, or mission that is too involved for you to do alone, teamwork usually provides the answer. In teamwork, a group of people, or fellow cadets, is there to help you complete it. As you will soon discover in the following case study, distributing food to the needy can be a huge mission. However, with good leadership and effective teamwork, the task can be accomplished. Find out if that is what actually happened.

Teamwork also gives you the opportunity to interact with other cadets. In most organizations that you will encounter, the members of a team or group will probably come from different backgrounds and will have different interests. But, by

> **Key Note Terms**
>
> **teamwork** – The cooperative effort or action on the part of a number of people working together, especially to achieve a common goal
>
> **cooperate** – to act or work with another or others

working together as a cohesive unit, everyone tries harder to get along with each other in a productive and professional manner. By working cooperatively with your teammates, you can improve your individual leadership, followership, and communication skills and abilities.

Another very important aspect of teamwork is that it builds friendships and fosters esprit de corps, or feelings of unity and pride for the team. When people feel united, everyone works together to complete the mission.

Your Role in Teamwork

A chain is only as strong as its weakest link. The links in the chain are you and your teammates. Without you and your team members, the chain would break. In much the same way, your role (and the roles of everyone else) keeps the team strong.

Your main role in teamwork is that of being a good follower. As you learned in the section on followership, even leaders have responsibilities to someone and that makes them followers, too. A good follower takes instruction and authority well.

The following story illustrates the responsibilities of leaders to their subordinates and how teamwork affects the outcome of a mission. As you read it, think about how the squad leader applied these responsibilities; then, answer the following questions. Was the squad leader:

- **Decisive?**
- **Appreciative of his subordinates' efforts?**
- **Developing initiative in his subordinates?**
- **Caring, sensitive, and compassionate?**
- **Communicating effectively with his subordinates?**

The Senior Army Instructor (SAI), Major Mason, wanted his cadet battalion to distribute food to the needy at Thanksgiving. He asked for a volunteer to research, plan, and present a report to him and the cadet battalion staff on the best way to accomplish this mission.

Although several leaders expressed an interest, the SAI selected Jim, a junior and fairly recent enrollee into JROTC, whose leadership potential was very impressive. Major Mason gave Jim the order on the first of October and told him he had until the first of November to complete the project.

Although Jim's squad was a group of 12 cadets with very different and independent ideas and backgrounds, they could be counted on to work well together and to complete their tasks. Jim was their squad leader because he consistently displayed outstanding leadership—not only in JROTC but also in student government and extracurricular activities as well—and he knew how to motivate people to get things done.

The same day Jim received the order he called a meeting of his squad and told them about the project. Everyone began to speak excitedly and all at once. "What about calling the Salvation Army?" "Yea, that's right. They know a lot about that stuff." "My mom can get dry goods from the store where she works."

Jim waited until everyone quieted down before continuing. "Those are all great ideas. I think we can put together an excellent report, but we need to get organized. I have broken the mission down into parts and would like to know what you each think you can do. Some of the jobs are big enough for two or three of you to work together. If you have any other suggestions, please mention them."

At the end of the meeting, Jim gave out the tasks. He charged Tony and Michelle with finding a place from which to distribute the food. Roger and Orlando were to find out how and where to get community support and donations. Mark was to prepare sample announcements for the school newspaper and for the public address given at school each morning, informing the other students about their efforts.

Jim had Tina and Larry work out a plan on how to collect food donated by students and where to store the food products. Joe was to keep an inventory of the collected foods. Based on Joe's inventory, Margo was to divide the food into packages for the families who came to collect a donation. Sandy and Leigh Ann were to devise a parking plan and lay out the area for the lines to form on the day of the distribution. Gail was to obtain the addresses of homeless shelters and other areas letting the needy know when and where to come when the plan was set. After everyone did their part of the planning and gave the information back to Jim, he would prepare a **staff study** for the SAI and cadet battalion staff.

Key Note Term

staff study – a detailed report that describes an action or event and how it can be accomplished

Each team member or pair within the squad worked hard to develop their section of the overall plan. In some instances, they came up with several alternatives for doing their jobs. After discussing those alternatives as a group and obtaining Jim's decision on the best way to do them, they completed the parts of the project. They knew that on the day of execution they would be responsible for executing the portion of the plan that they helped to develop.

With still a few days remaining before the first of November, Jim collected the results of the squad's hard work and thanked them for their outstanding effort. He wrote up a draft report concluding the research, verified each part with the squad member or members who researched it, and finalized the report.

After reading the report, Major Mason said, "You and your squad did a commendable job. A lot of planning went into this report; it is very complete and it includes some very sound information. I'll put your squad in charge of making the formal arrangements for carrying out the project and I'll have the cadet battalion commander assign other cadets to your squad to assist in the areas that you've identified. As a result of your efforts, I'm certain that this will be a very successful community project."

If you cannot or do not take the responsibility to do your part of a task, you may fail in your endeavor to complete it. If a team cannot or does not work together as a cohesive, cooperative unit, it may fail. However, if every member of a team used their beliefs, knowledge, and actions, and did their part as a follower or as a leader, most likely the team would accomplish its task and successfully complete its mission. Individual responsibility, self-reliance, followership, and teamwork are all important measurements of success.

Stages of Group Development

To make your team more effective, you also need to be aware of the stages of development each group experiences. They are referred to as the forming, storming, norming, and performing stages.

Forming

Forming is characterized by a great deal of uncertainty about the group's purpose (why are we here), structure (why am I here) and leadership (why is he/she in charge). Members are not sure how they are to behave. You know when you have moved on the second stage when the members of the team stop thinking of themselves as individuals and begin to think of themselves as part of a group.

While in the forming stage it is important to ensure the purpose of the group is clearly stated and what role each member plays toward the accomplishment of that purpose. The group will need to discuss what behaviors will be acceptable to the group (timeliness, decision-making process, interruptions, voting procedures, and so on).

Storming

The storming stage is one of intragroup conflict. Members accept the existence of the group, but there is resistance to the rules that are imposed on individuality. There is also conflict over who will control the group.

Different bases of power begin to show themselves through alliances, absenteeism, disagreements, and little focus on the completion of task. You will be aware of moving through this stage when there is a relatively clear hierarchy of leadership within the group.

When the group enters the storming stage it will be important for the leader to revisit the purpose of the group and each member's role. The leader will need to be an effective listener to make sure the root cause of the conflict is clearly stated. He/she will need to address the issues and provide effective informative feedback to help the group through this storming stage and into the norming stage.

Norming

The third stage is one in which close relationships are established and the group begins to develop a strong cohesiveness. You are aware when the group has successfully moved through this stage when the members have assimilated a common set of expectations of what defines member behavior.

Continual coaching and supportive behavior is needed during the norming stage until the group has agreed to accept willingly those norms. Then the leader needs to know when to step back and let the group lead the way to performing the task.

Performing

The fourth stage is performing. The group at this point is fully functioning and accepted. Group energy has moved from getting to know and understand each other to performing the task at hand.

Moving Through the Stages

Each group moves at its own speed through each of these stages. The more skilled in interpersonal skills each team member is, the easier it is to move to the performing stage. You cannot, however, be efficient in this process by directing the team members to jump from the forming stage to the performing stage. There are, however, interventions that the leader may use to help the group progress through these stages.

Conclusion

In this lesson you covered the fundamental leadership concepts of individual responsibility to yourself and to others on a team, the benefits of self-reliance, the traits of good followership, and the importance of a team and teamwork. All of these concepts are part of becoming a leader and all are equally important to the successful completion of a mission.

In the following lesson, you will learn about project management. You will learn how to identify critical issues associated with project management stages, understand how to use appropriate tools in managing a project, and learn and practice a variety of techniques required to manage projects successfully.

Lesson Review

1. Why is self-reliance an important part of individual responsibility?

2. Why must good leaders also be good followers?

3. What are the four stages of team development?

4. Considering your last team project, how would you characterize your team leader, and how would you have done things differently?

Chapter 4

Project Management

Key Terms

Gantt chart
implementation
PERT chart
project management

What You Will Learn to Do

- Use a Gantt chart to plan a project

Linked Core Abilities

- Take responsibility for your actions and choices
- Apply critical thinking techniques

Skills and Knowledge You Will Gain Along the Way

- Describe project management stages
- Identify the critical components needed for successful project management
- Explain how to use Gantt and PERT charts
- Define the key words contained in this lesson

Introduction

Projects have definite beginnings and endings. That makes them somewhat different from ongoing work and requires special management skills. Your project team may be composed of people outside those you supervise; however, you will be responsible for supervising their work on the team. All the knowledge and skills you have learned thus far in your JROTC program will come to play when given the opportunity to become a project team leader.

This lesson helps you identify critical issues associated with project management stages, understand how to use appropriate tools in managing a project, and learn and practice a variety of techniques required to manage projects successfully.

The Stages of Project Management

The four-stage model for **project management** includes the definition; planning; **implementation,** and follow-up stages.

In the definition stage, you organize the data, sort complex information, and clarify the goals in consideration of the organization's goals (see Figure 4.8.1). In the planning stage, you think ahead, seek expert advice, maintain objectivity, and identify subdivisions of the project.

In the implementation stage you monitor the performance, establish contingencies, and plan for prevention. Finally, the follow-up stage requires you evaluate the results and make recommendations.

Key Note Terms

project management – the process of planning, organizing, staffing, directing, and controlling the production of a system

implementation – to give practical effect to and to ensure actual fulfillment by concrete measures

Figure 4.8.1: Clarifying goals is just one part of the definition stage of project management.
Courtesy of John Henley/Corbis Images.

Tools for Project Management

It is important for you to set objectives and establish a basic strategy for achieving the objectives with regard to issues like time, cost, and so forth. It is also important for you to break the project down into subunits or steps once the extent of the project goals are determined. You will need to develop a *project schedule* and identify the *sequence* in which actions should take place.

Gantt Chart

One way of displaying the time relationship of the steps in the project is by using a **Gantt chart** (see Figure 4.8.2). Henry Gantt, an industrial engineer, introduced this procedure in the early 1900s. The chart shows the flow of activities in sequence.

To create a Gantt chart you must list the steps required to complete the project and the estimated time for each step. The steps are listed down the left side with time intervals given along the bottom. When the chart is finished, one can see the minimum total time for the project, the sequence of steps, and the possible overlapping of steps. You will need to watch for overuse of resources.

PERT Chart

Another useful tool in project management is the **PERT chart** (see Figure 4.8.3). PERT stands for Program Evaluation and Review Technique, and this planning method helps the project team to:

- **Be mutually aware of the process and sub-goals**
- **Contribute to and share in the decision made about how, when, by whom activities are done**
- **Make more efficient use of resources by concentrating effort and time on critical tasks rather than devoting time to subtasks while tasks of greater priority lack available people**

Figure 4.8.2: A Gantt chart.
Courtesy of SAS Institute, Inc.

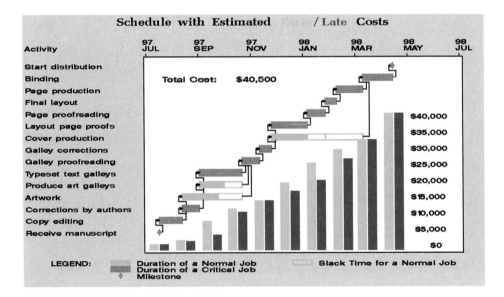

Key Note Terms

Gantt chart –the standard format for displaying a schedule graphically consisting of a horizontal bar chart with time as the horizontal axis and either resources, jobs, or orders as the vertical axis

PERT Chart – a term used to refer to a network diagram, which is a graphical illustration of the relationship between project activities

- **Reevaluate the project while it is underway**
- **Reallocate resources to cope with unexpected blocks to task accomplishment or to take advantage of unanticipated success in meeting some subgoal**

PERT is a group-analysis flow chart procedure that begins with *identifying the sequences of dependent activities*. You begin at the end, such as the following:

- **Before we can arrive at the picnic grounds, we must travel there in the car**
- **Before we can travel in the car, we must fill up the gas and check the oil**
- **Before we do that, we must have traveled to the service station**
- **Before we can start out for the service station, we must have loaded all the supplies in the car except the ice, which we can get at the gas station**

So we draw a network of activities, each of which ends in an event.

Another example of this is your getting up each morning to go to school. Suppose you need to be at school no later than 8 a.m. You would list all the events that need to take place from the time you wake up to the time you arrive and the length of time it takes you to do each event. You would then count back from 8 a.m. to determine what time you would need to set your alarm clock.

> **Note**
>
> The Critical Path Method (CPM) is a variation of PERT.

Putting all this together is your responsibility as the project team leader. You will need a working knowledge of these tools, good communication skills, and skills for setting expectations. You must provide continual evaluation and follow-up using the appropriate leadership style. Your knowledge of how to lead a meeting will also come in hand here. As you can see, it is time to put it all together so you can lead your project team and manage the project.

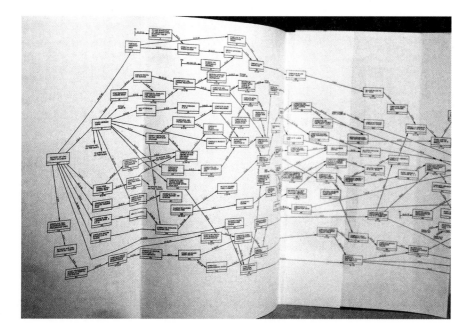

Figure 4.8.3: A PERT chart.
Courtesy of Six Cats Research, Inc.

Conclusion

In this lesson, you learned to identify critical issues associated with project management stages, understand how to use appropriate tools in managing a project, and learn and practice a variety of techniques required to manage projects successfully.

Next, you will learn about mentoring. Mentoring programs can help you explore new interests in helping others, further develop your personal skills, and stay excited about school.

Lesson Review

1. **What are the four stages of project management?**

2. **How can a Gantt chart assist in managing a project?**

3. **How is a PERT chart different than a Gantt chart?**

4. **Discuss how either of these management tools could have helped with your last project.**

Lesson 9

Mentoring

Key Terms

bias
mentee
mentoring
socioeconomic
stereotypes

What You Will Learn to Do

- Outline a plan to mentor another cadet

Linked Core Abilities

- Take responsibility for your actions and choices
- Treat self and others with respect

Skills and Knowledge You Will Gain Along the Way

- Describe the roles and responsibilities of a mentor
- Identify seven ways mentors can gain the trust and respect of subordinates and/or mentees
- Describe the four functions of a mentoring program
- Define the key words contained in this lesson

Introduction

This lesson presents a mentoring program designed to help you explore new interests in helping others, further develop your personal skills, and stay excited about school. Mentoring activities will center around building trust and developing positive self-esteem through sharing and working together with your subordinates, peers, or other teenagers and children in one-to-one relationships. The mentoring role is a major commitment on your part. In addition to comprehending the concept of self-identity, you must also understand the skills necessary in a mentoring relationship and work to acquire those skills. Finally, you must have an awareness of culturally diverse issues which can affect you, your mentoring program, and your community.

A dynamic **mentoring** program in your cadet battalion or school is one that encourages the development of caring partnerships. Every mentoring program requires the presence of positive role models to support high school mentors as they build positive interpersonal relations both in and out of school-based experiences. In this lesson, we will briefly look at how mentoring identifies with Army JROTC and your position as a cadet leader and mentor. Then, we will examine in detail how mentoring pertains to your development as a high school student entrusted with the responsibility to help others.

Key Note Term

mentoring – a sustained one-to-one relationship which promotes human development by regular, joint participation in structured activities

The Starfish

As an old man walked the beach at dawn, he noticed a young man ahead picking up starfish and flinging them into the sea. Finally catching up to the youth, he asked the young man why he was doing this. The answer was that the stranded starfish would die if left until the morning sun.

"But the beach goes on for miles and there are millions of starfish," countered the old man. "How can your effort make a difference?"

The young man looked at the starfish in his hand and then threw it to safety in the waves. "It makes a difference to that one," he said.

Mentoring in Relationship to Army JROTC Leadership

The concept of mentoring includes the roles of the teacher, role model, coach, and counselor. Mentors, however, are more than teachers and coaches; they are trusted guides and counselors. As a mentor, *you are not a trained counselor*. Leaders as mentors are responsible for molding and developing individuals into proficient, cohesive teams.

Genuine respect is a key element in any mentoring program. Subordinates must be able to respect their leaders if they want to trust them as their guides and counselors. To obtain this trust and respect, leaders as mentors must

- **Set a good example; role modeling and setting examples for subordinates to follow are extremely important**
- **Commit themselves to their subordinates and be fully committed to the complete development of those who are in need of some form of structured guidance in their lives**
- **Possess the commitment of guardians and the duty of tutors**
- **Have a personal stake in the positive and long-term development of those they are trying to help**
- **Be sensitive to the feelings of their subordinates, yet be responsible for training them intensively**
- **Develop the capacity to delegate authority in order to watch subordinates learn hard, valuable lessons through trial and error**
- **Provide adequate and timely feedback to ensure the success of their subordinates' development process**

Mentoring: What's It All About?

Entering into a mentoring relationship can be rewarding and exciting. It even can be a little scary. There are responsibilities involved that require maturity, compassion, and sometimes tough decisions. In this new adventure you are about to begin as a mentor, use your head, trust your instincts, listen to your heart, and it will be the experience of a lifetime. A mentor is someone who

- **Acts like an older brother or sister**
- **Generates respect and trust**
- **Helps mentees expect success**
- **Teaches by example and direction**
- **Admits to making mistakes, facing difficult tasks, and "not being perfect"**
- **Provides a positive role model**
- **Has something positive to contribute**
- **Participates in activities designed to motivate mentees**
- **Listens without judging**
- **Does fun things**
- **Tutors and helps to build good study habits**
- **Helps mentees develop a desire to attend/stay in school and improve school attendance**
- **Inspires others to set achievable goals**

Mentoring Functions

There are four mentoring functions that can guide you through this new adventure: listening, coaching, educating, and role modeling.

Listening

The most important function of the mentor may be to listen (see Figure 4.9.1). Many young people today do not have anyone at home who will take the time to listen to them. When there is someone with whom to "talk out" the situation, however, people are better able to sort out their difficulties and arrive at their own solutions.

Coaching

Coaches give praise for a job well done, encouragement when the going gets tough, and constructive criticism when they need to make changes (see Figure 4.9.2). It is always easier to deal with the negatives when you know there are some positives.

Educating

Being a tutor is another responsibility of a mentor. Sometimes it may seem easier to do something for another person; however, that person will benefit more if he/she does it for themselves with only guidance from the mentor. One way to give a person control is to teach them the skills to take care of themselves (see Figure 4.9.3).

Role Modeling

Mentors can help their mentees develop values, standards, and goals by allowing themselves to be seen as "real people" and by sharing personal beliefs and values. Mentors can also introduce their mentees to others whom they hold in high regard (see Figure 4.9.4).

Roles and Responsibilities of Mentors

The roles of mentors will vary with every situation. The following list is not all inclusive, but it gives you an idea of the different kinds of roles that mentors perform in typical mentoring programs.

Figure 4.9.1: Take the time to listen.
Courtesy of Paul Barton/Corbis Images.

Figure 4.9.2: A little encouragement can go a long way.
Courtesy of Jose Luis Pelaez, Inc./Corbis Images..

Figure 4.9.3: Share your knowledge.
Courtesy of John Henley/Corbis Images.

Figure 4.9.4: Meeting a hero can change your life.
Courtesy of Mannie Garcia/Retuters/Corbis Images.

- Be aware of the impact that culture, **socioeconomic** status, experiences, etc., have on how the mentee sees and processes information. Become comfortable with the fact that the mentee may be different from you and may approach evaluating, perceiving, acting, and behaving differently than you do.

- Be careful to respect the mentee's orientation and not to impose your values, assumptions, perceptions, and **biases** on the mentee. Be aware of your own attitudes, beliefs, and feelings and how these filters may bias your judgment.

- Help your mentee to accomplish tasks, but be careful not to hold preconceived ideas about what that person can or cannot do. Recognize limitations but do not attempt to replace the mentee's personal efforts. Always remember that you are there to *assist*, not to *do* the task.

- Acquire specific knowledge about the mentee with whom you work. If you find out that he/she has major challenges at home, school, and/or place of employment, be careful not to ask too many questions about any uncomfortable situations. If you encounter a situation that you do not feel comfortable handling, seek help or guidance from your instructors.

- Teach the mentee to respond to verbal rewards. Do not give gifts as a means of positive recognition and do not become emotionally attached. If the relationship becomes personal to the degree you are not able to be objective, withdraw and refer the mentee to another mentor. If a mentee makes a habit of bringing you gifts, discourage that habit. Always read any notes given to you by the mentee. Sometimes because of their learning style, mentees may not be able to vocalize their challenge but they are able to put it in writing. Never respond back in writing. If the notes are of a personal nature, discourage that habit. One or two positive words like "Congratulations!" or "Well done!" may be appropriate.

Although your roles as a mentor may change with the situation, your responsibilities will remain constant throughout the mentoring program. The following list describes specifically what the program expects of you. We mentioned at the beginning of this lesson that being a mentor is not an easy task. As you read through these responsibilities, identify those areas where you must increase your self-awareness and/or develop the necessary attributes of self-esteem to be an effective mentor. Accomplishing these responsibilities will require a high degree of self-identity and maturity.

- **Help your mentee to make assessments about behavior, thoughts, and actions as that individual tries new activities. Help the mentee see the benefits of trying and taking risks with new behaviors. Give support when necessary.**

- **Be clear, concise, direct, and consistent with feedback.**

- **Help the mentee generate a variety of responses or alternatives to situations.**

- **Do not make promises you cannot keep. Do not use the word *promise* to your mentee (as you will be taking responsibility). Make "I" statements to your mentee of what you are willing to do. For example, "I will help you find out the easiest and most effective way for you to study."**

- **Coordinate all planned activities with your instructors, the cooperating agency, other mentors, and the mentee.**

- **Prepare for and complete the tasks you agreed to do.**

- **Follow the rules of your battalion and school while working with the mentee.**

- **Make arrangements to contact the mentee's guardians, parents, teachers, and so on for permission to take that person on special activities.**

- **If you cannot perform a task that you agreed to do at the prescribed time, reschedule it for another time.**

- **Do not break confidentiality by sharing the mentee's concerns with others. However, confidentially should always be overridden if the situation calls for it. A competent mentor maintains confidences and does not discuss personal interviews with other cadets or people. *If the challenge is beyond your scope, contact a qualified person.* It is critical that you use concrete procedures in serious cases. *If a life-threatening situation arises:***

  - **Inform your mentee that you will notify a competent adviser because you *care*.**

  - **Encourage the mentee to go with you to the adviser to explain the situation. If the mentee refuses, insist that he or she go. Explain that you are not only concerned, but that the seriousness of the situation requires the mentee to seek counsel. If the mentee still refuses, clearly state, "I will seek advice alone from (state the name of the adviser)."**

> ### Note
> If the challenge is beyond your scope, contact a qualified person. If a life-threatening situation arises, notify an adviser immediately.

Using Effective Communication Skills

Participating in a mentoring relationship is not the time to misunderstand the use of a word, a gesture, or an emotion. Mentors must thoroughly understand the importance of using effective communication. The proper application of listening, nonverbal communication (such as body language), and verbal communication skills—as well as "I" messages—are critical to a successful mentoring program.

Any relationship must begin with communication in one form or another. The quality of that relationship often depends on the quality of the communication. Much of the communication we use in our daily lives involves some negative habits. Imagine how you feel when someone nags, reminds, criticizes, threatens, lectures, advises, or ridicules you. Many times the person doing this to you is not aware of the feelings these actions cause. Whether we are aware of these habits or not, they promise to lessen the quality of our relationships.

Study the following communication jammers and identify the ones you use most often. Then, try to determine why they are not helpful in maintaining satisfying relationships.

- **Ordering, commanding.** The phrases *You must, You will,* or *You have to* are a great way to create a power struggle, implying that you are superior. They are usually successful in producing anger and resistance. A favorite counter to these phrases is "Make me." Therefore, you will find it is more helpful to ask for cooperation with your mentee and to give choices, such as: "I would appreciate . . .," "It's your choice; you can either . . . or . . .," or "Would you rather . . . or . . .?"

- **Warning, threatening.** The phrases *If you do that, you'll be sorry* or *You'd better not do that if you know what's good for you* invite testing, threats, and hostility. Do not use them unless you want to fight with your mentee. The consequences and action methods are more effective. Simply state what you plan to do and then do it. There are no further reminders: just act, don't talk.

- **Moralizing, preaching.** When you use the "shoulds," "oughts," or "musts," the mentee may hear only the control part and may resist without considering the reasons or consequences. It is much more effective to listen and to problem-solve; for example, "Have you thought what might happen . . .?" or "What do you think might happen if . . .?"

- **Proposing alternatives, giving solutions.** Use "Now, if it were up to me . . ." or "What you should do is . . ." when you propose alternatives and help the mentee to find solutions, both important elements of mentoring responsibilities. However, in circumstances similar to counseling someone using the directive approach, there are several mentee behaviors for which you should be on the lookout. They are as follows:

  - Often, the person resists your proposals

  - You do not want the mentee dependent on you; instead, you want the individual to think for herself/himself

  - If the mentee takes your suggestion and it does not work, that person may hold you responsible

- **Lecturing, giving logical arguments.** When trying to prove your point with the facts, such as "You're wrong here" or "Yes, but . . .," people are often well aware of the facts and resent being told them again and again. Trying to persuade with facts is usually not effective. Instead, helping your mentee to explore the goals, alternatives, and consequences of a proposed action gives you much more influence in guiding the person.

- **The put-downs—judging, ridiculing, blaming, name-calling, sarcasm, shaming.** Some people use phrases like *How stupid, You're just lazy, It's all your fault, That's an immature point of view,* or *Okay, big shot* to motivate others by making them feel inadequate or inferior. However, these phrases normally succeed only in putting people on the defensive as they try to protect their self-image. The common responses are to return criticism, seal off feelings, or shut down communications and cooperation. It is important to separate the behavior you disagree with from the person's character and worth. It is harder to be specific about what you want without dragging the person's dignity through the mud, but far more effective.

- **Playing psychologist, analyzing and diagnosing.** When using the phrases "The problem with you is . . ." or "You're just jealous," you can embarrass, frustrate, or threaten people because you are indicating that you know what their motives are or have figured them out. This technique is another way to shut off communication and guarantee the person will not share difficult matters with you. Besides, if your interpretation is wrong, the person will most likely become angry.

- **Consoling.** "It's not really that bad," "You'll feel better in the morning," or "Don't worry, it'll all work out" are phrases a consoling person uses when trying to keep from getting involved. These phrases treat the other person's feelings lightly. Helping the person to explore alternatives and listening are more helpful. Sometimes, people are not looking to solve a problem; instead, they are complaining just to let off steam. Then, when you offer a solution, you could complicate the issue, anger them, or make the situation larger than what it really is.

Listening Skills

As mentors, you must understand the value of listening. Listen carefully for "feeling words" such as sad, happy, embarrassed, frustrated, alone, hurt, angry, bored, jealous, confused, and so on. Realize that everyone has feelings and they need to have ways in which to express them.

To ensure proper and effective communications with your mentee, you must first be able to identify what and how you feel while listening to your mentee. Then, learn what the mentee actually felt. These feelings may be the same or they may be different. For example, the mentee may be feeling depression, but you may feel frustration when hearing these words because you do not know how to help.

Additionally, understand some of the **stereotypes** related to listening. It is only natural for people to form different opinions about something. Oftentimes, these individual opinions will disagree with the opinions of others. It is your job as a mentor to know how feelings, stereotypes, and opinions reflect upon your mentee's values, attitudes, and behavior. Be able to identify these characteristics in a mentoring relationship and determine how you can use them to become a better mentor.

Nonverbal Communication Skills

Know the importance of nonverbal communications and the impact it has on others. Observe how your mentee listens; then, uses body language (see Figure 4.9.5) and eye contact. Remember, how your mentee says something is frequently more important than what he or she says. The behavior that this person displays sometimes expresses more meaning than words.

"I" Messages

"I" messages are statements, beginning with "I," that tell how you feel about a certain situation. They are the most appropriate way to express your feelings whenever a conflict arises. They show concern in a calm and respectful way. Plus, they focus the communication on your feelings and expectations rather than those of the other person, in this case your mentee.

Key Note Term

stereotypes – an oversimplified opinion, belief, or viewpoint; a person, group, event, or issue considered to typify or conform to an unvarying patter or manner; lacking any individuality; a standardized mental picture that is held in common by members of a group and that represents an oversimplified opinion, affective attitude, or uncritical judgment

Figure 4.9.5: Body language can tell you a lot about how people feel about themselves.
Courtesy of Corbis Images.

Whenever we focus attention on the other person's feelings and expectations, whether by accident or on purpose, the communication often takes on a blaming and accusatory tone. "I" messages express what the conflict is to the other person and how this conflict affects you.

Think about the last time you were in an argument. Did you use "I" messages? It sounds easy, but it takes a lot of practice. A typical "I" message has three parts, shown in parentheses, which can come in any order.

"I feel (*state feeling*) when you (*describe specific behavior*) because (*state how it affects you*)."

To reinforce your understanding of "I" messages, review both examples below. The "you" messages are first, followed by the appropriate "I" messages.

Example #1:

"You promised you'd never tell anyone. I knew I shouldn't have told you. You can't ever keep a secret."

"I feel hurt when you tell something I told you in secret because I didn't want anyone else to know."

Example #2:

"You're never organized or dependable. You can't be counted on."

"I get really upset whenever you back out on something, especially at the last minute because it leaves me stuck holding the bag."

Exploring Alternatives

What would you do if your mentee came to you with a difficult situation and wanted you to help? In most situations, your job is not to find the solution for the mentee but to help that person develop solutions to handle the issue. When you assist someone in exploring alternatives, it is always helpful to follow a pattern similar to the one below. The key words in this exploring alternatives model are *brainstorm*, *assist*, *choose*, *commitment*, and *follow-up*.

- **What is the difficulty and what are the alternatives? The mentor and mentee should *brainstorm* as many ways of handling the situation as possible.**

- **What are the consequences of each alternative? The mentor should *assist* the mentee in evaluating the pros and cons for each alternative.**

- **What is the best alternative? The mentee must *choose* what he/she thinks is best.**

- **When is the best time to put the plan into action? The mentee, under close coordination and supervision of the mentor, must make a *commitment* to begin using the best alternative as soon as the situation permits.**

- **Is there evaluation? Yes! The mentor must set a time to *follow up* and evaluate how the mentee is accomplishing the plan.**

When helping your mentee to choose a solution, especially if that person seems stuck, you can offer suggestions as other possible alternatives. However, do not put the person down for not accepting your ideas and do not take his or her responsibility away to solve the issue. After all, if your efforts fail, that person may hold you responsible or may not do as you suggested. Keep the mentoring relationship a learning process to help with future problems, as needed.

> **Note**
>
> Remember, developing positive mentoring relationships is not about *winning* but *solving* the conflict.

> **A Hundred Years**
>
> A hundred years from now it will not matter what my bank account was, the sort of house I lived in or how spotless it was, or the kind of car I drove. But the world may be different because I was important in the life of another.

> **Note**
>
> Commitment is easy during the good times; *it is during the rough times when mentors are truly tested.* And sometimes, the best thing a mentor can do for a mentee is *just be there.*

Conclusion

As a mentor, there are many difficult situations that you may encounter in mentoring relationships: prejudices, handling stress, coping with loss, and understanding the issues of troubled families. These topics are vitally important to your job because they are becoming increasingly commonplace in today's lifestyles. If you have questions regarding any of these issues, discuss them with your instructors.

Summarized below are the qualities of a successful mentor. Follow these qualities carefully, display maturity, show compassion, use your head, trust your instincts, listen to your heart, and you will make your mentoring opportunity the experience of a lifetime.

- **Know your job; be flexible and open-minded**
- **Know and use communication skills effectively, such as the**
  - **Ability to listen and accept different points of view**
  - **Ability to empathize with another person's struggle**
- **Apply effective leadership skills such as decision making, problem solving, and goal setting; possess the ability to see solutions, opportunities, and barriers**
- **Be personally committed to working with people; be available and supportive**
- **Show respect for individuals; display honesty, patience, trust, and a warm and caring attitude**

There are many important things to accomplish in life, and helping someone to help themselves is one of them. Remember, it sometimes takes a while to get something done right. What is important, however, is to keep trying and to *never give up*.

Lesson Review

1. **What is a mentor?**
2. **What are the four functions of mentoring?**
3. **List three responsibilities of a mentor.**
4. **What do you do if the problem is beyond your scope or a life-threatening situation?**

Chapter 5

Leading Others

Platoon Drill

Key Terms

cover
flank
formations
interval
line
pivot

What You Will Learn to Do

- How to command a platoon

Linked Core Abilities

- Communicate using verbal, nonverbal, visual, and written techniques

Skills and Knowledge You Will Gain Along the Way

- Describe the correct response to the commands when forming and marching the platoon
- Compare platoon drills and squad drills
- Match drill commands to platoon formations
- Define the key words contained in this lesson

Introduction

By now you should be familiar with stationary movements, basic steps, marching techniques, and squad drill. The introduction of platoon drill is designed to give you a better understanding of the discipline and coordination that is required of a large group to perform well in drill. Platoons execute certain drills in the same way that squads do. These drills include Inclining Around, Resting, Changing intervals in lines, Dismissing, Marching to the Flanks, Counting Off, and Marching in the Opposite Direction. This lesson describes the platoon movements that are unique to each formation.

Key Note Terms

formation – the arrangement of people or elements of a unit in a prescribed manner

line – a formation in which people or elements are side by side or abreast of each other

flank – the right or left side of any formation as seen by a person (or element) within that formation

Platoon Formations

The platoon has two prescribed formations: line and column; however, the platoon may be formed into a file or a column of twos from a column formation. When in a line formation, the elements (squads) of a platoon are numbered from front to rear; in a column formation, they are numbered from left to right.

For the most part, platoon drill merely provides the procedures for executing drill movements in conjunction with other squads formed in the same formation. Individual drill movements and the manual of arms are executed as previously described while performing as a squad member during the conduct of platoon drill.

When the platoon drills as a separate unit or as part of a larger unit in a line formation, without officers present, the post for the platoon sergeant is three steps in front of and centered on the platoon. When in column formation, the post for the platoon sergeant is three steps to left flank of and centered on the platoon.

The post for the platoon sergeant with the platoon leader present is one step to the rear and centered on the platoon in line or column formation.

When assuming his post in column from a line formation with the platoon leader present, the platoon sergeant faces to the left in marching (on the command of execution "face") and marches in the most direct route to his post. He then halts and faces to the right. When assuming his post in line from a column formation, he faces to the right in marching (on the command of execution "face") and marches in the most direct route to his post, halts centered on the platoon, and faces to the left.

When control of the formation is being exchanged between the platoon sergeant and the platoon leader, the platoon sergeant will *always* travel around the right flank (squad leader) of the formation when marching from post to post. The platoon leader will *always* travel around the left flank of the formation when marching post to post.

On the command *open ranks, march*; *backward, march*; *right (left) step, march*; *forward, march* and on commands that cause the platoon to change interval in line, he moves at the same time (with the appropriate step) so as to maintain proper position.

The leader of the first squad serves as the base when the platoon is a line formation. The leader of the fourth squad serves as the base when the platoon is in a column formation.

If the platoon is authorized a guidon, the bearer's post is one step in front of and two 15-inch steps to the right of and facing the person forming the platoon. When the formation is faced to the right for a marching movement, he executes in the same manner as explained in Appendix H, except that his post is three steps in front of and centered on the squad leaders. If the platoon leader is present and at his post, the bearer's post is one step to the rear and two 15-inch steps to the left of the platoon leader.

When the platoon drills as a separate unit, in a line formation, the post for the platoon leader is six steps in front of and centered on the platoon; when in a column formation, the platoon leader is six steps to the left flank and centered on the platoon. When marching as part of a larger formation, his post is one step in front of and centered on the squad leaders

Figure 5.1.1 shows platoon formations.

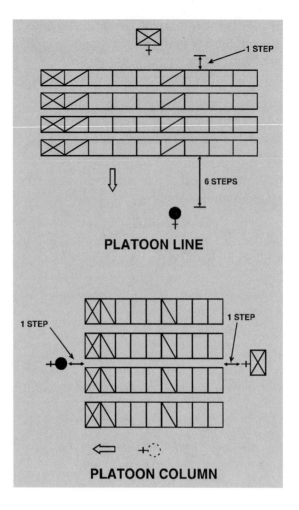

Forming the platoon

A platoon forms basically in the same way as a squad. The platoon sergeant assumes the position of attention and commands "fall in." On that command, the first squad leader and the first squad (when formed) are three steps in front and centered on the platoon sergeant. The other squad leaders then **cover** on the first squad leader at the correct distance, which they obtain by estimation.

Members of the first squad fall in on their squad leader as they would in squad drill; however, members of the other squads fall in on their squad leader, assume the position of attention, and turn their heads and eyes to the right. They obtain correct **interval** by taking short steps forward or backward, align themselves on the cadet to their right, sharply turn their heads and eyes to the front as in the position of attention, and obtain proper interval by taking short steps left or right to cover on the cadet in front of them. Members of these other squads do not raise their left arms unless the cadet to their immediate left has no one on which to cover.

When appropriate, the platoon leader may form the platoon. The procedures are the same as described above except that the first squad forms six steps in front of and centered on the platoon leader. The platoon sergeant forms at his or her position to the rear of the platoon. If the platoon leader is not present for the formation, the

Key Note Terms

cover – the distance between cadets in a column, measured by the cadet raising the left arm to the front and making sure the shoulder of the cadet in front is at the length of the arm plus 4-6 inches

interval – a space between actions; the lateral space between personnel in a formation, measured from right to left with close, double, and normal spacing

platoon sergeant steps forward three steps (making a total of six steps in front of the platoon) and assumes the duties of the platoon leader from that position.

Breaking Ranks

When the situation requires one or more individuals to leave a platoon formation or to obtain specific instructions from the platoon leader, the platoon leader directs "Cadet Private _____, front and center" or "the following personnel front and center: Cadet Private _____, Cadet Private _____, and so on." If you hear the leader call your name, come to the position of attention, reply "here, sir (sergeant)," take one 15-inch step backward, halt, face to the right (left) in marching, and exit the formation by marching to the nearest flank. After you clear the formation, double time to and halt two steps in front and centered on the platoon leader.

Counting Off

The platoon counts off in the same manner as a squad while in a line or column formation, except that members of all squads in that formation count in unison.

Changing Intervals

The platoon changes interval in a line formation in the same manner as the squad.

To change interval when the platoon is in a column formation at the halt, the right file stands fast and serves as the base. All other cadets execute the movement as previously described. To obtain close interval from normal interval, the third squad takes one step right, the second squad takes two steps right, and the first squad takes three steps right. To obtain normal interval, the procedures are the same except that the squads take the same number of steps to the left.

To change interval when the platoon is marching in a column, the leader gives the preparatory command "close interval" when the right foot strikes the marching surface and the command of execution "march" the next time the right foot strikes the marching surface. On "march," the base squad (right file) takes one more 30-inch step and then executes a half step.

All other cadets take one more step, simultaneously execute a column half right, and march until they obtain close interval. They execute a column half left and assume the half step when abreast of the corresponding cadet of the base squad. On the command "forward, march," all cadets resume marching with a 30-inch step. The platoon leader could also give the commands "mark time, march" and "platoon, halt."

To resume marching at normal interval, the platoon leader gives the preparatory command "normal interval" as the left foot strikes the marching surface and the command of execution "march" the next time the left foot strikes the marching surface. On the command "march," the platoon members obtain normal interval in the same manner prescribed for close interval except that they each execute column half left and then column half right.

To obtain double interval from normal interval, the procedures are the same as from close interval to normal interval. To obtain normal interval from double interval, the procedures are the same as obtaining close interval from normal interval.

Aligning the Platoon

This process is similar to aligning a squad. The command for alignment *is* "dress right, dress." On the command of execution "dress," the first squad leader stands fast and serves as the base. Other squad leaders estimate correct distance between their units and the squad in front of them. The cadets in the first squad obtain exact interval as they did in squad drill. All other squads execute as the first squad except that each cadet raises the left arm only for uniformity and covers on the cadet in front by glancing out of the corner of the left eye.

To obtain exact alignment, the platoon leader marches (on the command of execution "dress") by the most direct route to a position on line with the first squad, halts one step from the squad leader, and faces down that line. The platoon leader then verifies the alignment of the first squad and instructs cadets (calling them by name or number) to move forward or back as necessary to form an even line.

After aligning the first squad, the platoon leader faces to the left (right) in marching, takes two (or three) short steps to the second squad, halts, faces down that line, and aligns that squad in the same manner as the first squad. The platoon leader follows this same procedure for the remaining squads. When finished with the last squad, the platoon leader returns to the position centered on the platoon, halts perpendicular to the formation, faces to the left (right), and commands "ready, front."

Covering and Recovering

To align the platoon in a column formation, the commands are "cover" and "recover." On the command "cover," the fourth squad leader stands fast and serves as the base. The squad leaders, with the exception of the left flank squad leader, raise their arms laterally and turn their heads and eyes to the right. The members of the fourth squad raise their arms horizontally (as in squad drill) to the front and cover on the cadet to their front at the correct distance.

Cadets of the third, second, and first squads raise their left arms horizontally to the front (for uniformity only), cover on the person to their front, and, at the same time, glance out of the corner of their right eyes to align on the cadet to their right.

To resume the position of attention, the platoon leader gives the command "recover." On this command, cadets return sharply to the position of attention.

Opening and Closing Ranks

A platoon opens ranks from a line formation while at the halt. The command is "open ranks, march," and the platoon may execute it from any of the prescribed intervals.

On the command of execution "march," the front rank takes two steps forward, the second rank takes one step forward, the third rank stands fast, and the fourth rank takes two steps backward. If additional ranks are present, the fifth rank takes four steps backward, the sixth rank takes six steps backward, and so on. After taking the required number of steps, platoon members do not raise their arms to align themselves. If the platoon leader wants the exact interval or alignment, he or she commands "at close interval (at double interval), dress right, dress" and "ready, front."

The command to close ranks is "close ranks, march." On the command of execution "march," the first rank takes four steps backward, the second rank takes two steps backward, the third rank stands fast, and the fourth rank takes one step forward. Also, on the command of execution "march," the platoon leader and platoon sergeant take the approximate number of steps to maintain their correct positions.

Resting and Dismissing the Platoon

The platoon rests in the same manner as prescribed for the squad.

The procedures for dismissing the platoon are basically the same as prescribed for the squad. The following differences exist.

When the platoon leader commands "platoon sergeant," the platoon sergeant faces to the right in marching and inclines around the squad leaders, halts three steps in front of and centered on the platoon, and faces to the right. The platoon leader then commands "take charge of the platoon," they exchange salutes, and the platoon leader is no longer a part of the formation. The platoon sergeant takes three steps forward, halts, faces about, and carries out the platoon leader's instructions.

The platoon sergeant may release the squads to the control of the squad leaders by commanding "take charge of your squads." The platoon sergeant and squad leaders exchange salutes and the platoon sergeant is no longer a part of the formation. Without leaving their positions, the squad leaders then command "fall out."

Marching the Platoon

The platoon marches in the same manner as prescribed for the squad.

When marching in line, the first squad leader serves as the guide; when marching in column, the fourth squad leader is the guide.

When marching in line, each member maintains alignment on the cadet to the right by glancing out of the corner of the right eye; when marching in column, each member of the first, second, and third squads maintains alignment on the cadet to the right.

Changing Direction

During a march, a platoon will need to change direction at some point. There are several ways to do this, including a 90- or 45-degree turn, marching to the rear or incline, or counter column, march. The following sections help describe how these are done.

90- or 45-Degree Turns

The platoon changes the direction of marching basically the same as the squad. During a column movement, the base element is the squad on the flank in the direction of the turn.

To change direction 90 degrees, the command is "column right (left), march." On the command of execution "march," the base squad executes the movement as in squad drill except that the squad leader takes one 30-inch step and then takes up the half step. The squad leader continues marching with the half step until the other squad leaders come abreast. The other squad leaders must maintain correct interval, execute a 45-degree **pivot**, and continue marching in an arc.

As these squad leaders come on line with the base squad leader, they take up the half step. When all squad leaders are even, they step off with a 30-inch step without command. All other platoon members march forward on the command of execution and execute the column movement at approximately the same location as their squad leaders and in the same manner.

To change direction 45 degrees, the command is "column half right (half left), march." On the command "march," the platoon executes the movement in the same manner as for a 90-degree turn except that everyone makes a 45-degree turn.

Marching to the Rear or Inclining

The platoon marches in the opposite direction ("rear, march") and inclines around an object ("incline around") in the same manner as the squad.

Counter Column, March

When space is limited and the platoon leader wants to march the platoon in the opposite direction with the squad leaders at the head of their squads, the platoon leader would command "counter column, march." Figure 5.1.2 shows your way through this procedure.

On the command "march":

- **The first squad marches forward three steps, executes a column right, marches across the front of the platoon, and executes another column right just beyond the fourth squad.**

- **The second squad steps forward one step, executes a column right, marches forward, and executes another column right between the third and fourth squads.**

- **The third squad executes two short column lefts from the halt and marches between the remainder of the third squad and the second squad.**

- **The fourth squad marches forward two steps, executes a column left, marches across the front of the platoon, and executes another column left between the first and second squads.**

- **As the third squad leader marches past the last cadet in the third squad, the entire squad begins to march at half step. After marching past the last cadet in each file, all other squads incline to the right and left as necessary, obtain normal interval on**

Figure 5.1.2: Counter column, march command.
Courtesy of US Army JROTC.

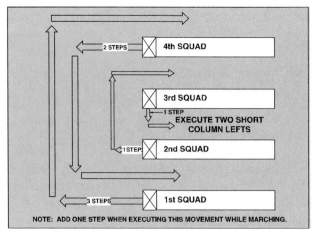

Chapter 5 Leading Others

the third squad, and begin to march with the half step. When all squads are even with one another, they begin marching with a 30-inch step without command.

During the movement, the platoon leader marches alongside of the first squad, and the platoon sergeant marches one step to the rear and centered between the second and third squads.

When marching, the platoon leader gives the preparatory command "counter column" as the left foot strikes the marching surface. On the command of execution "march," the platoon executes the movement basically the same as from the halt, except that the squad takes one additional step to ensure that the pivot foot is in the correct place to execute the movement.

Marching to the Flank

The platoon marches to the flank in the same manner as the squad.

Forming a File and Re-Forming

A platoon forms a single file from the left, right, or as designated, and only from the column formation and the halt. The command is "file from the left (right), march" (or "file in sequence 3-2-4-1, march").

On the preparatory command, the squad leader of the designated (or lead) squad gives the supplementary command "forward." The other squad leaders command "stand fast."

On the command of execution "march," the lead squad marches forward. The stationary squad leader next to the lead squad looks over the shoulder nearest the moving element. When the second from the last cadet in the lead squad is abreast, that stationary squad leader commands "column half left (half right)." When the last cadet in the lead squad is abreast and his or her right foot strikes the marching surface, the stationary squad leader commands "march."

On the command of execution, the squad leader next to the lead squad executes the column half left (half right), inclines to the right without command, and follows the last cadet of the lead squad at the correct distance. The other squad members march forward and execute the same movements as their squad leader. The remaining squads form the file in the same manner, one after another.

A platoon may also form a file and execute a column movement at the same time from a column formation. The execution is similar to that described previously, except the command is "file from the left (right), column left (right), march." After the platoon leader's preparatory command, the lead squad leader commands "column left (right)" instead of "forward." The other squad leaders also command "column left (right), march" at the appropriate time.

The platoon re-forms to the original column formation only from the halt. The command is "column of fours to the right (left), march." On the preparatory command, the squad leader of the base squad commands "stand fast." All other squad leaders command "column half right (half left)."

On the command of execution "march," the base squad stands fast; all other squads execute the column half right (half left) at the same time. As each of the moving squad leaders reach a point that ensures correct interval on the element to their left (right), they automatically incline to the left (right) and command "mark time, march" and "squad, halt" so that their squad is abreast of the base squad when halted.

Forming/Re-Forming a Column of Twos

A platoon forms a column of twos from the right or left when in a column of fours at the halt. The command is, "column of twos from the left (right), march." The basic elements of the movement are similar to forming a column of twos in a squad formation.

On the preparatory command, the squad leaders of the two lead squads command "forward." The other two squad leaders command "stand fast." On the platoon leader's command "march," the two lead squads march forward. The squad leader who is next to the lead element gives the command to start both remaining squads in motion. Looking over the shoulder nearest the moving elements, the squad leader gives the preparatory command "column half left (half right)" when the second from the last cadet is next to him or her and gives the command "march" when the right foot of the last cadet strikes the marching surface.

On the platoon leader's command of execution, both squad leaders execute the column half left (half right), incline to the right (left) without command, and follow the last cadets of the lead squads at the correct distance. Other members of the remaining squads march forward and execute the same movements as their squad leaders.

The platoon may also form a column of twos and execute a column movement at the same time from a column formation. The command is "column of twos from the left (right), column left (right), march." The squad leaders of the lead squads command "column left (right)" instead of "forward." The squad leader of the next squad gives the command "column left (right);" however, that leader then executes a column half left (half right). The remaining two squad leaders stand fast.

On the platoon leader's command "march," the lead squads execute the column left (right). The squad leader next to the lead squad gives the command to start the remaining squads in motion. Looking over the shoulder nearest the moving elements, the squad leader gives the preparatory command "column left (right)" when the second from the last cadet is next to him or her, and gives the command of execution "march" as the right foot of the last cadet strikes the marching surface (at the pivot for column left or the first time the last cadet's right foot strikes the marching surface after the pivot for column right). Although the command is "column left (right)," the outside squads execute a column half left (half right).

To re-form the original column formation, the platoon must be at the halt. The command is "column of fours to the right (left), march." On the preparatory command, the squad leaders of the lead squads command "stand fast." The trailing squad leaders command "column half right (half left)."

On the platoon leader's command "march," the lead squads stand fast. The trailing squad leaders execute slightly more than the column half right (half left) at the same time. As the trailing squad leaders reach a point that ensures correct interval on the element to their left (right), they incline to the left (right) without command. The squad leader nearest the stationary lead squads commands "mark time, march" and "squads, halt."

Conclusion

Your cadet battalion will spend many hours practicing the individual, squad, and platoon drill movements. Being able to execute them correctly will build confidence and teamwork as well as ensure that your unit looks as good as it can in ceremonies. To excel in *Leadership Lab* requires dedication in learning the steps and drills, the proper use of commands and the command voice, and thorough preparation on the part of the drill leader.

In the next lesson, you will learn what responsibilities go along with being a leader.

Lesson Review

1. What drills do platoons execute?
2. What does the platoon do when the sergeant commands "fall in"?
3. When marching in line, which squad leader serves as the guide? When marching in a column, which squad leader serves as a guide?
4. Define the term *pivot*.

Lesson 2

Taking Charge–Knowing Your Responsibilities as a Leader

Key Terms

implement
observe
plan

What You Will Learn to Do

- Perform the duties of a team leader, squad leader, platoon sergeant, or platoon leader

Linked Core Abilities

- Take responsibility for your actions and choices

Skills and Knowledge You Will Gain Along the Way

- Describe the duties and responsibilities of the different leadership positions within a platoon
- Explain the four steps leaders should use when assuming a new leadership position
- Demonstrate the responsibilities of a team leader or other higher position in drill
- Define the key words contained in this lesson

Introduction

This lesson helps you developer a style of leadership by describing the basic responsibilities of a team leader, squad leader, platoon sergeant, and platoon leader. By applying the traits, principles, factors, and values of leadership to your responsibilities as a role model, coach, and counselor, you will be able to obtain the best possible results from your team.

Learning How to Lead

Soon you will be taking charge of a unit and facing the difficult task of leading people. There are certain techniques and steps that will help you to adjust to your new assignment. Because first impressions are usually lasting ones, these steps will help you to make a better first impression. Regardless of the level of development of your followers, especially in drill, your actions and behavior must be consistent with appropriate leader behavior.

After all, your actions and behavior are the main factors that will determine the morale of your team members and the degree they are willing to work as a team to accomplish your goals. Taking charge of a group and turning them into a synchronized drill unit is no easy task. To guide you in assuming a new leadership position and in building a cohesive team, follow the four proven steps that leaders use to ensure a smooth and successful beginning:

- **Observe/assess**
- **Plan**
- **Implement**
- **Follow-up/evaluate**

Knowing Your Responsibilities as a Leader

An effective organization is essential for mission accomplishment. A prerequisite for a unit to function with maximum efficiency is that individuals within the unit function together effectively. The solution is to develop and maintain teamwork. To achieve this, it is partially a product of one's duties, responsibility, and authority. The other element is one's relationships with peers, supervisors, and followers.

To achieve the goal of every team member working side by side effectively and efficiently, leaders must have a complete understanding of their duties and responsibilities.

The following sections outline the responsibilities for team leaders, squad leaders, the platoon sergeant, and the platoon leader. At some point during your JROTC experience, your instructors will assign you to one or more of these positions. Specific duties in your cadet battalion (as outlined in the Cadet Handbook) may be different from these; however, they present you with guidelines illustrating what you can expect from your immediate chain of command.

In the middle of the school year, George moved out of town. The senior Army instructor gave his platoon leader's position to Michelle, the platoon sergeant. Michelle felt confident that she could handle the position because she had done very well as platoon sergeant. Although she knew what was required of a platoon leader, she was nervous about taking George's place because everyone in the platoon liked him very much.

As platoon sergeant, Michelle had closely **observed** how George led the platoon. One of the reasons for his popularity was that he would personally correct a squad or an individual if a drill movement was not performed well. The platoon members considered George to be a very good coach because he made them feel special to receive his attention.

However, Michelle knew that George's relationship with the platoon often caused resentment with the squad leaders, who interpreted George's actions as indications that they were not doing, nor could not do their jobs. Therefore, the squad leaders did not like his interference. They knew what they were responsible for and how to do it when given the chance.

Michelle often had to smooth things out between George and the squad leaders. She would explain to the squad leaders that his actions were not meant as criticism while suggesting to George that he should let the squad leaders do their jobs and stop stepping on their toes.

From her observations, Michelle decided to make a **plan** to change the situation when she became platoon leader. After all, every leader has an individual style and she wanted more harmony within the platoon.

She would use her chain of command more than George had and would let the squad leaders correct any problems she saw in platoon drill. But, she also wanted the cadets to work as hard for her as they did for George. After some thinking, she came up with a great idea. Her father managed one of the local movie theaters and she worked for him on the weekends. What if she exchanged a few hours of work for discounted tickets and food?

After discussing her plan with the squad leaders, who enthusiastically approved it, Michelle told the platoon her idea on her first day of drill. "I realize that it's hard switching leaders in the middle of the year and that we're all going to miss George, but I'm going to do my best to take over where he left off. One area where I believe we can still improve is squad drill. So, I've decided to hold a contest to reward the squad that consistently performs the best each month. Each member of that squad will receive one discounted movie pass and reduced prices on food at the Park Six Cinema. Our SAI, the platoon sergeant, and I will be the judges. Now let's get down to practice."

After just one month, Michelle was pleased to see that her transition to platoon leader had been successful. She did not have as many problems with the squad leaders as George had, and the new platoon sergeant confirmed that they were happier with her style of not interfering. The JROTC instructors even thought the squads performed a little better as a result of the contest and her leadership.

Responsibilities of Team Leaders

Team leaders are the first in the chain of command. There are generally two team leaders to a squad, referred to as Team Leader A and Team Leader B. Both team leaders are responsible for the formation, appearance, and training of their team members. Team Leader A must also be ready to assume control of the squad in the absence of the squad leader. They assist their squad leaders as directed and must

---

Key Note Term

observe – the act of recognizing and noting a fact or occurrence

---

Key Note Term

plan – to formulate an action for the accomplishment or attainment of an explicit purpose

---

Figure 5.2.1: To be a good leader, you must always set a good example. This includes good grooming, straight posture, and a can-do attitude.
Courtesy of US Army JROTC.

- **Set the example at all times (see Figure 5.2.1)**

- **Know the number, names, and personal information on all assigned personnel**

- **Assist team members with matters related to JROTC activities (when possible) and refer them to the squad leader for assistance if they are unable to handle/resolve an issue**

- **Be thoroughly familiar with individual and squad drill; inspect team members during formations and class assemblies to ensure they know what is required of them**

Responsibilities of Squad Leaders

Squad leaders are responsible to their platoon leader and platoon sergeant for the appearance, conduct, training, and discipline of their squad. They ensure that each squad member learns, does what is expected, and maintains high standards of behavior. Squad leaders must

- **Set the example at all times.**
- **Know the number, names, and personal information on all assigned personnel.**
- **Counsel/assist squad members with matters related to JROTC activities and help them to find solutions to other matters (when possible); refer them to the platoon sergeant or platoon leader for assistance if they are unable to handle/resolve an issue.**
- **Develop responsibility and leadership in team leaders and be the first person that they turn to for assistance and advice.**
- **Form the squad correctly. Make an accurate report by name of those persons present and absent during common hour activities, company platoon/formations, and other cadet battalion activities.**
- **Be thoroughly familiar with individual, squad, and platoon drill. When conducting drill, instruct/demonstrate the movement, allow time for individual performance and then supervise team leaders and squad members to ensure they perform properly.**
- **Inspect their team leaders and squad members at all times ensuring they know what is required of them (see Figure 5.2.2).**

Responsibilities of a Platoon Sergeant

The platoon sergeant functions as the platoon executive and administrator; therefore, the platoon sergeant must

- **Set the example at all times**
- **Form the platoon when prescribed by the platoon leader; submit absentee reports to the company first sergeant**
- **Assist the platoon leader in supervising the squad leaders while maintaining a close relationship with them**
- **Develop a spirit of teamwork within the platoon**
- **Learn the names of everyone in the platoon and use their names when addressing them**

Figure 5.2.2: Let those under your command know what's expected of the, and perform regular inspections.
Courtesy of US Army JROTC.

- Provide assistance/counseling to personnel in the platoon, especially when requested by the platoon leader or a squad leader

- Assist the platoon leader in training the platoon

- Be completely informed of all platoon matters to assume control of the platoon in the absence of the platoon leader

Responsibilities of a Platoon Leader

The platoon leader is a very desirable position in the cadet battalion. If you are a platoon leader, you have a platoon of cadets for whom you are directly responsible. Primarily, your job is one of leadership, training, and discipline. You also have the opportunity and privilege to be a role model, coach, and counselor. You must

- Keep the company commander appraised of the status of the platoon at all times.

- Establish and maintain command and control of the platoon at all times; organize and maintain an effective chain of command.

- Provide assistance/counseling to personnel in the platoon, especially when requested by a squad leader or the platoon sergeant, and/or when necessary for performance or disciplinary reasons.

- Conduct an inspection of the platoon at formations.

- Use the chain of command to accomplish tasks; work mainly with the platoon sergeant and the squad leaders.

- Know all cadet regulations and ensure that all members of the platoon also know and follow them.

- Enforce the orders from superiors whether you agree with them or not; however, if you think an order is morally or ethically wrong, discuss it with your chain of command and, if necessary, your instructor staff. Do not complain or gripe in the presence of subordinates. Develop a spirit of teamwork so as to instill respect, obedience, and cooperation in the platoon.

- Know all phases of drill and ceremonies; be able to supervise and conduct platoon drill and, if you are the senior officer present in a formation, be able to conduct company drill.

- Set high standards of personal appearance and conduct for yourself. Remember, the platoon leader sets the example for the platoon to follow.

- Make an effort to resolve all leadership, training, and disciplinary problems at your level; however, if you cannot solve a problem, seek the advice and/or assistance of the company commander, company executive officer, or first sergeant.

Conclusion

For a platoon to function effectively and efficiently, team members, team leaders, squad leaders, the platoon sergeant, and the platoon leader must

- **Clearly understand their duties and responsibilities**
- **Know exactly what is expected of them**

Only when those actions occur to the extent that leaders and platoon members are comfortable can teamwork, productivity, and mission accomplishment take place. At that point, the energy of everyone in the platoon is now available for work.

Remember, however, that followers will always observe the actions and behavior of their leaders very closely; therefore, successful leaders must be able to put that energy to work to build cohesive teams, establish high levels of morale, and create a climate where followers are willing to accomplish missions. Plus, when taking charge of a unit, successful leaders must know how to make a lasting impression; they must observe, plan, **implement**, and follow up.

In the following lesson, you will learn about company formations and movements. You will learn about company drill formations and movements "without arms," which indicates you will not be carrying weapons.

Key Note Term

implement – to give practical effect to and ensure actual fulfillment by concrete measures

---

Chapter 5

Lesson Review

Lesson Review

1. Why is it important to understand your responsibilities as a leader?
2. List three responsibilities of a platoon sergeant.
3. What creative way can you think of to entice your squad to be their best?
4. Where can you find a list of specific duties?

Lesson 3

Company Formations and Movement

Key Terms

arc
base
double time
guide
mark time
mass formation
post

What You Will Learn to Do

- Execute company drills

Linked Core Abilities

- Communicate using verbal, nonverbal, visual, and written techniques
- Take responsibility for your actions and choices

Skills and Knowledge You Will Gain Along the Way

- Describe the correct responses to commands when forming and marching the company
- Identify the different types of company formations and related specific drill commands
- Identify the locations of the key platoon and company personnel in company formations
- Define the key words contained in this lesson

Chapter 5

Introduction

This lesson covers company drill formations and movements "without arms." Your knowledge and recall of squad and platoon drill from previous lessons is vitally important in understanding this information. Pay special attention to the differences between platoon and company drill and to the roles of key personnel in company drill.

In this lesson, you will build upon your knowledge of individual drill movements, squad drills and platoon drills in order to conduct company drill.

Company Drill

Company drill provides the procedures for executing platoon drill in conjunction with other platoons in the same formation. For drill purposes, a company consists of a company headquarters and two or more platoons.

Key Note Term

base – stationary platoon on which others align; right-most platoon in mass and line formation; front platoon in column formation

Key Note Term

mass formation – a drill formation where the elements of a company-sized or larger unit assemble; or are abreast of each other, at close interval and in column

Drill tips

- When the company commander directs that the company "open or close ranks," "extend march," "close on the leading platoon," or "prepare for inspection," platoons execute the movements on the command of the platoon leaders and not on the directives of the company commander. The platoon leaders command the movement in sequence beginning with the **base** platoon.

- The company has four prescribed formations: company in line with platoons in line, company in column with platoons in column, company in column with platoons in line (used primarily for ceremonies), and a company mass formation. However, the company may form into a column of twos in the same manner as the platoon. (Graphics of these formations are with their corresponding text.)

- The company normally forms in a line formation; however, it may re-form in column when all personnel can identify their exact position in the formation.

- The company forms basically the same as the platoon. On the command "fall-in," platoons form in line, centered on and facing the person forming the unit, with five-step intervals between platoons.

- When in a line or a **mass formation**, the right platoon serves as the base; when in a column formation, the lead platoon serves as the base.

- The first sergeant assumes the position of the company commander if there are no officers present.

- Members of a company break ranks in the same manner as in platoon drill except that the individuals called from the formation form on the company commander rather than on the platoon.

Forming the Company

The company has four prescribed formations:

- **Company in line with platoons in line**
- **Company in column with platoons in column**
- **Company in column with platoons in line (used primarily for ceremonies)**
- **Company mass formation**

The company may also be formed into a column of twos in the same manner as the platoon.

The company normally forms in a line formation; however, it may re-form in column when each man can identify his exact position (equipment grounded) in the formation.

The company forms basically the same as the platoon. On the command "FALL IN (*At Close Interval*), FALL IN," the platoons form in line, centered on and facing the person forming the unit, with five-step intervals between platoons.

> **Note**
>
> To have the company assemble in a company mass formation the command is "Mass Formation, FALL IN." Before giving the commands the person forming the unit announces the interval and the number of personnel in the front and designates the base man. In this situation, the first sergeant and platoon sergeants travel around the right flank of the formation when moving from post to post. The commander and platoon leaders travel around the left flank of the formation when moving from post to post.

The company may be formed by the first sergeant and platoon sergeants or by the company commander and platoon leaders. When possible, the platoons assemble near the formation site before the arrival of the first sergeant or company commander. If the company is formed by the noncommissioned officers, the platoon leaders normally observe the procedures from a position to the rear of their platoons.

When the company is formed by the noncommissioned officers, the following procedures apply.

- **The first sergeant posts himself nine steps in front of (center) and facing the line where the front rank of each platoon is to form. He then commands "FALL IN (*At Close Interval*), FALL IN."**

- **On the command of execution, the platoons form in the same manner prescribed in platoon drill. Each platoon sergeant faces his platoon while the platoons are forming and directs his platoon to adjust (if necessary) and align on the platoon to its right at the correct interval. After the platoon is formed, the platoon sergeants face about.**

- **When all of the platoon sergeants are facing to the front, the first sergeant commands (if appropriate) "Inspection, ARMS; Ready, Port, ARMS; Order (*Sling*), ARMS." He then directs (if appropriate) "RECEIVE THE REPORT." The platoon sergeants face about and command "REPORT." Having received the report, the platoon sergeants face about. When all platoon sergeants are facing to the front, the** first sergeant commands "REPORT." The platoon sergeants turn their head and eyes toward the first sergeant, salute and report in succession from right to left. The first sergeant turns his head and eyes toward the reporting platoon sergeant and returns each "*Salute*" individually. Having received the report from the platoon sergeants, the first sergeant faces about and awaits the arrival of the company commander if the commander is scheduled to receive the company.

- When the company commander has halted at his post, the first sergeant salutes and reports, "*Sir, all present,*" or "*Sir, all accounted for,*" or "*Sir, (so many) men absent.*" The company commander returns the *Salute* and commands POST. The first sergeant faces about and marches to his post three steps to the rear and at the center of the company, halts, and faces about. The guidon bearer steps forward three steps. The platoon sergeants face to the right in marching and assume their posts to the rear of their platoons (if the platoon leader is not present, they step forward three steps). The platoon leaders march around the left flank of their platoons and assume their posts by inclining facing to the front. The company executive officer assumes his post two steps to the rear of the first sergeant.

Key Note Term

post – to take a position

When the company is formed by the company commander, the procedures are the same as forming with the noncommissioned officers except that the platoon leaders form their platoons and the first sergeant, platoon sergeants, and guidon bearer fall in at their posts (see Figure 5.3.1). The command **post** is not necessary. If a platoon sergeant is to fill the post of platoon leader, he takes a position six steps in front of and centered on the platoon.

On the command "fall in," the platoons form in the same manner prescribed in platoon drill. Each platoon sergeant faces the platoon while the platoons are forming and directs the platoon to adjust (if necessary) and align on the platoon to its right at the correct interval. Once formed, the platoon sergeants face about.

> **Note**
>
> If the first sergeant commands "at close interval, fall in," the members of the platoon form at close interval; however, they maintain the five-step interval between platoons.

When all of the platoon sergeants are facing to the front, the first sergeant directs (if appropriate) "receive the report." The platoon sergeants face about and command "report." The squad leaders report as previously described in platoon drill.

Figure 5.3.1: Company in line formation with platoons in line.
Courtesy of US Army JROTC.

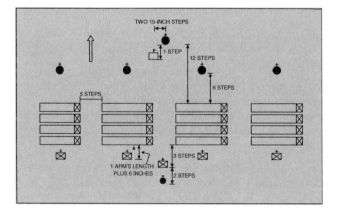

Having received the report, the platoon sergeants face about. When all platoon sergeants are facing to the front, the first sergeant commands "report." The platoon sergeants salute and report in succession from right to left. The first sergeant returns each salute individually. Having received the report from the platoon sergeants, the first sergeant faces about and awaits the arrival of the company commander.

If the company commander does not receive the company, the first sergeant commands "post." On this command, the platoon sergeants and guidon bearer step forward three steps. Simultaneously, the first sergeant faces about, steps forward three steps, and occupies the position of the commander.

If the company commander receives the company from the first sergeant, after the company commander halts at the post, the first sergeant salutes and reports, "sir, all present," or "sir, all accounted for," or "sir, (so many) absent." The company commander returns the salute and commands "post." The first sergeant faces about and marches to the post three steps to the rear and at the center of the company, halts, and faces about. The guidon bearer steps forward three steps.

The platoon sergeants face to the right in marching and assume their posts to the rear of their platoons (if the platoon leader is not present, they step forward three steps). The platoon leaders march around the left flank of their platoons and assume their posts by inclining and halting, already facing to the front. The company executive officer assumes a post two steps to the rear of the first sergeant.

When the company commander forms the company, the procedures are the same as above except that the platoon leaders form their platoons and the first sergeant, platoon sergeants, and guidon bearer fall in at their posts. The command "post" is not necessary.

Changing the Interval

The company changes interval in the same manner as prescribed for the platoon. When the company commander wants the company to obtain close interval in a line formation while maintaining a five-step interval, the company commander directs "close on the base platoon at close interval." The platoon leaders face about and command "count, off." After the platoons have counted off, the platoon leaders command "close interval, march." The second, third, and fourth platoon leaders command "right, face" and in succession command "half step, march." They halt at the five-step interval and face the platoon to the left.

If the company commander gives "close on the third platoon at close interval," the platoon leaders on the right of the designated platoon have their platoons obtain close interval, face their platoons to the left, march (at the half step) forward until they obtain the five-step interval, halt, and face their platoons to the right.

When the company commander wants the company to obtain normal interval from close interval in a line formation while maintaining a five-step interval, the company commander directs "extend on the base platoon at normal interval." The platoon leaders face about and march (at the half step) their platoons to a position that ensures the five-step interval between platoons after they have obtained normal interval.

After halting and facing the platoons to the left, the platoon leaders command "count, off." The platoon leaders then command "normal interval, march." If necessary, the platoon leader verifies the interval as described in *Opening and Closing Ranks*.

Aligning the Company

To align the company in a line formation, the company commander directs "have your platoons dress right." On the directive, all platoon leaders face about. The right flank platoon leader commands *"dress right, dress"* and aligns the platoon as described in platoon drill.

After the right flank platoon leader has verified the alignment of the first rank, the platoon leader to the left commands "dress right, dress." That left platoon leader then faces to the half right in marching, moves to a position on line with and one step to the left of the left flank cadet of the first rank, and faces left down the line. After aligning the first rank, that platoon leader centers himself or herself on the first rank, faces to the right in marching, takes two short steps, halts, executes left face, and aligns the second rank.

The platoon leader aligns the last two ranks in the same manner as the second. After aligning the last rank, the platoon leader faces to the left in marching, returns to a position at the center of the platoon, halts perpendicular to the formation, faces to the right, commands "ready, front," and faces about. All platoon leaders to the left of the second platoon take the same actions as the second platoon leader.

To align the company in column, the company commander directs "have your platoons cover." On this directive, the first platoon leader faces about and commands "cover." The other platoon leaders command "stand fast." The first platoon covers as in platoon drill. The other platoons then execute the movement in succession as soon as the platoon to their front has completed the movement.

Opening and Closing Ranks

To open ranks, the company commander directs "have your platoons open ranks and dress right." On the directive, all platoon leaders face about. The right flank platoon leader commands "open ranks, march." When the platoon has completed the movement, the right flank platoon leader then commands "dress right, dress" and aligns the platoon the same as in platoon drill. After the right flank platoon leader aligns the first rank, the platoon leader to the left commands "open ranks, march" and "dress right, dress." All platoon leaders to the left of the second platoon take the same actions as the second platoon leader.

To close ranks, the commander directs "have your platoons close ranks." On the directive, all platoon leaders face about and in sequence from right to left command "close ranks, march." The platoons execute the movement the same as in platoon drill. After the platoons have completed the movement, the platoon leaders face about.

Changing the Direction of March of a Column

The company changes the direction of march basically the same as the squad and platoon. The commands are "column right (left), march" or "column half right (half left), march." The base element during a column movement is the lead platoon and the squad on the flank, in the direction of the turn.

When at the halt, the lead platoon leader repeats the company commander's preparatory command. Succeeding platoon leaders give the supplementary command "forward." On the command of execution "march," the lead platoon executes the movement as described in platoon drill; succeeding platoons execute the movement on their platoon leader's command at approximately the same location.

While marching, units execute the movement as described from the halt except that the succeeding platoon leaders give the supplementary command "continue to march" rather than "forward."

The company executes rear march and inclines in the same manner as the platoon (see Figure 5.3.2).

When executing counter column march from the halt, the lead platoon leader repeats the preparatory command. Succeeding platoon leaders give the supplementary command "forward." On the command of execution "march," the lead platoon executes the movement as described in platoon drill, and marches through the other platoons. Succeeding platoons execute the movement on the platoon leader's command at approximately the same location.

When units execute the movement while marching, the leader gives the command of execution as the left foot strikes the marching surface. Platoons execute the movement basically the same as from the halt except that the succeeding platoon leaders give the supplementary command "continue to march" rather than "forward." The guidon bearer faces to the left in marching from the halt or executes a

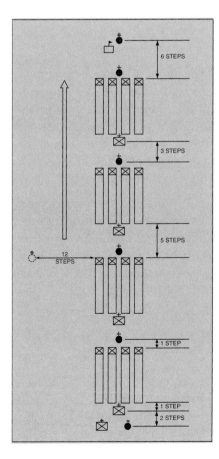

Figure 5.3.2: Company in column with platoons in column.
Courtesy of US Army JROTC.

column left in marching, marches by the most direct route outside of the formation, and moves to a position in front of the lead platoon as it clears the rear of the company.

Correcting the Distance Between Platoons

To obtain correct distance when the company is marching in column or is in a column at the halt, the company commander directs "close on leading platoon."

Key Note Term

mark time – to march in place, often given as a drill command

When at the halt and on the directive "close on leading platoon," the platoon leader of the lead platoon commands (over the right shoulder) "stand fast." The succeeding platoon leaders command (over the right shoulder) "forward, march," "**mark time**, march," and "platoon, halt" when they obtain correct distance.

While marching and on the directive "close on leading platoon," the platoon leader of the lead platoon commands (over the right shoulder) "half step, march." The succeeding platoon leaders command (over the right shoulder) "continue to march" and "half step, march" as soon as they obtain the correct distance. The company commander commands "forward, march (halt)" as soon as all platoons have obtained the correct distance and are marching at the half step.

Forming a Column of Twos and Re-Forming

The company forms a column of twos basically the same as the platoon. The company commander must allow sufficient time for the platoon leaders and the squad leaders of the lead platoon to give supplementary commands before giving the command of execution.

The command for this movement is "column of twos from the right (left), march." The lead platoon leader repeats the preparatory command. Other platoon leaders give the supplementary command "stand fast." On the company commander's command of execution "march," the lead platoon executes the movement as in platoon drill. Other platoons execute the movement on their leader's command. Succeeding platoon leaders give their commands in order to follow with the prescribed five-step distance between platoons.

Re-forming into a column of fours is executed only at the halt. The command for this movement is "column of fours to the left (right), march." On the company commander's command of execution, all platoons execute the movement simultaneously as described in platoon drill. As soon as the platoons are re-formed, the platoon leaders march the platoons forward and obtain the five-step distance between platoons.

Forming a Company Mass

The company may form in mass from a company in column (platoons in column) when halted or while marching (see Figure 5.3.3). The company must be at close interval ("close interval, march") before the commander can give "company mass left, march."

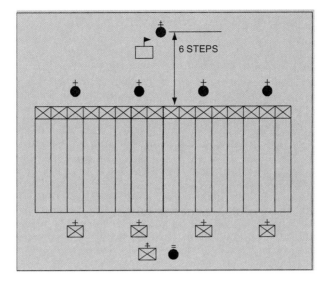

Figure 5.3.3: Company in mass formation.
Courtesy of US Army JROTC.

On the preparatory command "company mass left," given at the halt, the lead platoon leader commands "stand fast." The platoon leaders of the succeeding platoons command "column half left." On the command of execution "march," the lead platoon stands fast. The other platoons execute the column half left and then execute a column half right on the command of the platoon leaders to a point (line) that ensures the platoons will be at close interval alongside the platoon to their right when halted.

As the platoons come abreast of the base platoon, the platoon leaders command "mark time, march." While the platoon marks time, the members adjust their positions to ensure alignment on the cadet to their right. The platoon leaders allow their platoons to mark time for about eight counts and then command "platoon, halt." On the command of execution "march," the company commander and guidon bearer face to the right (left) in marching and reposition themselves centered on the company.

Aligning a Company Mass

As soon as the company commander forms the company in mass, he or she gives the command "at close interval, dress right, dress."

On the command of execution "dress," the platoon leader of the right platoon marches by the most direct route to the right flank and verifies the alignment of as many ranks as necessary to ensure proper alignment in the same manner as aligning the platoon. When finished, the right platoon leader returns to a position one step in front of and centered on the third squad, halts and faces to the right; then the platoon leaders and platoon sergeants position themselves in line with the third squad of their platoon by executing one 15-inch step to the right.

When the right platoon leader has returned to that position, the company commander commands "ready, front."

Changing the Direction of March of a Mass Formation

The company changes the direction of march in mass basically the same as a platoon column movement. When executed from the halt, the commander faces in the desired direction of march, looks toward the formation, and commands "right (left) turn, march."

On the command of execution "march," the platoon leaders face to the half right (left) in marching and continue to march in an arc until parallel to the new direction of march. Then they begin marching with the half step, dressing on the right (left) flank platoon leader until the leader commands "forward, march." The right (left) guide (the base squad leader in the direction of turn) faces to the right (left) in marching and immediately takes up the half step.

All other squad leaders (front rank) face to the half right (left) in marching and continue to march in an arc until they come on line with the guide. At this time, they begin marching with the half step and dress (glancing out of the corner of the eye) in the direction of the turn until the leader commands "forward, march." On that command, the dress is automatically to the right. All other members march forward and execute the movement in the same manner as their squad leaders.

When executed while marching, the movement is in the same manner as from the halt except that the company commander faces about (marching backward) to give the command "right (left) turn, march." The commander then faces about and completes the turning movement. After the company has completed the turn, the company commander faces about, commands "forward, march," and again faces about.

Forming a Column from a Company Mass

To form a company in column from a company mass at the halt, the command is "column of platoons, right platoon, column right (column half right), march." The right platoon leader gives the supplementary command of "forward (column right or column half right)," and the other platoon leaders command "stand fast." On the command of execution "march," the right platoon marches in the direction indicated. All other platoons follow (in sequence) in column, executing column half right and column half left on the commands of the platoon leaders.

To execute the movement when marching, the company commander commands "column of platoons, right platoon, **double time**, march." On the preparatory command, the right platoon leader gives the supplementary command "double time," and the other platoon leaders give the supplementary command "continue to march." On the command of execution "march," the right platoon marches in double time. Other platoon leaders (in sequence) command "column half right, double time, march" and "column half left, march" to bring the succeeding platoons in columns with the lead platoon.

The platoon leader and the platoon sergeant reposition themselves after the supplementary command, but before the command of execution.

Key Note Terms

arc – anything shaped like a curve, bow or arch; a curved line

guide – one that leads or directs another's way

Key Note Term

double time – to march in the cadence of 180 steps or counts per minute with a 30-inch step

Forming a Company in Column with Platoons in Line and Re-Forming

To form a company in column with platoons in line from a column formation at the halt, the command is "column of platoons in line, march." The platoon leader of the lead platoon commands "column right." All other platoon leaders command "forward." On the command of execution "march," the lead platoon stands fast, and the second platoon executes a column right, marches 12 steps past the right file of the first platoon, and executes a column left (see Figure 5.3.4). As they come in line with the base platoon, the platoon leader commands "mark time, march." After the platoon has marched in place for eight counts, the platoon leader commands "platoon, halt."

The succeeding platoons execute a column right at approximately the same location as the platoon to their front, execute a column left and then half in the same manner as the second platoon. When the platoons have halted in position, the company commander commands "left, face." On that command, the platoon leaders and platoon sergeants face in marching and assume their posts.

When executed while marching, the movements are basically the same as from the halt except that the commander gives the command of execution as the right foot strikes the marching surface. The lead platoon leader commands "mark time." On the preparatory command, the second platoon leader commands "column right," and the succeeding platoon leaders command "continue to march."

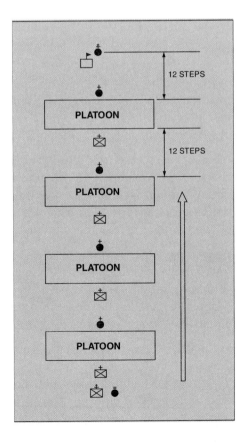

Figure 5.3.4: Company in column with platoons in line.
Courtesy of US Army JROTC.

On the command of execution "march," the lead platoon executes mark time and marches in place (approximately eight counts) until the platoon leader commands "platoon, halt." The other platoons execute the movement in the same manner as from the halt.

To re-form in column with platoons in column, the company commander commands "right, face; column of platoons, left platoon, march." On the command "right, face," the platoon leaders and platoon sergeants face in marching and resume their posts in column. On the preparatory command "column of platoons, left platoon," the left platoon leader commands "forward, (column left [half left])." All other platoon leaders command "column half left."

On the command of execution "march," the left platoon executes the movement. The other platoon leaders give the appropriate commands for following the lead platoon at the correct distance. If necessary, the platoons following the second platoon automatically adjust the length of their step to ensure correct distance from the platoon to their front.

Dismissing the Company

Dismiss the company only at attention. Either the first sergeant or the company commander may dismiss the company.

When the first sergeant dismisses the company, the company commander commands "first sergeant." The first sergeant marches by the most direct route to a position three steps from and directly in front of the company commander. After the first sergeant halts, the company commander commands "take charge of the company" and they exchange salutes.

Upon termination of the salutes, the platoon leaders and executive officer leave the formation. The platoon sergeants face to the right in marching and take their posts (platoon leader's position) six steps in front of and centered on the platoon by marching around the right flank of the platoon, inclining, and halting already facing to the front. The first sergeant steps forward three steps and faces about.

When all platoon sergeants are at their posts, the first sergeant commands "take charge of your platoons." The platoon sergeants salute. The first sergeant returns all salutes with one salute. After they exchange salutes, the first sergeant and guidon bearer leave the formation. The platoon sergeants then dismiss their platoons as in platoon drill.

When the company commander dismisses the company, he or she commands "take charge of your platoons." The platoon leaders salute. The company commander returns all salutes with one salute. After they exchange salutes, the company commander, guidon bearer, first sergeant, and executive officer leave the formation. Each platoon leader faces about and commands "platoon sergeant."

The platoon sergeants face to the right in marching, incline around the squad leader(s), halt three steps in front of and centered on the platoon leader, and face to the right. Each platoon leader then directs "take charge of the platoon." They exchange salutes and the platoon leaders leave the formation. The platoon sergeants step forward three steps, face about, and dismiss the platoons as in platoon drill.

Conclusion

Company drill is yet another link in the chain of drill movements of *Leadership Lab*. A weak link can break a chain, so make certain that you have reviewed this information well. It is important that you are familiar with all of the positions and formations of company drill before you can move up to the next links in the chain—leadership responsibilities at the company and battalion level and battalion drill.

In the next lesson, you will learn how to form, inspect, and dismiss a battalion.

Lesson Review

1. What are the four types of company formations?
2. What is the standard formation when commanded to "fall in"?
3. Where do platoon leaders take up position when the company forms in line?
4. What is *double time*?

Chapter 5

Lesson Review

Lesson 4

Forming, Inspecting, and Dismissing the Battalion

Chapter 5

Key Terms

en route
facilitate
respective

What You Will Learn to Do

- Execute battalion drills

Linked Core Abilities

- Communicate using verbal, nonverbal, visual, and written techniques
- Take responsibility for your actions and choices

Skills and Knowledge You Will Gain Along the Way

- Identify the different types of battalion formations and related specific drill commands
- Describe the correct responses to battalion drill commands
- Describe the correct responses to inspection commands
- Identify the locations of the key platoon, company, and battalion personnel in battalion formations
- Define the key words contained in this lesson

Introduction

This lesson covers battalion drill formations "without arms" and inspections. Your knowledge and recall of company drill from previous lessons will be vitally important in understanding this lesson. Pay special attention to the differences between the roles of key personnel (at the platoon, company, and battalion levels) in battalion drill.

This lesson teaches you the formations and inspection procedures for battalion drill. Battalion drill provides the procedures for executing company drill in conjunction with other companies in the same formation. For drill purposes, a battalion consists of a headquarters section (or the battalion staff), Colors, and two or more companies.

Drill Tips

- The battalion has two basic formations: a line and a column. There are several ways the battalion commander or staff can arrange the separate elements within either formation.

- The right flank unit serves as base when in a line formation; the lead element is the base when in column.

- To **facilitate** the forming of a larger unit, the commander normally alerts the subordinate units of the desired formation, time, place, route, uniform, and the sequence in which the units will form.

- Unless the S-3 has previously marked the position of the right guides at the formation site, the right guards report to the site and receive instructions prior to the arrival of the cadets.

- The commissioned staff forms in one rank at normal interval and centered on the commander. The commander-of-troops normally arranges the staff members in numerical order (S-1, S-2, S-3, S-4, and so on) from right to left as he or she faces the battalion.

- When enlisted staff personnel form as part of the officer staff, they form two steps to the rear of their **respective** staff officer.

- The command sergeant major forms one step to the rear of the commissioned staff and centered on the commander, or one step to the rear and centered on the Colors when in a battalion mass formation.

Key Note Term

facilitate –to ease the accomplishment of a task

Key Note Term

respective – related, belonging, or assigned

Formations

The battalion has two basic formations: a line and a column (see Figure 5.4.1).

Separate elements may be arranged in several variations within either formation: the battalion may be formed in line with the companies in line with platoons in line, or battalion in line with companies in column with platoons in line (Figure 5.4.2).

From those formations, the battalion may be positioned in a battalion in column with companies in column, or companies in mass, or companies in column with platoons in line.

This page illustrates the basic ways the battalion commander, commander-of-troops, or staff can arrange the battalion's separate elements into a line, column, or mass formation.

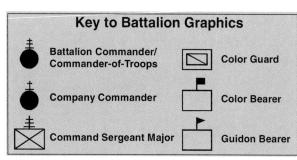

Figure 5.4.1: Key to battalion graphics.
Courtesy of US Army JROTC.

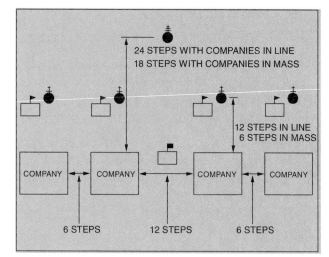

Figure 5.4.2: Battalion in line with companies in line or mass.
Courtesy of US Army JROTC.

The battalion may be formed in line with companies in line and platoons in line, or battalion in line with companies in column with platoons in line.

From either of those formations, we can position the battalion as follows: in a battalion in column with companies in column, or companies in mass, or companies in column with platoons in line (see Figure 5.4.3).

When the battalion participates as a separate element of a larger formation, or space is limited, the battalion can form in a mass formation (see Figure 5.4.4).

Forming and Dismissing the Battalion

To facilitate the forming of a larger unit, the commander normally alerts the component units as to the desired formation, time, place, route, uniform, and the sequence in which the units will form. Unless the right guide's position at the formation site has been previously marked, the guides report to the site and receive instructions before the arrival of the troops.

The commissioned staff forms in one rank, at normal interval and centered on the commander. Staff members are normally arranged in their numerical order from right to left. When enlisted staff personnel form as part of the officer staff, they form two steps to the rear of their respective staff officer. The command sergeant major forms one step to the rear and centered on the Colors.

Forming the Battalion

The adjutant is responsible for the formation of cadets. To do this, the adjutant takes a position at the right flank of the line on which the units are to form and faces down the line. The adjutant remains facing down the line until all units are formed and then marches to a post midway between the line of cadets and the proposed position of the battalion commander. If guides are used, the adjutant moves to a post as soon as the guides are in position and aligned.

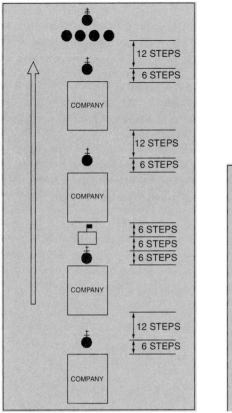

Figure 5.4.3: Battalion in column with companies in column or mass. Courtesy of US Army JROTC.

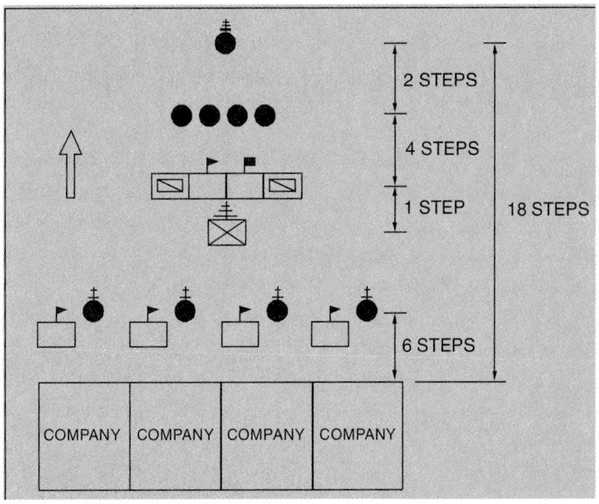

Figure 5.4.4: Battalion in mass formation. Courtesy of US Army JROTC.

As the battalion commander and staff approach, the adjutant commands the units to attention, faces the commander, salutes, and reports, "Sir, the battalion is formed."

The battalion commander returns the salute and commands "post." The adjutant marches forward, passes to the battalion commander's right, and takes a post as the right flank staff officer. The battalion commander then commands actions as desired.

Normally, the Colors are positioned at the center of the battalion when formed in line or column, and four steps to the rear of the staff when formed in mass.

Dismissing the Battalion

To dismiss the battalion, the battalion commander directs "take charge of your units." The company commanders and battalion commander exchange salutes. The battalion commander returns all salutes with one salute and then dismisses the staff. In a battalion mass formation, the platoon leaders form as the first rank of cadets. The right flank platoon leader serves as the guide.

Inspecting the Battalion

When inspecting the battalion, the adjutant forms the battalion in line with companies in line and platoons in line.

The adjutant forms the cadets, reports, and takes a position with the staff as previously described. After the adjutant joins the staff, the battalion commander directs "prepare for inspection." Unit commanders face about and give the same directive. The platoon leaders prepare their platoons for inspection in the same manner as in company drill.

When all platoons in each company have completed open ranks and dress right, the company commanders face the battalion commander. When all company commanders are again facing the battalion commander, the battalion commander commands "at ease."

Because of the time involved in inspecting a battalion, the battalion commander normally directs the staff to inspect the companies while he or she inspects the Colors and makes a general inspection of the battalion.

As the battalion commander (or the designated staff officer) approaches a company, the company commander faces about, salutes, and reports "Sir, ___ Company is prepared for inspection." The inspecting officer then proceeds to the first platoon to be inspected. The company commander takes a position to the left of the inspecting officer.

Conducting the Inspection

Conducting an *in-ranks inspection* of units in battalion drill uses the same procedures as in company drill. However, since we did not cover those procedures previously, the following information applies.

Forming for Inspection

The formation for inspecting personnel and equipment in ranks is company in line with platoons in line. With the company in a line formation, the company commander directs "prepare for inspection." Platoon leaders then face about, open ranks, and align the company. When all platoon leaders are facing the front, the company commander commands "at ease."

The company commander may direct the first sergeant and executive officer to accompany him or her during the inspection. If they do so, they take a position at normal interval (close interval if the company is at close interval) to the left of the company commander.

Inspecting the Cadets

During the inspection, the guidon bearer, officers, and noncommissioned officers who are not in ranks assume the position of attention as the inspecting officer approaches their positions. They resume the at ease position after being inspected (if armed, they do not execute inspection arms).

The company commander begins the inspection by stepping forward and inspecting the guidon bearer. The company commander then faces to the half left as in marching and proceeds to the right of the line. While approaching the right flank platoon, the platoon leader commands over the right shoulder "platoon, attention." After the company commander halts directly in front of the platoon leader, the platoon leader salutes and reports, "Sir, the platoon is prepared for inspection." The company commander returns the salute and inspects the platoon leader.

The company commander then directs the platoon leader to lead him or her through the inspection, faces to the half left in marching, and halts directly in front of the squad leader of the first squad. As the company commander faces to the half left in marching, the platoon leader faces to the right in marching, inclines, and halts directly in front of the second cadet in the first squad and on line with and at normal interval (close interval) to the right of the company commander. The other platoon leaders execute the same actions as the company commander approaches their platoons.

As soon as the platoon leader and company commander have halted in front of the first two cadets, the platoon leader commands "second, third, and fourth squads, at ease." When moving from cadet to cadet during the inspection, the company commander and platoon leader (as well as the executive officer and first sergeant) simultaneously face to the right in marching, take two short steps (one step if the company is at close interval), halt, and face to the left.

After the company commander has inspected the last cadet in the front rank, the platoon leader hesitates momentarily and allows the company commander to walk in front while inspecting the front rank from the rear. As the company commander inspects the rear of each rank, the platoon leader commands the next squad to attention. Then, as they begin to inspect the next rank, the platoon leader commands the last rank inspected to stand at ease.

Normally, when inspecting the rear of each rank, the company commander conducts a walking inspection. As the commander inspects the rear of the last cadet in each rank, he or she turns and halts directly in front of the squad leader of the next rank. The platoon leader turns and halts directly in front of the second cadet. The executive officer and first sergeant march past (behind) the company commander and assume their positions to the left.

Inspection with Arms

As the company commander halts directly in front of and facing the individual being inspected, the individual executes inspection arms. If the company commander wants to inspect the individual's weapon, he or she will inspect it first, then the individual's uniform and appearance. As soon as the company commander grasps the weapon, the individual releases it and resumes the position of attention. When the company commander finishes inspecting the weapon, he or she returns it in the same manner as receiving it.

In the event the company commander does not inspect the weapon, the cadet remains at inspection arms until the company commander moves to and is facing the next cadet. Then, the previously inspected cadet executes ready, port arms, and order arms.

Completing the Company/Platoon Inspections

When the company commander finishes inspecting the platoon sergeant, the platoon leader commands the platoon to attention and overtakes the company commander **en route** back to the front of the platoon. The platoon leader halts facing to the front (six steps in front and centered on the platoon) and exchanges salutes with the company commander. The company commander (executive officer and first sergeant) faces to the right in marching and moves to the next platoon.

> **Key Note Term**
>
> **en route** – in motion towards a destination

As soon as the company commander clears the first platoon, the platoon leader faces about, commands "close ranks, march" and "at ease," then faces about and executes at ease. After the company commander completes the inspection of the last platoon, he or she returns to the post at the center of the company and commands the company to attention.

> **Note**
>
> In the event a platoon has already been inspected, or it is still waiting to be inspected, and the battalion commander arrives, invite him or her to inspect the platoon.

Completing the Battalion Inspection

When the battalion commander and staff officers have completed their inspections and are en route back to their posts, the company commanders bring their units to attention, close ranks, and put their companies at ease. When the battalion commander and staff reach the front of the formation, the inspection is complete.

Conclusion

Now that you have reviewed battalion formations and inspections, you can see how each echelon continues to build upon previously learned skills. These new skills will enable you to perform drill in larger units. Study and practice will make your drill performance outstanding. Remember, knowledge is one of the most important elements of effective leadership.

The following lesson offers a review of drill procedures.

Lesson Review

1. What are the two basic types of battalion formations?
2. What is the standard formation when commanded to "fall in"?
3. What is the correct procedure for forming the battalion for inspection?
4. What is the correct procedure for inspecting arms in ranks?

Review of Drill Procedures

Key Terms

drill
formations
inspection
marching
stationary movements

What You Will Learn to Do

- Carry out responsibilities in a drill ceremony

Linked Core Abilities

- Communicate using verbal, nonverbal, visual, and written techniques
- Take responsibility for your actions and choices

Skills and Knowledge You Will Gain Along the Way

- Identify four steps that leaders should follow when starting a new leadership position
- Compare major duties of a team leader, squad leader, platoon sergeant, and platoon leader
- Define the key words contained in this lesson

Introduction

Using **drill** tips, **formations**, locations of key personnel, and lists of drill positions and/or movements, this lesson highlights some of the key elements of drill techniques and formations from previous lessons. Specifically, it reviews

- **Stationary movements**
- **Steps and marching**
- **Squad and platoon drill**
- **Company drill**
- **Battalion drill and inspections**

If you identify any movements in this lesson for which you are uncertain of the correct procedures on how to execute them, you should refer to the appropriate lesson, your Cadet Handbook, and/or Field Manual 3-21.5 for those procedures. Remember, depending on your position in the cadet battalion, one of your responsibilities as a senior cadet is to know—and possibly teach—drill. As a leader, you must set that example.

Stationary Movements

The individual positions and **stationary movements** are the basic skills required in drill. You learn these positions and their correct execution before proceeding to other drill movements. These basic skills are necessary to master because they are the building blocks for other movements used during *Leadership Lab*. Additionally, they are important because they help to develop discipline and self-confidence in individuals and the unit as a whole by ensuring uniformity of movement and overall effectiveness and efficiency.

Steps and Marching

The two basic steps used in **marching** are the 30-inch step and the 15-inch step. Use combinations of these steps, movements, and halts alone or in groups.

The following provides helpful drill tips for steps and marching.

- **When at a halt, start all marching movements from the position of attention**
- **Except for "route step, march" and "at ease, march," execute all marching movements while "marching at attention"**
- **Marching at attention is the combination of the position of attention and the procedures for the prescribed step executed simultaneously**
- **When executed from the halt, all steps except "close interval, march," "right step, march," and "about, face" begin with your left foot**
- **Unless otherwise specified, use 30-inch steps for marching forward**

Key Note Terms

drill – executing a predefined set of movements

formations – groups of people aligned in a specific pattern

Key Note Term

stationary movements – drill movements executed while remaining in place

---

Key Note Term

marching – a precise stepping movement designed to facilitate the efficient movement of formations

---

- Execute all marching movements in the quick time cadence except for the command "double time, march"

- Marching is a five-step process: preparatory command step; intermediate or thinking step; command of execution step; another step after the command of execution; and execution of movement

- Execute all 15-inch step movements for a short distance only

---

A Quick Review

The stationary movements are as follows:

- Position of attention
- Rest positions: parade rest, stand at ease, at ease, and rest
- Facing movements: left (right), face and about, face
- Saluting

The basic steps and marching movements are as follows:

- Halt
- Quick and double time (30-inch step)
- Rest movements in marching (30-inch step)
- Forward and backward step (15-inch step)
- Right (left) step (15-inch step)
- Changing step and marching in place

Squad Drill

To execute squad drill, you must first know how a squad forms and what your responsibilities are when it forms. After you have mastered these techniques, learning how to march in uniformity (and precisely) with other cadets is important in being part of a sharp drill squad. The following drill tips will help you to better understand some general information about squad drill.

- **While executing drill as a squad member, perform individual drill and stationary movements as described in those lessons**

- **When a squad forms in a line, its members are numbered from right to left; when in a column, from front to rear**

- **When the squad drills *as a separate unit and is in a line formation*, the squad leader takes a position three steps in front of and centered on the squad**

- **When it drills *as a separate unit and is in a column or column of twos*, the squad leader's position is three steps to the left and centered on the squad**

- **When the squad drills *as part of a larger formation*, the squad leader occupies the number one (base) position of the squad**

Squad Formations

The squad has two prescribed formations: line (or rank) and column (or file); however, your squad leader may form the squad in a column of twos from a column formation. Squad formations are shown in Figure 5.5.1.

Notes

- An arrow indicates the direction the squad is facing and/or moving
- A boxed "X" is the *squad leader*; boxed slashes are *team leaders*
- Squad sizes may vary with each unit

Marching the Squad

The following tips apply when marching the squad.

- **The squad normally marches in a column, but for short distances, it may march in a line formation**
- **To form a column formation from a line formation, the command is "right, face"**
- **When a column formation is at close interval, the squad may march for short distances at the half step**

Review Notes

The basic stationary drill movements in squad drill are as follows:

- Falling in
- Obtaining intervals: normal, close, and double
- Changing intervals
- Counting off
- Rest and dismissal

Platoon Drill

The following drill tips will help you to better understand some general information about platoon drill. Platoons execute certain drills in the same way that squads do. These drills include the following:

- **Inclining Around**
- **Changing Intervals in Lines**
- **Counting Off**
- **Dismissing**
- **Marching to the Flanks**
- **Marching in the Opposite Direction**
- **Resting**

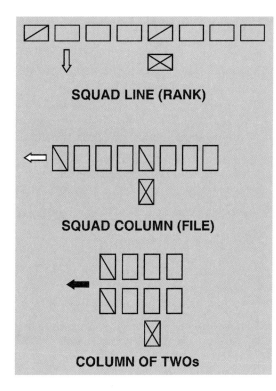

Figure 5.5.1: Squad formations.
Courtesy of US Army JROTC.

SQUAD LINE (RANK)

SQUAD COLUMN (FILE)

COLUMN OF TWOs

For the most part, platoon drill merely provides the procedures for executing movements in conjunction with other squads formed in the same formation.

- When a platoon forms in a line, its squads are numbered from front to rear; in a column, from left to right.

- Execute individual drill movements as previously described while performing as a squad member during the conduct of platoon drill.

- When the platoon drills *as a separate unit and is in a line formation,* the platoon leader takes a position six steps in front of and centered on the platoon. The platoon sergeant's position is centered on the platoon and one step to the rear of the last rank.

- When it drills *as a separate unit and is in a column formation,* the platoon leader's position is six steps on the left flank and centered on the platoon. The platoon sergeant's position is one step behind and centered between the second and third squads.

- When the platoon drills *as part of a larger unit,*

  - *And is in a line formation,* the platoon leader's position is six steps in front of and centered on the platoon. The platoon sergeant's position is one step to the rear and centered on the platoon.

  - *And is in a column formation,* the platoon leader's position is one arm's length plus six inches in front of and centered between the second and third squad leaders. The platoon sergeant's position is one step behind and centered between the second and third squads.

- The first squad leader serves as the base when the platoon is in a line formation; the fourth squad leader serves as the base when in a column.

Platoon Formations

The platoon has two prescribed formations: line and column; however, your platoon leader may form the platoon in a column of twos from a column. See Figure 5.2.2 for platoon formations. Use the following to interpret the symbols used in those formations.

- **An arrow indicates the direction the platoon is facing and/or moving**
- **A circle with an attached cross is the *platoon leader*; a boxed "X" with an attached cross is the *platoon sergeant*; boxed "X's" are *squad leaders*; boxed slashes are *team leaders***
- **Platoon sizes may vary with each unit**

Marching the Platoon

The following apply when marching the platoon.

- **The platoon marches in the same manner as prescribed for the squad**
- **When marching in line, the first squad leader serves as the guide; when marching in column, the fourth squad leader is the guide**

Figure 5.5.2: Platoon formations.
Courtesy of US Army JROTC.

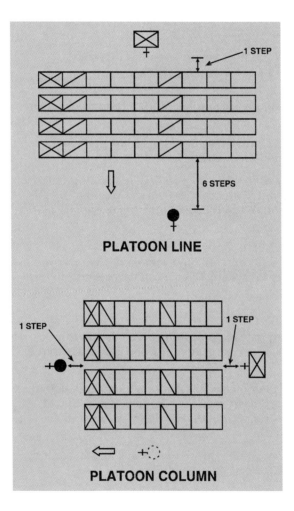

- When marching in line, each member maintains alignment on the cadet to the right by glancing out of the corner of the right eye; when marching in column, each member of the first, second, and third squads maintains alignment on the cadet to the right

Review Notes

The basic drill movements in marching the squad are as follows:

- Changing direction: column left (right), march; column half left (right), march; rear, march; and incline around
- Marching to the flank
- Forming a column of twos and re-forming

The movements in platoon drill are as follows:

- Falling in
- Breaking ranks
- Counting off
- Changing intervals
- Aligning the platoon
- Covering and recovering
- Opening and closing ranks
- Rest and dismissal

The basic movements in marching the platoon are as follows:

- Changing direction
- Marching to the flank
- Forming a file and re-forming
- Forming a column of twos and re-forming

Movements in company drill include the following:

- Forming and aligning the company
- Changing interval
- Opening and closing ranks
- Changing direction of march of a column
- Correcting distance between platoons
- Forming a column of twos and re-forming
- Forming and aligning a company mass
- Forming a column with platoons in line
- Dismissing the company

Company Formations and Movement

Company drill provides the procedures for executing platoon drill in conjunction with other platoons in the same formation. For drill purposes, a company consists of a company headquarters and two or more platoons. The following drill tips will help you to better understand some general information about company formations and drill.

- **The company normally forms in a line formation; however, it may re-form in column when all personnel can identify their exact position in the formation.**

- **The company forms basically the same as the platoon. On the command "fall-in," platoons form in line, centered on and facing the person forming the unit, with five-step intervals between platoons.**

- **When in a line or a mass formation, the right platoon serves as the base; when in a column formation, the lead platoon serves as the base.**

- **The first sergeant assumes the position of the company commander if there are no officers present.**

- **Members of a company break ranks in the same manner as in platoon drill except that the individuals called from the formation form on the company commander rather than on the platoon leader.**

- **When the company commander directs that the company "open or close ranks," "extend march," "close on the leading platoon," or "prepare for inspection," platoons execute the movements on the command of the platoon leaders and not on the directives of the company commander. The platoon leaders command the movement in sequence beginning with the base platoon.**

Company Formations

The company has four prescribed formations: company in line with platoons in line, company in column with platoons in column, company in column with platoons in line (used primarily for ceremonies), and a company mass formation. The company, however, may form into a column of twos in the same manner as the platoon.

Figure 5.5.3 shows formation illustrations. Use this illustration to interpret the following formation figures.

> **Notes**
> - An arrow indicates the direction the company is facing and/or moving
> - The symbol with the pennant is the company commander's guidon bearer
> - Company sizes may vary with each unit
> - The company marches, rests, and executes eyes right in the same manner as the platoon

Figure 5.5.4 shows a company in line with platoons in line.

Figure 5.5.5 shows a company in a column with platoons also in a column.

Figure 5.5.6 reflects a company in a column with platoons in a line.

Figure 5.5.7 shows a company in a mass formation.

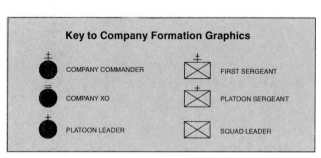

Key to Company Formation Graphics

Figure 5.5.3: Key to company formation graphics.
Courtesy of US Army JROTC.

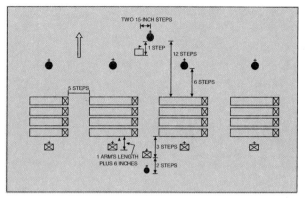

Figure 5.5.4: Company in line with platoons in line.
Courtesy of US Army JROTC.

Battalion Drill and Inspections

Battalion drill provides the procedures for executing company drill in conjunction with other companies in the same formation and for conducting an in-ranks **inspection**. For drill purposes, a battalion consists of a headquarters section (or the battalion staff), Colors, and two or more companies. The following drill tips will help you to better understand some general information about battalion formations and drill.

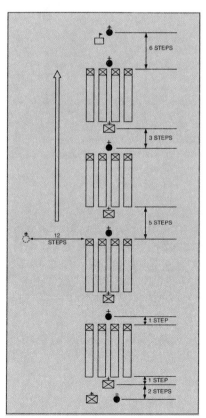

Figure 5.5.5: Company in column with platoons in column.
Courtesy of US Army JROTC.

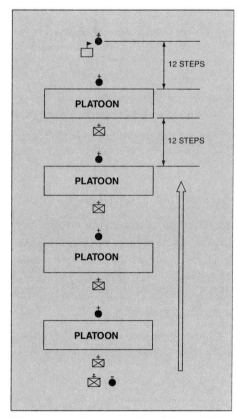

Figure 5.5.6: Company in column with platoons in line.
Courtesy of US Army JROTC.

Figure 5.5.7: Company in a mass formation.
Courtesy of US Army JROTC.

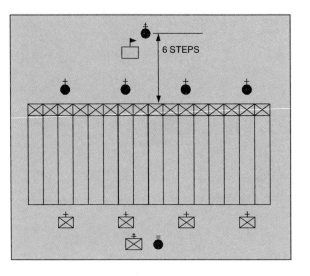

6 STEPS

- The right flank unit serves as base when in a line formation; the lead element is the base when in column.

- To facilitate the forming of a larger unit, the commander normally alerts the subordinate units of the desired formation, time, place, route, uniform, and the sequence in which the units will form.

- Unless the S-3 has previously marked the position of the right guides at the formation site, they report to the site and receive instructions prior to the arrival of the troops.

- The commissioned staff forms in one rank at normal interval and centered on the commander. The commander-of-troops normally arranges the staff members in numerical order (S-1, S-2, S-3, S-4, and so on) from right to left as he or she faces the battalion.

- When enlisted staff personnel form as part of the officer staff, they form two steps to the rear of their respective staff officer.

- The command sergeant major forms one step to the rear of the commissioned staff and centered on the commander or one step to the rear and centered on the Colors when in a battalion mass formation.

Battalion Formations

The battalion has two basic formations: a line and a column. There are several ways the battalion commander or staff can arrange the separate elements within either formation. Shown below are the basic ways the battalion commander, commander-of-troops, or staff can arrange a battalion's separate elements into a line, column, or mass formation. Use the symbols in Figure 5.5.8 to interpret the battalion formation illustrations.

The battalion may be formed in line with companies in line and platoons in line, or battalion in line with companies in column with platoons in line (see Figure 5.5.9).

From either of those formations, you can position the battalion in a battalion column with companies in column, or companies in mass, or companies in column with platoons in line (see Figure 5.5.10).

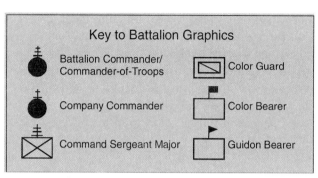

Figure 5.5.8: Key to battalion graphics.
Courtesy of US Army JROTC.

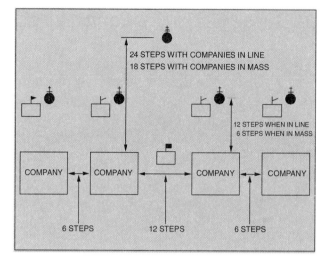

Figure 5.5.9: Battalion in line with companies in line or mass.
Courtesy of US Army JROTC.

When the battalion participates as a separate element of a larger formation, or space is limited, the battalion can form in a mass formation (see Figure 5.5.11).

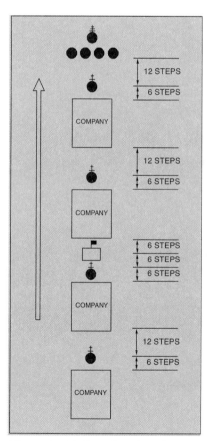

Figure 5.5.10: Battalion in column with companies in column or mass.
Courtesy of US Army JROTC.

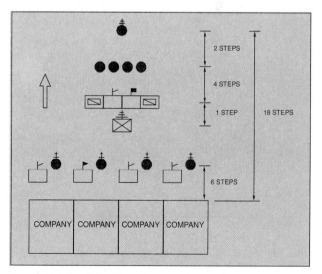

Figure 5.5.11: Battalion in mass formation.
Courtesy of US Army JROTC.

Conclusion

In this lesson, you had the opportunity to review some of the key concepts of drill, beginning with individual stationary movements and progressing up to battalion drill and inspections. As you make this progression, you can see how each echelon—squad to platoon, platoon to company, and company to battalion—builds on previously learned skills. To perfect drill, it takes many hours of practice and lots of discipline. Therefore, you must study and practice the tips and formations presented in this lesson as well as the detailed procedures for executing the various drills and commands. Only through study and practice will you be ready to teach and set the example for your subordinates in proper drill procedures.

In the following lesson, you will learn stationary movements with the M-1903 rifle.

Lesson Review

1. Why is it important for cadets to know and understand drill procedures?

2. What is the prescribed formation for marching?

3. Identify some of the differences between platoon and company formations.

4. What is the basic battalion formation for conducting inspection?

Stationary Movements with the M-1903 Rifle

Key Terms

balance
barrel
bolt
bolt handle
butt
chamber
cocking piece
hand guard
keeper
lower band
muzzle
port arms
sight
sling
sling swivel
stacking swivel
stock
trigger guard
upper band

What You Will Learn to Do

- Execute the manual of arms with the M-1903 rifle

Linked Core Abilities

- Communicate using verbal, nonverbal, visual, and written techniques
- Take responsibility for your actions and choices

Skills and Knowledge You Will Gain Along the Way

- Describe the correct response to commands for "order arms" and "reset positions"
- Describe the correct responses to commands to "port arms" and "present arms"
- Describe the correct responses to commands for "inspection of arms"
- Describe the correct responses to commands for "right and left shoulder arms"
- Describe the correct responses to commands to "sling and unsling arms"
- Describe the correct responses to commands to "stack and take arms"
- Define the key words contained in this lesson

Introduction

Executing drill with arms uses and builds on the same basic skills you learned in drill without arms. These drills and movements with the M-1903 rifle are important to master because you will be able to apply them in ceremonies, reviews, and drill competitions. Correct execution of them, combined with a lot of pride and practice on your part, can lead to a precision drill team.

This lesson introduces you to the procedures for executing the manual of arms with the M-1903 rifles. Specifically, it covers the correct response to the following commands for order arms and rest, present and port arms, inspection arms, right and left shoulder arms, sling and unsling arms, and stack and take arms.

The M-1903 Springfield Rifle

The M-1903 Springfield rifle was the primary rifle used by our American Expeditionary Forces during World War I in Europe. The magazine held five .30 caliber rounds and had a maximum effective range of about 850 yards, and an effective range of more than 3,500 yards. During World War II, the M-1903 was phased out and replaced by the M-1. The M-1903 drill rifle used by Army JROTC units today is the same one used by our Doughboys over a century ago in Europe. These rifles have been demilitarized for safety and are only functional for precision drill. The firing pins have been cut off or removed, and the barrels have been welded shut and filled with lead. Originally, the M-1903 weighed 8.69 pounds, but after demilitarization they weigh about 9.25 pounds. Most have the front and rear sights removed to ensure your safety. They still measure 43 inches, unless a butt pad is added to protect the surface of the floors. The pad adds an inch to the overall length.

Care and maintenance is relatively simple. These rifles still require security measures and must be locked up when not in use. Use a stiff bristle brush and damp cloth to clean debris from the stock. Do not add protectants to the stock because they will make the rifle slippery and difficult to grasp during drill. Clean the bore with a bore brush and lightly oil with cleaning patch. Remove all debris from the chamber, bolt, magazine feed, and barrel using a rag. Add a very light coat of oil to all metal parts to prevent rust. Be sure to wipe off all excess oil.

Use the following drill tips when executing drill with arms:

- At the halt, your leader initiates all movements from order arms, which is the position at attention.

- Execute all precision movements in the cadence of quick time.

- The command port arms must be given prior to the command for double time.

- Execute facings, alignments, and short distance marching movements from order arms. When the leader commands these movements while you are at order arms, automatically raise your rifle about one inch off the ground on the command of execution. When you complete them, automatically return the rifle to order arms.

- Execute facing movements at order arms only. When you execute facings to establish the direction of march, do so before the command for the manual of arms. After you complete a marching movement, the leader commands order arms prior to the command for the facing movement.

- While at the halt, all drill movements are initiated from order arms or sling arms, these are the positions of attention.

- All drill movements are executed with head up and eyes straight ahead as in position of attention.

Order Arms and Rest

Order arms is the position of attention with the rifle (see Figure 5.6.1). Assume the position of order arms on the command of execution "attention" from any of the rest positions and from the commands "fall in" or "order, arms," except from inspection or sling arms.

At order arms, place the **butt** of the rifle on the ground, with the toe of the butt on line with the toe of your right shoe and touching it. Keep the rear **sight** to the rear. Secure the rifle with your right hand in a "U" formed by your fingers (extended and jointed) and thumb. Hold the rifle by the **hand guard** just above the **lower band**.

Figure 5.6.1: Order arms.
Courtesy of US Army JROTC.

Keep your right hand and arm behind the rifle so that your thumb is along the seam of your trousers

Rest Position with the M-1903

Your leaders command the rest positions with the rifle and you execute them much the same as individual drill, with the following additions:

- On the command "parade, rest," grasp the hand guard below the upper band and thrust the **muzzle** forward, keeping your right arm straight (see Figure 5.6.2)
- Execute stand at ease in the same manner as parade rest with the rifle, except turn your head and eyes toward the unit leader
- On the commands of "at ease" or "rest," keep the butt of the rifle in place

Port and Present Arms

Port arms on the command "port arms." Present arms on the command "present arms." **Port arms** from order arms is a two-count movement (see Figure 5.6.3). The command is "port, arms." On the command of execution, grasp the hand guard of the rifle with your right hand and raise the rifle diagonally across your body. With the left hand, grasp the **balance** so that the rifle is approximately four inches from your belt. Hold your right elbow down without strain. On the second count, grasp the rifle again with the right hand at the small of the **stock**. Hold the rifle diagonally across your body with your right forearm horizontal and your elbows at your sides.

Execute order arms from port arms in three counts (see Figure 5.6.4). The command is "order, arms." On the command of execution, move your right hand up and across your body and grasp the hand guard firmly just above the lower band, without moving the rifle. On the second count, release the hand guard with your left hand and lower the rifle to your right side until it is approximately one inch from the ground. Guide the rifle to your side by placing the left hand at the **upper band**, fingers and thumb extended and joined, palm to the rear. On the third count, cut the left hand sharply to your side and lower the rifle gently to the ground, resuming the position of order arms.

Figure 5.6.2: Parade rest.
Courtesy of US Army JROTC.

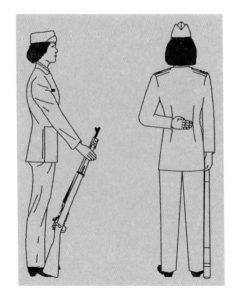

Figure 5.6.3: Port arms.
Courtesy of US Army JROTC.

Figure 5.6.4: Order arms from port arms.
Courtesy of US Army JROTC.

Present Arms

Present arms from order arms is a three-count movement. The command is "present, arms." On the command of execution, execute both movements of port arms. On the third count, twist the rifle with the right hand and move the rifle to a vertical position approximately four inches in front of and centered on your body. Lower the rifle until the left forearm is horizontal, keeping your elbows at your sides, as shown on the left side of Figure 5.6.5.

> **Note**
>
> Incline the muzzle of the rifle slightly backward to ensure the barrel is vertical.

Order arms from present arms is a four-count movement. The command is "order, arms." On the command of execution, return the rifle to port arms. Counts two, three, and four are the same as for port arms.

Figure 5.6.5: Present arms.
Courtesy of US Army JROTC.

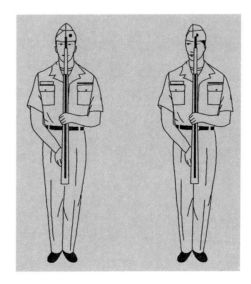

You may also assume port arms on the way to or from present arms from right or left shoulder arms. Present arms from or to port arms is a one-count movement.

When rendering reports or courtesy to an individual from order arms, execute present arms as mentioned above, except turn your head and eyes toward the individual addressed (see the right side of Figure 5.6.5). Execute order arms automatically upon acknowledgment of the salute.

When rendering courtesy to an individual while marching with the rifle at right shoulder arms, left shoulder arms, or port arms, and not in formation, execute present arms and continue marching. After acknowledgment of the salute, automatically return to the original position.

Inspection Arms

Inspection arms from order arms is a three-count movement (see Figure 5.6.6). The command is "inspection, arms." On the command of execution, execute port arms in two counts. On count three, release the small of the stock with your right hand and move the right hand forward, grasping the **bolt handle** with your thumb and forefinger. Turn the bolt handle up, draw the **bolt** back to the rear, and glance into the **chamber**. Raise your head and eyes back to the front. Continue to hold the bolt handle with your right hand.

The only command your leader may give from inspection arms is port arms. On the command "port," push the bolt forward, turn the bolt handle down, and grasp the rifle at the small of the stock, placing the index finger of the right hand on the **trigger guard**. On the command "arms," pull the trigger and resume port arms.

Actions during an Armed Inspection

Use the following procedures for an inspection with rifles. As the inspector halts and is directly in front and facing you, automatically execute *port arms* and *inspec-*

Figure 5.6.6: Inspection arms.
Courtesy of US Army JROTC.

tion arms. If the inspector wants to inspect the rifle, he or she will inspect the rifle first, then your uniform and appearance. As soon as the inspector grasps the rifle, you release the rifle and immediately snap to position of attention. When the inspector has finished inspecting the rifle, it is returned to you in the the same manner it was received. You receive the rifle by grasping the balance with your left hand and the bolt handle with the right hand. You then execute *port arms* and *order arms*. If the inspector does not want to inspect the rifle, you remain at *inspection arms* until the inspector has halted and is facing the next individual. Most inspectors will ask questions about your uniform, but during an armed inspection they expect you to know the model of your rifle and the serial number.

The purpose of inspection arms is to prepare the rifle for inspection and ensure there are no rounds in the chamber. A port arms also ensures the rifle has not been damaged during routine drill practice by checking the operation of the bolt and trigger mechanism.

Right (Left) Shoulder Arms

Shoulder arms on the command "right/left shoulder arms." Right shoulder arms from order arms is a four-count movement (see Figure 5.6.7). On the command of execution, execute the same movements as for the first count of port arms from order arms. On the second count, release your right hand and grasp the heel of the butt of the rifle between your first two fingers, with your thumb and index finger touching. On the third count, twist the rifle with your right hand and place it on your right shoulder, not changing the grasp of your right hand.

At the same time, move your left hand to the small of the stock and guide the rifle to your shoulder. Keep your fingers and thumb extended and joined, with your palm turned toward your body. The first joint of your left forefinger should touch the rear of the **cocking piece**. Keep your wrist straight and your left elbow down. On the fourth count, move your left hand back to your side as in the position of attention. Keep your right forearm horizontal with your right upper arm against your side and on line with your back.

Order arms from right shoulder arms is a four-count movement. On the command of execution, press the butt down quickly and guide the rifle diagonally across your body. At the same time, twist the rifle to keep the sights up. Grasp the rifle at the balance with your left hand while retaining the grasp of your right hand at the butt. On the second count, release your right hand, move it up and across your body and grasp the hand guard just above the lower band. The third and fourth counts are the same as the second and third counts from port arms to order arms.

Left Shoulder Arms

Left shoulder arms from order arms is a four-count movement (see Figure 5.6.8). On the command of execution, execute port arms in two counts. On the third count, release the grasp of your left hand and place the rifle on your left shoulder with your right hand, keeping your right elbow down. At the same time, grasp the butt with your left hand in the same manner as for right shoulder arms. On the fourth count, lower your right hand smartly to your side to the position of attention.

Figure 5.6.7: Right shoulder arms.
Courtesy of US Army JROTC.

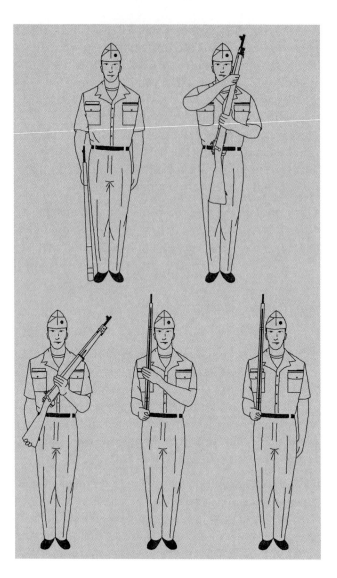

Figure 5.6.8: Left shoulder arms.
Courtesy of US Army JROTC.

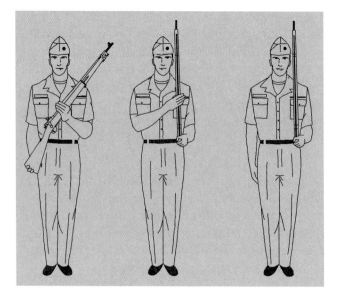

Order arms from left shoulder arms is a five-count movement. On the command of execution, move your right hand up and across your body and grasp the small of the stock, keeping your right elbow down. On the second count, release your left hand and carry the rifle diagonally across your body with your right hand. At the same time, grasp the rifle at the balance with your left hand, resuming port arms. Counts three to five are the same as order arms from port arms.

Changing Positions

Port arms to right shoulder arms is a three-count movement. The command is "right shoulder, arms." On the command of execution, slide the right hand to the right and grasp the butt. Counts two and three are the same as counts three and four from order arms. When marching, the leader gives the command as the right foot strikes the ground.

Port arms to left shoulder arms is a two-count movement. The command is "left shoulder, arms." On the command of execution, execute left shoulder arms in the same manner as counts three and four from order arms. When marching, the leader gives the command as the left foot strikes the ground.

Right shoulder arms to left shoulder arms is a four-count movement. The command is "left shoulder, arms." On the command of execution, execute the first count the same as in order arms. On count two, release the butt of the rifle with the right hand and grasp the small of the stock as in port arms. Counts three and four are the same as from port arms. When marching, give the command as the left foot strikes the ground.

Left shoulder arms to right shoulder arms is a five-count movement. The command is "right shoulder, arms." On the command of execution, execute port arms in two counts. Counts three, four, and five are the same as from port arms. When marching, the leader gives the command as the right foot strikes the ground.

You execute present arms from right shoulder arms or left shoulder arms while in formation from the halt only. On the command of execution, assume port arms from either shoulder and then execute present arms in one count from port arms.

To resume right (left) shoulder arms from present arms, on the command of execution, execute port arms in one count and then execute the counts as prescribed from port arms.

> **Note**
>
> Experienced cadets should be able to execute the 15-count manual of arms in unison: from order, to right shoulder, to left shoulder, to present, to order arms. The command is "fifteen count manual, arms."

Sling and Unsling Arms

Performing drill with a rifle takes practice and coordination. Many of the positions and movements you just learned with the **sling** of your M-1903 rifle can be done with the sling loose. Knowing how to drill with your rifle when the sling is loose is equally important in being a sharp drill unit.

Sling Arms

From the order arms position with the rifle slings tight, the command for sling arms is "sling, arms." On the command of execution, raise the rifle vertically and place the rifle butt on your right hip. Cradle the rifle with your right arm and with both hands loosen the **keeper** and adjust the sling. For rifles with a latched keeper on the sling that are operated with one hand, place the rifle on the right hip as previously described, hold it in place with the right hand, use the left hand to loosen the keeper, and adjust the sling. After the sling is adjusted, sling the rifle on your right shoulder in the most convenient manner. Assume the position of attention by grasping the sling with your right hand and by keeping your right forearm horizontal and the rifle vertical. If the sling is already loose, sling the rifle in the most convenient manner (see Figure 5.6.9).

Key Note Term

keeper – slide for adjusting slack in rifle sling

Drill Tips

- You may execute all individual or unit drill movements, except stack arms, while at sling arms.

- Remain at sling arms during all rest movements.

- You execute stack arms with the slings loose from order arms only.

- When in formation at sling arms, execute the hand salute on the command "present, arms."

- When acting as a platoon leader or platoon sergeant, carry your rifle at sling arms during all drills and ceremonies. This also applies to acting squad leaders when their squads drill as separate units.

- When all members of a unit are carrying their rifles at sling arms, only the platoon leaders and platoon sergeants execute present arms. They do not execute unsling arms..

Figure 5.6.9: Sling arms.
Courtesy of US Army JROTC.

Unsling Arms

To return the rifle to the order arms position, the command is "unsling, arms." On the command of execution, reach across the body with the left hand and grasp the sling at the shoulder. Unsling the rifle in the most convenient manner and assume order arms.

If the leader desires the sling to be tightened, he/she commands "adjust, slings." On the command of execution, unsling and cradle the rifle, adjust the sling, and automatically assume the order arms position. For rifles with a latched keeper on the sling that are operated with one hand, place the rifle on the right hip as previously described, hold it in place with the right hand, use the left hand to loosen the keeper, and adjust the sling. If you are already at order arms with a loose sling when the leader commands "adjust, slings," immediately cradle the rifle, adjust the sling, and return to order arms.

Saluting While at Sling Arms

To salute while at sling arms, the command is "present, arms." On the command of execution, reach across your body with your left hand and grasp the sling just above the right hand. Release your right hand and execute the hand salute (see Figure 5.6.10).

To end the hand salute, the leader commands "order, arms." On the command of execution, lower your right hand smartly to your side and grasp the sling at the original position. After grasping the sling with your right hand, release it with your left hand, returning it smartly to your left side as in the position of attention.

> **Note**
>
> When rendering reports or courtesy to an individual while at sling arms, use the same rules that apply for the hand salute in stationary drill.

Executing Port Arms from Sling Arms

The command for this movement is "port, arms." On the command of execution, reach across the body with your left hand and grasp the sling at the shoulder. Lift the rifle by the sling, swing it to the front of your body, and grasp the small of the stock with your right hand. Release the sling and grasp the rifle at the balance with your left hand, keeping your elbows at your sides with the right forearm horizontal (see Figure 5.6.11).

Figure 5.6.10: Saluting while at sling arms.
Courtesy of US Army JROTC.

Figure 5.6.11: Executing port arms from sling arms.
Courtesy of US Army JROTC.

Resume sling arms on the command of "sling, arms." On the command of execution, grasp the sling near the upper **sling swivel** with your left hand. Release the right hand and swing the rifle back onto your shoulder by inserting the right arm through the sling, immediately resuming the position of sling arms.

Adjust Slings to Right Shoulder Arms

During casing and uncasing the colors it is necessary to tighten the rifle slings and go to right shoulder arms. This is normally done without commands. Execute port arms from sling arms. Position the rifle on your right hip as described in sling arms then tighten the sling. Return to port arms and execute right shoulder arms.

Executing Inspection Arms from Sling Arms

The command for this movement is "inspection, arms." On the command of execution, first execute port arms (in the same manner as you did with the sling tight); then execute count three in the same manner as inspection arms from order arms (see Figure 5.6.12).

To resume sling arms, use the same procedures as described above for port arms.

> ### Key Note Term
>
> **sling swivel** – metal loop for connecting sling to stock

Figure 5.6.12: Executing inspection arms from sling arms.
Courtesy of US Army JROTC.

Stack and Take Arms

Stack arms on the command "stack arms." Take arms on the command "take arms." Execute "stack, arms" from order arms only. You execute this movement while at normal interval in a squad line or column formation. The leader designates the stackpersons by numbers (2-5-8-11) when in a line formation and by squads (second or third) when in a column formation.

On the command of execution, the cadet on the left of the stackperson grasps the rifle at the lower portion of the front hand guard. The cadet on the left then passes it in a vertical position to the right front (about 30 degrees) to the stackperson who grasps it with the left hand at the upper portion of the front hand guard (see Figure 5.6.13).

The stackperson places the heel of the rifle butt between his/her feet with the **barrel** to the front, muzzle outward, and raises the **stacking swivel** with the thumb and forefinger of the left hand. That person then swings the butt of his/her rifle two feet in front and six inches to the right of the right of his/her right toe. At the same time, the stackperson shifts the right hand to the stacking swivel of the rifle and engages it with that of the left rifle. The stackperson's rifle is on the right (see Figure 5.6.14).

The cadet on the right of the stackperson steps to the left with his/her left foot, keeping the right foot in place. At the same time, that cadet bends to the left front, grasps his/her rifle with the left hand at the front hand guard, and places the right hand at the small of the stock. He/she then slides the left hand up to move the stacking swivel, engaging it with the free hook on the swivel of the stackperson's rifle (see Figure 5.6.15).

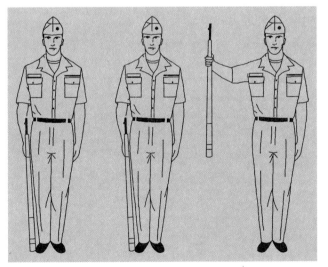

Figure 5.6.13: Passing left rifle to stackperson.
Courtesy of US Army JROTC.

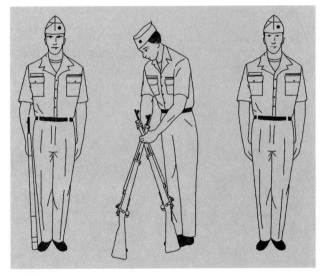

Figure 5.6.14: Stacking center and left rifles.
Courtesy of US Army JROTC.

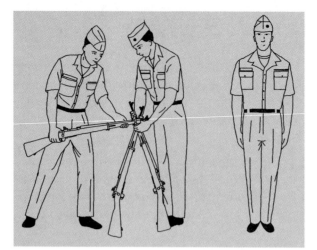

Figure 5.6.15: Passing right rifle to stackperson.
Courtesy of US Army JROTC.

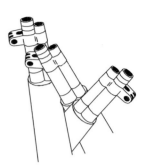

Figure 5.6.16: Stacked rifles barrel alignment.
Courtesy of US Army JROTC.

The cadet on the right side of the stackperson then rotates the rifle outward so that the barrel rests in the angle formed by the other two rifles and above the bayonet stud on the left rifle (see Figure 5.6.16).

That same cadet then pulls the rifle butt inward until the stack is tight and the butt of the rifle is in line with the butt of the rifle between the stackperson's feet. He/she then lowers the butt to the ground and resumes the position of attention (see Figure 5.6.17).

Cadets with other rifles pass them to the nearest stack on their right. When passing extra rifles to the stack grasp the front hand guard with your right hand and while holding the rifle vertical, fully extend your arm to your right front. When the cadet on your right has grasped the rifle at the balance with his/her left hand, release your right hand and resume the position of attention.

When you have received a rifle from the cadet on the left, keep it vertical and move it in front of you, with your left hand at the balance. Grasp the front hand guard with your right hand as described above. If you are the stackperson, place the rifle on the stack, trigger guard outward, at a sufficient angle from the vertical to keep it in place. If the second squad is the stack squad, extra rifles are passed to the left.

Figure 5.6.17: Completed stacking movement.
Courtesy of US Army JROTC.

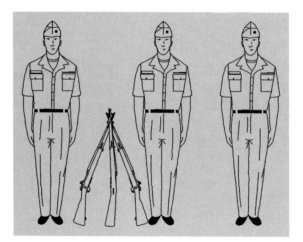

To take arms, the command is "take, arms." On the command of execution, the stackperson passes each extra rifle toward its bearer.

> **Note**
>
> Each person holds the rifles passed in the same manner described for passing them to the stack: left hand at the balance followed by right hand at the front hand guard.

When you receive your rifle, resume the position of order arms by guiding and steadying the rifle with your left hand as in the next-to-last count of order arms.

After the extra rifles have been passed, the stackperson grasps his/her rifle and the rifle of the cadet on his/her left. The cadet on the right of the stackperson steps to the left as in stacking, secures his/her rifle, and resumes the position of order arms.

The stackperson then disengages the two remaining rifles, grasps the left rifle at the lower part of the front hand guard, and passes it to the left front. The cadet to the left grasps the rifle at the front hand guard with his/her right hand and lowers it to the ground, resuming order arms. The stackperson resumes order arms after the cadet on the left has received his/her rifle.

Conclusion

This lesson covered the procedures for executing the manual of arms with the M-1903 rifle while at sling arms and when carrying it with the sling tight. Precise drill movements with a rifle require a lot of practice and hard work, but the outcome may be rewarding for you and your cadet battalion: winning local, state, and/or national drill competitions. Take a moment to look at a video of the national drill competitions held at Daytona Beach, a news video of the Old Guard as members from that unit guard the Tomb of the Unknown Soldier, or the opening of the movie *A Few Good Men* to see firsthand examples of just how good precision drill can be.

In the next lesson, you will learn stationary movements with the M-1 rifle. Much of what you learned in this lesson will help you in the following lesson.

Lesson Review

1. What are the correct movements for "order arms?"
2. What are the correct movements for "present arms?"
3. What are the correct movements for "inspection arms?"
4. What are the correct movements for "right shoulder arms?"

Lesson 7

Stationary Movements with the M-1 Rifle

Key Terms

balance
barrel
butt
port arms
sling
stock
trail arms
trigger guard

What You Will Learn to Do

- Execute the manual of arms with the M-1 rifle

Linked Core Abilities

- Communicate using verbal, nonverbal, visual, and written techniques
- Take responsibility for your actions and choices

Skills and Knowledge You Will Gain Along the Way

- Describe the correct response to commands for "order arms" and "rest positions"
- Describe the correct responses to commands to "port arms," "present arms," and "rifle salute"
- Describe the correct responses to commands for "inspection of arms"
- Describe the correct responses to commands for "right and left shoulder arms"
- Describe the correct responses to commands to "sling and unsling arms"
- Describe the correct responses to commands to "stack and take arms"
- Define the key words contained in this lesson

Introduction

Executing drill with the M-1 rifle uses and builds on the same basic skills you learned in drill without the use of arms. The positions and movements with the M-1 rifle are important to master because you will apply them in ceremonies, reviews and when carrying your rifle during other phases of training. With a lot of pride and practice on your part, correct execution of these movements may lead to a precision drill team.

This lesson introduces the procedures for executing the manual of arms with the M-1 rifle (see Figure 5.7.1).

Note

Because of the many similarities between the manual of arms for the M-1 and the M-1903, in various places throughout this lesson you are referred back to pages in the previous lesson so that you can see illustrations of those procedures.

Drill Tips

- Execute fall in with the rifle at order arms.

- The term "at the **balance**" refers to a point on the M-1 rifle just forward of the **trigger guard**.

- You normally execute facings, alignments, and short distance marching movements from order arms. Right (left) step, backward march, open and close ranks, and close and extend interval march are short distance movements. To march units forward for similar short distances, the drill leader may give forward march from order arms. After receiving these commands, automatically assume **trail arms** on the command of execution for the duration of the movement. Return the rifle to order arms upon halting.

- Before starting any other marching movement, the drill leader must face the troops in the desired direction of march and then have them bring their weapons to right shoulder, port, or sling arms by the appropriate command. After the formation completes a marching movement, and the drill leader desires to execute a facing movement, first have the weapon brought to order or unsling arms, and then give the command for the facing movement.

- With your left hand at the balance, hold the M-1 rifle with your thumb and fingers, including the **sling** in your grasp. Extend and join your fingers forming a "U" with your thumb.

- The cadence for rifle movements is quick time.

- Before your drill leader commands "fall out," you must be at attention at order, port, stack, or unsling arms.

Key Note Terms

balance – position just forward of the magazine floor plate on the underside of the rifle stock

trigger guard – metal strip surrounding trigger mechanism to prevent accidental firing

trail arms – fingers and thumb closed around the front hand guard, rifle butt raised about three inches off the ground and stock inclined at an angle of 30 degrees.

sling – strap for carrying rifle over back and shoulder

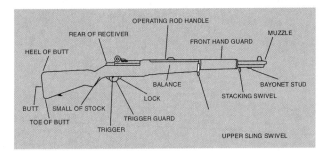

Figure 5.7.1: M-1 rifle.
Courtesy of US Army JROTC.

- When at a position other than sling arms, come to **port arms** for double time.

- Execute the manual of the M-1 while at the position of attention, but you may execute any position from another, except inspection arms, trail arms, and sling and unsling arms—which you execute from order arms. Plus, you can only execute port arms from inspection arms.

- The position of *diagonally across the body* means that the **barrel** is up, the heel of the butt is on line with your right hip, and the barrel is at such an angle that one point of it is in front of the juncture of your neck and left shoulder. Hold the rifle at a height that allows your right forearm to be horizontal when you grasp the small of the **stock** with your right hand. Grasp the rifle at the balance with your left hand, keeping your left elbow at your side. The distance of the rifle from your body (belt) should be about four inches.

Order Arms and Rest

Order arms is the position of a cadet at attention with the rifle. Assume the position of order arms on the command "squad (platoon), attention" from any of the rest positions except fall out, on the command "fall in," and on the command "order, arms" from any position except inspection arms and sling arms.

At order arms, maintain the position of attention except for your right arm and the M-1. Place the **butt** of the rifle on the ground with the barrel to the rear and the toe of the rifle butt against your right shoe, on line with the front of your right shoe (see Figure 5.6.1). Grasp the front hand guard with your right hand in a "U" formed by your fingers, extended and joined, and your thumb. Hold the tips of your index finger and thumb on line with the forward edge of the front hand guard. Keep your right hand and arm behind the rifle so that your thumb is along your trousers seam (see Figure 5.7.2).

Figure 5.7.2: Order arms.
Courtesy of US Army JROTC.

Rest Positions with the M-1

The rest positions with the M-1 are commanded and executed as without arms, with the following exceptions and additions:

- On the command "parade, rest," keep the toe of the rifle butt on line with the front of your right shoe, and hold the rifle butt against it. Slide your right hand upward, regrasp the front hand guard just below the stacking swivel, and straighten your right arm so the muzzle is inclined straight to the front. Place your left hand behind your back, just below the belt line, with your fingers and thumb extended and joined and your palm to the rear. Thrust the rifle out at the same time you move your left foot (see Figure 5.6.2).

- Execute stand at ease with the M-1 in the same manner as parade rest, except turn your head and eyes toward the leader.

- On the commands "at ease" or "rest," keep your right foot in place and hold the M-1 as in parade rest, except that you may relax your right arm slightly. When at sling arms, follow the procedure outlined later in this lesson.

Trail Arms

When at the position of order arms, you execute the position of trail arms on the command of execution of a march command when no other command precedes the preparatory command for the movement.

For instructional purposes, a leader may use the command "trail, arms" to teach the position at the halt. On the command of execution, grasp the rifle with your right hand, with your fingers and thumb closed around the front hand guard. Raise the rifle butt about three inches off the ground and incline the rifle forward at an angle of 30 degrees. Execute this movement in one count.

Carry the rifle in that position until the leader gives "order, arms." On the command of execution, lower the rifle to the ground with your right hand and resume the position of order arms.

Port and Present Arms

Port arms on the command "port arms." Present arms on the command "present arms." Port arms from order arms is a two-count movement (see Figure 5.6.3). On the command of execution, raise the rifle diagonally across the body with the right hand, grasping the balance with the left hand so that the rifle is about four inches from your belt. Hold your right elbow down without strain. On the second count, regrasp the rifle with your right hand at the small of the stock. At port arms, keep your right forearm horizontal, your elbows in at your sides, and the rifle diagonally across the body about four inches from you.

Execute order arms from port arms in three counts. On the command of execution, move your right hand up and across your body and grasp the front hand guard without moving the rifle (see Figure 5.6.4). On the second count, release your left hand from the balance and lower the rifle to your right side with your right hand so that the butt is about three inches from the ground. Place your left hand on the rifle in the vicinity of the stacking swivel with your fingers and thumb extended and joined, palm to the rear, to steady the rifle and hold the barrel vertically.

On the third count, lower the rifle gently to the ground with your right hand and then sharply move your left hand to your side, resuming the position of order arms.

Present Arms

Present arms from order arms is a two-count movement (see Figure 5.7.3). On the first count, carry the rifle to the center of your body with your right hand, keeping the barrel to the rear and vertical and your right elbow down. Grasp the rifle and sling at the balance with your left hand, keeping your forearm horizontal and elbow against your body. On the second count, grasp the small of the stock with your right hand. The distance of the rifle from your body should be about four inches from your belt.

Order arms from present arms is a three-count movement. Execute the first count by grasping the rifle at the front hand guard with your right hand, keeping your elbow down and at your side. On the second count, lower the rifle with your right hand, completing the second and third counts as in order arms from port arms.

Executing Port Arms from Present Arms

Execute port arms from present arms in one count. Raise and twist the rifle with your right hand, moving the muzzle to the left, and regrasp the rifle at the balance with your left hand.

Executing Present Arms from Port Arms

Execute present arms from port arms in one count. Lower and twist the rifle with your right hand, moving the rifle to a vertical position, and regrasp it at the balance with your left hand.

Figure 5.7.3: Present arms.
Courtesy of US Army JROTC.

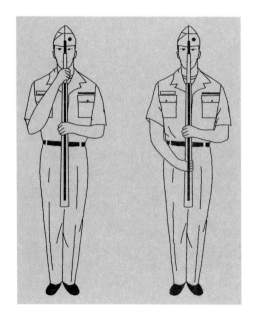

Rifle Salute

You may execute a rifle salute from order arms (see Figure 5.7.4), trail arms, right shoulder arms, or left shoulder arms. For instructional purposes, the drill leader may use the command "rifle, salute." The rifle salute is a two-count movement.

Executing a Rifle Salute from Order Arms

When at order arms, on the first count, move your left arm across your body. Then, with your forearm and wrist straight, fingers and thumb extended and joined, and palm down, touch the rifle at a point between the stacking swivel and the muzzle with the first joint of your forefinger. If not in ranks, turn your head and eyes toward the person or the Colors you are saluting. On the second count, sharply move your left hand away to your side and turn your head and eyes back to the front (see Figure 5.7.4).

Executing a Rifle Salute from Trail Arms

When saluting at trail arms, the movements are identical with those for saluting at order arms except hold the rifle in the trail arms position.

Executing a Rifle Salute from Right Shoulder Arms

At right shoulder arms, execute the movement by moving your left arm across your chest and touching the first joint of your forefinger to the rear of the receiver. Hold your left elbow so that the lower edge of your left forearm is horizontal. Hold your fingers, thumb, and wrist as described for order arms above, with your palm down. The second count of the rifle salute at right shoulder arms is similar to the return from the rifle salute at order arms (see Figure 5.7.5).

Figure 5.7.4: Executing a rifle salute from order arms.
Courtesy of US Army JROTC.

Figure 5.7.5: Executing a rifle salute from right shoulder arms.
Courtesy of US Army JROTC.

Executing a Rifle Salute from Left Shoulder Arms

At left shoulder arms, execute the movement by moving your right arm across your chest and touching the first joint of your forefinger to the rear of the receiver. Hold your right elbow so that the lower edge of your forearm is horizontal. Hold the fingers, thumb, and wrist as described in order arms above, with your palm down. The second count is similar to the return from the rifle salute at right shoulder arms.

> **Note**
>
> The next to the last count of order and right shoulder arms is not a rifle salute but is used for steadying the rifle. You execute a rifle salute with the palm of your hand down and the side of the first joint of your forefinger touching the rifle.

Inspection Arms

Inspection arms from order arms is a four-count movement that you execute *only* from order arms. The first two counts are the same as in going to port arms. On the third count, release your left hand from the balance and, with your fingers closed, palm in, and forearm horizontal, place your left thumb on the operating rod handle and push it to the rear until it is caught by the operating rod catch. At the same time, lower your head and eyes enough to look into the receiver (see Figure 5.7.6). On the fourth count, having found the receiver empty or having emptied it, raise your head and eyes to the front and at the same time regrasp the rifle at the balance with your left hand.

Port arms is the only command that the drill leader may give from inspection arms. On the preparatory command, with your fingers extended and joined, and palm in, place the rear edge of your right hand against the operating rod handle and move it

Figure 5.7.6: Inspection arms.
Courtesy of US Army JROTC.

slightly to the rear. Then, depress the follower with your right thumb and allow the bolt to move forward slightly, overriding the rear portion of the follower. On the command of execution, remove your right thumb from the receiver and at the same time release the operating rod handle. Pull the trigger with your forefinger and regrasp the small of the stock as in the position of port arms.

> **Note**
>
> Leaders should execute inspection arms as a safety precaution when they form and dismiss their units.

Right (Left) Shoulder Arms

Shoulder arms on the command "right/left shoulder arms." Right shoulder arms from order arms is a four-count movement. On the command of execution, execute the first count of port arms. Hold your right elbow down without strain. On the second count, regrasp the rifle at the butt with your right hand; the heel of the butt should be between your first two fingers and thumb, your fingers closed around the stock, and your thumb and index finger touching.

On the third count, place the rifle on your right shoulder with the grasp of your right hand unchanged. Release your left hand from the balance and use it to guide the rifle to your shoulder by placing your left hand at the small of the stock, thumb and fingers extended and joined, palm toward your body, and the first joint of your left forefinger touching the rear of the receiver. Keep your left elbow down. On the fourth count, sharply move your left hand back to its position by your side as in attention. At right shoulder arms, keep your right forearm horizontal and your right elbow against your side and on line with your back (see Figure 5.6.7).

The return to order arms is a four-count movement. On the command of execution, press the rifle butt down quickly and move the rifle diagonally across your body, turning the butt so as to keep the barrel up. Grasp the rifle at the balance with your left hand, retaining the grasp of your right hand on the butt (count one). On the second count, move your right hand up and across your body and grasp the front hand guard. Execute the third and fourth counts in the same manner as the second and third counts in executing order arms from port arms.

Right shoulder arms from port arms is a three-count movement. On the first count, re-grasp the rifle at the butt with your right hand as you would in coming to right shoulder arms from order arms. The last two counts are the same as the last two counts in moving from order arms to right shoulder arms.

Port arms from right shoulder arms is a two-count movement. The first count is the same as the first count from right shoulder arms to order arms. On the second count, regrasp the rifle with your right hand at the small of the stock in the position of port arms.

Left shoulder arms from order arms is a four-count movement. On the command of execution, execute port arms in two counts. On the third count, place the rifle on your left shoulder with your right hand, keeping your right arm pressed against your body. At the same time, re-grasp the butt with your left hand in a manner similar to grasping the butt with your right hand in right shoulder arms. On the fourth count, sharply move your right hand to your side as in the position of attention (see Figure 5.6.8).

Port arms from left shoulder arms is a two-count movement. On the first count, move your right hand up and across the body and grasp the small of the stock with your right hand, keeping your right arm pressed against your body. On the second count, carry the rifle diagonally across your body with your right hand, and regrasp the balance with your left hand as in the position of port arms.

Order arms or right shoulder arms from left shoulder arms is a five-count movement. On the first two counts, bring the rifle to port arms. On the last three counts, execute the steps for order arms or right shoulder arms.

Sling and Unsling Arms

Performing drill with a rifle takes practice and coordination. Knowing how to drill with your rifle when the sling is loose is equally important in being a sharp drill unit.

Sling Arms

A leader gives the command "sling, arms" only from order arms or unsling arms. Do not execute this movement in cadence. If the sling is not adjusted, on the command of execution, place the butt of the rifle on your right hip and cradle the rifle in the crook of your right arm. Adjust the sling with both hands and then sling the rifle on your right shoulder in the most convenient manner. When at sling arms, grasp the sling with your right hand, keeping your right forearm horizontal and holding the barrel of the rifle vertical (see Figure 5.6.9).

If the sling is already adjusted when the leader gives the command of execution, sling the rifle in the most convenient manner.

Unsling Arms

On the command of execution for "unsling, arms," remove the rifle from your right shoulder in the most convenient manner and assume the position of order arms, steadying the rifle with your left hand.

> **Note**
> When assuming order arms, the sling remains loose.

Before executing precise movements, the leader must command "adjust, slings." On the command of execution, tighten the sling from the position described above for loosening the sling.

Saluting While at Sling Arms

To salute while at sling arms, on the command of execution for "present, arms," grasp the sling with your left hand to steady the rifle. Keep the palm of your left hand to the rear and your forearm horizontal. At the same time, release the sling with your right hand and execute the first count of a hand salute (see Figure 5.6.10). Then, on the command of execution for order arms, sharply move your right hand and arm to your side as in the position of attention and resume the original position of sling arms.

Executing Rest Positions While at Sling Arms

Execute parade rest and at ease while at sling arms in the manner described for order arms, but keep the rifle slung, held with your right hand. On the command "rest," you may unsling the rifle. On the preparatory command of squad or platoon, take the position of parade rest at sling arms.

Stack and Take Arms

Stack arms on the command "stack arms." Take arms on the command "take arms." The members of the squad stack arms from their positions in line at normal interval on the command of "stack, arms." After the squad counts off, the leader designates the stackpersons by numbers (2-5-8-11) before giving the command to stack arms. Only those squad members with other people on each side of them can be designated as stackpersons.

On the command of execution, the cadet on the left of the stackperson grasps his/her rifle at the lower portion of the front hand guard and passes it in a vertical position to the right front (approximately 30 degrees) to the stackperson, who grasps it with the left hand at the upper portion of the front hand guard (see Figure 5.6.13). The stackperson places the butt of the rifle between his/her feet, with the barrel to the front and the muzzle outward; then, with the thumb and forefinger of his/her left hand, the stackperson raises the stacking swivel.

The stackperson then swings the butt of his/her own rifle about two feet in front and six inches to the right of his/her right toe. At the same time, the stackperson shifts his/her right hand to the stacking swivel of his/her rifle and engages it with that of the left rifle. The stackperson's rifle is on the right (see Figure 5.6.14).

The cadet on the right of the stackperson steps to the left with his/her left foot, keeping the right foot in place. At the same time, that cadet bends to the left front, regrasping his/her weapon with the left hand at the front hand guard and the right hand at the small of the stock. This cadet then slides his/her left hand up to manipulate the stacking swivel, engaging it with the free hook of the swivel on the stackperson's rifle (see Figure 5.6.15).

The cadet on the right of the stackperson then rotates his/her rifle outward so that the barrel rests in the angle formed by the other two rifles and above the bayonet stud on the left rifle (see Figure 5.6.16). This cadet pulls the butt toward him/her until the stack is tight and the butt is in line with the butt of the rifle between the stackperson's feet. The cadet then lowers the butt to the ground and resumes the position of attention (see Figure 5.6.17).

Cadets with other rifles pass them to the nearest stack on the right. When passing extra rifles to the stack, grasp the front hand guard with your right hand and, holding the rifle vertical, fully extend your arm to your front. When the cadet on your right has grasped the rifle at the balance with his/her left hand, release your right hand and resume the position of attention. When you receive a rifle from the cadet on your left, keep it vertical and move it in front of you, with your left hand at the balance; grasp the front hand guard with your right hand and, if you are not the stackperson, pass it to your right as described above. If you are the stackperson, place the rifle on the stack, trigger guard outward, at a sufficient angle from the vertical to keep it in place.

The squad in line behind the stacks takes the rifles on the command of "take, arms." On the command of execution, the stackperson passes each extra rifle toward its bearer. Cadets hold the rifles in the manner described for passing them to the stack. After cadets receive their weapons, they resume the position of order arms.

After the extra rifles have been passed, the stackperson grasps his rifle and the rifle of the cadet on his left. The cadet on the right of the stackperson steps to the left as in stacking, secures his/her rifle, and resumes the position of order arms.

The stackperson then disengages the two remaining rifles, grasps the left rifle at the lower part of the front hand guard and passes it to his/her left front. The cadet on the left grasps it at the front hand guard with the right hand and lowers the rifle to the ground, resuming order arms. The stackperson resumes order arms after the cadet on the left has received his/her rifle.

Each cadet comes to order arms by guiding and steadying the rifle with his/her left hand as in the next to the last count of order arms.

Conclusion

This lesson covered the procedures for executing the manual of arms with the M-1 rifle while at sling arms and when carrying it with the sling tight. As you learned in Lesson 6, precise drill movements with a weapon require a lot of practice and hard work, but the outcome may be rewarding for you and your cadet battalion: winning local, state, and/or national drill competitions. Review the video of the national drill competitions held at Daytona Beach or the opening of the movie *A Few Good Men* to see firsthand examples of just how good precision drill can be.

The following lesson discusses the manual of arms for the saber and the scabbard.

Lesson Review

1. What are the correct movements for "present arms"?

2. What are the correct movements for a rifle salute from the position of "order arms"?

3. What are the correct movements for "inspection arms"?

4. What are the correct movements for "take arms"?

Lesson 8

The Saber and the Scabbard

Key Terms

cant
guard
pistol belt
port
saber
scabbard

What You Will Learn to Do

- Execute the manual of arms with the saber and the scabbard

Linked Core Abilities

- Communicate using verbal, nonverbal, visual, and written techniques
- Take responsibility for your actions and choices

Skills and Knowledge You Will Gain Along the Way

- Describe the parts of a saber and a sword
- Explain the proper way to wear the saber
- Describe the correct responses to commands for "inspection of arms"
- Describe the correct responses to commands for the "standing manual of arms"
- Describe the correct responses to commands for the "marching manual of arms"
- Define the key words contained in this lesson

Chapter 5

Introduction

This lesson introduces you to the manual of arms for the saber. After you have mastered these procedures, you will have added another important skill to your knowledge as a drill leaders and as a cadet officer in JROTC. You will be able to demonstrate this skill during ceremonies or competitions for your cadet battalion.

The Saber

Key Note Terms

saber – a heavy cavalry sword with a one-edged, slightly curved blade

pistol belt – a belt designed to carry a holster, pistol, ammunition pouches and or other field equipment

scabbard – a sheath for a saber or sword, or other similar arm

guard – the portion of the belt (handle) of a saber or sword that protects the hand

Cadet officers who participate in ceremonies with cadets under arms may be able to wear the saber. The **saber**, shown in Figure 5.8.1, is carried on the left side of the body and attached to the **pistol belt** by the **scabbard** chain with the **guard** of the saber to the rear. When using a saber, remember that precise execution of it enhances the status of the wearer. Poor or inexact execution, however, is particularly obvious at ceremonies.

The infantry, revolutionary saber is slightly different than the infantry sword (Figure 5.8.2) carried by platoon sergeants and first sergeants during ceremonies with cadets under arms. Although the manual of arms for the saber and sword are the same, we will refer only to the saber for the remainder of this lesson.

Standing Manual of Arms

Execute standing with the saber (sword) using the procedures described in the following sections.

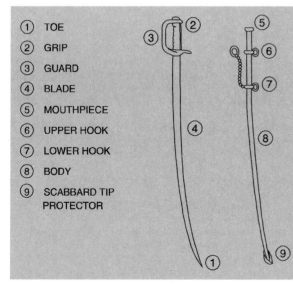

1. TOE
2. GRIP
3. GUARD
4. BLADE
5. MOUTHPIECE
6. UPPER HOOK
7. LOWER HOOK
8. BODY
9. SCABBARD TIP PROTECTOR

Figure 5.8.1: Saber and scabbard.
Courtesy of US Army JROTC.

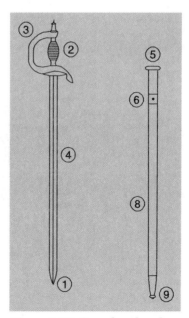

Figure 5.8.2: Sword and scabbard.
Courtesy of US Army JROTC.

Attention

When in formation, assume the position of attention before the command "draw, saber" and after the command "return, saber." Place your hands behind the trouser seams with the thumbs touching the first joint of the forefingers (see Figure 5.8.3).

Draw Saber

On the preparatory command "draw," grasp the scabbard with the left hand and turn it clockwise 180 degrees, tilting it forward to form an angle of 45 degrees with the ground. Take the saber grip in the right hand and pull the saber about six inches from the scabbard. The right forearm should now be roughly parallel to the ground (see Figure 5.8.4).

On the command of execution "saber," pull the saber out of the scabbard and hold it in a *carry saber* position. Hold the saber with the inner blade-edge riding in a vertical position along the forward tip of the right shoulder (see Figure 5.8.5).

Carry Saber

To execute *carry saber*, the cadet officer must first be at the position of *attention*. Hold the saber in the right hand keeping the wrist as straight as possible with the thumb along the seam of the trouser leg. Ensure that the point of the blade rests inside the point of the shoulder and not along the arm. Hold the saber in this position with the thumb and forefinger grasping the grip. Steady the saber with the second finger behind the grip.

Figure 5.8.3: Standing at attention.
Courtesy of US Army JROTC.

Figure 5.8.4: Draw saber.
Courtesy of US Army JROTC.

Figure 5.8.5: Carry saber position.
Courtesy of US Army JROTC.

Chapter 5 Leading Others

You will want to assume the *carry saber* position under the following situations:

- **When giving commands**
- **When changing positions**
- **When officially addressing (or when officially addressed by) another officer, if the saber is drawn**
- **Before returning the saber to the scabbard**
- **When giving the preparatory command for—and while marching at—*quick time*.**

Present Arms

Execute *present saber* from the *carry* position when serving in the capacity of commander-of-troops or in a command that is not a part of a larger unit. On the preparatory command of "present," of the command "present, arms," bring the grip of the saber to a position approximately four inches from the nose (at the rate of two counts). Hold the saber outward so that the toe is approximately six inches from the vertical (see 1, Figure 5.8.6).

On the command of execution "arms," lower the right hand (at the rate of two counts) with the flat of the blade upward, the thumb extended on the left side of the grip, and the toe of the saber about six inches from the marching surface (see 2, Figure 5.8.6).

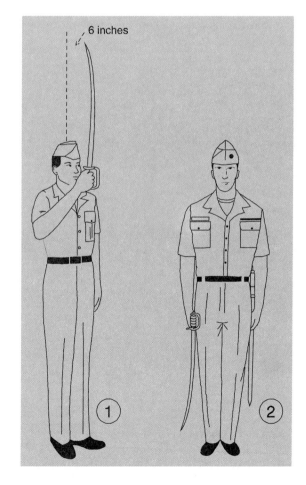

Figure 5.8.6: Present saber.
Courtesy of US Army JROTC.

On the command "order, arms" return the saber to the *carry saber* position. Ensure that whenever the saber is at the *order arms* position, it is straight and not at an angle inward or outward in relationship to the body.

> **Note**
>
> When not in formation, keep the saber in its scabbard and use the hand salute.

Parade Rest

Assume this position without moving the saber from the *order arms* position. At the command of execution, move the left foot about 10 inches to the left of the right foot, and place the left hand in the small of the back, fingers extended and joined, palm to the rear (see Figure 5.8.7). On the command of execution "attention," return the left hand and foot to the position of *attention*.

Return Saber

Execute "return, saber" from *carry saber* in three counts.

1. **On the preparatory command "return" of the command "Officers, return, saber," bring the saber to a vertical position (see 1, Figure 5.8.8). Hold the forearm (wrist) parallel to the marching surface about three inches from the body with the guard pointed to the left.**

2. **On the command of execution "saber," three actions take place simultaneously:**

   - **Pivot the saber downward toward the guard.**

   - **At the same time, grasp the scabbard with the left hand just above the upper hook.**

Figure 5.8.7: Parade rest.
Courtesy of US Army JROTC.

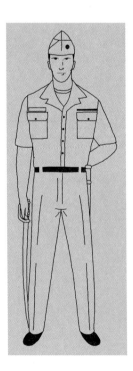

- Tilt it forward and turn it clockwise 180 degrees.

- The scabbard should form a 45-degree angle with the ground, and the saber bearer turns his or her head to the left and looks down to observe the mouthpiece of the scabbard (the shoulders remain squared to the front and level). As smoothly and as quickly as possible, insert the saber in the scabbard and stop so that about 12 inches of the blade is showing. The right forearm (wrist) should be horizontal to the marching surface and three inches from the body. (See 2, Figure 5.8.8.)

3. At the command of execution "cut" of the command "ready, cut," thrust the saber smartly into the scabbard. Rotate the scabbard so that its tip protector is forward; then come to attention (see 3, Figure 5.8.8).

Marching Manual of Arms

While marching, carry the saber with the inner blade-edge riding in a vertical position along the forward tip of the right shoulder, as shown in Figure 5.8.9.

Eyes Right While Marching

Execute the command "eyes, right" while marching at carry saber as follows (see Figure 5.8.10). Give the command "ready" as the right foot strikes the marching surface (no action is taken).

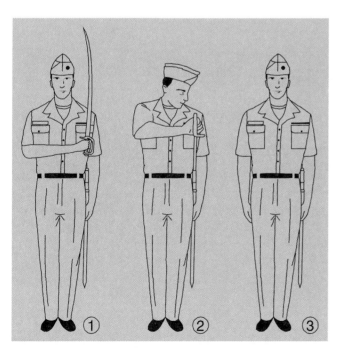

Figure 5.8.8: Return saber.
Courtesy of US Army JROTC.

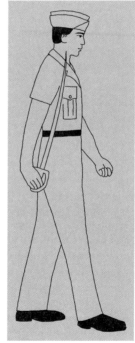

Figure 5.8.9: Carry saber position— marching.
Courtesy of US Army JROTC.

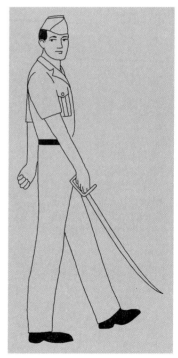

Figure 5.8.10: Eyes right while marching.
Courtesy of US Army JROTC.

Lesson 8   The Saber and the Scabbard

The second time the right foot strikes the marching surface, give the command "eyes" and bring the saber to the count one position of *present arms* (or *present saber*). No action is taken the third time the right foot strikes the marching surface. The fourth time the right foot strikes the marching surface, give the command "right." As that foot strikes the surface, turn your head sharply to the right at a 45-degree angle and bring the saber downward.

While marching at *present saber*, swing the right arm naturally (nine inches to the front and six inches to the rear) in a vertical plane, flexing the wrist to keep the toe of the blade level (about six inches) above the marching surface. This requires extending the wrist on the forward movement and elevating the wrist on the rearward movement.

Ready Front While Marching

Execute "*ready, front*" by first giving the command "ready" as the right foot strikes the marching surface (no action is taken). The second time the right foot strikes the marching surface, give the command "ready" a second time (again, no action is taken). Return the saber to the order position while maintaining a natural arm swing as the right foot strikes the marching surface the third time. The fourth time the right foot strikes the marching surface, give the command "front." Turn your head sharply to the front as the right foot strikes the surface and return the saber to the *carry* position the next time the left foot strikes the marching surface.

Port Arms

Execute "**port,** arms" on the preparatory command "double time" of the command "double time, march." Assume this position only from the *carry saber* position. Swing the right arm naturally across and six inches in front of the body. **Cant** the saber 45 degrees from the vertical with the guard pointed to the left. The left hand grasps the scabbard (see Figure 5.8.11).

Exercise extreme caution when double timing with the saber in the *port arms* position. To end the double-time cadence, command "quick time, march," and return the saber to the *carry* position.

Conclusion

Saber drill distinguishes the key positions within a formation, enhances the leadership status of the saber bearer, and increases the showmanship of drill. It is important to correctly drill with the saber since poor or inexact execution is particularly obvious at ceremonies.

Figure 5.8.11: Port arms.
Courtesy of US Army JROTC.

This lesson concludes the chapter, "Leading Others." At any time, refer back to these lessons if you need a refresher about platoon drills, company formations and movements, and more.

Lesson Review

1. Describe the correct movements to "draw saber."

2. What are the correct movements to "present arms?"

3. What are the correct movements to "return saber?"

4. What is the correct position to carry a saber while marching?

Leadership Principles

Lesson 1

Power Bases and Influence

Key Terms

coercive power
defensive
developmental
expert power
legitimate power
referent power
relinquishing
reward power

What You Will Learn to Do

- Outline a personal plan to build strong relationships with team members

Linked Core Abilities

- Take responsibility for your actions and choices
- Apply critical thinking techniques

Skills and Knowledge You Will Gain Along the Way

- List the different types of power and influence
- Describe the appropriate application of power and influence
- Discuss how individual and system power can be used to increase performance
- Define the key words contained in this lesson

Introduction

Leaders can often experience tremendous confusion as they exercise power and influence. If they provide too little influence, their followers will drift aimlessly. If they exert too much power, the follower will shut down. In this lesson you learn about the bases of power available to leaders and how to use them effectively. You will also learn about four different approaches to influencing.

Understanding Power and Leadership

Power is the capacity to which you can influence someone else to behave in accordance with what or how you want them to. The amount of power you have is contingent on the level of dependency that person has on you; the greater the dependency, the greater the power. You only have power if you have something that the other person wants. As a high school student living at home, you are highly dependent on your parents for financial support. After you graduate and get a job, the level of dependence significantly decreases.

The two concepts of leadership and power are closely intertwined yet have important differences. Leadership focuses on the attainment of a goal. Power does not need to have a goal, just dependence. Leadership most often refers to a downward influence and power does not. Power is focused on gaining compliance.

Source of Power

A leader can experience confusion and frustration when trying to gauge how and when to exert power (see Figure 6.1.1). Leaders use to draw their power from the fact that they were the "boss." The followers were dependent on the leader for distribution of rewards and punishments; however, you have learned that leading from the position of boss with these controls can yield average performance. To energize followers, leaders must grasp a broader understanding of and relationship to power. Five power bases from which power is yielded include coercive, reward, legitimate, expert and referent.

Coercive power is defined as a power that is yielded by fear—fear that negative results might occur if one does not comply. Fear is generated from the belief that someone might inflict pain, restrict movement or withhold basic needs.

Reward power is seen when people comply with the wishes of another because they may be given something of value in return—there is a positive benefit for doing so.

Legitimate power is given to the person in the position within the hierarchy. Positions of authority can use both coercive and reward power. Most often, because of the position they hold, the followers listen and comply.

Expert power comes from the result of specific expertise, knowledge, or special skills. Those who exert expert power are seen as the expert in the field (such as technology, medicine, politics, and religion) and their advice is sought after and followed.

Figure 6.1.1: Know how and when to exert power and leadership.
Courtesy of US Army JROTC.

Referent power is based on admiration. This power is used often in the advertising world. Tiger Woods is admired by the world and can influence what people buy through his endorsement of the product. The product is purchased in hopes to be seen more like him.

Table 6.1.1 shows examples of the different types of power covered in this lesson.

Understanding Influence

Influence can be thought of as power in action. It is difficult to know how much influence to exert with followers and in tcams. The challenge is to know when and how to exercise more or less influence on the follower or the team. There are four types of influence available to the leader: controlling, relinquishing, developing, and defensive.

<table>
<tr><td colspan="2">Table 6.1.1: Examples of Power</td></tr>
<tr><td>Coercive</td><td>The person yells at others, so you want to avoid making him/her angry.</td></tr>
<tr><td>Reward</td><td>The person gives rewards to people, so you want to trade favors with him/her.</td></tr>
<tr><td>Legitimate</td><td>The person is the supervisor and you are the subordinate; he/she has the right to ask for compliance.</td></tr>
<tr><td>Expert</td><td>The person has the knowledge and experience in the task at hand, so you defer to his/her judgment.</td></tr>
<tr><td>Referent</td><td>You really like this person and search for opportunities to do things for him/her.</td></tr>
</table>

Key Note Term

referent power – a type of power that is used to influence others

Controlling is a one-way approach. It involves exerting pressure, using authority or attempting to persuade someone into doing something the way you feel it should be done.

It is best to use this approach when you have all or most of the facts, experience, or knowledge related to the problem at hand; there is an emergency situation or speed is important; the resistance to a course of action is low; and/or the need to develop collective commitment and understanding is low.

Even if you have all the facts, unless others recognize your expertise (expert power) they will resist the controlling approach. There are a few situations where any one person has all the facts or knowledge related to the problem. None of us is as smart as all of us. And finally, this method is less effective when there are expectations of employee involvement.

Relinquishing is also a one-way approach and it involves giving up influence and reducing one's contribution or role in the situation. The leader may accommodate or comply with the wishes of others. This one-way approach puts others in the influencing position.

It is best to use this approach when the team has most of the facts and experience related to the problem, the problem is highly personal and not work-related, and/or the team is highly motivated and can learn from the experience.

Be careful that you are not using the relinquishing approach to avoid "rocking the boat." Sometimes discussions are hard and people are not always happy. Don't use this approach to avoid dealing with the issue. If you have been controlling and feel the need for change, don't run all the way to this point to compensate for previous behavior.

The **developmental** approach is a two-way or mutual approach. It involves sharing opinions or facts. This approach is used most often when there is a need for consensus.

This approach is best used when the individuals involved do not have all the experience and knowledge about the situation, collective commitment is important, there is resistance or a difference of opinion, and/or new ideas are needed.

A word of caution. The developmental approach takes more time and energy on the part of everyone. Some may feel this is a rather soft approach and may be uncomfortable with it. It is important that you have strong communication and listening skills.

The **defensive** approach occurs when the person withdraws from the situation. This withdrawal is visible by someone leaving the room or invisible by tuning people out. The person in this behavior cannot be influenced or influence others.

This approach is best used when there is insufficient information to explore the issue any further, and/or there is a legal, moral, or ethical consideration that prevents discussion of the issue. But patience is important here. Don't continue to push and if withdrawal occurs; be willing to come back at another time to better understanding of the situation.

Different situations require you to select the appropriate approach; used appropriately, each approach can be effective. Effective two-way communications and a win-win attitude about conflict are key ingredients to the developmental approach and most often the benefits of the developmental approach outweigh the others. In the developmental approach process there is a great amount of give-and-take of information, ideas, and opinions between the leader and the follower or the team. If disagreement exists, instead of saying you don't agree, explore the reasons behind the idea. You could ask "Why do you think that is important? What would happen if we did that?" The assumption that one person is right or wrong is set aside and all ideas are considered. There is a desire to hear what is being said. Clearly this is not the type of influence you are most likely familiar with. You might be more used to the controlling (being told what to do) or the relinquishing (withdrawing from the discussion). You might also be used to how those two approaches feel to you; after you experience the developmental approach as either the leader or the follower, you will want to lead or follow that path again.

As a leader in an organization you will often feel caught between the needs of your organization and the needs of your team because the two are not always the same (see Figure 6.1.2). The beginning of this lesson defined power as "the capacity to influence people," and you learned about where power comes from and different approaches to influencing others. You can broaden this definition and its application. An expanded definition of power can be "the capacity to influence the larger system to survive and adapt." It is important that you know how to use the power and influence you have in your organizational role as well as the role of team/unit leader. You will have information from different parts of the organization and can see the total picture more clearly than either the team or the organization. It is your responsibility to facilitate integration of both viewpoints.

Leaders can serve an integrating function by moving back and forth between working with their teams and working with other team leaders in the organization. When you are with your team you are working independently from other team leaders. You will use your influencing skills within your team. You will focus on what is working, what the team needs, and what difficulties the team is

Figure 6.1.2: Use your influence when necessary.
Courtesy of US Army JROTC.

experiencing. When you are meeting with other team leaders, however, there is a sharing of what they have heard while working with their own teams.

The potential knowledge pool for team leaders is substantial. Team leaders create a forum for sharing information with each other and effecting the organization as a whole. Often this is known as gaining "critical mass."

Conclusion

In this lesson you learned about the bases of power available to leaders and how to use them effectively. You also learned about four different approaches to influencing people.

In the next lesson, you will learn about the different styles of leadership, and which one might be right for you.

Lesson Review

1. List and give brief explanations of the five power bases.
2. Compare and contrast relinquishing and developing influence.
3. What is the difference between leadership and power?
4. What is the main downside to controlling influence?

Styles of Leadership

Key Terms

directing
delegating
leadership style
participating

What You Will Learn to Do

- **Assess personal leadership style**

Linked Core Abilities

- **Take responsibility for your actions and choices**
- **Apply critical thinking techniques**

Skills and Knowledge You Will Gain Along the Way

- **Describe different styles of leadership**
- **Explain which leadership styles are best suited for different situations**
- **Identify ways to improve management skills**
- **Define the key words contained in this lesson**

Chapter 6

Introduction

Key Note Terms

directing – a leadership style where the leader tells team members what to do and how to do it

participating – a leadership style where the leader consults with, obtains advice from, or asks the opinions of one or more followers before making a decision

delegating – a leadership style where the leader delegates problem-solving and decision-making authority to a teammate or to a group of followers

leadership style – patterns of behavior that a leader uses to influence a team or group of followers

To command respect and obedience as a leader, you must be prepared to lead. Because your actions and attitudes set the example for others to follow, you must also be ready for any type of situation that may occur. Therefore, how you lead—or your style of leadership—can mean the difference between success or failure of a mission. This lesson introduces you to three basic leadership styles: **directing**, **participating**, and **delegating**. You will have the opportunity to develop a style that works for you as you progress in rank in Army JROTC.

Leadership Styles

Leadership styles are the pattern of behaviors that one uses to influence others. You can influence others in many different ways. Those patterns will be perceived by others as your **leadership style**.

It's important to understand the differences between autocratic and democratic styles of leadership as well as sources of leadership behavior. Autocratic leaders use positional power and direct authority to influence others; democratic leaders use personal power and involve their followers in the decision-making and problem-solving processes. You can use a continuum with autocratic on one end and democratic on the other to learn if your style is either one or the other. When the historical perspective of leadership was discussed in the lesson, "Leadership Reshuffled," you learned that leadership styles did not have to be an either/or set of behaviors. In fact you learned that the situation the leader was faced with affected his/her choice of behaviors.

Think of your classmates who are leaders: the student body president, the cadet battalion commander, and group project leaders (see Figure 6.2.1). These individu-

Figure 6.2.1: Your student body president is just one of many leaders in your school.
Courtesy of Tom Stewart/ Corbis Images.

als have certain responsibilities so they can accomplish their goals. The manner in which they carry out those responsibilities and the way they interact with others is their style of leadership. The three basic leadership styles are directing, participating, and delegating.

Directing Style

Leaders use the directing leadership style when they tell their team members what they want done and how, when, and where they want it done, without getting others' advice or ideas (see Figure 6.2.2). They then supervise closely to ensure team members follow their directions precisely.

This style is clearly appropriate when

- **Time to complete the mission is short and only you know what needs to be done and how to do it**
- **You must lead people who lack experience at a certain task and you must direct their behavior**

Normally, most people will not resent this close supervision because you will be giving them exactly what they need and want.

> **Note**
>
> Sometimes people think that leaders are using the directing style when they yell, scream, threaten, or intimidate followers. This is not a directing style; it is simply an abusive, unprofessional way to treat people. Do not confuse emotion or anger with styles of leadership.

Figure 6.2.2: Use the directing style of leadership when your team needs to know what to do.
Courtesy of Tom Stewart/ Corbis Images.

Case 1

Marla knows exactly what her position is all about. She gets excited whenever an instructor assigns her a project because she knows that she can get it done. Sometimes, she even suggests projects to her instructor. Based on her ideas, the instructor usually assigns them to her and her team.

Marla is highly motivated and has very structured work habits. She likes to map out a project in which everything is her decision. She then tells her team members how to do each step of their tasks according to her direction. She watches everything that her team members do, and if they appear to be doing a task differently from her plan, she criticizes them.

Marla got upset once when a teammate was caught stealing. At first, she was afraid to talk to that person about the incident, and she did not know what to say to her peers who had also heard about it. Finally, after asking herself how she would like to be treated if she were the one involved, she called a team meeting.

At the meeting, Marla informed everyone that all team members make mistakes, not only as a team but also as individuals. She hoped that if they ever had any problems, they would turn to her and/or to another team member for help. They agreed.

Participating Style

Leaders use the participating style when they consult with, obtain advice from, or ask the opinions of one or more followers before making a decision. Although leaders may ask for such information or recommendations (see Figure 6.2.3), they are still the ones who make, and are responsible for, the final decision.

This style is appropriate for leadership situations when those whom you are leading are fairly competent and support your goals. Allowing them to participate can be a powerful team-building process. It will increase confidence and support if everyone has a part in developing the final plan.

Do not think that obtaining good advice from a teammate or using another member's plan or idea is a sign of weakness on your part. It is a sign of strength that your

Figure 6.2.3: The participating style is used when you get input from other team members.
Courtesy of Jose Luis Pelaez, Inc./Corbis Images.

followers will respect; however, you are responsible for the quality of your plans and decisions. If you believe that your follower's idea is not a good one, you must reject it and do what you believe is right, regardless of pressure to do otherwise.

Delegating Style

The delegating style is the most efficient. It requires the least amount of your time and energy to interact, direct, and communicate with your team members. Leaders use the delegating style when they delegate problem-solving and decision-making authority to a teammate or to a group of followers (see Figure 6.2.4).

This style is appropriate when

- **Dealing with mature followers who support your goals and are competent and motivated to perform the task delegated**

Figure 6.2.4: You can delegate authority to responsible team members.
Courtesy of Charles Gupton/Corbis Images.

- **Certain key members of your team are able to analyze a problem or situation, determine what needs to be done, and do it**

Remember, you are still responsible for the results of their actions and decisions.

> ### Case 3
>
> Brian is an easygoing person. He wants to complete projects with plenty of time left so that he and his friends on the team can relax. After he assigns tasks to each of his team members, he lets them figure out the best way to complete the tasks—without giving them any help, direction, or supervision. Plus, he rarely makes any decisions.
>
> Then, when the time comes to complete the project, he still turns it in even though parts of it are not finished. When the final grade comes back, his group makes the lowest mark in the class, prompting an instructor to ask, "Why wasn't your project done?"
>
> Brian passes the blame on to his team members by saying, "They didn't complete their parts as they should have. I don't believe that I should have to be responsible for or receive a bad grade because of their sloppy efforts."
>
> When the other team members find out their grades, they approach Brian: "Why didn't you tell us everything that we were supposed to do? We could have worked harder and done it better if we had just known."

Keep in mind that no one style is superior to another one. What works in one situation may not work in another. You must develop the flexibility to use all three styles and the judgment to choose the style that best meets the situation and the needs of your team. In fact, you may want to use all three styles or different styles as the need arises:

- **With different followers or in different situations**
- **When you receive a new project, you receive new personnel, or your supervisor changes**
- **If the competence, motivation, or commitment of your team changes**

Do not fall into the trap of believing that there are some leadership techniques that must always work. You must evaluate every situation carefully when choosing the right style. Keep in mind that the best strategy in one situation may be inappropriate in another.

Situational Leadership Model

Ken Blanchard and his colleagues built on existing research and continued discussions with successful leaders on how the follower affected leadership behaviors. They developed the Situational Leadership Model from their research. This model identifies four leadership styles (sets of behaviors) and four developmental levels of the followers and the relationship between the two.

> To learn more about Ken Blanchard, his background, his books, and his company, go to www.kenblanchard.com.

The leadership styles in this model are based on the leader providing either directive or supportive behaviors.

Directive behavior is defined as how much structure, control, and supervision the leader provides to the follower.

Supportive behavior is defined as how much praise, listening, and facilitating the leader provides to the follower.

These styles also vary in three ways: the amount of direction given; the amount of encouragement and support provided; and the amount of involvement the follower has in decision making.

The four styles are known as follows:

Style 1	Directing
Style 2	Coaching
Style 3	Supporting
Style 4	Delegating

They are similar to the three styles discussed earlier in this lesson.

The behaviors that are present when using style 1 will be more directive and less supportive. The follower will be told what, how, when, and where to do the task. There is little to no involvement from the follower in decision making. Communication is one-way.

The behaviors present when using style 2 will be providing equal amounts of directive and supportive behaviors. Here, the leader will provide lots of direction but will ask the follower for ideas and suggestions. A more two-way communication style exists; however, the leader is still in control of the decisions.

Style 3 behaviors are high supportive and low directive. While using this style the leader allows the follower to take control of the day to day decisions. The leader's job is to listen and facilitate the problem-solving process. The decision-making process begins to shift from the leader to the follower.

Style 4 requires low supportive and directive behaviors. Here the leader behaviors change to allowing the follower to make the decisions on how to solve an agreed on situation or task.

You learned earlier in this lesson that there is no one best way to lead. The most effective leader matches his/her behaviors to the situation and the follower. The amount of decision making and involvement the leader allows the follower depends on the situation or the task (have they ever been in this situation before or done this task before) and the level of confidence and competence (how sure of and how skilled in performing the task) the follower possesses.

Now that you know the four leadership styles and the pattern of behaviors in each, turn to the four developmental levels of the followers. These levels are based on the competence (the level of knowledge to do the task) and commitment (a combination of confidence and motivation).

The development level of the follower is based on his/her level of competence and confidence. There are four developmental levels:

Level 1	low
Level 2	low to moderate
Level 3	moderate to high
Level 4	high

Level 1 exists when the follower has a high level of commitment (very motivated and confident) with a low level of competence (knowledge of how the task is to be done). An example of this situation can be your first day of drill in the *Leadership Lab*. You were probably excited and motivated to perform as a platoon leader or sergeant. You did not know how to perform this task, but you were committed to making it happen. It required your leader to give you exact directions on how to do the task. You listened and did what you were told so you could learn the routines. The leader matched his style of leadership to your development level.

Level 2 happens after you have been given direction and you have practiced enough to feel competent to perform the task. Your level of commitment to practice begins to drop. You are getting somewhat bored with the repetition of drill. This level is described with having low commitment and some competence. The leadership style now needs to change from directing to coaching. Letting you get involved in the process and asking for ideas, suggestions, or shared leadership will be more effective at this time. The focus here is to keep your confidence on the rise while recharging your commitment. You are not ready to take charge yet and the leader recognizes you still need direction and practice to be able to perform outstandingly.

Level 3 occurs when you have high competence (the ability to perform well) but your commitment level is not consistent. The supporting leadership style is more appropriate now. It is time to get you involved in making the task happen and shifting the responsibility from the leader to the follower. Again, the follower can perform the task, but for some reason is not highly committed to making it happen. The focus is to keep the performance high *and* consistent.

Level 4 is when the follower is highly committed and highly competent in performing the task. The follower not only knows how to perform the task well, but *wants* to perform the task well. The leader will focus on recognizing the performance.

As you progress through the JROTC program, you will be asked to take a leadership role in the *Leadership Lab* where you can practice the directing, coaching, supporting and delegating role with new cadets. You will also be involved in service community projects that will allow you to practice the leadership styles. These assignments will be made based on *your* performance and developmental level. You will be very competent at drilling tasks; however, this may be the first time you will experience a leadership role. You will be energetic and motivated because you know how to drill; however, the task of leading others in drill is new to you and you will need direction from your instructor so you can build your competence and commitment through the process. As you become better skilled in matching leadership style to developmental level, your instructor will begin to coach, support, and finally delegate the role of leadership to you.

In a leadership position you must assess your team's capability to perform its mission, and then develop a plan that accomplishes it. You should use the style that your experience tells you is most appropriate after you have assessed the team's level of competence, motivation, and commitment to accomplish its mission.

A good rule of thumb to follow is to be flexible in your thinking. Approach each leadership situation as an opportunity to improve your leadership potential, ability, and style.

Conclusion

As you have learned, leadership styles are the pattern of behaviors that one uses to influence others. You now know that you can influence others in many different ways. Those patterns are perceived by others as your leadership style.

The next lesson discusses management skills. You will learn the five principles of management and will compare management and leadership styles.

Lesson Review

1. **Compare and contrast the directing, participating, and delegating styles of leadership.**
2. **Which directing style do you feel best suits you as a leader? Why?**
3. **List the four styles of the situational leadership model.**
4. **Choose two developmental levels of followers and explain them.**

Management Skills

Key Terms

management
mandatory
procrastinate
resources
visualize

What You Will Learn to Do

- Assess personal management skills

Linked Core Abilities

- Take responsibility for your actions and choices
- Apply critical thinking techniques

Skills and Knowledge You Will Gain Along the Way

- Identify five management principles
- Compare management skills and leadership skills
- Define the key words contained in this lesson

Introduction

Good **management** is an essential tool of leaders in the performance of their duties and responsibilities. The skillful execution of basic management principles by leaders is seldom an accident. It is normally the result of clear purpose, earnest effort, and intelligent direction. This lesson defines management, introduces you to five basic management principles (planning, organizing, coordinating, directing, and controlling), and compares management to leadership.

Good management is also the sound use of the available means (or **resources**) to accomplish a task. It requires careful planning by a leader to employ those resources to achieve the desired results. Because it is rare that leaders will have everything they need or want, they must strive to succeed with what they have. As you will see, the principles of management have broad application to many leadership situations.

Management Defined

Management is the process of planning, organizing, coordinating, directing, and controlling resources such as people, material, time, and money to accomplish a mission; however, the presence of these resources does not guarantee success or mission accomplishment. How well the leader uses these resources is much more important than the fact that the resources are available.

Of all the resources available to the leader, people are the most important. Because leaders must use people to coordinate time, material, and money, this resource is the foundation for the use of the other three. Leaders can control and/or influence this vital resource by properly applying techniques such as the principles and factors of leadership.

We can divide the five management principles into two stages: preparation and execution. During the preparation stage, a leader must plan, organize, and coordinate. During the execution stage, a leader must direct and control. The execution stage cannot begin until after the leader has made plans, developed the necessary organization to accomplish those plans, and completed all required coordination.

Planning

Planning is the basis for the problem-solving and decision-making processes; what goes on in planning affects what is done in those two processes. Leaders spend many hours in planning the activities of their organization. They must consider what the objectives are and how they are going to accomplish them.

When planning, leaders must **visualize**, examine, consider, realize, and reflect on the factors involved in accomplishing the mission. Planning is not an easy process as it requires a lot of work. To help, there are four basic steps to planning.

- **Define the objective. In this step, leaders begin to determine the tasks and conditions that are necessary to complete the objective. Timing is very important. Leaders must ensure that their team members can do all tasks within the specified time frame.**

- Study the situation.
- List and examine possible courses of action the leader could take.
- Select the course of action that will achieve the objective.

Additionally, there are four factors that leaders must consider when using the planning process to make and implement plans.

- **Time.** Leaders must consider time as they plan events, meet deadlines, and set goals; then they make plans and execute tasks according to an established time schedule. Effective leaders will schedule their time and the activities of their team to meet these events, deadlines, and goals.
- **Effort.** Leaders must exert effort to get things done. You cannot expect results if you do not work at putting your plan into action. Successful leaders are energetic. They work hard to accomplish goals; you should exercise that same type of effort.
- **Patience.** Patience is an ingredient that all leaders must possess. It is hard to be patient when challenges occur. To solve a difficult situation, you should reexamine the facts, coordinate with people who may be helpful, and readjust the plan, if necessary. Most important, do not give up. Exercise patience and maturity while the designated people carry out the plan.
- **Objective attitude.** An objective attitude is the ability to see and consider the different sides of an issue or situation. It involves being flexible, listening to opposing points of view, making compromises, or making changes when necessary. Your objective attitude determines how much time, effort, and patience you are willing to exert to ensure mission accomplishment.

Finally, leaders must plan or estimate approximately how many people (or man-hours) they will need to accomplish the objective. Before selecting these people or defining specific tasks, leaders must consider the requirements of the objective against the capabilities of their team members.

Organizing

Organizing is the process of creating the conditions necessary to effectively execute your plans. It involves systematically defining the tasks and arranging the resources with respect to the achievement of your objective. There are five factors involved in organizing:

- **Determine/fine-tune each task.** Identify all the tasks and subtasks that the team must do to accomplish the objective. Be specific. Develop detailed lists to record them and set measurable standards for each task/subtask.
- **Select personnel.** After you have a detailed list of tasks and subtasks, assign people to them. You should base your assignments on what each task/subtask requires versus the capabilities of your team members.
- **Develop a working structure.** With a detailed list of tasks completed and people assigned to do them, you are ready to organize the list sequentially. Determine which tasks your team must do first, second, and so on until you have included everything necessary to carry out the plan. The next step, setting priorities, goes hand-in-hand with this step. You and your teammates cannot do everything at once.

- **Set priorities.** Because some tasks are more important than others or you must start them before others because of their degree of difficulty, organize a to-do list in terms of priority for every task and subtask you have identified. Establish priorities in categories such as priority A, priority B, priority C, and so on, for each item on the to-do list. Do the A priorities first, then the Bs, the Cs, and so on.

  Allow sufficient time for each team member to do the job well. Not planning sufficient time for each task could result in the work being half-done or done "slipshod." Finally, you should develop a system for checking each other and ensuring that team members accomplish their tasks according to set standards and on time.

  A common fault among many people is that of spending too much time on tasks that are unimportant. Another fault is the tendency to **procrastinate**, or to put off those things that need to be done. When studying for an exam or doing a project, do you find yourself putting it off until the last minute? Then you have to rush just to get the material studied or the project finished. Know what is **mandatory** and what is not when setting priorities and organizing your time.

- **Allocate resources.** In the final step of your organizing process, you must ensure that you have identified all required resources necessary for completing the objective, set aside all available resources, and planned for obtaining those that are not available.

Key Note Terms

procrastinate – to put off or delay

mandatory – something that absolutely must be done

Coordinating

Coordination is the active process of establishing contact and then keeping in constant touch with everyone involved to ensure the successful accomplishment of the objective (see Figure 6.3.1). Coordination is an essential part of the planning process. Plans that are not properly coordinated cannot be properly executed, directed, or controlled.

A good rule of thumb to follow is to coordinate with everyone you think might be involved somehow or at some point in completing the objective. Through coordination, leaders secure the cooperation of people not under their direct control. A key to effective coordination is the use of friendly persuasion and mutual cooperation.

Figure 6.3.1: Keep in contact with team members to ensure the objectives are being accomplished.
Courtesy of US Army JROTC.

Directing

Directing is the active process by which a leader issues instructions to achieve a predetermined objective. The leader uses two common methods of directing: written or spoken. Be sure to include all the necessary details and information in your directions. In an office situation, many supervisors may decide to direct through the written word by passing out memos. After you have told everyone by written or spoken directions what is expected of them, you must supervise to ensure that they go by the rules you have laid down. There are four basic types of directing that leaders use.

- **Demand.** A straightforward statement telling what must be done, who must do it, and when it must be done. For example, you tell cadets unexcused absences will not be tolerated.

- **Request.** A milder, more tactful approach to reaching the objective. The results usually would be the same if you requested, instead of demanded, specific behavior. In the demand example, you would ask your cadets to please provide reasons for each absence.

- **Suggestion.** This type of directing is used only when a suggestion is strong enough to get the job done. It relies on the manners and good taste of those to whom you make the suggestion. Here the leader suggests what should be done but does not say, when, by whom, or how it should be done. You may suggest to cadets it is preferable to provide an authorized excuse for any absence as soon as possible.

- **Volunteer.** Leaders rarely use this method except when they want to get someone to do something that they cannot require them to do. Because volunteering means to offer assistance, you would ask your cadets who are consistently absent to schedule a counseling session to discuss problems they are having in attending class.

Controlling

Controlling is when leaders compare the tasks that their team members are actually doing to the tasks that they had directed and planned the team to do at any point in the project. Remember, you have direct control over the managerial actions of your teammates.

Then, based on your team's progress, your options may include proceeding with the way the plan is progressing, modifying the plan and continuing on with it, or stopping the action and starting over again. As the leader, it is your responsibility to ensure that the objective is met within the required standards and according to the established deadlines. Controlling is continuous until you complete the task.

Management versus Leadership

Leadership deals with the personal relationship of one person to another. It is the way a leader influences subordinates to accomplish the mission. Management, then, is a set of activities or behaviors performed by those in senior positions to obtain, direct, or allocate resources to accomplish goals and tasks. A good leader will think and plan in a rational manner in order to efficiently utilize the talent and skills of the individuals that make up the team.

How do leadership and management relate? You must realize that although they are separate processes, you will almost never use them separately. At lower levels, you lead through face-to-face dealings with your people. You are still a manager, but higher levels of authority in the chain of command control most of the physical resources.

As leaders get promotions, they control more resources. Instead of just leading a group, they may now be responsible for the overall operation of the organization. For example, if you were the assistant manager at a fast-food restaurant, you would be behind the counter with your kitchen crew making sure they were performing their jobs correctly and in a responsible manner. If you were promoted to manager, you would not have as much face-to-face contact with the kitchen crew. Instead, you would be more concerned with putting together work schedules, hiring, and ordering food supplies and equipment. You would then check with your assistant manager to make sure that the employees were doing their jobs.

Time Management

In the reality of life, time will be one of your most valuable resources. As a leader, you must learn to use time wisely and to your best advantage. You may choose to write down a schedule so you can allocate the proper amount of time for each task you need to do (see Figure 6.3.2).

Most everyone can benefit from time-saving techniques that will make them more efficient managers of time. The following list addresses various time-saving techniques. Keep these techniques in mind and try to incorporate as many of them as you can in your everyday life. By following these tips, you will become a more effective time manager and a better leader.

- **Goal setting is the first and foremost key to success. The key points and the importance of goal setting were covered earlier in this lesson. Try posting notes around your area that will remind you of your goals.**

Figure 6.3.2: Keeping a schedule can help with time management.
Courtesy of Dex Images/ Corbis Images.

- Learn to set priorities. After you set your goals, determine your priorities. Learn to do first things first.

- Identify your attention span and schedule/do work accordingly.

- Thoroughly plan your work. In planning, learn to delegate authority. This will help so that you do not waste time and effort.

- Make use of your spare time.

- Learn to say no to yourself and others.

- Examine old habits that may prevent efficiency.

- Do not strive for absolute perfection.

- Learn to outline.

- Use a desktop or pocket diary.

- Use a file system.

- Set time limits on meetings.

As a leader, you also need to be aware of time wasters. Create an effective time management environment within your team—both you and your team members should learn to avoid these pitfalls. The most common time wasters are as follows:

- Lack of organization

- Lack of priorities

- Lack of delegation

- Unclear objectives

- No plan available and no, or little, time spent planning

- No coordination

- No teamwork

- Procrastination

- Lack of self-discipline

- Lack of feedback

- Interruptions

These management tips will help you to become a leader who is more efficient in managing your time as well as your team.

Conclusion

Becoming a leader means learning to manage your resources—people, money, material, and time—to their fullest extent. You must also continue to search for more effective ways of improving your management techniques. Whether you use the principles of management in your everyday life or as a member of the JROTC program, you must use them to your best advantage.

People with authority have the responsibility of leading and managing. To succeed, they must exercise leadership when dealing with subordinates while at the same time properly managing the resources of their organization.

Next, you will learn about the importance of communication. You will learn about the process of communication, the barriers to that process, the power of emotional intelligence, and the process of exchanging feedback.

Lesson Review

1. What is the most important resource available to a leader? Why?
2. List the five basic principles of management.
3. What are the four basic types of directing?
4. Choose one time-waster and discuss how this affects your life.

Lesson 4

Communication

Key Terms

communication
decodes
emotional intelligence
encodes
feedback
message
transference
transmitted

What You Will Learn to Do

● Adapt communication to give direction and provide feedback to others

Linked Core Abilities

● Communicate using verbal, nonverbal, visual, and written techniques
● Treat self and others with respect

Skills and Knowledge You Will Gain Along the Way

● Discuss how communication is important for effective leadership
● Explain the basic flow and purpose of informal communication
● Review the major elements of a communication model
● Review how to overcome barriers of effective communication
● Define the key words contained in this lesson

Introduction

It's not what you say, but what you do. This statement highlights the philosophy that actions speak louder than words. You are a model for others. They watch what you do and, if they admire you, will imitate your actions. Communicating is sending a message through a process that allows the receiver to understand the message as you intended. Many things affect this process. In this lesson, you will learn about the process of communication and the barriers to that process, the power of emotional intelligence, and the process of exchanging feedback.

The Communication Process

Even though your actions speak louder than the words you use, words still influence others. To be effective, there must be an understanding of what is heard and alignment of actions with what you are saying. Effective communication is important in our lives. It is the number one cause of interpersonal conflict; we spend over 70 percent of our waking hours communicating through some means (writing, reading, listening, speaking).

Communication is defined as the transference and understanding of a meaning. Note the two words **transference** *and* understanding. It is not enough to just send a message. For the communication to be successful, it must be understood. This is no easy task.

First, someone has something they want to say, that is, a **message** to be sent. Then the sender **encodes** this message. That means the sender puts it into some symbolic form to be transmitted. After the message is encoded, it is **transmitted** through some medium. This could be written, spoken, nonverbal gestures or expressions, paper, television, audiotape, and so on. The receiver then **decodes** the message. He/she must put the message in some symbolic form that they understand. Finally, through **feedback**, the sender determines whether the message was received as intended (see Figure 6.4.1).

Sounds easy, doesn't it? Well, it is much more complicated than that, and that is why most communication is not understood and often creates conflict. There are many hidden barriers affecting the process.

For example, the encoding and decoding process is greatly affected by the sender and receiver's skills, attitude, and knowledge. His/her skills in reading, writing, listening, and reasoning influence what is said, how well it is said, and with what meaning it is sent or received. In an earlier lesson, you learned that attitudes can

Key Note Terms

communication – sharing of information

transference – the act of transferring

message – a communication transmitted between persons by written or spoken words, signals, and so on

encodes – converts

transmitted – sent from one person to another

decodes – translates

feedback – verifying that a message was received in the manner it was intended

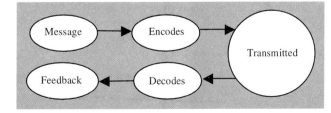

Figure 6.4.1: The communication process.
Courtesy of US Army JROTC.

affect your behavior. When you are communicating, your attitude can affect the tone of your voice, the words you choose to use, and the readiness to listen. Your knowledge about the topic also has an impact on how well you can communicate about the message.

Additional barriers exist. We often filter what we say; we drop things out of the message based on what we think the listener needs to know or wants to know. We choose what to say. We listen selectively; we listen for what we want to hear. We are overloaded with information to the point of not knowing how to organize or use all this information. We might be defensive or apprehensive about the message and not want to hear what is being said. Languages, accents, and jargon affect what we hear and what we think it means. Is it any wonder we have difficulty being understood?

You will be building your skills around communication in speaking and writing techniques in other lessons. One barrier discussed in this lesson is one's emotions and how they interfere in the communication process. This can be done by understanding **emotional intelligence**.

Emotional Intelligence

Emotions are real. They create a need to react in a situation that faces us. When faced with a dangerous situation, the brain quickly tells the rest of your body that something is not right and that it is time to either run away or stand and fight. Emotions cannot be checked at the door and forgotten until the day is over. If you have a disagreement with your parents before school, the emotions around that disagreement are influencing your behavior the rest of the day, possibly the week. They will influence what you hear, what you say, and how you behave. They will become barriers to understanding or sending a message.

People who have a high degree of emotional intelligence have a greater degree of influence. Their behaviors reflect they are aware of what the emotion is that is present, understand why that emotion is there, and are able to separate the emotion and the reaction so they can manage the emotion rather than the emotion managing them.

There are five competencies or skills to managing your emotions: self-awareness, self-regulation, self-motivation, empathy, and effective relationships. These are covered in the following sections.

Self-Awareness

Self-awareness is the ability to feel an emotion and understand where it is coming from. Read the following list. What would you be feeling if you were in the following situations?

- **A slow line at the video store**
- **Making a presentation in class**
- **A surprise birthday party**
- **Being told on Friday that you cannot go to the ballgame on Saturday**
- **A phone call from an old friend**

Different emotions can happen in similar situations. The slow line may not be a problem if you are not in a hurry; however, add to that situation that you have only a few minutes to get home on time or your parents will be grounding you for a week.

Now that you have identified the feeling that is going on inside you in those situations, think about the consequences those feelings might bring. For example, the slow line and your need to be home on time could bring about your making comments to the people in front of you if they are not ready to ring up their purchase. Or it might make you moody and be abrupt with your friends who are waiting in the car for you.

The emotion will drive different actions or consequences. You need to know what the emotion is (fear, frustration, anger, disappointment) and why it exists (what consequences the situation might bring, therefore how you might react to the emotion).

Self-Regulation

Self-regulation is the ability to control that emotion. Do not ignore or push aside the emotion, rather recognize it and deal with it effectively. Take a pause between the emotion and your reaction to it. And more important, identify what you are telling yourself at that time—self-talk.

What you tell yourself goes immediately to your subconscious where it increases or decreases your anger or other emotions. Repeated negative self-talk leads to exaggerated and irrational thinking. Have you ever said these things to yourself?

- **They always take me for granted**
- **I'm always late**
- **No one ever helps me**
- **No one ever listens to me**
- **It will always be this way**
- **Everything I do is wrong**
- **I never get a passing grade**

Now think about why you say those things to yourself. For example, if you are always late, why are you late? Are you only late at certain times? Be more specific about your being late. After you have identified why you say those things to yourself, you can begin to identify the emotions around the reasons you are late. It could be that you are not getting to bed early enough to get a good night's sleep. It could be that you are not prepared for that class. It could be that you don't like that particular teacher. Whatever the reason, after you have identified it, you can change the self-talk from "I'm always late" to "I am late because I do not get enough sleep." The next question would be "Why don't I get enough sleep?" "Must be because I don't start my homework until after dinner." "What can I do to start my homework earlier so I can get a good night's sleep?" You see, a series of questions can get to the root of the problem, which is driving negative self-talk and negative behaviors.

Self-Motivation

Self-motivation is the ability to change the way you think about things to get them done. There are things about our lives, school, family, and community that we don't enjoy doing. But they must be done. Learning to connect to those things in a positive way is a big part of emotional intelligence. Can you identify a few things about school that make you feel uncomfortable or bored? Now answer the next two questions: Why are these things important? How might you think about these things differently so that you can take greater satisfaction in them?

Empathy

Empathy is the ability to share your feelings with others more openly so they will open up and trust you, improving communication overall. Think of someone you are close to. Someone you tell everything to. Do you trust that person? Do they trust you? Then think of someone you tell very little to. What is your trust level with them? Each relationship will build a different trust level; however, it begins with you. The greater the trust, the more open the communication. The more open the communication, the greater the trust. Kind of like the story, Which came first, the chicken or the egg?

The four levels of communication are shown in Table 6.4.1.

With some people, you never get past the first two levels. To open the trust and communication you will want to reach the fourth level.

Effective Relationships

Effective relationships are about what occurs from your ability to be self-aware, to self-regulate, to self-motivate, and to create empathy with others. It creates an enthusiasm, which is contagious. It is about finding those things you love about what you are doing and creating such an energy level around those things that dealing with those things you don't like can be easier. Earlier we thought about things you did not like about school. Now think about things you like best in school. What makes those things so appealing?

The communication process of sending and receiving a message is successful when the message is understood. Many barriers exist that get in the way of our message being understood. Your behaviors speak louder than your words. Your overall communication is increased by your ability to engage in your emotions, rather than keeping them at bay. Emotional Intelligence allows you to become aware of

Table 6.4.1: The Four Levels of Communication	
Superficial	"Hi! How you doing?"
Fact	"It is raining."
Thought	"I think you are good at that."
Feeling	"I feel you don't care about your homework."

emotions, regulate their consequences, find ways to motivate ourselves to complete tasks we may not like to do, feel empathy with others, and build effective relationships—all increasing the likelihood that the message sent is the message received.

Exchanging Feedback

Although feedback is seen as the final loop back to the sender, it is present throughout the process. How and when to give feedback is important to the process. Having a high degree of emotional intelligence increases the effectiveness of providing and receiving feedback.

Feedback is something you give as well as receive. Whether the gift is welcome or not depends on knowing when and how to share your reflections so that others accept, value, and seek out your point of view. When you give feedback in a caring and skillful way, you open a window on the world.

In the give-and-take of effective feedback, you need the skills to create a zone of safety in which honest and constructive information can be exchanged. Those who are people-smart are adept at inviting others to give them constructive feedback. They are also talented at getting invited by others to give feedback. They are able to give feedback that is constructive and enlightening.

You might have had bad experiences with feedback. Perhaps you were on the receiving end of too much criticism from people in authority (parents, teachers, supervisors) or felt put down by peers when most vulnerable. However, you can structure the feedback process in ways that create a sense of safety for yourself and for others.

To receive feedback, you need to let others know that you want it; that you are receptive to hearing both the positive and negative story. To avoid being overburdened by too much feedback, you need to be specific in your request for feedback. Specify why you want the feedback, what areas you want feedback in, and how much feedback you want. The following is one example of how to ask for feedback.

> "Sarah, the more I'm learning about leadership, the more I'm coming to understand that receiving feedback is important to making me a better leader specifically, listening to others ideas. I really want to make a difference in our unit and I want to understand how my behavior affects the team. I'd like you to help me with this by sharing your honest opinions with me. Would you be willing to do that?

> "You can help me today by answering two questions. What are some things I do that make it easier for you to convey your ideas, and what is one thing I could do differently?"

Compare the previous request for feedback to this one:

> "Sarah, the team leader told me I needed to get some feedback from others about my listening skills. I listen to others, don't I?"

Getting feedback from only one source could lead you down the wrong corrective road. Getting the feedback and agreeing with it are two separate things. That is why you want to broaden your circle of feedback sources. Your Success Profiler is a good tool to use to receive feedback from any sources around the same questions. Also, posing the same questions to a number of people can validate what you are told. If most of the people you ask have similar input, you can assume there is some validity in their comments, even if you are uncomfortable with it.

If you are not ready to receive feedback (or if someone else is not ready to receive your feedback) you will most likely deny, discount, or defend yourself instead of listening to it. To be invited to give feedback entails four key behaviors. You need to

- **Ask for permission**
- **Share rather than insist**
- **Time your input**
- **Check others' perceptions**

By asking permission to share feedback, you can set the stage for your input and assess the recipient's readiness to listen. Some ways to seek permission might be:

- **Is this a good time for you to hear some feedback about . . .**
- **Would you be open to hearing some input about . . .**
- **I have some input on how you handled . . . Would you like to hear them?**
- **May I share some reactions with you about . . .**

Finding the right time and the right level of receptivity will enhance the likelihood the feedback will be heard. That is the same for you as the receiver. If it is not a good time for you to receive feedback, let them know that and agree to a better time and place.

Share your feedback in a form of a hypothesis rather than to insist that it is a fact. There might be a reason behind the behavior you were not aware of. By not insisting you are right, you help your recipient trust you and feel safe. The following is an example:

> Sarah has accepted your offer to share some feedback about her presentation to the class. You had noticed that Sarah was speaking very fast and seemed to be cramming in too much information into the presentation. You ask: "I was wondering if you felt pressured to cover every aspect of the topic in your presentation?" When Sarah agrees that this was the case, you ask: "If you could only address three main points, what would they be? Why?"

The timing of the feedback is essential to it being heard. Feedback is most effective when it is immediate. Old stuff is not relevant. Memories fade quickly. Whenever possible go for an instant replay while the behavior in question is fresh; however, being sensitive to the circumstances is important as well. Providing feedback in public can be embarrassing. Think through the impact that the time and setting will have so you can reduce distractions and increase the usefulness of your input.

Checking the recipient's perceptions about your feedback is a final closing point to the feedback process. Ask them how they felt about what you said: was there agreement or disagreement, was your input helpful or confusing, and/or does the person need more information? Use effective listening skills such as paying attention to people's words and body language and asking for clarification of their reactions.

If there has been miscommunication or feelings have been hurt, often clarification can help the situation.

Feedback is most useful if it is constructive, concise, and specific. People are more open to positive feedback than negative. If you can tell them what they are doing right, they will most likely listen and repeat the behavior in the future. Informative feedback includes specific behaviors, is limited, and provides suggestions.

Global statements are not correctable. Specific behaviors are correctable. Compare the following two statements:

Global. You have an attitude problem.

Specific. You sounded rather impatient at the team meeting today.

Behaviors can lead to some conclusions about personal values that can be misinterpreted. Be sure you avoid being personal and dig deep to find the behavior that needs to be challenged. Look at the following examples:

Personal. You are sloppy and disorganized.

Behavior. There is a lot of clutter in your locker. How do you find what you need?

Personal. You are lazy.

Behavior. You often procrastinate, don't finish the task, and return late from breaks. Why do you think you do this?

Personal. You are well organized.

Behavior. You are consistent in your prioritizing of assignments, setting deadlines, and keeping materials readily available.

In each of these examples, the specific behaviors convey more information than the personal statements. People can hear the message more easily, can see the behaviors you are speaking about, and are not confronted with labels that provide no direction, either good or bad.

Have you ever been confronted with a list of things you do wrong? You might start off with a high degree of listening, but after a while it gets difficult. Keep your feedback focused on the main point.

Show your concern for the recipient's growth by suggesting ways to build on strengths and overcome deficits. Your suggestions should be specific, realistic, positive, and tactful. For example,

"You often interrupt when others are speaking. When you do that to me, it makes me feel you do not value what I have to say. I think you would be a more effective team member if you practiced better listening skills. Would you be willing to work on this during the next team meeting? When you feel yourself ready to speak before the other person is finished, could you take a deep breath and hear them out? If you would like, I can sit next to you and if you begin to interrupt someone, I can gently tap your arm so you are aware of your behavior."

When you follow up on your feedback, the recipient feels you care. In the example you just read, you could continue the feedback process after the team meeting by asking:

"I saw you really working at this today. You caught yourself the first time and stopped, apologized, and took a deep breath. When I tapped your arm, you were able to sit back in your seat and let the team talk through the problem. By the end of the meeting you seemed much more comfortable in waiting your turn to speak. You also did a great job summarizing what others had said. How did it feel to you when you were able to stop yourself and let the others finish? Was it helpful to have me tap your arm? What would you like to do next?"

If you were not at the meeting, you could follow up by asking:

"How did the meeting go? Were you able to practice your deep breathing? How did that work for you? What do you think you need to do next?"

Feedback is an important part of the communication process. Emotional intelligence is an important part of feedback. Being able to manage your emotions and to give and receive informative feedback reduces many of the barriers to effective communication.

Conclusion

Communication skills take practice, but when you understand the basics and use these skills often, you can present your message in an understandable manner and get/receive feedback in a positive way.

The next lesson discusses motivation. You will learn the 14 principles of motivation and see how individual performance within a group is influenced by expectations, ability, and motivation.

Lesson Review

1. Describe the communication process.
2. List the five competencies for managing your emotions. Do you have one at which you excel? Which one and why?
3. Why is it important to exchange feedback?
4. Define the term *emotional intelligence.*

Lesson 5

Motivation

Key Terms

alleviate
complement
intangible
prejudicial

What You Will Learn to Do

- Employ motivation strategies that inspire others to achieve goals

Linked Core Abilities

- Take responsibility for your actions and choices
- Treat self and others with respect

Skills and Knowledge You Will Gain Along the Way

- Identify how individual performance within a group is influenced by expectations, ability, and motivation
- Explain the 14 principles of motivation
- Define the key words contained in this lesson

Chapter 6

Introduction

Leaders spend a great deal of time and effort studying the technical aspects of their jobs; however, to lead effectively, they must also know what makes people tick. By studying human behavior, leaders learn why people act and react in certain ways. Plus, leaders who care about their subordinates and are attentive to their needs are more able to influence them in accomplishing unit goals. This lesson identifies those basic needs, and it explains how they can be satisfied.

Studying human behavior helps leaders acquire the knowledge they need to better understand themselves and those they lead.

It is important that leaders learn why human beings act and react in certain ways and to identify various types of behavior. They also must learn how to influence the behavior of subordinates so that their personal goals **complement** or reinforce the goals of management.

Key Note Term

complement –
complete

Leaders' Concern for Group Needs

Leaders must provide purpose and goals for the group. By selecting the best course of action to reach a goal, they provide purpose. By explaining the reasoning behind decisions and demonstrating their own enthusiasm for the task, they provide direction and assistance in accomplishing the goal (see Figure 6.5.1). This direction should also include information on the required standards of performance.

Leaders must realize that, although they are recognized as leaders because of their position, they will not be accepted until they earn the respect and confidence of the group by satisfying its needs. Successful leaders, therefore, must be more concerned with the well-being of their people than they are with themselves. They must go out of their way to give time, energy, and counsel to help their subordi-

Figure 6.5.1: Explain the reason behind a decision to help keep followers motivated.
Courtesy of US Army JROTC.

nates live up to their potential. By constantly showing this level of concern to their subordinates, these leaders receive a high degree of respect and loyalty from their subordinates along with their desire to accomplish team goals.

> **Note**
>
> Unselfish leaders avoid providing for their own comfort and personal advancement at the expense of others. Leaders should place the comfort, pleasure, and recreation of subordinates before that of their own. It is difficult to respect leaders who seek their own comfort over that of their subordinates or who hoard credit for achievement made possible by subordinates. True leaders place themselves last in priority and share the dangers and hardships with their subordinates.

Motivating by Satisfying Needs

Needs form the basis for actions. They motivate people to behave in certain ways and to do certain things. Consequently, motivation is a total process that is determined by the interaction of human needs, the situation, and the combination of personal and group needs. The leader's part within this interaction includes the following:

- **Thoroughly understand human needs and stay directed toward satisfying them. Keep a broad point of view on human nature and motivation. Do not hold to a narrow view that people are motivated only by fear or believe the opposite, that people are all good and will always be motivated to do the right thing. Instead, a complex array of forces can motivate people, and leaders must be open to every situation.**

- **Satisfy individual and group needs by establishing goals or tasks for individuals and groups to reach, leading to goal/task accomplishment.**

- **Understand how to motivate to obtain the behavior and conduct (confidence, competence, professionalism, and so on) needed from subordinates.**

- **Establish and maintain loyalty and teamwork within the unit.**

- **Create a caring climate within the unit—one that promotes trust and respect as well as an understanding and acceptance of the "why" of subordinates' actions.**

- **Create self-motivation in subordinates; this is the most powerful and lasting form of motivation. Most people can become self-motivated if taught leadership attributes.**

Principles of Motivation

Although there is no simple formula for motivation, you can understand a basic view of what motivates people. Keep in mind that this view is a simplification for you to use as a guide. It assumes that needs motivate people and that a person's motivation to reach a goal depends on whether the person perceives that the goal will satisfy any of those needs. Realizing that different people react to varying needs will allow you to arrive at appropriate decisions and actions in a particular situation.

People are motivated by many forces, including values, self-interest, kindness, worthy causes. Some of these forces are internal, such as fears and beliefs. Some are external, such as danger; the environment; a chance for promotion; or pressures from a senior, subordinates, or one's family. Forces combine to determine what a person is motivated to do in a given situation.

Because needs form the basis for actions and leaders must motivate by understanding these needs, leaders must understand how needs drive individuals, people, or groups to action. The following is a discussion of 14 practical principles (guidelines) that flow from this basic view of motivation.

> **Note**
>
> Do not confuse these principles with the 11 leadership principles.

Principle 1

Make the needs of subordinates coincide with unit tasks and missions.

Subordinates will have a natural desire to work to satisfy their own needs. When leaders link these interests and needs with those of the group, they have a powerful way to motivate.

Principle 2

Reward individual and team behavior that supports unit tasks and missions.

The opportunity to win a reward is a sound motivator. A ribbon, a medal, a certificate, or a letter are only small tangible objects, but they mean a great deal to someone psychologically (see Figure 6.5.2). These rewards have motivating power because they are a way of satisfying social and higher needs. Awards symbolize a proud achievement. After the higher needs are awakened by such rewards, the motivation to keep working for more recognition normally increases.

Rewards can also include a simple "well done" or a "pat on the back," a promotion, or a favorable evaluation.

Figure 6.5.2: Being rewarded for a job well done can keep motivation high.
Courtesy of US Army JROTC.

Principle 3

Counsel subordinates who behave in a way that is counter to unit tasks, missions, and standards.

The previous two examples were the "carrot" or the reward approach. This principle is the opposite; it is the "stick." Use this principle only when it is necessary to motivate people who do not respond to positive motivation. Before resorting to this approach, however, be certain that the task, mission, or standard was clearly communicated prior to the infraction.

Every leader in the chain of command must be involved in the discipline of the organization. This shows subordinates that even their immediate supervisor has the power of "the stick." Each case requiring counseling or disciplinary action also provides an opportunity to teach subordinate leaders how to counsel and take disciplinary action. Remember, conduct reprimands, counseling sessions, and other corrective actions as privately and as quickly as possible after an infraction. Do not humiliate or embarrass someone in front of others.

Principle 4

Set the example in all things.

If leaders show their subordinates how to act, they are teaching them at the same time. If leaders follow regulations and unit operating procedures, they are demonstrating the expected policies to be followed. By doing these actions, leaders are also proving their own degree of self-discipline.

A word of caution is in order here. No one is superhuman, and subordinates do not expect that. While they want leaders to set the example in all things and to share hardships with them, they do not want their leaders to take unnecessary risks. If they see leaders taking unnecessary risks, they may lose confidence in their judgment, affecting the morale, cohesion, and discipline of the unit.

Principle 5

Develop morale and esprit within the unit.

Morale is the mental, emotional, and spiritual state of an individual. It is how a person feels—happy, hopeful, confident, appreciated, worthless, sad, unrecognized, or depressed. Morale has a tremendous impact on motivation. High morale strengthens courage, energy, and the will to get things done. Because everything a leader does affects morale in one way or another, a leader must always be aware of how his or her actions and decisions affect it. Give subordinates something to hope for, because hope builds morale.

Esprit means team spirit; it is the spirit, soul, and state of mind of the unit. It is a product of cohesion; the overall consciousness of the unit that the subordinate identifies with and feels a part of.

Principle 6

Give subordinates tough problems and challenge them to wrestle with them.

Coach subordinates on their problem-solving, decision-making, planning, and implementing skills. This principle

- **Encourages (by teaching and coaching) the development of junior leaders**
- **Motivates people who must carry out the plan**
- **Makes communication clearer, which gives everyone a better understanding of the mission and what they must do as individuals and as a team to achieve it**
- **Creates an open, trusting communication bond between the members of the chain of command**

Principle 7

Have subordinates participate in the planning of upcoming events.

Participating in the planning of future events can be a highly motivating experience. By contributing ideas to a plan, subordinates then have a personal interest in seeing the plan succeed. Plus, it improves communication, which improves teamwork. Improved communication also gives everyone a clearer picture of the objective so that they can use their initiative to achieve it. Clear understanding of the mission and the plan prevents ill-founded rumors and fears based on a lack of knowledge.

Also, by involving subordinates in planning, leaders show that they recognize subordinates' abilities and appreciate them. Recognition and appreciation from respected leaders are powerful motivating forces.

Principle 8

Alleviate causes of the personal concerns of subordinates so that they can concentrate on their jobs.

Everyone has a unique combination of experience, values, character traits, knowledge, and skills, causing a person to have a unique way of dealing with life. Things that seem of no importance to leaders may be of critical importance to subordinates.

Some people may have family problems that leaders must empathize with before they can help them. Others may not know how to handle money, have meaningful relationships, stay out of trouble, balance the demands of school or work with the needs of the family, or grow professionally and personally.

Leaders should strive to help their subordinates as much as they can by keeping them informed of situations and decisions, encouraging feedback, and through counseling if necessary. For those people who are having real or perceived challenges, these difficulties will cause them to worry, consume their energy, and prevent them from being productive. To help **alleviate** these causes of personal concerns, leaders should teach subordinates how to handle their lives in a healthy, constructive way.

Principle 9

Ensure that subordinates are properly cared for and have the tools they need to succeed.

Simply put, this principle means caring for subordinates. Leaders at all levels of the chain of command must do all they can to help subordinates meet their physical, safety, social, esteem, and self-fulfillment needs. Teach them all you know. You want them to have the right values, character traits, knowledge, and skills because these are the tools that will allow them to grow and to live happy, productive lives.

Key Note Term

alleviate – to relieve

Principle 10

Keep subordinates informed about missions and standards.

Keep clear, open communications with subordinates so that they can accomplish their mission as a team and use initiative in the absence of orders.

Principle 11

Use positive peer pressure to work for you, the leader, and the unit.

Peer pressure can be a powerful motivating force, but leaders must be careful how they apply it. If not used properly, it can backfire with serious consequences. On the other hand, positive peer pressure that is based on professional norms and values is healthy.

Principle 12

Avoid using statistics as a major method of evaluating units and motivating subordinates.

Statistics in themselves are not necessarily bad or good. Leaders should use them sparingly and carefully because they are only the "mask" and may present a false image. They are surface indicators or symptoms that leaders need to check into further. Perhaps they indicate a serious problem; perhaps not. Leaders simply do not know until they look into the true causes of the symptoms.

Improper use of statistics has a devastating effect on trust, morale, and motivation. Valid evaluation systems and effective leaders require much more than statistics. They require ways to get beneath the "image" to the real substance—the true strengths and weaknesses that influence effectiveness and the real leadership causes of those strengths and weaknesses. Good leaders make the time to get out and to see the real substance of a unit.

Principle 13

Make the jobs of subordinates as challenging, exciting, and meaningful as possible.

Make each subordinate feel special. Experience and study have proven that people need meaningful work. They need to believe that what they are doing, even if it is tiring and unpleasant, is necessary and important. When people feel that their jobs are important and that they have responsibility, they feel needed and motivated. This principle encourages the delegation of authority. This "power-down" approach helps leaders get the best out of their subordinates. Leaders give responsibility to subordinates who have the skill and will to handle it, and they strive to make subordinates feel that they are as responsible as them for achieving unit standards and goals.

Principle 14

Do not tolerate any form of prejudicial talk or behavior.

Racial, sexual, or other **prejudicial** talk and behavior are contrary to the principles on which America was founded. If a person feels that he or she is the object of prejudice, that person's motivation can be seriously damaged. Prejudice can also destroy teamwork, cohesion, and discipline within a unit.

> **Key Note Term**
>
> **prejudicial** – to form an opinion without knowing or in spite of the facts

Although these 14 principles of motivation are different from the 11 leadership principles, there are similarities. Did you recognize any?

Building Motivation

People will have little motivation to do something if they believe they cannot succeed. Likewise, if they are not convinced that good performance is the best way to satisfy their needs, their motivation will be low and they will have little or no interest in doing their best. However, when subordinates are convinced that their chances for success are good enough to warrant the effort, this belief will help them to achieve their own goals (or needs) as well as those of the group. Therefore, leaders must know their subordinates' capabilities, establish challenging goals within those capabilities, and employ them in accordance with those capabilities (one of the leadership principles). Leaders can also build confidence by offering support, encouragement, and assistance.

Creating assurance that good performance will be rewarded is based on three factors:

- **The leader has a consistent record of checking and evaluating performance**
- **The leader has an equally consistent record of using rewards in respect to improving performance**
- **The leader knows that some team players feel that completion of the task itself is sufficient reward**

Tangible and Intangible Rewards

People work for the opportunity to receive tangible (a plaque) or **intangible** (a "pat on the back") rewards and need to believe that their work is necessary and important. If supervisors never compliment them on a job well done, however, it is easy for subordinates to feel that they never do good work or that their leaders are not interested in their work. Either of these beliefs can destroy motivation.

On the other hand, if leaders recognize and confirm each person's importance and value to the organization, motivation will be strong. Highly motivated teams with high morale usually have leaders who take a personal interest in them and are understanding.

People resent a lack of respect and will respond with that same disrespect by doing only what is necessary to get by. Leaders must build bonds of mutual respect, trust, confidence, and understanding that are fundamental to a disciplined, cohesive team.

Conclusion

This lesson explained one of the most important aspects that you, as a leader, must know to do your job properly—the understanding of human nature and how that understanding impacts on what you must know about yourself, your job, your subordinates, and your unit. This knowledge will give you a stronger foundation for what you must be and what you must do; then, what you do as a leader—the application of these skills—flows from this "being" and "knowing" foundation.

Invisible threads weave together many of the techniques and attributes of leadership. This lesson illustrated how understanding needs is intertwined with a leader's values, ethics, and character and with various leadership traits and principles. Your knowledge and proper application of human nature is essential; it is the bedrock of your character as a leader.

This concludes the chapter, "Leadership Principles." Through the lessons in this chapter, you have learned about power and influence, different styles of leadership, and communication skills. You have also learned what it takes to manage your team and the importance of motivation.

Lesson Review

1. Compare and contrast tangible and intangible rewards.

2. How do the 14 principles of motivation compare to the 11 principles of leadership? What are the similarities? What are the differences?

3. Choose one of the 14 principles of motivation and explain it.

4. Why is it important to establish and maintain loyalty and teamwork within the unit?

Unit 1: Citizenship in Action
Correlated to:
McRel Standards for Civics, Life Work, Thinking and Reasoning, Working with Others and Self Regulation

McRel Standards	Unit 1: Citizenship in Action
CIVICS STANDARDS (C) **What are the Basic Values and Principals of American Democracy**	
C 8. Understands the central ideas of American constitutional government and how this form of government has shaped the character of American society	Department of Defense, 91–101; The Active Army, 102–112; Army Reserve Components, 113–121; The United States Navy, 122–132; The United States Air Force, 133–142; The United States Marine Corps, 143–149; The United States Coast Guard and Merchant Marine, 150–164; The Peace Corps, 165–184
C 9. Understands the importance of Americans sharing and supporting certain values, beliefs, and principles of American constitutional democracy	The Stars and Stripes, 55–62; Proudly We Sing: the National Anthem, 63–68
C 10. Understands the roles of volunteerism and organized groups in American social and political life	The Peace Corps, 165–184
How Does the Government Established by the Constitution Embody the Purposes, Values, and Principles of American Democracy?	
C 16. Understands the major responsibilities of the national government for domestic and foreign policy, and understands how government is financed through taxation	Department of Defense, 91–101; The Active Army, 102–112; Army Reserve Components, 113–121; The United States Navy, 122–132; The United States Air Force, 133–142; The United States Marine Corps, 143–149; The United States Coast Guard and Merchant Marine, 150–164; The Peace Corps, 165–184
What is the Relationship of the United States to other nations and to world affairs?	
C 22. Understands how the world is organized politically into nation-states, how nation-states interact with one another, and issues surrounding U.S. foreign policy	The Peacc Corps, 165–184
What are the Roles of the Citizen in American Democracy?	
C 24. Understands the meaning of citizenship in the US, and knows the requirements for citizenship and naturalization	The Active Army, 102–112

Copyright © 2004 McREL
Mid-continent Research for Education and Learning
2550 S. Parker Road, Suite 500
Aurora, CO 80014
Telephone: 303/337-0990
www.mcrel.org/standards-benchmarks

McRel Standards	Unit 1: Citizenship in Action
C 27. Understands how certain character traits enhance citizens' ability to fulfill personal and civic responsibilities	The Peace Corps, 165–184; AmeriCorps, 185–193
C 28. Understands how participation in civic and political life can help citizens attain individual and public goals	The Past and Purpose of the Army JROTC, 8–13; The Active Army, 102–112; Army Reserve Components, 113–121; The Peace Corps, 165–184; AmeriCorps, 185–193
C 29. Understands the importance of political leadership, public service, and a knowledgeable citizenry in American constitutional democracy	The Past and Purpose of the Army JROTC, 8–13; The Active Army, 102–112; Army Reserve Components, 113–121; The Peace Corps, 165–184; AmeriCorps, 185–193
LIFE WORK STANDARDS (LW)	
LW 2. Uses various information sources, including those of a technical nature, to accomplish specific tasks	The Peace Corps, 165–184; AmeriCorps, 185–193
LW 5. Makes general preparation for entering the work force	Army JROTC – The Making of a Better Citizen, 3–7; The Signs of Success, 31–41; Your Personal Appearance and Uniform, 42–54; The Peace Corps, 165–184; AmeriCorps, 185–193
LW 7. Displays reliability and a basic work ethic	The Signs of Success, 31–41; Your Personal Appearance and Uniform, 42–54; The Peace Corps, 165–184; AmeriCorps, 185–193
LW 8. Operates effectively within organizations	The Past and Purpose of the Army JROTC, 8–13; Moving Up in the Army JROTC (Rank and Structure), 14–30; The Signs of Success, 31–41; Your Personal Appearance and Uniform, 42–54; American Military Traditions, Customs and Courtesies, 69–76; Basic Command and Staff Principles, 77–89; The Peace Corps, 165–184; AmeriCorps, 185–193
THINKING AND REASONING STANDARDS (TR)	
TR 3. Effectively uses mental processes that are based on identifying similarities and differences	American Military Traditions, Customs and Courtesies, 69–76
TR 4. Applies basic trouble-shooting and problem-solving techniques	The Peace Corps, 165–184; AmeriCorps, 185–193
TR 6. Applies decision-making techniques	The Signs of Success, 31–41; The Peace Corps, 165–184; AmeriCorps, 185–193

McRel Standards	Unit 1: Citizenship in Action
WORKING WITH OTHERS STANDARDS (WO)	
WO 1. Contributes to the overall effort of a group	The Stars and Stripes, 55–62; Proudly We Sing: the National Anthem, 63–68; American Military Traditions, Customs and Courtesies, 69–76; Basic Command and Staff Principles, 77–89; The Peace Corps, 165–184; AmeriCorps, 185–193
WO 3. Works well with diverse individuals and in diverse situations	Basic Command and Staff Principles, 77–89; The Peace Corps, 165–184; AmeriCorps, 185–193
WO 4. Displays effective interpersonal communication skills	American Military Traditions, Customs, and Courtesies, 69–75; Basic Command and Staff Principles, 77–89; The Peace Corps, 165–184; AmeriCorps, 185–193
WO 5. Demonstrates leadership skills	Basic Command and Staff Principles, 77–89; The Peace Corps, 165–184; AmeriCorps, 185–193
SELF REGULATION STANDARDS	
SR 1. Sets and manages goals	The Signs of Success, 31–41; Your Personal Appearance and Uniform, 42–54
SR 2. Performs self-appraisal	Army JROTC – The Making of a Better Citizen, 3–7; The Signs of Success, 31–41; Your Personal Appearance and Uniform, 42–54
SR 4. Demonstrates Perseverance	The Signs of Success, 31–41
SR 5. Maintains a healthy self-concept	Your Personal Appearance and Uniform, 42–54
HISTORY STANDARDS	
H8. Understands the institution and practices of government created during the Revolution and how these elements were revised between 1787 and 1815 to create the foundation of the American political system based on the U.S. Constitution and the Bill of Rights.	Origins of the US Army, 103–104

Unit 2: Leadership Theory and Application
Correlated to:
McRel Standards for Life Work, Thinking and Reasoning, Working with Others, Self Regulation, and Physical Education

McRel Standards	Unit 2: Leadership Theory and Application
LIFE WORK STANDARDS (LW)	
LW 1. Makes effective use of basic tools	Stationary Movements with the M-1903 Rifle, 445–459; Stationary Movements with the M-1 Rifle, 460–471; The Saber and Scabbard, 472–479
LW 2. Uses various information sources, including those of a technical nature, to accomplish specific tasks	Be technically proficient, 224–225; Taking Charge—Knowing Your Responsibilities as a Leader, 406–412
LW 4. Studies or pursues specific job interests	Be technically proficient, 224–225
LW 5. Makes general preparations for entering the work force	Be technically proficient, 224–225; Leading Meetings, 348–360
LW 6. Makes effective use of basic life skills	Be Technically Proficient, 224–225; Development, 284–291; Goal Setting 292–295
LW 7. Displays reliability and a basic work ethic	Leadership Defined, 196–201; Leadership from the Inside Out, 207–220; Principles and Leadership, 221–235; Taking Charge—Knowing Your Responsibilities as a Leader, 406–412
LW 8. Operates effectively within organizations	Leadership Defined, 196–201; Leadership from the Inside Out, 207–220; Principles and Leadership, 221–235; Sexual Harassment/Assault, 236–245; Steps from the Past, 247–250; Roles of Leaders and followers in Drill, 251–256; Using your Leadership Skills/Taking Charge, 257–260; Stationary Movements, 261–265; Steps and Marching, 266–272; Squad Drill, 273–282; Goal Setting 292–295; Leading Meetings, 348–360; Supervising, 361–368; Team Development, 369–377; Taking Charge—Knowing Your Responsibilities as a Leader, 406–412; Company Formations and Movement, 413–425; Forming, Inspecting and Dismissing the Battalion, 426–432; Stationary Movements with the M-1903 Rifle, 445–459; Stationary Movements with the M-1 Rifle, 460–471; The Saber and Scabbard, 472–479

McRel Standards	Unit 2: Leadership Theory and Application
THINKING AND REASONING STANDARDS (TR)	
TR 2. Understands and applies basic principles of logic and reasoning	Project Management, 378–382; Management Skills, 496–503
TR 3. Effectively uses mental processes that are based on identifying similarities and differences	Platoon Drill, 395–405; Review of Drill Procedures, 433–444
TR 5. Applies basic trouble-shooting and problem-solving techniques	Sexual Harassment/Assault, 236–245; Negotiating, 332–335; Decision Making and Problem Solving, 337–347; Supervising, 361–368; Team Development, 369–377; Project Management, 378–382; Management Skills, 496–503
TR 6. Applies decision-making techniques	Pressures to be Unethical, 216–218; Development, 284–291; Supervising, 361–368; Project Management, 378–382; Taking Charge—Knowing Your Responsibilities as a Leader, 406–412; Management Skills, 496–503
WORKING WITH OTHERS STANDARDS (WO)	
WO 1. Contributes to the overall effort of a group	Leadership Defined, 196–201; Leadership from the Inside Out, 207–220; Sexual Harassment/Assault, 236–245; Steps from the Past, 247–250; Roles of Leaders and followers in Drill, 251–256; Using your Leadership Skills/Taking Charge, 257–260; Stationary Movements, 261–265; Steps and Marching, 266–272; Squad Drill, 273–282; Goal Setting 292–295; Performance Indicators, 309–331; Decision Making and Problem Solving, 337–347; Leading Meetings, 348–360; Supervising, 361–368; Team Development, 369–377; Project Management, 378–382; Platoon Drill, 395–405; Company Formations and Movement, 413–425; Forming, Inspecting and Dismissing the Battalion, 426–432; Stationary Movements with the M-1903 Rifle, 445–459; Stationary Movements with the M-1 Rifle, 460–471; The Saber and Scabbard, 472–479; Power Bases and Influences, 481–486; Styles of Leadership, 487–495; Management Skills, 496–503; Motivation, 513–521
WO 2. Uses conflict-resolution techniques	Negotiating, 332–335; Decision Making and Problem Solving, 337–347; Supervising, 361–368; Project Management, 378–382

McRel Standards	Unit 2: Leadership Theory and Application
WO 3. Works well with diverse individuals and in diverse situations	Leadership Defined, 196-201; Leadership from the Inside Out, 207-220; Sexual Harassment/Assault, 236-245; Celebrating Differences—Culture and Individual Diversity, 297-308; Negotiating, 332-335; Decision Making and Problem Solving, 337-347; Supervising, 361-368; Team Development, 369-377; Project Management, 378-382; Mentoring, 383-393; Power Bases and Influences, 481-486; Styles of Leadership, 487-495; Management Skills, 496-503; Communication, 504-512; Motivation, 513-521
WO 4. Displays effective interpersonal communication skills	Leadership Defined, 196–201; Leadership from the Inside Out, 207–220; Principles and Leadership, 221–235; Sexual Harassment/Assault, 236–245; Steps from the Past, 247–250; Roles of Leaders and Followers in Drill, 251–256; Using your Leadership Skills/Taking Charge, 257–260; Celebrating Differences—Culture and Individual Diversity, 297–308; Performance Indicators, 309–331; Negotiating, 332–335; Decision Making and Problem Solving, 337–347; Leading Meetings, 348–360; Supervising, 361–368; Team Development, 369–377; Project Management, 378–382; Mentoring, 383–393; Taking Charge—Knowing Your Responsibilities as a Leader, 406–412; Power Bases and Influences, 481–486; Styles of Leadership, 487–495; Management Skills, 496–503; Communication, 504–512
WO 5. Demonstrates leadership skills	Leadership Defined, 196–201; Leadership Reshuffled, 202–206; Leadership from the Inside Out, 207–220; Principles and Leadership, 221–235; Sexual Harassment/Assault, 236–245; Roles of Leaders and followers in Drill, 251–256; Using your Leadership Skills/Taking Charge, 257–260; Celebrating Differences—Culture and Individual Diversity, 297–308; Performance Indicators, 309–331; Negotiating, 332–335; Decision Making and Problem Solving, 337–347; Leading Meetings, 348–360; Supervising, 361–368; Team Development, 369–377; Project Management, 378–382; Mentoring, 383–393; Taking Charge—Knowing Your Responsibilities as a Leader, 406–412; Review of Drill Procedures, 433–444; Power Bases and Influences, 481–486; Styles of Leadership, 487–495; Management Skills, 496–503; Communication, 504–512; Motivation, 513–521

McRel Standards	Unit 2: Leadership Theory and Application
SELF REGULATION STANDARDS	
SR 1. Sets and manages goals	Leadership Defined, 196–201; Leadership from the Inside Out, 207–220; Principles and Leadership, 221–235; Development, 284–291; Goal Setting 292–295; Celebrating Differences—Culture and Individual Diversity, 297–308; Leading Meetings, 348–360; Supervising, 361–368; Team Development, 369–377; Project Management, 378–382; Power Bases and Influences, 481–486; Styles of Leadership, 487–495; Management Skills, 496–503
SR 2. Performs self-appraisal	Leadership Defined, 196–201; Leadership Reshuffled, 202–206; Leadership from the Inside Out, 207–220; Principles and Leadership, 221–235; Sexual Harassment/Assault, 236–245; Celebrating Differences—Culture and Individual Diversity, 297–308; Performance Indicators, 309–331; Supervising, 361–368; Team Development, 369–377; Project Management, 378–382; Mentoring, 383–393; Taking Charge—Knowing Your Responsibilities as a Leader, 406–412; Power Bases and Influences, 481–486; Styles of Leadership, 487-495; Management Skills, 496-503; Communication, 504-512; Motivation, 513-521
SR 3. Considers risks	Pressures to be Unethical, 216–218; Staying Safe, 242–244; Negotiating, 332–335; Project Management, 378–382
SR 4. Demonstrates perseverance	Making the Change, 200; Goal Setting 292–295; Negotiating, 332–335; Decision Making and Problem Solving, 337–347; Team Development, 369–377; Power Bases and Influences, 481–486; Styles of Leadership, 487–495; Management Skills, 496–503; Motivation, 513–521
SR 5. Maintains a healthy self-concept	Making the Change, 200; Staying Safe, 242–244; Goal Setting 292–295; Supervising, 361–368; Project Management, 378–382; Motivation, 513–521

McRel Standards	Unit 2: Leadership Theory and Application
PHYSICAL EDUCATION STANDARDS (PE)	
PE 1. Uses a variety of basic and advanced movement forms	Stationary Movements, 261–265; Steps and Marching, 266–272; Squad Drill, 273–282; Goal Setting 292–295; Company Formations and Movement, 413–425; Forming, Inspecting and Dismissing the Battalion, 426–432
PE 3. Understands the benefits and costs associated with participation in physical activity	Review of Drill Procedures, 433–444; Stationary Movements with the M-1903 Rifle, 445–459; Stationary Movements with the M-1 Rifle, 460–471
PE 5. Understands the social and personal responsibility associated with participation in physical activity	The Saber and Scabbard, 472–479
HEALTH STANDARDS (H)	
H 5. Knows essential concepts and practices concerning injury prevention and safety	Staying Safe, 242–244; Stationary Movements with the M-1903 Rifle, 445–459; Stationary Movements with the M-1 Rifle, 460–471; The Saber and Scabbard, 472–479
US HISTORY STANDARDS (USH)	
USH6. Understands the causes for the American Revolution, the ideas and interests involved in shaping the revolutionary movement, and reasons for the American victory	Steps from the Past, 247–250

Glossary

Academic award. Recognition given to an individual cadet for scholastic achievement or excellence.

Air Expeditionary Force. The largest deployable operational unit of the US Air Force.

Air Expeditionary Wing. Tactically self-contained, deployable wing-size unit.

Air Superiority. Affording freedom of action to friendly and allied forces while denying the same to the enemy.

Air Wing. The Air Force's basic operational unit.

Align. To arrange in a line; alignment: the arrangement of several elements on the same line.

Anthems. A song of gladness, praise, devotion, or patriotism.

Athletic awards. Recognition given to an individual for athletic participation or excellence.

Battalion. A military unit made up of two or more companies or batteries and a headquarters that is commanded by a lieutenant colonel, is the smallest unit to have a staff, and is administratively self-sufficient.

Battle Dress Uniform. A camouflage uniform worn by members of the US Army, Army National Guard, Army Reserve, and Army ROTC.

Battlespace. The three-dimensional battle area above, upon, and below the surface of the ocean.

Bisecting. To cut or divide into two equal parts.

Bombardment. To attack with bombs, explosive shells, or missiles; to attack persistently.

Cadet. A high school student enrolled in leadership and citizenship activities through the Junior Reserve Officers' Training Corps (JROTC).

Candor. Impartiality, fairness; frankness, openness.

Cannon salutes. The firing of a salute by a battery of guns or cannons to honor a person of military, national, or civic importance or to honor a significant national event.

Challenges. To arouse the interest of one's actions or efforts; to stimulate; the quality of requiring full use of one's abilities, energy, and resources; to demand identification from someone before they are allowed to enter or pass.

Chevron. Insignia consisting of stripes meeting at an angle to indicate (enlisted) grade or rank.

Citizen-soldiers. Members of the National Guard or Army Reserves.

Class A uniform. A service uniform that consists of an Army green coat, trousers or slacks; a long or short sleeve shirt; a black four-in-hand tie or black neck tab; and other authorized accessories.

Class B uniform. A service uniform that is the same as the Class A uniform except the service coat is not worn. The black tie and black neck tab are required when wearing the long sleeve shirt; both tie and tab are optional with the short sleeve shirt.

Colors. The U.S. national flag.

Combatant. Engaged in combat.

Command by Negation. Orders to continue operations until told to stop.

Commerce. The exchange or buying and selling of commodities on a large scale involving transportation from place to place.

Commitment. A pledge or promise to do something; dedication to a long-term course of action.

Community service. Any form of service provided for the community or common good.

Company. A subdivision of a military regiment or battalion that constitutes the lowest administrative unit. It is usually under the command of a captain and is made up of at least two platoons.

Conflict resolution. The solutions utilized by a society to settle disputes in a cohesive manner.

Coordinating staff. Principal staff assistants to the commander.

Counterland. Missions interdicting enemy supplies and providing close air support to the Army.

Countersea. Missions targeting enemy ships and submarines operating in proximity to land.

Counterintelligence. Actions taken by intelligence personnel or units to prevent an enemy from gathering information about friendly forces, to deceive the enemy, to prevent sabotage, or to gather political and military information.

Course of action. A decision on how to proceed; a plan.

Courtesies. An act of politeness or gracious manners; the use of polite gestures or remarks.

Culturally diverse. The presence of multiple and different cultural groups and their behaviors within an organization or institution.

Customs. A long-established practice followed as a matter of course among people, oftentimes considered an unwritten law or repeated practice.

Cutter. Small armed vessel in government service.

Decoration. An indication of honor, such as a badge, medal, or ribbon.

Doctrine. A principle (or creed of principles) relating to a specific belief, subject, theory, or branch of knowledge; the fundamental policy or standard for a principle or set of principles on a specific subject, theory, or branch of knowledge; something that is taught.

Dress. To attire with a certain degree of uniformity; an appearance appropriate or peculiar to a particular time.

Echelon. An arrangement of a body of troops in the form of steps; a section of a military group; an organizational level of importance.

Ecosystem. A community of organisms and its environment functioning as an ecological unit.

Enlisted. Relating to or constituting the part of the military force below officers.

Ensign. A flag that is displayed or flown from an aircraft, ship, or boat as the symbol of nationality.

Esprit de corps. The common spirit or feeling of pride found in the members of a group and inspiring enthusiasm, devotion, and strong regard for the honor of the group.

Ferrule. A decorative metal cap attached to the end of a shoulder cord to prevent fraying; a metal ring or cap attached to the end of a staff or handle to give strength or to protect it against splitting.

Fitted. To adapt to the proper size or shape.

Financial grant. A sum of money given by the government or some other organization to fund such things as education or research.

Flagged. A ship registered to a particular nation.

Formal inspection. An official examination of JROTC units that takes place on a prescribed schedule.

Forward from the Sea. U.S. Naval strategy to project power in the littoral regions of the world.

Garrison cap. Headgear that may be worn with the Class A or B uniforms. For JROTC, the braid (piping used for identification purposes) will have a cord edge of the same material as the cap (or Army green shade 344).

Garrison flag. Type of flag flown on holidays and important occasions; 20 feet by 38 feet.

Gigline. Line formed by the seam of the shirt aligned with the zipper flap and the edge of the belt buckle on certain JROTC uniforms.

Half-staff. The position of the flag about half-way down from the top of the pole or staff, used to honor and pay respect to military and nationally important deceased persons. Also used as a distress signal.

Halyard. A rope or tackle used for hoisting or lowering.

Hemmed. To fold back and stitch down the edge of a garment.

Individual award. Recognition given to an individual for outstanding academic, athletic, or military achievement, or for excellence in competition, contribution to unit goals, or outstanding service.

Initiative. The power to begin or fellow through energetically with a plan or task; determination.

Insignia. An emblem, badge, medal or other distinguishing mark of office, honor, or position; denotes grade and branch; may also indicate capacity and duty assignment in the US Army.

Intermodal. Being or involving transportation by more than one form of carrier during a single journey.

JROTC. A program that teaches high school students the values of good citizenship while giving them a brief introduction to the US Army.

Leadership. The ability to influence, lead, or guide others so as to accomplish a mission in the manner desired.

Logistics. The aspect of military science dealing with the procurement, maintenance, and transportation of military materiel, facilities, and personnel.

Marine Air Ground Task Force. Organizational concept that makes the Marines uniquely light and lethal.

Marine Expeditionary Brigade. Combat organization constituted from Maritime Prepositioned Squadrons.

Marine Expeditionary Force. Largest combat organization composed of a Marine Division and Marine Air Wing.

Marine Expeditionary Unit. Smallest combat organization, forward deployed with the amphibious ready group.

Maritime. Of, relating to, or bordering on the sea.

Maritime Prepositioned Squadron. Small flotilla of cargo ships stationed close to hot spots of the world.

Mess. A group of people, usually in the military, who regularly eat meals together; the place where such meals are served.

Military award. Recognition given to an individual for participation in JROTC-sponsored activities or for leadership excellence.

Militia. A citizen army—as distinct from a regular army or a body of full-time, professional soldiers—that is usually controlled by the individual states and subject to call during an emergency by the government of a country.

Miscellaneous award. Recognition given to an individual for participation in school or community service activities or in activities that enhance the JROTC program.

Mission. A specific job given to a person or group of persons to accomplish.

Mobilize. To assemble, prepare, or put into operation (personnel, units, equipment, and so on) for war or a similar emergency.

Motivate. Provide a need or a purpose that causes a person to want to do something.

Motivation. A force that moves a person to action; often inspired by an idea, fact, event, or goal.

Nap. A soft, fuzzy finish or cloth formed by short fibers raised on the surface.

National Defense Act. Enacted in 1916, this act officially created the Reserve Officers' Training Corps (ROTC) of which Junior ROTC is a part.

National march. "The Stars and Stripes Forever" as recognized in the U.S. Code of Federal Regulations.

Nonaccession. The policy or practice of not accepting personnel directly from traditional officer or enlisted entrance sources.

Noncombatant Evacuation Operation. Specialized Marine mission to rescue civilians from combat zones.

Nonprofit group. A group or organization designed not to make or intended to make a profit.

Nonsubdued. Bright and shining, not dull or flat, such as polished brass pin-on insignia.

Numbered Air Force. The Air Force's largest operational unit.

Numbered Fleets. Forward deployed forces of the U.S. Navy.

Officer in Tactical Command. Commands warfare functions within the battlespace.

Operating Forces. The combatant arm of the U.S. Navy.

Operations Plan. Military plan of action for future potential crisis or contingencies.

Operational commands. Commands performing the primary mission of the service as distinguished from support commands.

Operational Maneuver from the Sea. Using the ocean as maneuver space to surprise the enemy.

Opportunities. Favorable or advantageous circumstances or a combination of circumstances.

Partnership. A legal relation existing between two or more persons contractually associated as joint principals in a business.

Pennant. A long, narrow flag tapering to a point or a swallowtail at the end.

Personal staff. Officers who work under the immediate control of the commander.

Platoon. A subdivision of a company-size military unit normally consisting of two or more squads or sections; the leader is usually a second lieutenant.

Position of honor. A military courtesy of usually keeping seniors to your right while walking or sitting.

Post flag. Type of flag used for everyday occasions; 10 feet by 19 feet.

Precedence. The act or right of preceding or placing in order according to rank or importance; priority.

Pre-inspection. An informal examination before an official or formal inspection.

Principle Warfare Commanders. ADC, ASuW, ASW, and Strike Warfare Commanders.

Reporting. Presenting oneself to a senior.

Reserve Corps. Trained military members available to augment active duty forces in times when activated.

Responsibility. The quality of being responsible, trustworthy, and accountable for your actions.

Ruffles and flourishes. A drum and bugle salute, usually to honor military or civil officials.

Salute. A sign or form of exchange used to greet or to show respect and recognition.

Sealift. Ocean transportation.

Self-propelled. To have the ability within itself to move.

Service-learning. An environment where one can learn and develop by actively participating in organized service experiences within one's community.

Shore Establishment. Organization that recruits, organizes, trains, equips, and supports Navy operating forces.

Shoulder marks. A pair of broad pieces of stiffened cloth worn on the shoulders of the Class A or Class B uniforms to display the insignia of grade; blank shoulder marks do not display an insignia of grade so that pin on insignia may be used instead.

Sized. The physical dimensions, proportions, magnitude, or extent of an object. Any of a series of graduated categories of dimension whereby manufactured articles, such as shoes and clothing, are classified.

Special staff. Assist the commander in professional, technical, and other areas of interest in the command.

Specialist. A person who devotes himself to a particular occupation or field of study; the enlisted grade in the army corresponding to a corporal.

Specified. To state explicitly or in detail.

Squad. The smallest unit in the army organization composed of a varying number of personnel, depending on the type of element, and led by a noncommissioned officer.

Staff. Another word for flagpole used to carry unit guidons or colors.

Standard. A term now interchangeable with "the Colors," although formerly it was used for flags of mounted, motorized, and mechanized organizations.

"The Star-Spangled Banner." The national anthem of the United States, written by Francis Scott Key.

Storm flag. Type of flag flown in bad weather; 5 feet by 9½ feet.

Strategic. Of or relating to the large scale or global planning and conduct of military strategy, movements, and/or operations essential to the effective conduct of war; of great importance within an integrated whole or to a planned effect.

Strategic Attack. Striking enemy Centers of Gravity to destroy their will and ability to fight.

Strategic Triad. Nuclear deterrent force of land-based bombers and missiles and fleet ballistic missile submarines.

Subordinate. A person lower in rank or grade.

Succession. The order of persons next in line for an office or rank that is held by another.

Symbol. Something that represents something else by association, resemblance, or convention, especially a material object used to represent something invisible.

Tactical. Of or pertaining to tactics.

Tarnish. To dull the luster of; discolor.

Task force. Structured force designed to perform a specific task or mission.

Team. A group of persons approximating one half of a squad and normally led by a junior noncommissioned officer.

Theater. A large geographic area (including its land, sea, and air) in which active military operations are coordinated and conducted.

Traditions. The passing down of elements of a culture (such as knowledge, beliefs, or customs) from one generation to another.

Uncasing. Removing the case from the Colors that are attached to a staff.

Unconventional. Not bound by or in accordance with international agreements dealing with a specific subject, such as the rules or laws of warfare or the use of nuclear, biological, or chemical weapons or energy.

Uncovered. To remove a hat or other headgear; to be bareheaded or without a cover.

Under arms. To carry or be furnished with, or to have attached to the person, a weapon or the equipment pertaining directly to a weapon, such as a pistol belt or pistol holster.

Underway Replenishment. Logistic supply method that allows ships to maintain forward Navy presence.

Union. The emblem in a flag symbolizing unity, such as the blue rectangle and stars on the U.S. flag.

Unique. Being the only one of its kind.

Unit award. Recognition given to a JROTC program for being an honor unit or an honor unit with distinction.

Vertical Envelopment. To flank or surround the enemy using air, ground, and surface assets all at once.

Volunteer. A person who voluntarily undertakes or expresses a willingness to undertake a service; one who enters into military service voluntarily.

Unit 2

Glossary

Actions. Behavior or conduct.

Agenda. Schedule of items to be discussed at a meeting addressing who, what, when, where, and how.

Alleviate. To relieve.

Approach. To draw closer to.

Arc. Anything shaped like a curve, bow, or arch; a curved line.

Assess. To pass judgment or assign value.

At ease. Command to relax the body while remaining silent in place and not assuming any particular position.

Attendee. A meeting participant.

Attention. A military position in which a person stands erect, with arms at sides, heels together, and eyes straight ahead; position of readiness to execute other movements; a command to take that position.

Attributes. A quality or characteristic (such as a belief, value, ethic, character trait, knowledge, or skill) that belongs to a person or thing; a distinctive personal feature.

Balance. A counterbalancing weight, force, or influence; position just forward of the magazine floor plate on the underside of the rifle stock.

Barrel. Metal tube for aiming and firing ballistic projectile.

Base. Stationary platoon on which others align; right-most platoon in mass and line formation; front platoon in column formation.

Behavior. The manner of conducting oneself.

Beliefs. A personal truth; mental acceptance or conviction of particular truths of someone or something.

Bias. A mental leaning; partiality, prejudice, bent.

Bolt. Breeching mechanism for loading, locking, and removing cartridges from rear of barrel.

Bolt handle. Lever mechanism for moving rifle bolt to open and close cartridge chamber.

Bribery. The act of giving or offering to, or accepting money, property, or a favor from someone in a position of trust to persuade or influence that person to act dishonestly.

Butt. Bottom end of the rifle stock designed to rest against shoulder.

Cadence. The uniform rhythm in which a movement is executed or the number of steps or counts per minute at which a movement is executed.

Cant. To tilt to one side; to slant.

Censure. An opinion or judgment that criticizes or condemns sternly.

Chamber. The opening towards the rear of the barrel for inserting and removing cartridges.

Close interval. Elbow's distance between troops in rank formation.

Cocking piece. Lever mechanism extending from bolt that primes the firing pin.

Coercion. The act, process, or power of forcing someone to act or think in a given manner, such as by using force or threats as a form of control.

Coercive power. Power that is yielded by fear.

Cohesive. Sticking together.

Column. A formation in which people or elements are arranged one behind the other; to form up in files, facing forward the width of the formation.

Command of execution. The part of a drill command that tells when the movement is to be executed (carried out).

Command voice. A properly given command should be understood by everyone in the unit.

Communication. Sharing of information.

Complement. Complete.

Conceptual skills. Capacity for sound judgment, problem-solving, critical/creative thinking, and moral reasoning.

Conclude. To close the meeting by summarizing what was discussed and agreed.

Constructive criticism. A comment that is meant to improve or help.

Contingencies. Chances or possible occurrences.

Convictions. A strong persuasion or belief.

Cooperate. To act or work with another or others.

Correction. To make or set right.

Counseling. An interchange of opinions, perceptions, and ideas.

Cover. The distance between cadets in a column, measured by the cadet raising the left arm to the front and making sure the shoulder of the cadet in front is at the length of the arm plus 4–6 inches.

Cultivate. To foster the growth of.

Cultural diversity. The presence of multiple and different cultural groups and their behaviors within an organization or institution.

Culture. Civilization.

Date rape. Sexual assault perpetrated by the victim's escort during an arranged social encounter.

Decodes. Translates.

Dedication. Loyalty to a cause, ideal, or system; to commit oneself to a particular course of thought or action.

Defensive. Withdrawing.

Delegating. A leadership style where the leader delegates problem-solving and decision-making authority to a team-mate or to a group of followers.

Development. To get gradually stronger and better; to make known in detail.

Developmental. Sharing opinion of fact.

Dilemma. An argument presenting two or more equally conclusive alternatives against an opponent.

Directing. A leadership style where the leader tells team members what to do and how to do it.

Direction. An explicit instruction.

Discipline. Orderly, obedient, or restrained conduct; training that corrects, molds, or perfects the mental faculties or moral character.

Discrimination. To show preference for or prejudice against.

Diversified. To produce variety.

Doctrine. A principle (or creed of principles) relating to a specific belief, subject, theory, or branch of knowledge; the fundamental policy or standard for a principle or set of principles on a specific subject, theory, or branch of knowledge; something that is taught.

Double interval. Two arms' distance between troops in rank formation.

Double time. To march in the cadence of 180 steps or counts per minute with a 30-inch step.

Drill. The execution of certain movements by which individuals and/or units are moved in a uniform manner from one formation to another or from one place to another; movements are executed in unison and with precision; executing a predefined set of movements.

Dysfunctions. Impaired or abnormal functioning.

Emotional intelligence. The ability for one to monitor their emotions and use information about those emotions to guide one's thinking and actions.

En route. In motion towards a destination.

Encodes. Converts.

Ethics. Rules, principles, or standards that guide individuals or groups to do the moral or right thing in accordance with accepted principles of right or wrong.

Ethnic. Of, pertaining to, or characteristic of the basic groups of people with a common history, language, culture, and identity.

Evaluation. To appraise or find the value of.

Executing. To carry out or put into effect; to do what is required.

Expert power. Power resulting from specific expertise, knowledge, or special skills.

Facilitate. To encourage participation; to ease the accomplishment of a task.

Facing. Pivoting movement executed while stationary to orient the body left, right, or opposite the current position.

Favoritism. The showing of special favor.

Feedback. Verifying that a message was received in the manner it was intended.

File. To form up in a column.

Flank. The side of the formation, either left or right; the right or left side of any formation as seen by a person (or element) within that formation.

Flexibility. Adaptable to change.

Followership. Accepting the guidance or leadership of another; the capacity or willingness to follow a leader.

Formation. Patterned arrangement of troops; the arrangement of people or elements of a unit in a prescribed manner; group of people aligned in a specific pattern.

Gantt chart. The standard format for displaying a schedule graphically consisting of a horizontal bar chart with time as the horizontal axis and either resources, jobs, or orders as the vertical axis.

Goals. The purpose toward which an endeavor is directed; an objective.

Guard. The portion of the bolt (handle) of a saber or sword that protects the hand.

Guide. One that leads or directs another's way.

Halt. Command to bring moving formation to standstill.

Hand guard. Metal barrel cover; protective grip forward of the rifle stock.

Impartial. Fair and unprejudiced.

Implement/Implementation. To give practical effect to and ensure actual fulfillment by concrete measures.

Improving. To make better.

Inclusionary. To invite or include.

Inflection. The rise and fall in the pitch and the tone changes of the voice.

Influencing. To exercise or have physical or moral influence on; used in leadership to mean getting people to do what you (as leaders) want them to do; it is the means or method to achieve two ends, operating and improving.

Inspection. Visual evaluation.

Intangible. That which has a value not dependent on physical makeup.

Interpersonal skills. Ability to work with and positively relate to other people.

Interval. The lateral space between personnel in a formation, measured from right to left with close, double, or normal spacing; a space between actions.

Intuitions. Instinctive knowledge or feeling; immediate perceptions.

Keeper. Slide for adjusting slack in rifle sling.

Leadership. The ability to influence, lead, or guide others so as to accomplish a mission in the manner desired.

Leadership style. Patterns of behavior that a leader uses to influence a team or group of followers.

Legitimate power. Power given to the person in the position within the hierarchy.

Line. To form up in ranks, facing forward the length of the formation; a formation in which people of elements are side by side or abreast of each other.

Lower band. Metal band located halfway along rifle barrel.

Management. The act of managing; control or direction.

Mandatory. Something that absolutely must be done.

Maneuver. To perform a movement in military tactics (or in drill) normally to secure an advantage.

Marching. A precise stepping movement designed to facilitate the efficient movement of formations.

Mark time. To march in place, often given as a drill command.

Mass formation. A drill formation where the elements of a company-sized or larger unit assemble, or are abreast of each other, at close interval and in column.

Mentee. One who receives advice, especially officially or professionally.

Mentoring. A sustained one-to-one relationship which promotes human development by regular, joint participation in structured activities

Message. A communication transmitted between persons by written or spoken words, signals, and so on.

Minority. A racial, religious, or ethnic group different from the dominant group.

Motivation. Provide a need or a purpose which causes a person to want to do something; something that incites or has a tendency to incite to determination or action.

Muzzle. The open end of the rifle barrel from which the bullet exits.

Negotiation. An attempt to reach a win-win agreement.

Nonjudgments. Absence of judgments.

Normal interval. Single arm's distance between troops in rank.

Norms. A principle of right action binding on members of a group and serving to guide, control, or regulate proper and acceptable behavior; a pattern or trait taken to be typical in the behavior of a social group.

Objectively. Without prejudice; expressing or dealing with actual facts or conditions of someone or something without distortion by personal feelings, prejudices, or interpretations.

Observe. The act of recognizing and noting a fact or occurrence.

Operating. To work, function; to conduct or manage; used in leadership to mean actions that leaders do to accomplish the short-term mission and to get the job done on time and to standard.

Parade rest. Command to place feet apart, knees unlocked, and clasp hands behind the back in a somewhat relaxed position.

Participating. A leadership style where the leader consults with, obtains advice from, or asks the opinions of one or more followers before making a decision.

Perpetrator. One that carries out a crime or a deception.

PERT chart. A term used to refer to a network diagram, which is a graphical illustration of the relationship between project activities.

Philosophy. Discipline comprising as its core logic, aesthetics, ethics, metaphysics, and epistemology.

Pistol belt. A belt designed to carry a holster, pistol, ammunition, pouches, and/or other field equipment.

Pivot. To turn in position; to turn in place.

Plan. To formulate an action for the accomplishment or attainment of an explicit purpose.

Port. To carry a weapon diagonally across the body, with the muzzle (or blade) near the left shoulder.

Port arms. Movement to position rifle diagonally across body with right forearm horizontal and elbows at sides.

Post. To take a position.

Precision. Being precise, accurate, or exact.

Prejudice. An adverse opinion or leaning formed without just grounds or before sufficient knowledge.

Prejudicial. To form an opinion without knowing or in spite of the facts.

Preparation. The act or process of making something ready for use or service; getting ready for an occasion, test, or duty.

Preparatory command. The part of a drill command that states the movement to be carried out and mentally prepares personnel for its execution.

Principled negotiation. Negotiations based on the criteria for fair negotiations and focused on a win/win outcome.

Priority. Precedence, especially established by order of importance or urgency.

Procedure. A series of steps followed in a regular, definite order.

Procrastinate. To put off or delay.

Professionalism. The ability to do and to take pride in doing a job well; the conduct, aims, or qualities that characterize a profession or professional person.

Project management. The process of planning, organizing, staffing, directing, and controlling the production of a system.

Purpose. A desirable end or aim; something set up as an object or end to be attained.

Quick time. Standard marching pace at 120 steps per minute.

Rank. To form up line abreast.

Recrimination. A retaliatory accusation.

Referent power. A type of power that is used to influence others.

Relinquishing. Giving up; submitting.

Resources. A source of help or supply.

Respective. Related, belonging, or assigned.

Rest. A position where you remain standing with your right foot in place; in certain situations you may move or talk in this position unless otherwise directed.

Rest (marching). Relaxed form of march without a set cadence to conserve troops' energy.

Reward power. When people comply with the wishes of others to get something in return.

Rhythmic. A regular or orderly repetition of sounds or movements; steady; recurring with measured regularity.

Saber. A heavy cavalry sword with a one-edged, slightly curved blade

Salute. Act of raising right hand to eyebrow, fingers straight, hand slightly cupped and tilted forward, as a gesture of courtesy.

Scabbard. A sheath for a saber or sword or other similar arm.

Self-discipline. Training, regulating, or controlling oneself (or one's conduct, personality, performance, and so on) for the sake of personal improvement.

Self-evaluation. To, with, for, or toward oneself or itself.

Selfless. Having no concern for self; unselfish.

Selfless service. A willingness to put the welfare of others first; to sacrifice, if need be, even to the point of giving up one's own life, in service to the nation.

Self-reliance. The ability to make your own decisions confidently and independently.

Sexism. Behavior or attitudes, especially against women, that promote gender-based stereotypes or that discriminate based on gender.

Sexual harassment. The making of unwanted and offensive sexual advances or of sexually offensive remarks or acts.

Sight. Front and rear plates used to align rifle with target.

Sling. Strap for carrying rifle over back and shoulder.

Sling swivel. Metal loop for connecting sling to stock.

Snap. An immediate, sharp, precise response to a drill command.

Socioeconomic. Involving a combination of social and economic factors.

Stacking swivel. Metal loop on upper band of rifle.

Staff study. A detailed report that describes an action or event and how it can be accomplished.

Stationary movements. Drill movements executed while remaining in place.

Steps. The prescribed distance from one heel to the other heel of a marching soldier.

Stereotypes. An uncritical or formalized conception, notion, or attitude; an oversimplified opinion, belief, or viewpoint; a person, group, event, or issue considered to typify or conform to an unvarying pattern or manner; lacking any individuality; a standardized mental picture that is held in common by members of a group and that represents an oversimplified opinion, affective attitude, or uncritical judgment.

Stock. Part of a firearm where the barrel and lock are attached; framework securing firing mechanism while providing protected handling, aiming, and firing.

Supervising. To have the charge and direction of; to oversee and direct; keep tabs on; keep an eye on; keep under surveillance.

Supplementary command. An oral order given by a subordinate leader that reinforces and complements a higher order to ensure proper understanding and execution of a movement.

Support. To encourage or help.

Synergy. A joint action or force.

Tangible. Possible to understand or realize: the tangible benefits of the plan.

Teaching. To cause to know something or to know how; to accustom to some action or attitude.

Teamwork. The cooperative effort or action on the part of a number of people working together, especially to achieve a common goal.

Technical skills. Understanding and ability needed to perform assigned tasks.

Tenet. A principle, belief, or doctrine generally held to be true.

Tone. A sound of distinct pitch, loudness, vibration, quality, and/or duration; the particular or relative pitch of a word or phrase.

Trail arms. Fingers and thumb closed around the front hand guard, rifle butt raised about three inches off the ground and stock inclined at an angle of 30 degrees.

Transference. The act of transferring.

Transmitted. Sent from one person to another.

Trigger guard. Metal strip surrounding trigger mechanism to prevent accidental firing.

Tunnel vision. Extreme narrowness of viewpoint.

Unethical. Not doing the moral or right thing (normally a result of pressures or temptations from self-interest, peers, subordinates, or seniors); to violate established rules or standards of conduct.

Unison. In complete or perfect agreement; at the same time.

Upper band. Metal band located close to the muzzle of the barrel.

Values. A principle, standard, or quality considered worthwhile or desirable in a person or group; an ideal.

Visualize. To form a mental image.

Vulnerable. Capable of being wounded or injured; susceptible to being hurt.

Key Terms Index